**DO NOT REMOVE
CARDS FROM POCKET**

11 / 15 / 91

ALLEN COUNTY PUBLIC LIBRARY

FORT WAYNE, INDIANA 46802

You may return this book to any agency, branch,
or bookmobile of the Allen County Public Library.

DEMCO

Prince of the Magic Kingdom

Prince *of the* Magic Kingdom

Michael Eisner and the Re-Making of Disney

JOE FLOWER

John Wiley & Sons, Inc.
New York / Chichester
Brisbane / Toronto / Singapore

In recognition of the importance of preserving what has been written, it is a policy of John Wiley & Sons, Inc., to have books of enduring value published in the United States printed on acid-free paper, and we exert our best efforts to that end.

Library of Congress Cataloging-in-Publication Data

Flower, Joe.
    Prince of the magic kingdom : Michael Eisner and the re-making
of Disney / Joe Flower.
        p.   cm.
    Includes index.
    ISBN 0-471-52465-4 (alk. paper)
    1. Walt Disney Company—History.   2. Walt Disney Productions—
Reorganization.   3. Eisner, Michael, 1942—   .   4. Chief executive
officers—United States—Biography.   I. Title.
PN1999.W27F5   1991
384'.8'092—dc20
[B]   91-16601

Printed in the United States of America

10 9 8 7 6 5 4 3 2 1

Dedicated to Patrice—a challenge and a friend,
  a light and an amazement,
    my partner and mate

Acknowledgments

No one ever writes alone. Yet it never fails to astonish me, the outpouring of help that greets a project like this one. I would like to extend my deepest gratitude

To Kathy Hrastar, who labored uncounted hours calling people, writing letters, managing databases, transcribing interviews. Her help was prompt, uncomplaining, fastidious, intelligent, and continual. I could only wish such help on every writer.

To the other apprentices who helped me from time to time, and to Apprentice Alliance, for providing the connections.

To the young people in the Disney College Program, for providing insight into the workings of Disney World.

To the folks at Writers Connection, for their steady stream of information and encouragement.

To fellow writers George Leonard, Bill Novak, Richard Heckler, and the writers on WELL, for their words of wisdom.

To Kathy Garcia Egan, for helping out a friend in need.

To Tom Curran, for going beyond the call of duty.

To Paul Growald and Charles Ewell, for their patience.

To the people of Galilee Harbor, for providing a writing home.

To my agent, Jim Trupin, for making the connection.

To my parents, Burt and Fran, for their excitement and for conveying to me a love of the word.

To my sons, Abraham and Noah, for the wonderful gift of being exactly who they are.

To Roger Scholl, my editor, for his steady professionalism and sure hand.

I want to remember especially the open helpfulness and cheer of Randy Bright, a very special man, "imagineer," author of *Disneyland: Inside Story*, creator of many of the special shows and effects at EPCOT, for his many conversations. Soon after our last discussion, he was killed while cycling. He has been sorely missed by many people.

Similarly, I wish to remember Elton Rule, who was courteous enough to grant an interview in the midst of what turned out to be his final illness.

I would like to thank all those inside and outside the Walt Disney Company who took the time to give me interviews. Some of them requested anonymity, and so cannot be acknowledged directly, but they know who they are, and I greatly appreciate their contribution. Of those I can name, I would like to thank particularly Elliott Gould, Ted Danson, Nancy Stafford, Gary Pudney, Bill Blinn, Fess Parker, Charles Wickham, Peter Rummell, Lauren Schuler, Jim Jimirro, Saul Steinberg, Irwin Jacobs, Fred Pierce, and Ed Feldman for being extraordinarily helpful.

I extend my deepest thanks to Wall Street analysts Hal Vogel, Chris Dixon, Liz Buyer, and David Londoner for giving me their points of view.

To John Gardner, Peter Drucker, and Charles Hampden-Turner, for their discussions with me about the nature of change in human organizations.

To Peter Senge, for his ideas about systems thinking.

To Warren Bennis, for his thoughts on leadership.

To John Taylor, author of *Storming the Magic Kingdom: Wall Street, the Raiders, and the Battle for Disney,* for his advice and encouragement.

Contents

Introduction

"Mr. Flower? Please hold the line for Mr. Eisner." It was a phone call from Michael Eisner, the chairman and chief executive officer of the Walt Disney Company.

Eisner, the man who walks in the shoes of Walt, was calling me, it turned out, to tell me why he was not going to talk to me for the biography that I planned to write—a commitment, he said, to another author, if he should ever do a book. And he wasn't doing a book. With anybody. Not now, not for a long time. It wasn't time for a retrospective, he felt, because he wasn't finished yet.

In a dozen years as a writer I had interviewed thousands of people. I had done scores of stories on business executives. I had done many stories on people who, for this reason or that, would not talk to me. Michael Eisner was the first person ever to call me up to tell me that he would not talk to me.

His words strangely echoed those of Bill Novak over scones and coffee in Watertown, Massachusetts. Novak had coauthored the wildly successful *Iaccoca*. He had ghost-written Tip O'Neill's book, and Nancy Reagan's book, and coauthored *Mayflower Madam*. His agent had been after him to write about Eisner. "I can't do Eisner," he said. "He's too young. He's not finished."

Every story has a story behind it, the kind of stories writers trade when they get together to complain about their dismal, grinding, oddly romantic business. But the call from Eisner was just the beginning of the strange contradictions coiled in the heart of the Disney story.

There was, for instance, the question of access, of getting people to talk. It was far from the simple matter it had seemed at first. I had grown up with Disney, like any child of the '50s, and more closely than most. I was four when Disneyland opened, and went to it often enough as a child to track its changes, to still think of "It's a Small World" as "that new ride" two decades later. My father, an artist, had tried to get a job at Disney, and had often pointed out the studios standing just off the freeway. The Corcoran brothers, who played Davy Crockett's kids, and the

1

kids in *Old Yeller,* and numerous other "kid" characters in Walt's movies, went to my grade school.

More important, the Disney mythology had helped shape my way in the world of dream and nightmare and imagination, and had introduced me to the deep pull of myth long before Joseph Campbell and Robert Bly let the word out.

So, for me to write about Eisner and Disney, now as I turned 40, would not be like any other story. It would be an opening into innocence, into the child within.

Tracking the story down, I found that part, at least, to be true. There was something magical about Disney. I met people who swore they could never work anywhere else, people whose job it was to spin fairy tales into reality, to build giant toys, space ships, miniature worlds.

But I met something else as well—a corporation intent on the bottom line, a global entertainment conglomerate that could be as grasping, as controlling, as juiceless and impersonal as any company in America. This strange mix of the magical and the ruthlessly practical, of creativity and ferocity, took on, for me, a new sense of intrigue.

Eisner had said, "I won't discourage anyone from talking to you. If anyone tells you different, they have reasons of their own." But Eisner is the boss, and once they heard that he was not talking to me, few of those who worked for him would talk to me. Of the scores of people in and out of the company who replied, "Let me check with Michael," or "Let me check with Erwin"—Erwin Okun was Eisner's vice president of communications at Disney—not one later agreed to an interview. Many in the company, those who would never think to ask permission to speak their minds, did talk to me, in their offices, on the lot, in the animation buildings in Glendale, on the job in Orlando. Others, more circumspect, would talk only anonymously. One met me in front of a supermarket and drove 30 miles with me to a public beach for the interview. Others would talk only in their homes or apartments, or only if I turned the tape recorder off.

In the end, I relied on a wide variety of sources, written and oral, inside and outside the company. I conducted scores of interviews, and augmented them with stock analysts' reports, plus the company's own annual reports and SEC filings. I personally explored the extensive Disney properties in Orlando, Anaheim, and Long Beach, the animation workshops in Glendale and North Hollywood, and the company lot in Burbank, and culled published reports from the United States, Japan, and

Europe. I sent associates to sift the court records of Los Angeles and Orlando, and using computers, tapped into public database systems. The obstacles posed by Disney's lack of involvement forced me to be more resourceful, but in no way dried up my sources of information.

Disney is a strangely closed corporation. At the time I began work on this book, Walt Disney World had just celebrated Mickey's 60th birthday by inviting hundreds of journalists from all over the world, providing them with free hotel rooms, tickets, behind-the-scenes tours, meals, and an avalanche of information. Yet when I flew to Orlando myself, the press office would not even provide me with a basic press packet of information, much less arrange interviews for me, let me behind the scenes, or answer any of the accusations that the local press had leveled at them. It was a level of controlling paranoia I had never encountered in my years of writing about American business.

Writing about the difficulties of writing is usually a sophisticated type of whining. Writing is my job, it's my passion, and nothing worth doing is ever easy. But the story of the roadblocks that I encountered writing this book points to something fundamental about Disney. The contradiction between the magical charm of the Disney image and the aggressive abandon of the Disney company points to something deeper, a dichotomy at the core of Disney, a split in the seed that may yet be its undoing—the split between, on the one hand, imagination, energy, boldness, and the power of myth, and, on the other hand, the mindless greed of a major American corporation. The difficulty of writing this story rose out of Disney's still-troubled inner spirit.

This is not a corporate history.

It is a history of a deeply human struggle over ideas, values, and hopes for which men and women were willing to give themselves over, values at times so evanescent that some people could dismiss them as silly, values so deep that others became students of them, dedicated their careers to making them come alive, became enraged and embittered when they seemed to be violated, and turned poetic and inspired in their defense.

This is what is impressive about the name "Disney": no one is neutral. To a surprising degree, almost everyone I talked to in the course of writing this book had an opinion about Disney. Most people had a strong opinion, vividly expressed. Walt Disney was a genius or a charlatan, a hypocrite or an exemplar, a snake-oil salesman or a beloved father figure to generations of children, as well as to the child in generations of adults.

Those who managed the company after Walt's death were incompetent fools or skilled men who suffered only by comparison with the founder; they were dedicated to Walt's memory or they were witless slaves to a formula; they were risk-takers of an unusual scale or they possessed no vision. Michael Eisner and "Team Disney," as the new management calls itself, were heartless money-grubbers, or they were prudent developers of latent corporate assets; they were merely in the right place at the right time, or they were prodigiously talented; they were taking Walt's vision to the next stage, or they were strip-mining an American legacy.

Few American institutions, and certainly no American corporation, can command anything like the place in the public mind occupied by Disney. Most Americans do not have strong opinions about other companies of Disney's size, such as Xerox, National Medical Enterprises, or Rockwell; or even about other successful entertainment and media companies, such as Time Warner, MCA, or Paramount. Certainly no other American company carries the mix of expectations that Disney does, or has been able to carve itself such a strange, deep-setting hook of myth, magic, and values. No corporation is "about" something in so full and personal a way as Disney is. No corporation has excited so many letters to the editor, so much media coverage and even public demonstrations over its essence. For reasons rooted in mass psychology, the history of myth, and the changing face of America, this country cares deeply who is in charge of the Walt Disney Company and what they do with it.

At the center of this storm of opinion is Michael Eisner, one of the most peculiar men ever to run a major American corporation. The tall, gangly man with the lovably toothy, what-me-worry face charmed many people who saw in him a reincarnation of the beloved Walt. Others loved the exterior but distrusted the man behind it, seeing the "family man" image as a front for a voracious and arrogant global entertainment combine out to churn the money machine as fast as humanly possible. As Disney doubled and tripled in size, and the value of the stock increased 1,200 percent, Wall Street became enamored of Eisner, even while some analysts were privately reluctant to credit him with most of Disney's success.

Their reluctance stemmed from the same fact that had nearly blocked Eisner's rise to the chairmanship: he rose through ABC and Paramount, not through the "hard business" ranks, not from the financial sphere, not even from marketing, but from the creative side. He was a "story" man, whose skill lay in recognizing and developing creative ideas and people.

The Walt Disney Company had been founded by a charismatic creator, a "story" man. Walt Disney had laid down a theme and variations as solid as the opening lines of a Beethoven symphony. He had left a great many ideas and possibilities to be carried out by others—ideas that would need artists, sometimes even magicians. But he handed them to an orchestra of highly competent followers—sorcerer's apprentices who had the book of secrets, but not the inner wisdom to read its arcane symbols.

Walt Disney's theme was the structuring of mythic worlds. His variations led off into synthetic high adventure, future cities, structured environments, manufactured experiences, and the repeatable real moment. The reigning intellectuals of his time thought him a peripheral person, a talented hick with a knack for family entertainment. But his themes would turn out to be highly appealing to millions in the rapine and chaos of today's world.

After Walt's death, the company employed many creative people, but none of them were in charge, and the enterprise stuck to playing out the ideas Walt had been developing at his death. Over time, the company's development slowed, it attracted corporate raiders, and suddenly, in 1984, a decades-long deterioration became a crisis. In what amounted to a "friendly takeover," Walt's nephew Roy E. Disney teamed up with outside investors to install a lawyer, Frank Wells, as president, and a "story" man, Eisner, as chairman of the board. The men making this decision were not creative crazies. They were some of America's preeminent deal-makers, money men of the first water. In their opinion Disney was one company that didn't need one of their kind at the top. It needed a kiss of craziness. It needed a creative spark.

What that decision meant for Disney was seven years—so far—of unprecedented growth and profitability, some of it in unexpected and un-Disney-like directions. What it means for the rest of American business is less clear. It may be here—in creativity, in risk, in the urge to do something new—that American business has the most to offer the world, and that the example of Disney has much to offer American business.

I like Michael Eisner. I'll admit that right up front. No one told me to like him. Disney didn't publish this book or sponsor it in any way. I'm not trying to sell them a script. In fact, Eisner, and most of his Team Disney, wouldn't even talk to me.

My publisher didn't tell me to be nice to him. When you write about someone famous (especially someone rich, famous, and successful), publishers usually like it if you can dig up some dirt—alcoholism, sexual peccadillos, financial sleight-of-hand. If you can't find that, if your subject seems to be completely clean and above-board, the next best thing publishers hope for is that you can lambaste what he's doing. Publishers call it "controversy," and marketing departments love it.

Michael Eisner has made some mistakes. Some of the effects of Disney's success are worrisome, and the company's attitude toward labor has seemed, at times, insensitive. Yet I can't help but like Eisner as a human being.

This is not because he's famous. Famous people are just people, and their fame is at best a necessary evil of the career they have chosen, at worst a destroyer of all that is personal and treasured.

It's not because he has made sacks of money. If you think money defines life, then you might admire someone who has made a lot of it. But money doesn't define life. Rich people are not happier, more noble, more attractive, or easier to be around than anybody else. On the other hand, if you think people only make money by "ripping off" other people, then you might despise someone who has made a lot of it. Certainly many of the success stories of the '80s were stories of men who came to great wealth by impoverishing others, milking great corporations, shrinking enterprises, and destroying jobs. But it's equally possible to make money by creating new wealth, nurturing new enterprises, new jobs, new ideas. And I believe that is the case with Eisner and Disney.

It's not because he is powerful that I enjoy Michael Eisner. Power is reach. A powerful person affects a larger part of the world. We all have power of one sort or another—in our family relationships, at work, in our communities. What is truly interesting is not the fact that people have power, but how they use that power. Do they make their world better, stronger, gentler, more varied, more interesting, more humane? Do they create wealth or hoard it? Do they foment wonderfulness or hideousness?

I like Michael Eisner because he has done something unimaginable: he has become rich, famous, powerful, and admired at least in part by bringing the child inside him out into the open, by fighting for his instincts, often against the conventional wisdom.

In America, business is our field of struggle and play. It's the ground on which we choose to have our contests. Too often, we seem to think there are only two models for the person who wants to make a success on that ground. One model is the cool technocrat, full of formulas and case studies, the MBA working alchemy with numbers, chi squares, moving averages, and statistical filters, cerebral and Apollonian. The other model is the corporate buccaneer, rapacious, a gambler, visceral and Dionysian. Neither model is particularly cuddly. And more important, they do not stake out all the possibilities between them. Yet to be successful in business, we tell ourselves, means being either calculating or piratical. If you care about the heart, if you want to build things, if you have humane values and would like to improve some portion of the earth, business is not your field of play. Business is not for the creative or the sensitive. It is not possible, we tell ourselves, to mix ambition with a heart that is still beating.

Michael Eisner's career displays a third possibility, a possibility that is creative and powerful, that combines the traditional capabilities of powerful business leadership—such as a clear vision, the ability to communicate that vision, and the intelligence to process vast amounts of information from many sources at once—with the mind of a child—direct, fascinated, innocent, intuitive, enthusiastic, and capable of being astonished. Like a child, Eisner has a steep learning curve. Like a child, he will pursue an idea not because he has some scheme in mind, or because it was the most outrageous thing he could think of, but simply because he likes it.

So Michael Eisner's story, like many a classic Disney tale, has a moral, a model that we could profit from: in ourselves and others, competence is important. So are intelligence and vision. But equally important are fascination, intuition, innocence, and a path with heart.

When You Wish upon a Star

By 1966, Walt Disney, and the company he had built, had met with more success than most people ever even imagine. He had become one of the most famous people in the world, he was incredibly wealthy and one of America's most respected businessmen; and he had made hundreds of millions of people happy.

"Uncle Walt," with his moustache and kindly, wrinkled face, was seen in the United States and throughout much of the world as the creator or re-creator in animated films of dozens of fantastic tales and well-loved characters—Mickey Mouse, a scrappy rodent with a "nice guy" personality; Donald Duck, known for his flights of volcanic but ineffectual rage; Snow White and the Seven Dwarfs, each with his own particular slice of the human condition; Pinocchio, the wooden boy, so easily led astray, and his wise sidekick, Jiminy Cricket; Peter Pan, the perpetual boy; Goofy, the floppy dog full of clumsiness and wild emotion; and scores of pirouetting elephants, dancing skeletons, dandified pirates, and water-toting broomsticks.

In "live" films and television shows, Disney had presented such figures as Davy Crockett, Zorro, and Mary Poppins, and such adventure tales as *The Swiss Family Robinson* and *20,000 Leagues under the Sea*. His wildlife films had introduced popular audiences to animals from the frozen tundra to the fragrant jungles of the tropics. And Disney had gone beyond films. He had created in Disneyland an earthly paradise for children (as well as the child in every adult), where guests could actually visit Sleeping Beauty's Castle, meet Mickey Mouse in person, watch dinosaurs fight, and plunge beneath the polar ice pack in a submarine. Now, in 1966, Walt Disney had declared on his "Wonderful World of Disney" television show that he was hard at work planning another magical place—a real city of the future, where everything would be perfect.

Walt Disney had been well rewarded for all this creative energy. Universities, societies, and governments had showered Disney with over 700 commendations, proclamations, awards, and medals. The Hollywood establishment had given him 29 Academy Awards for his films and four Emmys for his television shows. Harvard, Yale, and the University of Southern California had bestowed honorary degrees upon him. France had awarded him the Legion of Honor, Mexico the Order of the Aztec Eagle. President Lyndon Johnson, politically his opposite, had only two years before pinned on his lapel the Medal of Freedom, the nation's highest civilian honor.

Disney was one of the wealthiest men in the entertainment industry. His 263,000 shares of Disney stock were worth over $18 million. His salary of $182,000 per year made him, according to *Fortune*, "one of the best compensated executives in the U.S." In addition, Walt Disney Productions owed him some $650,000 in deferred salary. Through a family company named Retlaw, he held a 10 percent interest in most recent Disney films. *Mary Poppins*, the charming tale of a magical English nanny liberating her charges from the strictures of their stuffy home into a world of fun and fantasy, brought him over $1 million by itself in 1965. Through Retlaw, he owned and took considerable profit from both of the railroads at Disneyland (the monorail and the steam train), and licensed the use of his name to Walt Disney Productions for merchandising purposes. *Fortune* estimated his income in 1965, through the Retlaw company, at more than $2 million, in addition to his salary and stock dividends. Altogether, the Disney family, including Walt and his wife, his brother Roy and his wife, his daughters Diane and Sharon and their husbands, and the grandchildren, owned 34 percent of Walt Disney Productions.

His technical accomplishments were as important a legacy as his wealth. Disney had done creative, pioneering work in animation, in the use of color and sound in film, and in television. He had invented the modern theme park, and demonstrated new possibilities in urban planning.

In the end, he had outlasted his more powerful rivals in the entertainment industry—the moguls of the great studios who, one by one, had been forced to relinquish their power and diminish their empires. The strong and diversified company that he had created stood in stark contrast to the rest of Hollywood. He had built a small empire. He had made it work. He had inspired it, expanded it, forced it into taking risks and being creative. He had made it consistently profitable—which could not be said of any of his rivals at the time. And, again in contrast to other Hollywood moguls, he had maintained absolute, unchallenged control over every detail of it.

Walter Elias Disney, the son of a struggling, restless proletarian Midwest father with a string of failures to his name—at construction in Chicago, at farming in Kansas, at orange-growing in Florida—began making crude cartoon shorts and advertisements in Kansas City in 1920, with a partner named Ub Iwerks. By 1923, he had gone bankrupt. He later commented, "It's important to have a good hard failure while you're young."

Walt's reaction to failure was the same that his father's had been: he moved. He left Kansas City for Hollywood, and tried to become a film director. Failing at that, he sent for Ub to join him and, with his brother Roy, went back into cartoons. They turned out a long series of increasingly sophisticated and successful silent cartoons until, in 1928, he lost control of his most popular character, a rabbit named Oswald, to a distributor.

It was a devastating blow after so many years of cranking out the little shorts week after week to meet punishing deadlines. But in a way that would become typical for him, the disaster moved Disney forward rather than backward. He was forced to create a substitute—a mouse named Mickey.

The mouse was a good character from the start—feisty, cheerful, a happy little survivor in a hostile world, reminiscent of Chaplin's tramp. But Mickey needed a boost, something to make him stand out above the competition. He got that boost in his third film, *Steamboat Willie*, the world's first animated movie with synchronized sound. The film's wild cheerfulness and the broad pranks with which Mickey rescued Minnie from the evil steamboat captain would have spoken to any audience of the time, but what made Mickey a phenomenon was the sound. "It growls, whines, squeaks, and makes various other sounds that add to its mirthful quality," said the *New York Times*. In the most famous scene Mickey uses a collection of animals as an orchestra, cranking the tail of a goat as a hurdy-gurdy, strumming the tail of a cat as a bass. Audiences were entranced, and Mickey was an overnight worldwide success.

Walt soon gave Mickey a coterie of costars, including Donald Duck, Pluto, and Goofy. At the same time he launched a new series of *Silly Symphonies*, which animated musical scores with dancing skeletons, trees, and rocks. This series also took off, and by 1932 Disney was producing it in Technicolor, another first. Slowly in the beginning, then more rapidly, Walt built a studio—Walt Disney Productions—on the success of his characters.

Walt's brother Roy, 13 years his senior, served as business manager of the enterprise. It was Roy who worried over the ledgers, arranged loans to cover the payroll, and fought for better terms from distributors. Their relationship had a repetitive form. Every time Walt would achieve some success, he would want to use it as a base from which to try something bigger, newer, more daring. And each time, Roy would fight it, on the sensible grounds that the expense and the risk were too great. Sometimes Roy was right—Walt's failed experiments cost the company millions of dollars over the years. Often enough though, Roy was wrong and in the end, Walt's successful experiments built the base of a completely new kind of entertainment empire.

In 1937, for instance, Walt took the leap into feature-length animated fantasy films. His first, *Snow White*, financed on the backs of the Mickey Mouse–Donald Duck shorts and the *Silly Symphonies*, turned out to be phenomenally successful.

As the '30s turned into the '40s, Disney built his future on the hope that he would repeat that success. He planned and built an entirely new studio in Burbank and plunged his artists into a string of full-length animated fantasies. Unfortunately, the full-length animated shows took too long to produce, and consumed too much money, for too uncertain a profit, to keep the studio going. World War II cut off his foreign markets, a strike tore his studio apart, and one beloved classic after another— *Pinocchio, Bambi, Fantasia, Song of the South*—lost money or eked out minimal profits. He barely escaped another bankruptcy by grinding out military and industrial training films. Yet, even in the difficult 1940s, Walt Disney rarely seemed to lose his phenomenal energy.

Walt was not a talented illustrator—after his first crude beginnings, all the animation was done by confederates. But he tinkered with the stories, told them and retold them to the animators, acted out the parts, grimacing, hooting, crawling on all fours, going over scene after scene. Similarly, he was no machinist, but he invented mechanical contraptions to make the filming of animated features more productive, or appear more realistic. One invention, for instance, was a multiplane camera: instead of photographing one inked "cel" held flat, the camera would shoot down through several planes of glass, each partially painted with elements of the foreground. As characters in the background walked through a forest or a castle, the foreground elements would shift, giving a three-dimensional impression.

Any energy and time that he didn't pour into his films, he lavished on other projects that might just be fun, and might turn into something he could use. He spent endless hours tinkering with trains, and had an entire one-eighth scale steam train built in the backyard of his house in Holmby Hills. He was fascinated by the possibility of making mannequins move realistically, studying the gears, motors, hydraulic links, and electric switching sets that might make robots look, walk, talk, even dance like people. On one occasion he hired the dancer and actor Buddy Ebson (who would later play Davy Crockett's sidekick) to do a dance routine on a small stage with one large graph matrix behind him and another to one side. Disney filmed the routine from several different angles and set out to analyze its motions, to see if they could be reproduced mechanically. Many of these experiments would one day contribute to the success of Disneyland.

The 1950s brought new life to Disney's enterprise. He found a movie niche that worked for him, one that combined four different kinds of films. The big money-makers were live-action films for a family audience. Most were historical adventures—*Treasure Island*, *The Story of Robin Hood*, *20,000 Leagues under the Sea*, *Davy Crockett—King of the Wild Frontier*, and *Johnny Tremain*. In the '60s Disney added toothless comedies that put bumbling Mr. Average in impossible situations, such as *Parent Trap*, *The Absent-Minded Professor*, and *The Happiest Millionaire*.

To these he added less costly animal pictures, True-Life Adventures and True-Life Fantasies, of which he made eight between 1948 and 1960. For these films, Disney sent explorer-photographers to the ends of the earth. Then he used narration and editing to anthropomorphize the wild animals in the footage, to make the lions, gazelles, chimpanzees, and seals into the flesh-and-blood equivalents of the ducks, mice and hippos his animation department had been turning out since the '20s.

Every few years, the Disney artists came out with another animated feature—11 between 1949 and 1967, including *Cinderella, Alice in Wonderland, Peter Pan, Lady and the Tramp*, and *Sleeping Beauty*. The combination—animated classics, live-action adventures, silly comedies, and wildlife films—proved a stable source of profit.

In the 1950s, Disney became the legendary right man at the right place and time. He caught and rode a demographic wave: the returning war veterans had produced over 4 million sons and daughters in 1946, and continued to break the 4-million mark for the next 18 years. Those years, 1946 to 1964, mark the bounds of the baby boom and, by no coincidence, of Walt Disney Productions' greatest financial success in films. During the peak of the baby boom, in the early and mid-'50s, millions of young, suburban families were avidly looking for safe, charming entertainment to which they could take their children. By the end of that period, the first of the baby boomers were in college, those at the crest of the wave were becoming teenagers, and Disney's world would never again be quite the same.

But while it lasted, the economics meshed elegantly with the demographics. The live films cost Disney, on average, less than $2 million to make, $1 million less than the lowest cost for an animated feature. Between 1953 and 1966, Disney released five animated features and over 50 live-action films. All five of the animated films, with their higher cost, appeared on *Variety*'s list of the top-grossing films of all time, as did 16 of Disney's live-action films. These 21 films grossed an average of more than $4 million—huge numbers for the time.

The Disney animated films, and the best of the live-action films, carried special value that began to emerge more clearly as the company matured. Because they were based on timeless tales that were not subject to fashion, because their production qualities were so high, because children formed a substantial part of their audiences, and because Disney had been careful to keep full control of them, the films could be released over and over, every five or seven years. And since the first release had paid off a film's expenses, almost all the money made on a rerelease was profit.

No one has ever quite been able to turn film-making into a risk-free money machine, but in the '50s and '60s, Walt Disney came very close. If, to the critics, the films were bland and predictable, neither Disney nor his audiences seemed to notice. Disney even denied that they were children's films. If the films drew the derision of intellectual elites at the *Nation* and other standard-bearers of all that was avante-garde, Walt didn't seem to mind. He at times seemed to wear their derision as a membership badge in some sort of commoner's club. He had been their darling for a brief moment in the '30s and '40s, when he was taking animation to new heights and beginning to explore the classic fables. He had flirted with them, and even tried to live up to his billing by producing his version of high-brow fare—*Fantasia*. This one-of-a-kind film choreographed fighting and dying dinosaurs to Stravinsky's *Sacre du Printemps*, dancing Chinese mushrooms to Tchaikovsky's *Nutcracker Suite*, and various devils and ghouls to Mussorgsky's *Night on Bald Mountain*. But the brief romance with the intellectuals had turned to mutual antipathy, and Walt had moved in other directions.

All his life Walt Disney was an enthusiast, plunging into one project after another, growing obsessed with a new technology, a new plan, a new possibility—and growing tired of what had gone before. And all his adult years Roy Disney resisted Walt's obsessions with sound, with color, with new techniques to increase the depth and power of animation, with daring subjects such as *Fantasia*. But Walt fought back, as if Roy's role in life was to provide Walt an obstacle to climb over or plow through.

The new Disney niche in films had barely begun to show its possibilities in the early '50s when Walt grew increasingly distant from it, and began to spend more and more time on his latest obsession—a new kind of leisure place, to be called "Disneyland," that went far beyond the conventional amusement park or fairground. What he had in mind was not quite like anything else in existence. He had difficulty getting other people to see what he saw—a place of fun and fantasy, neat and clean, relaxing—neither noisy and dusty and rank with greasy fumes, nor peopled by grizzled barkers and hard characters. This amusement park would be more like a park, with trees and flowers, benches and fountains. Rather than rides that merely spun people in the air or turned them upside down, the park would feature "attractions" built around stories. The rides would carry the "guests" through storyland, peopled with the characters from Disney's most popular movies.

Roy Disney failed to see any magic or sure profit in the idea, and refused to give Walt any of the studio's money. In fact, Roy originally campaigned against the plan, telling bankers and other potential investors that it was a money-losing proposition. He even told them that Walt Disney Productions would refuse to license the use of Walt Disney's own name to this "Disneyland" idea—an odd idea that would surely have been tested in court had Roy pressed the issue. Walt was forced to start a separate company, Walt Disney, Inc., to develop the idea. When Roy complained about the studio's right to the name, Walt renamed the company WED ("Walter Elias Disney") Enterprises. He called the creative designers and artisans who worked there his "imagineers."

Walt spent what money he had on the project; he even cashed in his life insurance for $100,000. But he needed, by his calculations, $2 million to open the gates. He got the money, finally, in a way that shifted the history not only of his own enterprises, but of the entertainment industry.

The first years of the 1950s had seen the destruction of the great Hollywood studios by what the studio heads saw as two implacable enemies: the federal government and the new medium of television. The power and freedom of action of the studios had rested on the fact that they controlled the movie process from beginning to end. From writers and actors to theaters and popcorn machines, it was a vertically integrated business. By refusing to deal with independent producers, and forcing actors, directors, writers, and producers into long-term contracts, they could control the supply of product. By owning the distribution companies and their own strings of theaters, they could control the retail sale of the product. Even independent theater owners could be made to sign package contracts that forced them to show all of a studio's product, the popular with the not-so-popular. But under the pressure of federal anti-trust action, in the late '40s the studios had sold their chains of theaters, and had lost much of their power to control the market. If the theaters were free to show any film that sold tickets, then independent producers had a market for their films. And if independent producers could provide work for writers, actors, and directors, then nobody could be forced to work for the big studios.

At the same time the growth of television created a powerful rival to the neighborhood theater. In 1946 there were only 6,000 television sets in American homes. By 1950 there were 6 million. The weakened movie studios saw television as a threat, and left production for the cheap and fast new medium to independents and to the networks themselves. The studios stuck to movies, and they were left flailing for new ways to attract customers.

But the industry's traumas had not deeply affected Disney. He had survived his rough years in the early '40s. For Disney, the loosening of the giants' control over distribution provided the opportunity to start his own distribution arm. And television became Disney's greatest ally for both marketing and financing.

In Hollywood in the early 1950s, the hope of the moguls was that television was just a passing fad. To encourage this possibility, the studios were trying to hold the line against selling theatrical movies to television. Disney himself held the same opinion. But by the fall of 1953 Walt was desperate for money to finance Disneyland, and had exhausted every means he could think of to raise it. He negotiated with the two major television networks, CBS and NBC, over various series ideas. But he insisted that the series be linked to an actual investment in Disneyland. Both networks turned him down.

ABC, however, was struggling to establish itself in a world ruled by the two larger networks. It needed some big names to draw viewers and affiliates. Disney's overture fitted their needs exactly. Roy Disney, by this time, had been gradually converted to the cause. In a meeting with Leonard Goldenson, Roy worked out a deal: Disney would produce a weekly anthology series for the network—television movies, specials, cartoons, and nature films. In return, ABC would join the studio in buying a majority interest in Disneyland. For a $500,000 investment and a $4.5-million loan guarantee, ABC-Paramount Theaters received 34.48 percent of Disneyland. Walt Disney Productions received an equal slice. Western Printing and Lithographing, Disney's publishing partner for two decades, received 13.79 percent for a $200,000 investment. And Walt himself received 17.25 percent for the $250,000 he had already contributed.

The series, at first called "Disneyland," became in time one of the longest-running series on television, and made ABC the peer of the other two networks on Sunday nights. "Disneyland" introduced the idea of the made-for-television movie, and eventually helped to popularize color television. It pushed network television entertainment to a higher standard of technical quality, as well as to larger budgets. And it demonstrated to the larger studios that television was not necessarily the movies' destroying angel, but another way to make a profit.

The Disneyland park, which opened in 1955 in Anaheim, California, financed by the "Disneyland" television show, was something entirely new: clean, bright, cheerful, and full of adventures, yet safe not only from accidents, but from surliness, boredom, and even surprise. Out of the flat, ordered rows of Orange County's citrus groves, Walt's bulldozers had fashioned a twelve-foot-high earthen berm in a rough triangle. Surmounted by a railroad track and planted with trees, the berm shut out the outside world, with its freeways and cars. Inside, an idealized "Main Street" of brightly colored Victorian shops and arcades opened onto a broad, leafy, central plaza and "lands" filled with characters and situations from Disney films—Adventureland, Frontierland, Fantasyland, and Tomorrowland. In the middle rose the centerpiece of the park, Sleeping Beauty's Castle. Each sight line and facade used the tricks of the set-designer's trade to make the buildings and environments—jungles, castles, riverboats, frontier forts, and moon rockets—seem larger, higher, finer, and altogether more solid than they really were.

Disneyland was an instant success. Within six months a million people had passed through its gates. Within nine months the venture had paid off its loans and was in the black. Within five years, Disney was able to buy out ABC's $500,000 investment for $7.5 million and consider it a bargain. Over the years, Disney expanded the park repeatedly, usually using money straight out of its own revenue stream. Disneyland became the mainstay of the profitability of Walt Disney Productions.

Disneyland drew most of its visitors from southern California. But, because of its continual presence on television, it became the Mecca of children across the country—and of adults from around the world. Soviet Premier Nikita Krushchev, on a visit to the United States, asked to go to Disneyland, and threw a tantrum when informed that, for security reasons, it would not be possible. Other celebrities counted themselves luckier. President Eisenhower got to skipper a jungle cruise boat, Senator Robert Kennedy and astronaut (later senator) John Glenn rode the Matterhorn together, India's Prime Minister Nehru strode down Main Street, Crown Prince (now Emperor) Akihito of Japan brought his wife Michiko, and Nat King Cole came with his son. Harry Truman refused to ride on Dumbo during his visit, since elephants symbolized the Republican cause. John Kennedy came to the Magic Kingdom, as did Richard Nixon, Jimmy Carter, Ronald Reagan, and Anwar Sadat.

Not everyone liked Disneyland. It drove some critics to vicious rhetorical charges. John Ciardi complained that a visit to Disneyland had exposed him to "the shyster in the backroom of illusion, diluting his witch's brew with tap water." Julian Halevy decried it in the *Nation* as part of the nation's "drift to fantasy," and accused Disney of reducing all the universe "to a sickening blend of cheap formulas packaged to sell. . . . Life is bright-colored, clean, cute, titivating, safe, mediocre, inoffensive to the least common denominator, and somehow poignantly inhuman. . . . One feels our whole mass culture heading up the dark river to the source—that heart of darkness where Mr. Disney traffics in pastel-trinketed evil for gold and ivory."

But others admired it extravagantly. Ray Bradbury, himself a noted fantasist, was an early and steadfast admirer. Critic Aubrey Menen felt that Disney had satisfied "the strongest desire an artist knows . . . to create a world of his own where everything is just as he imagines it."

Some of the greatest praise came from urban planners, such as James W. Rouse, a prime figure in the "New Town" movement. In a lecture at Harvard in 1963, Rouse said, "If you think about Disneyland and think about its performance in relation to its purpose; its meaning to people— more than that, its meaning to the process of development—you will find it the outstanding piece of urban design in the United States. It took an area of activity—the amusement park—and lifted it to a standard so high in its performance, in its respect for people, that it really has become a brand-new thing. It fulfills all the functions it set out to accomplish unself-consciously, usefully, and profitably to its owners and developers. I find more to learn in the standards that have been set and in the goals that have been achieved in the development of Disneyland than in any other single piece of physical development in the country."

Disneyland was profitable because it was a new, high-quality, inexpensive experience that fit the needs of the emerging baby boom families, and because its promotion was a stroke of genius. Every Sunday evening, in prime family time, "Disneyland" provided Disney what amounted to an hour-long commercial for both the company's theatrical films and the parks. The opening sequence always featured Sleeping Beauty's Castle, the central monument of Disneyland. Many of the shows were, in fact, promotional pieces—tours of Disneyland, trailers of Disney films, documentaries about the making of Disney films, clips from Disney films. Far from objecting to this blatant self-promotion, the industry awarded Disney an Emmy for a film about the making of *20,000 Leagues under the Sea*, and sponsors, including such giants as Coca-Cola and Johnson and Johnson, flocked to the show.

It was a prime example of synergy, years before the term became vogue. Each element—the parks, the movies, and the television show— gained energy and interest and form from the other two. It all tied together. Viewers could actually go to the wonderful place they had seen on television (which was true of few other places they saw on television). If they liked the park, they could relive the experience, and reconnect with that magical world, every Sunday night on television, for free. If they liked what they saw on television about a new Disney film, they could catch the film at their local theater. When they did go to the film, they were already preconditioned to like it by the television show about how it was made. And if they liked the film, they and their children would love the attraction made out of it at Disneyland.

These three elements of synergy—movies, television, and Disneyland—together launched yet another. In 1954 Disney hired Fess Parker—who claimed to be allergic to horses and leather clothes—and put him into a fringed leather jacket in a miniseries based on a collection of stories that a congressman from Tennessee had written about himself and distributed as campaign literature in the 1830s. The congressman's name was Davy Crockett. The shows were budgeted tightly—so tightly, in fact, that sketches were substituted for expensive location shots. But, partly because they had a catchy signature tune, the television films became a wild success, and immediately boosted ABC's ratings. Recut and knit into a single movie, *Davy Crockett—King of the Wild Frontier* became the box-office phenomenon of 1955. The movie's signature song rose to number one on the charts and stayed there for weeks. And all across the country little boys began to beg their mothers for coonskin caps, fringed jackets, and toy rifles.

Disney had been licensing trinkets imprinted with images of Mickey and Minnie and Snow White for decades. But consumer products had never brought in much money, and were never of much interest to Walt. The magnitude of the response to Davy Crockett changed all that, however. Card Walker, Disney's director of marketing, put Vince Jefferds in charge of consumer products, and soon stores across the country were inundated with caps, jackets, rifles, and all manner of paraphernalia marked with the official Walt Disney logo. Jefferds followed that with Donald Duck hats with bills that quacked, and a flood of other items—T-shirts, dolls, wind-up toys. On the heels of the success with the Davy Crockett song, Disney even went into the record business. Consumer products based on Disney characters, which had been, in the best years, a $3-million revenue source, became immediately worth $12 million per year and, by the early '80s, over $50 million per year.

So the money was flowing in from four directions: movies, television, Disneyland, and merchandise. What made it sweeter, and all the more secure, was the fact that Walt Disney controlled everything. Despite the complex financial underpinnings of Disneyland, Walt had complete control over every detail of the operation of the park. Every film and every television show had his name in large script above the title. While many of the other studios had given in and sold large portions of their film libraries to television packagers, Disney kept all rights. He even controlled the distribution of the films. In 1953 when RKO Radio, his usual distributor, showed less than avid enthusiasm for *The Living Desert*, his second True-Life Adventure, Disney countered by forming his own distribution company, Buena Vista. This completed the circle of control that Walt Disney had over his empire. No one would ever be able to show a Disney film in an "unsuitable" environment, double-bill it with the wrong film, or sell it into discount houses.

It was the same in other parts of the empire. No one could ever put Mickey on an obscene poster or a shabby piece of merchandise. No vendor could run an operation at Disneyland that was not spic and span, or hire employees who didn't meet Disney's standards of neatness or helpfulness.

Over the years, Disney studio public relations material had repeatedly talked about Disney's "warmth" and his love of children, and the "magic" and "wonder" of his films. One promotional piece called him "a very simple man—a quiet, pleasant man that you might not look twice at on the street. But a man—in the deepest sense of the term—with a mission. The mission is to bring happiness to millions."

Yet Walt himself did not see his mission, or his accomplishment, in such dreamy terms. When a *Los Angeles Times* reporter asked which of all his experiences had been the most rewarding, he replied without hesitation, "The whole damn thing. The fact that I was able to build an organization and hold it."

The control of that organization went beyond the matter of who counted the profits, or who got their name above the title. It made "Disney" into a brand name. Walt Disney liked to tell a story from early in his career, when he was trying to sell Mickey Mouse cartoons to a distributor, before Mickey had become famous. The distributor claimed that he could get other cartoons for less money, and the audience wouldn't know the difference. "Nobody knows you or your Mouse," said the distributor. The man then picked up a roll of Lifesavers candy off of his desk and showed it to Disney. "Everybody knows Lifesavers," he told Walt. "If you had a name like that, you would have no trouble selling your films."

Disney was struck by the little demonstration. He determined that people would know his name, and the names of his characters. The character's name would be very large on the advertising posters and the title slides, larger than the title of the film. And over the character's name, "Walt Disney's" or "Walt Disney presents" would always appear. People would learn to associate his name with a particular type of entertainment. Like "McDonald's" or "Holiday Inn," "Disney" became the significator of a well-defined, prepackaged, indefinitely repeatable experience. Just as people would pull into a McDonald's rather than a Sam's Hot Burgers because they knew exactly what they would get, people would go to a Disney film, buy a Disney record, or go to Disneyland because they knew what they were getting—good, clean, family fare with no sex, a minimum of violence, and a happy, satisfying ending.

Enough people liked the Disney formula to make Walt Disney a rich man. While the world seemed to be getting more and more violent and chaotic, Disney created a controlled, understandable world that could release adult and child from confrontations with modern terrors.

This was what made Disneyland so different from ordinary amusement parks. Amusement park rides merely jazz the senses. They have no meaning, ask no questions, and pose no answers. Disneyland, in contrast, was about something. Every "land" and every ride told a story—about pluckiness, the triumph of virtue, and the value of innocence. Every view held out a definite and at times explicit promise that the future would be better than the present, that the nasty evils of the past, like pirates and train robbers, were now laughable because they had been vanquished, that people the world over were fundamentally the same, benign and lovable.

The same was true of the Disney films. Sex and death, longing and sorrow, ecstasy and grief, time and change held no sway in the world of Disney. In the Disney films, being virtuous was enough to bring success in the end. If it was an adventure film, bravery counted, too, but courage was a natural attribute. All that was needed in addition to natural courage was a dash of cleverness and that peculiar brand of energy called "spunk." There was a buoyancy, an undefinable energy, to Disney's universe. The Disney brand identity gained much of its power and cohesiveness from its evident sincerity. Walt Disney always said that he just made films that he would like to see.

In fact, his entire empire was an extension of his personality—the flights of fancy, the fastidiousness, the prudery, the childlike enthusiasm, the firm denial of all that disturbed him. It was all there on blatant public display. Even the layout of Disneyland was a kind of autobiographical psychohistory in concrete and wood. The visitor enters through an idealized, turn-of-the-century midwestern Main Street. Main Street is enticing and comfortable, but beyond it life spreads out in wilder and deeper attractions, adventures, fantasies, the future, experiences that are scary, exhilarating, and fascinating. And around it all, stopping everywhere, is the great escape machine of the Midwest from the turn of the century: the steam train, ready to take you away.

Walt Disney was obsessed with creation, driven to build magical worlds not, as many artists are, out of paint and canvas, or words, or even film, but physically, out of concrete, wires, smoke, electricity, and highly programmed employees. And he drove his designers and engineers fiercely, as extensions of himself, to accomplish his aims.

Two weeks before Disneyland opened, he suddenly decided that the set and artwork of the hit fantasy film *20,000 Leagues under the Sea*, to be displayed in Tomorrowland, were not complete without the film's giant squid—alive and wiggling. He called imagineer Ken Anderson and told him to get it done by opening day. It was a ridiculous order. The monster lay in storage in the props department. Its skin had been hacked to shreds by James Mason and Kirk Douglas during the film's climactic struggle. Besides, it couldn't move on its own. A crew pulling on cables had caused the tentacles to wave and curl about for the cameras. But Anderson, fellow imagineer Bob Mattey, and their crews labored night and day on the project. Within a week Mattey had replaced the skin and the inner workings. Then he dug up an eight-cylinder Hudson engine and constructed a piston-and-pulley mechanism that could move the squid's tentacles. But even with Anderson and his people working long hours to paint the backgrounds, the frustrated imagineers still didn't beat the deadline. The park opened without the attraction. Yet a mere three weeks later the squid was wiggling on cue.

A year before the opening of the 1964/65 New York World's Fair, Pepsi approached Admiral Joe Fowler, Disney's park factotum and general attractions wizard, asking whether Disney could come up with a pavilion for them—a children's attraction that would promote UNICEF (the United Nations' Children's Fund). Fowler's organization was already working at top speed on three other major projects for the fair—a walking, talking Abe Lincoln for the State of Illinois, a "Progressland Pavilion" for General Electric, and a Ford "Magic Skyway" that would take guests from dinosaurs and cavemen to a city of the future. Fowler told Pepsi no. It couldn't be done. A year, he felt, was far too short a time.

When Walt caught wind of the conversation, he became irate, telling designer Dick Irvine, "I'll make those decisions. Tell Pepsi I'll do it!" The idea ballooned into "It's a Small World," whose animated dolls in cute native costumes have been singing their peppy tune of the togetherness of humanity at the Disney parks for a quarter-century.

Such incidents pepper any Disney biography, and any conversation with men and women who worked for him. Walt Disney repeatedly placed demands on his organization that could only be called crazy. And he repeatedly bet the company, and his own fortune, at times actually mortgaging his house and borrowing on his life insurance, to invest in untested ideas, driven only by his hunch that they would work, that the public would accept them.

But it was a madness that worked. People drove themselves to extraordinary lengths to make it work. Walt was a mad magnet pulling energy from everyone around him. Sometimes he didn't get what he wanted. But he always got more than he would have gotten by being "sane," "normal," satisfied with "business as usual."

Walt Disney was often called a "genius" (not least by his own public relations department), but he resisted the label. He knew he was not Mozart or Einstein. Yet the label fit in the sense that genius is not about rational ability. It is about the creative power to see new patterns, to find connections that others miss. Rational analysis is weighted toward the status quo, since that's where all the known data come from. Creative synthesis is able to create new things by finding a deeper kind of unity than the available data suggest. Walt Disney had that ability.

Genius often renders the artist nearly or completely incapable of working through an organization. Walt Disney's peculiar madness took just the opposite turn: he demonstrated four abilities any great leader possesses—creativity, energy, communication, and inspiration.

Like a muscle, creative ability grows with exercise. Walt Disney exercised his creative ability early and often. From childhood, he was forced to live by his wits and hard work, carrying newspapers door to door, hawking sodas on the trains, counting bottles in a jelly factory. He quickly learned that the better idea pays more. As an ambulance driver in France in the wake of the First World War, for instance, he painted a Croix de Guerre on his jacket, and soon was making money painting them on the jackets of his comrades. A fellow driver from Georgia had a thriving business in souvenirs, selling German helmets collected on the battlefields to homeward-bound doughboys. When the Georgian saw the camouflage that Disney had painted on his footlocker, he commissioned him to paint helmets at five francs each. Disney painted them in camouflage, then antiqued them with shellac. The Georgian then cut a "bullet" hole in each helmet, glued a little hair around the hole, dragged the helmet through the dirt, and sold it at a huge profit.

Later in his life Walt repeatedly found the next idea, pushed it further, took it the next step. This showed up in ways large and small. When imagineer Dick Irvine suggested glass-bottom boats in a lagoon in Tomorrowland, Disney said, "No, let's do a real submarine ride. Let's take them down and give them ports to look out of." Similarly, when Mickey Mouse was at the height of his popularity, Walt had him redesigned with more mobile eyes and more flexible body.

The energy and obsession that he poured into his projects are legendary within the Disney organization. As a child, he had always worked, whether milking the cows, selling newspapers on street corners, or taking photos of friends' children. As an adult, he rarely stopped working, arriving early and staying late, forced into taking vacations on doctors' orders more than once. He would regularly pay surprise visits to Disneyland, stand in line with the "guests," and take the rides himself, sometimes in the first car, sometimes in the last, looking for anything that might be out of place. The firehouse at Disneyland, near the train station on Main Street, has a small apartment upstairs. Disney would often spend the night there. In the morning the park workers would find notes scribbled on his distinctive blue paper stuck into their work places or in strategic spots around the park. The notes were instructions from "Walt": "Paint that curb," "Move that bench," "Replace these flowers." He had been up during the night, roaming around the park, looking for ways to improve it.

Walt Disney built a company culture that focused on the very highest quality. He would willingly toss out twenty minutes of animation—representing hundreds of hours of expensive and painstaking work—if, in his opinion, it did not help the film. That level of concern could extend almost anywhere within his domain, even to the script of the most ordinary film. The Disney archives include a script of a film called *Follow Me, Boys*, a cornball celebration of the Boy Scouts released a few weeks before Walt's death. He had long lost his major focus on the films that his studio produced. By the time the film was in production he was deep into his plans for Disney World in Florida, and his dream of a city of the future. He was moving forward with major expansions of Disneyland based on the attractions the company had done for the World's Fair. His health was failing him, and he was in pain much of the time. Yet the script of this minor film includes detailed marginal notes in Walt's hand, dealing with minutiae that would normally be in the domain of the film's director.

As Emerson noted, "All vigor is contagious." Walt's vigor became part of the culture of the company.

Walt Disney was a gifted storyteller. He could communicate his vision.

At every other studio in Hollywood, the root of the film-making process was a scriptwriter, sitting alone, typing. At Walt Disney Productions it was Walt, in a story conference, in the door of a drugstore, in a parking lot, telling the story, acting it out for his animators and gag men. His nephew Roy E. Disney remembers Uncle Walt visiting him when he was sick, sitting at his bedside, telling him the story of *Pinocchio*. "And it was just wonderful. He went on for half an hour or more, and he acted all the parts, and his eyebrows shot up and down. A year or two later, when the film was finished, I went to see it and, well, it was pretty bad. It was nowhere near as good as the story he told me. . . . Walt was better than most film-makers because one of his great talents was conveying what it was he wanted to other people."

But the storytelling was not just for making films. It was the foundation of the corporate life of his company. Whether he was telling an architect how he wanted his new studio to look, showing his subordinates what a trip to Disneyland should feel like, or projecting for potential investors how a new project would work, he was at bottom a storyteller, a man who created realities out of the ether and made them so real that other people could give them flesh.

When he needed money from the Bank of America to complete *Snow White*, the bank sent a representative to the lot to see the film. But there wasn't a lot to see yet. So Walt showed the completed bits and pieces to the banker, and simply told him the rest of the story. The banker, who had no experience evaluating films, sat silent through the whole demonstration. The worried Walt showed him out afterwards, and walked him out to his car—with still no word on whether the bank would back the film. As the banker was about to drive away, he told Disney, "That thing is going to make a hatful of money." The bank would loan the money. Walt's power of envisioning something, making the story real, had convinced him.

In the same way, he sold the story of Disneyland to potential sponsors and investors orally and visually. And he sold the Walt Disney story week after week to America, every Sunday night on television, by sitting down and talking. He was nervous about these television appearances. He thought his voiced squeaked and cracked. His Missouri accent bothered him, and he knew his diction wasn't the best. But people believed him. They could see what he saw.

Finally, he had the extraordinary capacity to draw from other people their utmost—their best work, their most creative thought, their last ounce of energy.

It is not too much to say that people who worked for Walt Disney did it at least partly out of love. They fell in love with the man and the visions he could create. Randy Bright, for instance, who would spend 30 years with the Disney company and come to be one of the chief imagineers, remembers the onset of the love affair vividly: "In 1959 while I was in college I started working part-time as a ride operator at Disneyland. I fell in love with it. When I worked on the *Columbia* sailing ship, at night we'd sail out around the Frontierland rivers and we'd anchor the ship out there during the fireworks at 9 o'clock. I'd look through the rigging and see the fireworks going off. I was in a different place, totally in a different world. There were no visual reminders that there was a hotel across the street, and a freeway a quarter mile away. Even then, in 1959, the land-scaping had filled in pretty well. The Frontierland river was really a very acceptable river. You could pretend you were Peter Pan in Neverland, Tom Sawyer on the Mississippi, or whatever you wanted. And I got paid for it. I was 20 years old."

Jim Jimirro, who would later found the Disney Channel, describes the impact of coming to work for Disney, years after Walt's death, with a similar warmth: "When you get an opportunity to be important at Disney it's really heady. Disney has an impact on people. How many people have the opportunity to work for a company that is revered by everybody else? Everybody has their favorite Disney movie, their favorite Disney experience. Everybody remembers their first experience with Mickey Mouse. So you're working with a company with so much pride. When people say, 'Where do you work?' and you say 'Disney,' immediately people want to express themselves. It's what we're all looking for, to be a part of something that people like, something that people believe in, something that makes a difference in people's lives."

Disney veterans and biographers tell stories of destroyed marriages and broken health among Disney's employees, yet people gave themselves willingly to Walt's frenzied energy. Such energy, and such demands for perfection, were woven into the culture of the company.

These four abilities—creativity, energy, communication, and inspiration—made Disney formidable. One nationwide poll asked businessmen to select the ten greatest American businessmen from the past. Walt Disney came in second only to Henry Ford, and well ahead of such creative giants and entrepreneurs as Andrew Carnegie, Thomas Edison, John D. Rockefeller, and Alexander Graham Bell.

On film or in the parks, Walt Disney wanted to build worlds that were, according to his taste, perfect worlds. That his taste happened to coincide with the least common denominator of American taste made his attempts very profitable.

But in the middle '60s it began to seem to his colleagues that he had gone too far. Beginning in the summer of 1964, the company bought 28,000 acres in central Florida, an area only slightly smaller than the city of San Francisco, to build another Magic Kingdom, along with other attractions, resorts, and hotels. The bulldozers had already begun their work down among the palmetto scrub, the cypress, the pine and fern, the stunted scruffy forest hung with Spanish moss, churning the swamps to muck, building a vast network of drainage canals, when Walt got side-tracked again. He began feverish studies that pointed toward a truly fantastic goal: he wanted to build not just a mythical kingdom, but an actual city, a kind of Oz among the swamps, that would be perfect in every way. There would be no crime, no slums, no poverty. Energy, transportation and everything else a city needs would be taken care of in the most clever, innovative, well-planned way. It would be a laboratory for city planning. He hired consultants to scour the country and the world for information, and cleared out a room behind his office to study their reports, quiz them, work on ideas. The project was called EPCOT— "Experimental Prototype Community of Tomorrow."

But Disney was in a race with time, and increasingly he knew it. For years the animators and story men and in-betweeners at Walt Disney Productions knew when Walt was coming down the hall because his cough—a loud, guttural "woof-woof"—preceded him everywhere. He smoked incessantly, and if the cigarettes gave him a persistent cough, that was only natural, a small price to pay for a minor pleasure. In the early 1960s he had shown increasing fascination with medical advances that could prolong life, and even with hopes for physical immortality. In those days cigarette packs carried no warning label: cigarette ads claimed that nicotine was a healthy way to reduce stress; and Walt Disney didn't believe that cigarettes could kill him. But by 1966, the cough had given way to cancer.

He drove his EPCOT researchers relentlessly, and spent more and more hours closeted with their reports, in between his stays at St. Joseph's Hospital across the street from the Burbank studio. As he felt death rumbling inexorably toward him, he began to panic. He hired researchers to look into the infant art of cryogenics—freezing bodies at the moment of death so that they might be brought alive again when the cure for their particular disease has been found. He did this not so that he might live forever, but so that he could come back to correct the mess that he was sure his brother Roy, and his other successors, would make out of EPCOT.

The last time he was released before his final hospitalization, in fact, he went straight to the studio and spent several hours in the secret room poring over the latest reports on EPCOT before coming out to wander around the lot and check on the business of the corporation. He was not fighting ghosts or struggling to live forever. He was doing the same thing he had done all his life. He was fighting his brother. He thought that if he didn't live long enough to build it himself, Roy would never build his city of the future.

Walt spent his 65th birthday, December 5, 1966, in the hospital, too sick to celebrate. The family gathered, afraid that he was dying. But the crisis passed, and over the following days he slowly improved. On the afternoon of the 14th his wife, Lillian, came to visit him, and in the evening his brother, Roy. Both went home elated, convinced that he was recovering. But in the small hours of the night sometime before dawn, something went dreadfully wrong. The doctors suddenly found themselves struggling in vain against an "acute circulatory collapse." For hours no one but the medical staff knew. Outside, the first light of false dawn pushed through the leaden skies of Los Angeles, across the newly-built Ventura Freeway, across the empty two-hundred-yard-wide concrete trough of the Los Angeles River, and lit up the silver water tank that towered over the Disney lot. Walt's famous signature was still there, the looping letters a dozen feet high. But Walt was gone. At 9:35, the sun fully up and the day begun, the doctors called Lillian. It was mid-day before the company announced his passing to the press. Walt Disney, "Uncle Walt" to millions, was dead.

2

Late Bloomer

Michael Dammann Eisner bloomed late. The man who would one day peer from the covers of *Time, Newsweek, Fortune,* and *Business Week* did little to distinguish himself until he was in his late 20s, married, and a father. Until well into his 30s, in any family history he would have been overshadowed by his ancestors.

He was born on March 7, 1942, in Mount Kisco, New York, a suburb 20 miles north of New York City. He came from old money (at least as this country counts it), from generations of upper-crust merchants and lawyers who dabbled in government and community service.

Michael Eisner's grandfather, J. Lester Eisner, typified the family. J. Lester grew up in a three-story frame house on expansive grounds on the banks of the Shrewsbury River in Red Bank, New Jersey. His father, Sigmund, had grown wealthy as a uniform manufacturer, making everything from Boy Scout uniforms to Army parachutes. After attending Phillips Exeter Academy and Harvard College, J. Lester first joined the family firm, then started his own trading company. He served in the First World War and returned as a major; he stayed on in the reserves and the National Guard as a lieutenant colonel—and afterwards styled himself "Colonel Eisner." In the Great Depression he served on, founded, or chaired a half-dozen state and local government commissions dealing with the crisis, once offering to serve without salary if necessary. When his parents died, he and his brother donated the family house to the town of Red Bank for use as a library. At the outbreak of World War II, he shipped off to London, and later to Paris, to organize transportation for the Army Reserve Corps. He was a joiner, an organizer. A member of a number of yacht clubs, the Harvard Club, the Army and Navy Club in Washington, and the American Club in London, he was knit into the working establishment of the country. He believed in making a contribution.

J. Lester Eisner's eldest son, Lester, Jr., attended Princeton and graduated from Harvard Law School. He married Margaret Dammann, the daughter of Milton Dammann, one of the founders of the American Safety Razor Company (eventually sold to Philip Morris). Margaret and Lester had two children, Margot and Michael. Not quite 30 when the Japanese attacked Pearl Harbor, Lester Eisner volunteered for the Army Air Corps, and emerged from the war as a captain. He was tall, and he looked much like his son would one day: the same floppy ears and dark curly hair, but the face more lean, saturnine, sometimes given to brooding. A more private man than his father, Lester, Jr., shifted his attention from one business to another, first starting a small airline and merging it with another with routes in Latin America, then producing trade shows at the Coliseum and other arenas in New York. What increased his fortune, though, was his sure-handed investment in New York real estate. A Republican, he would later shuttle between private business and high housing posts in the state and federal governments. During this time Margaret, in addition to being a mother, volunteered for public service, eventually becoming the president of a medical-research institute.

Michael lived the sheltered, serious childhood of a member of New York's elite, in a quiet, luxurious apartment three floors above Park Avenue on the prestigious Upper East Side, and in the family's "country place" in Bedford Hills, near Mount Kisco.

His life was carefully ordered. His parents took care to expose him to the proper kind of culture. They arranged for an art collector friend, Victor Ganz, to loan them a Picasso, *The Bullfight*, to hang on young Michael's bedroom wall. They took him to Broadway shows and to Leonard Bernstein's Young People's Concerts at the Philharmonic.

He went to school a few blocks south of the Park Avenue apartment at Allen-Stevenson School on East 78th Street, one of the city's most elite private schools. Founded in 1883, it was an all-boys school in a fine old four-story Georgian building. The school was known all over the city for its children's orchestra. Decades later Michael would still remember fondly his music teacher, Stanley Gauger. Michael played every sport, but as a student he was only average. He went to school every day outfitted in a tie, a button-down blue cap, and a blue blazer, with the escutcheon of the school in gold on the pocket bearing the school's symbol: the lamp of learning.

At home in the evening he came to dinner in a tie and jacket. Dinner was formal. The boy who would later be considered a television program-

ming genius was allowed to watch only one hour of television each day—
and that only after reading for two hours.

His parents only occasionally took him to the movies, where he could
escape to other worlds that were full of possibilities. He was no adoles-
cent movie maven. As childhood friend Susan Baerwald put it, "We all
went to movies, but it was nothing special. We both came from families
in the business world, and Michael didn't show any sign of steering from
that."

Yet, like most children of his generation, he was steeped in television
and movies. Television and Disney came of age as Eisner did. Eisner was
a member of the first generation to grow up with television, the first
generation that would be comfortable with television's peculiar plasticity
and its constant play with stories. In the mid-1950s, "Hopalong Cassidy"
and "The Lone Ranger" were joined on the television networks by Walt
Disney. When Michael was 12, "The Mickey Mouse Club," soon to be
the most popular kids' show on television, debuted on ABC. On Sunday
evenings Davy Crockett and his fellow Disney icons captured the hero-
hungry kid hearts of America on "Disneyland."

Eisner would later say that, like other children of his era, "I grew up
on Disney." But if he did, it was the Disney of "Disneyland" and "The
Mickey Mouse Club"—the Disney of television, not the Disney of the
great animated classics. These years were the peak of Walt Disney's
creativity. Off in California, in sunny Burbank, Disney had artists at the
drawing boards turning out *Cinderella*, *Alice in Wonderland*, and *Peter
Pan*. While Eisner was growing up, *Snow White*, *Pinocchio*, *Fantasia*,
Dumbo, and *Bambi* were reissued. Oddly, unlike most children of his
generation, Michael never saw any of them until he was married and had
a child of his own. He would later reflect on the world of animated
classics: "I wish I could say this was in my blood. It wasn't."

"Disneyland," the television series, often portrayed Disneyland, the place.
Several shows during the series' first year were full documentaries of the
building of Disneyland. Finally, during the summer between the series'
first and second years, Disneyland opened with a major live telecast.

On July 17, 1955, thousands of children and their parents, impatient
and excited, stood in a line on pavement that only months before had been
the soft tilled earth between fragrant rows of blossoming orange trees in
the southern California summer sun. In Disney's corporate mythology,
opening day at Disneyland would come to be known as "Black Sunday."

Some 35,000 people packed the park, many of them carrying one of the thousands of counterfeit tickets that someone had printed and sold. Others talked their way past the ticket-takers, claiming to be friends of Walt. Still others climbed over the back fence, helped over by locals with ladders out for a few quick dollars freelancing.

The landscaping was still sparse. In some areas, the cement was still wet. Some of the first people to venture onto Main Street's still-steaming asphalt had to leave their shoes behind, mired in the tar. Only a few rides were in operation. The "Canal Boats of the World" ride was nicknamed by Disney management the "Mud Banks of the World" because the quaint villages that were supposed to line its banks had not yet been built. The outboard engines of the boats, when they worked, drowned out what the guides were saying. A plumbers' strike had left the park critically short of drinking fountains, in what the press would call a scheme to jack up soda-fountain sales. Crowd control "experts," hired outside the firm, yelled at tourists and herded them about.

Still, it was a grand day. The governor, Goodwin Knight, was there to ride up Main Street with Walt Disney. Twenty-two television cameras recorded the festivities for nationwide telecast, claimed by ABC to be the first time more than three cameras were used to record any live event. Three emcees shared the announcing chores: Bob Cummings, Art Link-letter, and Ronald Reagan. Cummings at one point shouted, "I think that everyone here will one day be as proud to have been at this opening as the people who were there at the dedication of the Eiffel Tower." And when the speeches were done, America could watch the first group of children run screaming up Main Street and under the gates of Cinderella's Castle. Walt took his television audience on a walking tour of the brand new park: Main Street, Frontierland, and Fantasyland. The long telecast caught Sammy Davis, Jr., and Frank Sinatra driving the pint-sized cars of Autopia, and Irene Dunne trying and failing to smash a bottle of water across the bow of the *Mark Twain* in Frontierland. The whole event made a lasting impression on America.

Michael's parents assumed that he would, like his father, eventually go to Princeton. They also assumed that he would go on to law school, as well, perhaps Harvard, which had graduated his father, his grandfather, and his great uncle. So in 1956, when Michael Eisner was 14, his parents packed him off to live in one big room with two dozen other boys at Lawrenceville in New Jersey, one of the region's most prestigious boarding schools, known as a "feeder" for Princeton.

Founded in 1810, when James Madison lived in the White House, Lawrenceville School is eerily similar to the school that Eisner would feature in the 1989 Disney film *Dead Poets Society*. It looked from the outside like a vast wooded estate behind a high black-iron spiked fence. Inside, the white clapboard houses of the faculty sat apart from the main brick and stone buildings, roofed in slate. The neatly groomed paths and roads wound about under a leafy canopy of trees. Broad and plush fields accommodated the rush of soccer and football players. The campus sported dozens of tennis courts and the school's own golf course. Lawrenceville's central commons, the Circle, had been designed by Frederick Law Olmsted, designer of New York's Central Park.

The man who, within a few years, would begin to build a career based on an uncanny appreciation of the tastes of the average American spent his formative high school years carefully insulated from average people. Lawrenceville's tuition in 1956 was the same as nearby Princeton University—$3,000 per year. There were no black students at Lawrenceville and no women. Eisner rubbed shoulders only with white patrician males. Over the years Lawrenceville had graduated, among many other sons of the Establishment, Malcolm Forbes, Governor Lowell Weicker, and Saudi prince Turqi al-Faisal. Joe DiMaggio and Errol Flynn both had sons in young Eisner's class. It has since been home to a surprising number of people in the entertainment industry, including rock performer Huey Lewis, screenwriter-director Richard Tuggle (*Escape from Alcatraz* and *Tightrope*), network executive Brandon Tartikoff, and Richard Berger, whom Eisner would one day fire as head of production at Disney.

Lawrenceville was a rigorous school, with small colloquium classes and a seven-day week filled with activities, from compulsory chapel to varsity sports. Students only saw their parents at Thanksgiving, Christmas, and Easter vacations, one weekend each in the fall and spring quarters, two weekends in the winter. So, from the age of 14, Eisner had only intermittent contact with his father and mother. He did not have much contact with girls during the school year. In the summer he would see his friends in New York, and one summer he took ballroom dancing lessons with Susan Baerwald.

In a school with only 750 students, in a class of fewer than 200, there are plenty of niches for everyone. People don't easily get lost in the crowd. But Eisner did. His friends found him funny, a prankster and a joker. Yet he was no shining star. He joined the Periwig Club, the school's drama society, but he never captured a lead role. He joined the staff of the school paper one year, and the yearbook another, but he was not an editor. He made scholastic honors his first year, but never repeated that feat in his remaining three years. In those four years he grew beyond "strapping" to "towering," four inches over six feet, and he played and coached basketball, football, and tennis for the "houses" where he lived. Yet he was never a star player or team captain. He went out for fencing, since the sport requires reach. But fencing also demands a grace he didn't have, and he never made varsity.

He was known for his skill at "Gettysburg," a popular Civil War board game, for his wit, and for his innocent self-promotion. A Lawrenceville friend said, "You never heard about his family. He never suggested by his clothes or his style that his family had money to speak of. But when he accomplished something, recovered a fumble at football or won a tennis match, everybody would find out really fast, because he'd talk about it. He would have been the first to dance in the end zone, like they do today on television."

His teachers knew that if Michael Eisner were to find success at all, it would not be in academia. In November 1959, when SAT scores were in, he sat down with his school counselors and talked about college. Because of his less than sterling performance in the classroom, he had already given up hope of attending Princeton or Harvard. He had focused instead on McGill University in Montreal. Now even that seemed out of reach. He had sleepwalked through Lawrenceville, and as a result had failed at the principal task of students at such prominent prep schools: getting into an Ivy League college. He attended instead Denison University, a small (2,000-student) liberal arts college in Granville, Ohio.

It was almost an exile, although a pleasant one. Denison sits on a hillside, overlooking a valley in Licking County, Ohio, an hour's drive east of Columbus. With its flowering dogwoods, its stalwart brick buildings, and its chapel steeple crowning the hill, it looks like a tiny chunk of New England plopped down in the Midwest.

Eisner's failure to get into an Ivy League school may have been the best thing that could have happened to him. His time at Denison proved to be a startling break from the sheltered environment that he had lived in from birth.

Michael would never, it seemed clear now, be a lawyer like his father, his great uncle, or his grandfather. It had not been lost on him that his father never really enjoyed being a lawyer, and kept dabbling in one business after another, and then in government service, searching for something that would move him. Perhaps Michael could discover who he was, and what he was made for.

Eisner registered at Denison as a pre-med student. He wanted to be a doctor. But, after reading a Maxwell Anderson essay about "how what remains behind in societies is not the wars or the politics but the art," he found his imagination piqued. He felt himself drawn to the arts. In his third year he changed his major to theater. He tried to write plays, the first one to impress a pretty drama major who had caught his eye. The play, the story of two young lovers caught in a ski lift, was to star the drama major. The lead male part was roughly modeled on Eisner himself. The lead female character was a wild, sensual young woman, which the drama major was not. His play did not, apparently, win the girl's heart, but the world of entertainment began to win over Eisner. When confronted with the assignment of writing his philosophy of life for another class, he convinced the professor to let him write another play instead. Before he left Denison, he had written five more plays, which are packed away in his attic today.

At Denison, he continued to indulge and nurture his puckish, playful, impulsive, inquisitive side, interrupting his professors with strange questions and observations, points of view that were sometimes wildly different. Literature professor Dominick Consolo had been lecturing on *Moby Dick* for six days straight. It was one of his favorite subjects. Suddenly Eisner's hand shot up, and he posed an odd question: "What if this whole thing is a big fish tale?" Consolo reminded Eisner that the white whale was a mammal, not a fish. But Eisner persisted, pointing out how, looked at from a different point of view, this was not a ponderous epistle of morality, but an elaborate joke, a long, drawn-out satirical "fish story." Consolo remained unconvinced, even when Eisner made his theory the subject of a four-page paper. The paper earned Eisner a B and the sobriquet "Mr. What If."

This quest for the oddball point of view, the unsounded note, this playing with ideas, would become a major theme in Eisner's life. It would earn him praise, scorn, and puzzlement. It would gain him major assignments and jobs, and it would cost him as well, when others thought of him as childish or even silly.

In the summer of 1963, following his junior year at Denison, Eisner returned to New York to take a job as a page at NBC. He spent the summer deep inside the tall granite warren of Rockefeller Center, giving studio tours to tourists, ushering them into their studio-audience seats, standing watch for rowdies, keeping things moving properly, watching what excited the audience. It was his first contact with the arcane, powerful, impressionistic world of television. It was also his first contact with the world of studio tours, crowd control, and the care and feeding of the American tourist.

Despite this introduction, Eisner did not set out immediately to explore the world of entertainment. He had already written a half-dozen plays, and he thought of himself as a writer. Within a few days of his graduation from Denison, he was on the *Mauritania*, headed for Paris, to sit in the boulevard cafés, like Hemingway and Fitzgerald, and write his novel.

While the trip over was fun ("All the girls were getting out of college about that time. . . . I had a great time on that boat."), after ten days in Paris he decided that the life of the expatriate writer was ridiculous: "There were a lot of Americans in Paris who were hiding their American Express checks under their mattresses and going around acting real poor. It was like a game everyone was playing." He tired of the game and headed home. If he had not known it before, he had quickly discovered that he was no solitary creator. His creativity would have to take some other form, one more suited to his gregarious and curious personality.

Back in New York, Eisner landed another entry-level job in network television as an FCC logging clerk at NBC, meticulously recording for the government the endless minutiae of what went out on the air. Eight hours a day, 40 hours a week, he watched television. His boredom at the job was instant, and he began almost immediately looking for something else. Six weeks later he landed a position in the programming department at CBS. His job was to make sure the children's shows at CBS had all the commercials inserted in their proper spots. It was a step up, and it was a job that involved him more directly in the world of television.

Eisner spent almost two years doing the paperwork at CBS on endless commercials for breakfast cereals, Frisbees and toy robots. Finally, itching for a job with more possibilities, he put together a new résumé and began sending it out to the television community. He sent out over 200 résumés with a doggedness that remains one of his trademarks to this day. The single response he received turned out to be one of the most important communications of his life. It was from Barry Diller, only a year older than Eisner but already assistant to Leonard Goldberg, the vice president of programming at ABC.

Diller had no job available for Eisner, but the two decided to meet. Diller was impressed. He was convinced that Eisner showed real promise. In November 1966, Diller managed to get him a job in the programming department, working on specials for Ted Fetter. This was not a premium job. In the 1960s, ABC was considered a backwater network. It was so far behind CBS and NBC in the ratings that people in the industry habitually called it "the fourth network." Within ABC, specials was a backwater department; the network did few of them. And within the specials department, Eisner's job was itself a kind of backwater—he had few responsibilities as an assistant to a man who, it turned out, was already on his way out of the company.

But it was the open door that Eisner needed, the chance to begin to show what he could do. The job also proved to be the beginning of an 18-year alliance and rivalry between Eisner and Diller. While Diller himself had no power at ABC at this point, he had the ear of one of the powers at ABC. And he was the gate-keeper for that power. To get to Leonard Goldberg's office you had to walk through Barry Diller's office.

In 1967, Gary Pudney (today a partner in Paradigm Entertainment) joined ABC as director of specials and talent, taking over from Fetter in supervising the network's specials, as well as acting as ombudsman and recruiter for talent on all network shows. It was a new position. Pudney's job was to lure new talent, to establish relationships with major talents that were not yet in the network's orbit, to woo them and get them to do projects at ABC.

Michael Eisner was to be Pudney's new assistant. Diller had kept Goldberg aware of Eisner, and finally Goldberg had given Eisner to Pudney with orders: "Take this kid and see what you can do with him. If he works out, we'll find a place for him. If he doesn't, fire him." Eisner showed up for his first day of work with Pudney, his clothes disheveled, motorcycle helmet in hand, a rumply, tousle-haired kid with a cowlick. It turned out that Eisner showed up that way every morning, tie askew, suit in need of pressing, hair three sheets to the wind. Pudney thought him "goofy-looking." Yet while he thought of Eisner as clumsy, he also found him boyish, likeable, and possessed of an eager charm. And in Eisner's job, handling stars, it was important that he be likeable. Pudney soon began to see other assets in his young assistant. Eisner was willing and ready to do any task that came to hand, from picking up celebrities at the airport to spending night after night scouring the theaters and nightclubs of Manhattan for undiscovered talent. He had what Pudney would call a "supernatural enthusiasm" for the job: "It didn't make any difference how late or early the hours were, or where he had to go, or how late he had to stay up, or how many shows he had to go to. He had a great lust for the theater, and for comedy clubs." He was also, according to Pudney, smarter than anybody else around.

Despite his liberal arts education and romantic attraction to the arts, Eisner quickly became a pragmatist at ABC. "I noticed early on that there would be this great enthusiasm at ABC for 13 hours of Shakespeare," recalls Eisner. "But I also noticed that the guy who did the 13 hours would get fired. I'm a survivor, and I wasn't going to be fired."

Pudney came to think of Eisner, with his intelligence, enthusiasm, sense of organization, and charm, as a treasure. But Eisner was equally lucky in getting Pudney for a boss at this formative stage in his career. Unlike many ABC executives, it was Pudney's style to let subordinates get involved in things, take responsibility, put their hands on projects. Pudney gave Eisner the title "manager of specials and talent," and let him go to work. It was the only way to learn television, and Eisner learned rapidly. ABC, with Pudney, was Eisner's graduate school.

Working with the talent under Pudney, Eisner began to see something that many network executives did not: that talent was what drove the network. Find entertainers whom people want to watch, put them in projects that will let them show what they can do, and people will watch. Yet many network executives did not particularly like the entertainers they hired.

Variety shows were a big part of television in the late '60s. Every network had four or five running at a time. The country frothed with the energy of the young baby boom generation, and the networks competed desperately to come up with formats that would attract these young viewers. Yet network people still did not see any point in hanging out at night clubs, coffee-houses, and off-Broadway theaters, beating the bushes for new talent. Eisner did.

Morning after morning Eisner would get off the elevator at the 31st floor, motorcycle helmet in hand and the morning papers under his arm, looking more like a messenger than an executive. He would set the helmet down in his jumbled cubicle, filled with lithographs from ABC shows, the windows looking out toward Fifth Avenue and the back of Warwick Hotel. He would open his logbook and write in his notes from his latest foray down to the Village to see an act or musical. He would cut the reviews of new entertainers out of the paper and paste them in. He was "keeping the pulse." The logbook mirrored Eisner perfectly: it was big, a little disheveled, the pages dog-eared and coffee-stained. But it was also highly organized and filled with information.

Eisner would show the log to Pudney periodically, and discuss the acts that he had seen. And he would talk to Pudney about television and how it was changing. Many network people never watched television at home like other Americans, as if they were embarrassed by their own medium, as if they had been so inundated with rough cuts and screenings that they couldn't settle on the couch and be part of the audience. Every night that he stayed home, Michael would watch the shows, count the commercials, stopwatch the breaks.

Other nights would find him at ABC's production center on the West Side, sitting at the elbow of the video editors, splicing together shots, learning the craft by working with the craftsmen.

His second year with Pudney brought Eisner the first project he could call his own. It combined his newfound enthusiasm for working with entertainers with an interest that would blossom later: theme parks. At the time, ABC owned Marine World, which was then in Foster City, a half-hour south of San Francisco. Marine World was a favorite toy of Leonard Goldenson, the head of the network. Pudney asked Eisner to produce an in-house special to be called "Feelin' Groovy at Marine World." The special would feature the rock band The Young Rascals performing their recent hit "Groovin'." Eisner wanted to build the special around a major talent, and he decided to try to talk Bing Crosby into signing on for the show. Crosby lived in Pebble Beach, California, a short plane hop south of San Francisco. Eisner flew to San Francisco, got in touch with Crosby, and was able to talk him into narrating the show. The show pulled good ratings, and got the attention, especially, of Goldenson. Before long, ABC executives began to look for other assignments to give the young producer.

At this point in his career at ABC, Eisner made $16,000 to $18,000 per year. Pudney thought he was poor. The motorcycle and the thrown-on clothes hardly spoke of great wealth, and Eisner never talked about his family. Ever since Eisner had come to work for him, he had been inviting Pudney to dinner at his house, to meet his new wife, Jane. Pudney had put him off with various excuses for a year. He thought he would be intruding, and that it would embarrass both of them. "My God, I don't want to get myself into this," he thought. "God knows where they live, or how they live. The Bowery, or some place like that." Nevertheless, he finally agreed to come. The address Michael gave him was on East 81st Street near Lexington Avenue, a high-rent district then, as it is now. When he got there, Pudney discovered that Michael and Jane owned a brownstone townhouse furnished with antiques. Michael welcomed him amid the paintings and tasteful furniture, his tie askew and his cowlick standing up, and introduced his wife. Pudney immediately began calling her "Rita": her beauty and her striking red hair reminded him of Rita Hayworth. Michael had married her less than two years before. He was crazy about her. He had managed to parlay a business trip to Italy for a Sophia Loren special into a honeymoon in Venice, complete with singing gondoliers in the moonlight and visits to little glass-blowing shops.

Pudney and Eisner talked that night of things they had touched on before: the network and Eisner's ambitions. Eisner wanted someday to run ABC. He claimed to know exactly what he would do if he were in charge. But he was also fascinated by the movies. He would love, he said, to run a studio someday. He loved animation and dreamed of producing an animated series, or even a film. He also loved family entertainment, and was an admirer of Walt Disney. He felt he knew nothing about children's entertainment, so he had recently taken Jane and his six-month-old son Breck out to the old Bruckner Drive-In in the Bronx to see *Pinocchio*. It was his first encounter with Disney animated classics. "I'd never seen anything like it. It was fabulous. Sitting there, watching this marvelous puppet, I couldn't believe I was in the same field." Years later, he would focus on how jarring the experience was to a man who just a few years before had been putting commercials in "Quick Draw McGraw" cartoons: "I was in the car, with this terrible sound and terrible picture, but I just couldn't believe the difference. I couldn't believe how real it was. . . . Then you watch *Pinocchio* and all of a sudden a light goes on. I became obsessed with Disney and watched every one of the Disney movies."

At the same time that his Disney fascination developed, Eisner was becoming bolder in his efforts to get to know talent. Pudney continued to drum into him that talent was the key to success. In this business, he would tell his assistant, it's who you know, so get out there and get to know people. Eisner began meeting stars that he would work with over the decades, including Carol Burnett, a friend of Pudney's.

In network meetings about programming he was an odd duck, making references to dramatic unity, the Greek chorus or the *deus ex machina*. Half the time, Pudney admits, "I didn't know what the hell he was talking about." Eisner pushed for new ideas that would attract a younger audience. In doing so, he often said the right thing at the wrong time, and ended up with his foot in his mouth. He was sometimes out of place, and people became angry with him. But he was impossible to stay mad at. He began to gain a reputation in the company. Fred Pierce, who would become president of ABC television network while Eisner was there, says he became known as "a progressive, hard-driving executive that would get the job done, if he knew what the assignment was."

Pudney and Eisner drew in the talent in increasing numbers and built specials around them—stars such as Tom Jones, Engelbert Humperdink, and Johnny Cash. But Pudney began to feel that Eisner was underutilized. He told the people on the 37th floor—Leonard Goldberg and Barry Diller and Marty Starger—"This Michael kid is highly capable. He can do everything and we're not utilizing him to his fullest capacity. You have to let him develop some programs. He belongs in program development."

The brass listened, and in 1970 Eisner moved upstairs. In the preceding three years he had built a reputation within the company as a brilliant new voice, and he was about to begin a remarkable six-year odyssey that would grant him one of his dreams: his own studio.

Between 1970 and 1976, Eisner moved from New York to Los Angeles, and worked his way up ABC's corporate ladder through a series of job descriptions and titles, from "director of program development for the East Coast" to "senior vice president for prime-time production and development." At one time or another he became head of nearly every department of program development at ABC, from children's programming to daytime television, from variety to prime-time series. The rise would seem rapid to an outsider, and it was, but as the late Elton Rule, then president of ABC, put it, "That was a young man's business. It was very fast. Recognition was quick. Your skills could be shown quickly. They were on display for a lot of people to see."

People in the industry were already describing Eisner as "childlike." Some meant it as a compliment to his simplicity, charm, enthusiasm, and lack of corporate polish. Others referred to what they saw as a short attention span, although it may have been simple impatience. Married, a father, and a fast-rising corporate executive, Eisner still carried an ingenuousness, an artless directness so bald that many would mistake it for naiveté.

In part because of these traits, Eisner was given responsibility for all of the network's children's programming. He had always felt a special empathy for children, and he reveled in his new job. For two years, he spent most of his working hours watching children's cartoon shows. (From this he garnered some rare and valuable training, along with some training of dubious value: he can—and will, if prompted—sing from memory the theme songs of such cultural monuments as "Bugs Bunny," "George of the Jungle," "Tom and Jerry," and "Rocky and Bullwinkle.") He soon had designed his first animated series, built around two singing groups.

"We were in last place," he said later, referring to ABC's position in the Saturday morning kiddie ratings wars, "and I had heard about this group called the Jackson Five. I had nothing better to do, so I went to Las Vegas to hear them sing. It occurred to me that the Jackson Five would make a good animated show. Everything else on Saturday morning then was 'Scooby-Do' and 'Mighty Mouse.' The Jackson Five were real people. Also, I liked the story of how Diana Ross had discovered them in Gary, Indiana. After the Jacksons, we did an animated Osmond Brothers show. We went from third to first." To those two, he added a series of "Afterschool Specials."

He repeated his success in daytime programming, land of the soaps, by starting such hit series as "All My Children" and "One Life to Live"; then in prime time with television movies such as *Brian's Song*, and such series as "Barney Miller," "Happy Days," "Starsky and Hutch," "Baretta," and "Welcome Back, Kotter."

Eisner's taste, it turned out, was perfect for the task at hand. If he liked something, usually his audience would too. It worked in children's television, in daytime soap operas, and in prime time. Eisner sometimes attributes this instinct simply to his age, his membership in a cohort just ahead of the baby boom: "My biggest break was being born in 1942. When I was 21, that was the target audience for everything. When I was 35, the target audience was 35. I always felt and acted as though I was the audience." He had grown up with the medium, and now he had the opportunity to grow up with a network. He was lucky to land at ABC, which had nowhere to go but up. It was a network that was willing to try almost anything to gain a yard on its rivals, and it was willing to quickly recognize and reward anybody who helped them gain that yard.

These were the years that ABC, the perpetual also-ran in the ratings race, overtook its two great rivals and became the dominant television network in America. Between 1968 and 1983, the long-anemic network grew from 146 to 214 affiliate television stations and from 365 to 1,800 affiliate radio stations, while company profits shot up from $13.5 to $160 million on revenues that expanded from $600 million to $2.7 billion.

There were many parts to this extraordinary turnaround, but industry analysts agree that its engine was the decisions made, the risks taken, and the money invested in basic television programming. Much of the credit for this creative programming is commonly given to Fred Silverman, who became president of ABC entertainment late in 1975. But others point out that a number of the most popular shows were under development before Silverman arrived, and give Eisner the credit (or at least a share of it). Rule, for instance, said, "Mike's contribution to the turnaround was considerably more than he was given credit for." According to Fred Pierce, "Obviously it's a collaborative effort, but Eisner was basically the driving force behind ABC's turnaround." Rule agreed, saying in particular that "He's got to be given major credit for 'Happy Days.'"

"It was Eisner, for instance," Pierce points out, "who suggested that the 'Fonzie' character played by Henry Winkler on 'Happy Days' be brought to the forefront. This really helped the series explode and helped keep it on the air for seven or eight years. And a number of spinoffs developed out of the initial success of 'Happy Days' which were successful in themselves, such as 'Laverne and Shirley,' and 'Mork and Mindy.'"

The shows share a trademark of Eisner's. They are simple, almost cartoonlike in characterization, with a strong sense of story and larger-than-life, quirky, charming characters of no great depth or complexity. And, for the most part, they are upbeat. One might guess, if one didn't already know, that they were developed by a network executive who had cut his teeth on children's television. But they clearly fit the taste of the American television watcher. Despite his blueblood background, Eisner seemed to have an unusual ability to sense what middle America would enjoy seeing. According to Rule, "He shoots from his gut. He's got a good gut, a commercial gut—a good feel for the taste of the viewer." Diller would later say, "Michael has good taste, a good eye, and a good brain." Speaking of Eisner's time at ABC, Pierce says, "He had a terrific entertainment flair. He had a good feel for showmanship. He knew what would work and what was appealing." He showed this "flair" repeatedly at ABC, and it is this flair, more than anything else, that would become the backbone of his career.

Eisner always considered network programming, with its fast pace and incessant need for new material, to be his training ground. When he, Diller, and Brandon Stoddard were reinventing the television movie and miniseries concepts that Walt Disney had pioneered on Sunday nights two decades before, they churned out 75 movies a year: "It's a volume medium. You never have a chance to rest. . . . We learned how to survive in the creative bunker."

The pressure made them very different from the rest of Hollywood.

"Everybody thought we were inferior," Eisner has said. "We couldn't go to the better restaurants, and we certainly were not to be socialized with. But TV is actually a great training ground. The network business has a certain work ethic. When we moved to California, the movie business was much more lethargic. You'd wait until a great idea fell from the sky. If we had an idea we liked, we'd say, 'Let's go find somebody to do it.' "

It was at ABC, as well, that Eisner developed a singular, and some-times astonishing, executive style. Pierce describes him as "full of boyish enthusiasm. He had tremendous amount of drive. He would do whatever was necessary to get to the goal line. He never gave up on a project. For instance, he had an innate belief in 'Barney Miller' as a show. He stuck with it and kept it on the air. He had a tremendous enthusiasm for getting ABC to purchase the animated version of the 'Jackson Five.' " According to Brandon Stoddard (now president of ABC Productions), "Many times he said something was the greatest idea ever, and I knew it was just terrible. But his energy was so great that we'd get carried away and do it. His enthusiasm is greater than any human being's I know."

Eisner combined this enthusiasm, energy, and instinctive awareness of the audience with a businesslike feel for detail. Pierce even describes him as "buttoned up. He was always prepared. If he was going to make remarks at an affiliate convention, he was one of the few executives I knew who would write his own remarks and have them all prepared in a looseleaf notebook."

He combined enthusiasm and intense preparation with an affinity for risk. Rule said Eisner was "not afraid to take a shot. As a matter of fact, there was probably a time when he was not afraid to take chances to a fault. We're all searching for answers, and he would go a little overboard."

Eisner displayed yet another talent that would serve him well through-out his career. He had, according to Pierce, "an uncanny knack for picking very good, intelligent people who would not only support him but challenge him to get the job done. For example, he hired Tom Warner and Marci Carsey, who have gone on to become one of the most successful production teams in Hollywood." It was a knack he had developed early, scouting talent for Pudney: he could spot executive talent when it was still embryonic. Just as important, he could recognize his own limitations and find people to complement them—an ability that would become crucial when he took on Disney.

Eisner's executive style was not based on a theoretical concept he had picked up in a business school or from Dale Carnegie. It seemed to spring straight from his own personality. As Rule put it, "Mike is extremely bright. He's very high strung. All you have to do is be with him for five minutes, and you can feel it. He's all sweaty palms. He's very flamboyant. In a meeting it's pretty hard to keep him sitting. He tends to get up. He has to be moving around and gesticulating. He's a very mental-physical person and that's good. That's his way of expressing himself. He's kind of a big puppy dog; he's all over the place."

He was all over the place and, sometimes, over the edge. Another man who has worked for him says, "If he weren't Michael Eisner, you'd think this guy was a lunatic." Diller puts it less bluntly: "He's a little crazy, and that always helps. Anybody who is good in this business is a little crazy."

3

The Sorcerer's Apprentices

Like Davy Crockett, the Tennessee congressman, Walt Disney was one of those rare people who had created a legend for himself and made it stick. The country's reaction to his death was the reaction to the death of a legend. Teachers reported students bursting into tears at the news.

The night of Walt Disney's death, television commentator Erik Sevareid perhaps best summed up the feelings of the country when he remarked on network television that Disney "was an original, not just an American original, but an original, period. He was a happy accident, one of the happiest this century has experienced. . . . He probably did more to heal or at least soothe troubled human spirits than all the psychiatrists in the world. There can't be many adults in the allegedly civilized parts of the globe who did not inhabit Disney's mind and imagination at least for a few hours and feel better for the visitation. . . . What Disney seemed to know was that while there is very little grown-up in every child, there is a lot of child in every grown-up. . . . People are saying we'll never see his like again."

After Walt Disney's death, the *Los Angeles Times* echoed most of its peers when it remarked in an editorial that his "true joy must have come from seeing the flash of delight sweep across a child's face and hearing his sudden laughter, at the first sight of Mickey Mouse, or Snow White or Pinocchio."

Once Walt Disney the man was gone, Walt Disney the myth quickly took his place. The company began to deify Walt the day he died. Decades later most Disney veterans could recall exactly what they were doing, where they were standing, and who was with them when they heard the news.

Walt's place in the company quickly solidified—even rigidified. Randy Bright (later one of the chief designers of EPCOT) was working in the Disney University on a new employee orientation program at the time.

The employees stood around the coffee pot in shock, talking about Walt's death. Suddenly, Bright's boss disappeared from the group, only to return an hour later with a concept for "the Walt Disney tradition" at Disneyland. His basic premise, which the company soon adopted, was that the company would maintain Walt's philosophy and traditions throughout the park. Bright designed training programs that focused specifically on keeping the Walt Disney tradition alive in the company. He even produced a book of Walt Disney's quotes. "Anything that Walt said became chiseled in stone as part of the ten commandments," Bright said, "even though a lot of things that Walt was quoted to have said were written by his speechwriters."

While Walt's death cast a pall over Anaheim, the same was not true on Wall Street. Paradoxically, when Walt Disney died, the company's stock rose. Wall Street seemed to feel that, now that the brand was established, the demise of its founder only rendered it more stable. And the company seemed like a prime candidate for a merger. It was, after all, on sound financial footing. It had little debt. For the most part, the new attractions were paid for out of the till. The studio had its ups and downs, but was profitable in all but a few years. The company had bought 28,000 acres in Florida on the cheap, through agents and dummy companies. The towers and lakes and boardwalk streets of the new Magic Kingdom were already taking form among the kudzu and loblolly.

Still, all was not right in the Disney universe. In a sense, Walt Disney's very success was his gravest failure. Although Walt Disney Productions was a large organization, with hundreds of creative animators, writers, designers, engineers, and architects, its personality was an extension of Walt Disney himself. Without him, the company was leaderless and, in some ways, brain dead. There was no one who could take his place. He had shaped the organization to meet his own needs. People ambitious enough to want recognition in the world had largely elected not to work in his shadow. The good news for Walt Disney Productions had been that Walt was an autocratic visionary capable of thinking grand new thoughts and pushing them into reality. The bad news, now that Walt was gone, was that the company consisted of people who were used to working for an autocratic visionary: they had been trained to expect the big ideas and the big decisions to come from the top. In Walt's absence many of them were not able to create anything on their own. The danger was that the company would fall back on rote, doing things the way they had been done before. As Randy Bright put it, "Walt left an organization that wasn't used to making decisions. It was used to saying 'Well, Diz will tell us if this is right or not.' "

After Walt's death, 72-year-old Roy O. Disney, the president of the company, was named chairman. Donn Tatum became president, and marketing manager Card Walker was appointed executive vice president for operations. Together, the three became known as the "Disney Troika," and over the next five years they managed the company and oversaw the construction of the new Magic Kingdom in Florida.

Walt Disney Productions was not a well oiled machine capable of running on autopilot indefinitely. It was a herky-jerky congeries of divisions, projects, and joint ventures held together by Walt's personality, energy, and interests. His brother Roy, by his own admission, had none of his brother's genius for technical leaps, none of his passion for novelty, and little of his salesman's ability to intrigue potential investors. Roy had carried the business side of things for Walt Disney Productions, yet had little flair for the deal. He was the steady metronome to Walt's wild improvisation.

Roy did not attempt to run the company alone. He shrank from responsibility and sought consensus, creating layers of committees. At the top he established an executive committee that included himself, Card Walker, Donn Tatum, film producers Bill Anderson and Bill Walsh, Roy E. Disney, Jr., and Walt's son-in-law Ron Miller, a former college football star whom Walt had made a producer.

The committee system had inherent problems. The company operated like the Roman Catholic Church, but without a pope. Ward Kimball, one of the "Nine Old Men" (key animators from *Snow White* days), later remarked, "I think that any organization that was built by one man, one man's tastes and choices, will have a tough time adjusting to the rule of the committee, where decisions are split among a group of people. That's the advantage of having one man. Good or bad, he makes a decision and you run with it."

The company quickly fell out of balance. Walt Disney Productions had grown out of the peculiarly feisty interplay between Roy and Walt. Walt was never close to anyone, but his relationship to Roy was symbiotic, nurturing in its very antagonism. The brothers had fought since they were children. But while the other brothers had drifted away, and while Walt had little contact with his parents, he stuck with Roy. Eight years older than Walt, Roy kept Walt grounded. And Walt struggled his whole life against the grounding. In later years he would recall wetting the bed when they slept together as children, then remark, "and I've been pissing up his leg ever since."

Roy opposed every major move in Walt's career—his decision to make Mickey Mouse talk in synchronized sound, to offer the *Silly Symphonies* in color, to create full-length animated features, to produce series for network television, to build theme parks, to plan EPCOT. And his opposition went far beyond mere gentlemanly discussions to enlisting board members, potential investors, distributors, venture partners, and even Walt's wife Lillian in opposition to Walt. And over and over, Walt went forward in the teeth of such opposition, as if to prove his brother wrong, sharpening and perfecting his ideas to meet his brother's objections, making things work better than he would have if he had not been opposed.

Now only one side of that balance was left, and it was not the side that had pushed the company forward.

Roy put a brave face on things. He said, "It was Walt's wish that when the time came he would have built an organization with the creative talent to carry on as he had established and directed it through the years." Yet it was eight years before any of the company's television shows, training films, or promotional materials could actually mention outright that Walt was dead.

The company faced major challenges. One was to continue to make money off the mix of live and animated films, cornball comedies, adventure shows, and television fare that Walt had put together. The second was to develop the new Magic Kingdom in Florida, essentially an improved version of the California Disneyland. Beyond that was a truly daunting challenge. In his last year of life, Walt had promised the public a city of the future. The "Progressland" exhibit at the World's Fair—and the "Carousel of Progress" that it became at Disneyland—ended with what Randy Bright called "a huge, very lavish, ornate model of a city of the future." Walt had stood before nationwide audiences on "Walt Disney's Wonderful World of Color," pointer in hand, before large-scale plans and architectural renderings of the proposed city, as if the whole thing were all worked out down to the last fireplug. But in reality the city, the Experimental Prototype Community of Tomorrow, was nothing more than a concept and a pile of studies, reports, statistics, and sketches, in a secret room behind Walt's office. It was what the computer industry would come to call "vaporware." Walt had promised it, and something would have to be delivered. But for now, Walt's fantasy of a perfect city was carefully catalogued, cross-referenced, and put away.

Walt's organization and projects were now in the hands of men who were dedicated to his memory, ferocious in their desire to fulfill his dreams, competent, hard-working rational men who subjected every decision to the litany response, "What would Walt have done?" But they were not Walt. They did not have his peculiar madness. And without that peculiar madness, that "genius," things fell apart.

The splits, the arguments that Walt would have ended in an instant, were not long in coming. In 1968 heated arguments broke out over the direction of the design of the "Haunted Mansion" the imagineers were designing for Disneyland. Everyone at WED (imagineering) had a hand in the project. Imagineer Mark Davis said, "There were too many people. . . . We had a lot of confusion because Walt had not been gone all that long. . . . There were a lot of great ideas, but when you have too many people of equal clout, nobody's about to say, 'Hey, wait a minute! Let's do it this way,' which Walt would have done in a minute." Some wanted to soft-pedal the show, arguing that little kids were scared even by the witch in the "Snow White" ride. Others wanted to use every art that Disney could muster to produce a truly bone-chilling experience. Their refrain was, "People love to be scared."

The soft side won. In the original drawings, done while Walt was still alive, the delapidated, tilting mansion, its paint peeling, its windows shattered, peered through ancient scraggly oaks hung with Spanish moss. The new design was as neat and pretty as everything else in the Magic Kingdom, a "happy haunting ground" that scared only three-year-olds.

Simple arguments over concept and style actually split the organization and changed careers. For instance, the design of the Magic Kingdom in Florida differs from that of Disneyland. Disneyland employs the intimacy of forced-perspective architecture (in which the higher parts of the buildings are made smaller, so that the buildings seem taller than they really are). Disneyland is, in effect, an intimate, delicate, underscaled set design. In contrast, the buildings in Florida are real buildings, with full-sized upper stories.

When it came to designing the castle for the Magic Kingdom at Disney World, the imagineers divided into camps. Rolly Crump, Walt's chief designer for the New York World's Fair projects, was known for his ability to produce extraordinary attractions under great time pressure, and for his design of the "It's a Small World" attraction, including its whimsical facade. In Florida, he wanted to retain an intimate, forced-perspective, Disneyland-size Sleeping Beauty's Castle. Those who were running imagineering at the time, particularly Dick Irvine, the chief creative executive, wanted everything to be scaled up.

So Crump built a model of the castle scaled up to the size that they wanted and placed it next to the other buildings on the Magic Kingdom model to make his point. It seemed obvious to him that it overshadowed the rest of the park. But the other imagineers didn't agree, and eventually they built the castle full size. Crump felt defeated and devalued. Before long he left the organization.

Without an umpire, tensions developed not only between individuals with creative differences, but between segments of the company. One classic example was the tension between the park designers and the park operators. The park operators constantly pushed for higher-capacity attractions, even if they came at the expense of some of the careful detail of sight and sense that Walt had envisioned.

Ponies and pack mules, for instance, still roamed the outback of Disneyland, carrying one visitor per mule through man-made badlands. They were inefficient; they were hard to market; they needed high maintenance; they cost a bundle; and they were unpredictable. They would eat people's hats and bite women's pony tails. When the second phase of the "Nature's Wonderland Mine Train" opened, the pack mules were confronted with a series of new animated figures based on Walt's nature films, including a mechanical mountain goat that strolled and turned on the top of a peak. He looked realistic, to both the guests and the mules. When the mules saw the mountain goat for the first time, they stopped. The ride operators had to turn off the mountain goat, or the mules wouldn't walk under the peak.

The park operators wanted to get rid of the animals. The imagineers argued that there was something right and wonderful about the mules, the real stagecoach, and the real Conestoga wagons. They contributed to the realism and liveliness of Frontierland. They helped make Frontierland work as a living organism where pack mules passed by up on the hill, the mine train rolled along the edge of the river, and the *Mark Twain* steamboat churned by on the other side. There were Indian war canoes in the water, keel boats with the crews splashing water on one another, rafts crossing the river, and people playing on Tom Sawyer's Island. Everything played off of everything else.

But the operators won the battle. The live animals were packed off to a retirement ranch, to be replaced by the new Thunder Mountain thrill ride.

In the struggle for turf, the organization began to change shape.

Under Walt, Disney had been a flat, egalitarian organization with very few levels of hierarchy run by a usually benevolent dictator, a familial and clubby place where everybody was on a first name basis. Many people, including the company president, wore golf shirts to work.

The culture included some nearly flamboyant symbols of this attempt at equality. For instance, everyone flew first class. Even the lowest-level staff person sent on a temporary assignment to New York or Florida never had to rub knees with the hoi-polloi back in the coach section. And titles were unimportant. Randy Bright, for example, who was engaged in designing Disney World, was a "staff writer." Walt had hated titles. The culture at the company said, "You don't have to have a title. If you're important to the company you'll know it." But this egalitarianism had its dark side: there was a faceless anonymity to those who worked for Walt. As Bright put it, "Most of the artists thought that was okay as long as Walt was there. A lot of the top guys lived and died for the old man. When he died their whole reason for being changed."

The world outside Disney continually looked at titles in order to determine how important someone was in the Disney organization. And without Walt to tell them how important they were, the people in Disney began to need titles. For example, the secretary for Bright's boss, Marty Sklar, received a phone call from a major corporation that was sponsoring part of Disney World. At the time, Sklar was probably one of the five most influential people in the entire Disney organization. The caller requested Sklar's title to put on an invitation to a large public function which they were sending him. The secretary said, "We don't have titles here." The caller insisted. The secretary said, "He's a staff writer." There was a pregnant pause, and the caller said, "I'm sorry. We must have the wrong Marty Sklar."

During the '70s, as people increasingly tried to define what they meant to the organization now that Walt was no longer there to tell them, "real" corporate titles and wiring diagrams proliferated. As parts of the organization struggled for turf and hierarchies within the company grew, people in the organization began to refer to the past for support for their point of view. "What would Walt have done?" was asked repeatedly by the top managers in committee meetings, and it came to be the standard incantation at all levels of the company. But others chafed at this magic formula. "The people who said, 'This is what Walt would have done' were really highly traditional," according to Bright. "They were looking at the predictable side of what Walt would have done." Some studio regulars joked, "This is necrophilia. We're working for a dead man."

Another rift in the Disney continent started much earlier, and would surface much later in ways that would profoundly affect the future of the company. This was the rift in the Disney family.

The Disney brothers had competed ferociously, but they were connected by a nearly umbilical love. Yet Roy had succeeded in one way that Walt had failed: he had fathered a son. Walt felt he had no heir, and stories were rife in Hollywood and in the Disney family of the antipathy between Walt and his brother's son, Roy E. Disney, often called "Junior."

The stories focus on the early 1950s, when Walt was trying to find the funding for Disneyland, his brother was trying to stymie him at every turn, and the two men could not even bring themselves to speak to each other. Roy E. Disney at that time was in his early 20s, back from the service and full of self-confident mockery. He would twit his uncle about the "circus" he was trying to build. Crude teasing was not what Walt was looking for at that stage in his life. At the groundbreaking ceremony for Disneyland, over the noise of the bulldozers uprooting the first orange trees, the elder Roy is said to have approached Walt with a peace offer—Walt Disney Productions would buy out Walt's Disneyland interests for a half-million dollars. In the hearing of bystanders, Walt countered with an offer of 50 percent for a half-million, then added that he would cut his own share to 25 percent "on the condition that your son, Junior, here, signs up to work at Disneyland once the park is finished . . . as a clown. Did I tell you we plan to set up a circus sideshow in the park? Junior would do a real good job whooping it up as the back end of a horse." It was a deliberate and public humiliation.

Whether the stories of Walt's antipathy toward young Roy were true was less important than the fact that they were believed to be true. Other members of the Disney family and higher-ups in the company commonly referred to the younger Roy as "Walt's idiot nephew."

Walt's true attitude toward his nephew is not so easy to discern. He did, after all, make Roy a producer of television shorts and animal pictures. This is often mentioned dismissively, as if Roy were being banished to the minor leagues of the organization. But Walt Disney is perhaps the only movie mogul to have repeatedly made money from animal films. It is not likely that he thought of them dismissively at all. Furthermore, given Walt's obsessive character, it is unlikely that he thought of anything the studio produced so dismissively that he would put it in the hands of someone he did not consider intelligent, a good manager and a decent judge of artistic matters.

The elder Roy certainly held a reasonably high opinion of his son. He made him his heir and, after Walt's death, put him on the executive committee that ran the company, as well as on the board of trustees. By 1970, Roy E. Disney was in charge of all Disney nature films.

One man who did hold a decidedly low opinion of Roy E. Disney was Ron Miller. In the early 1950s, when he played tight end for the University of Southern California, Miller had gone on a blind date arranged by his roommate after a game at Stanford University. The woman turned out to be Walt Disney's daughter, Diane, who fell madly in love with the handsome six-foot-five-inch blond football player. They were married in Santa Barbara on May 9, 1954, with the father of the bride weeping openly. Miller did a stint in the Army, then played a season as tight end for the L.A. Rams. After watching him get battered on the field (and knocked unconscious once), and after watching what it did to his daughter's composure, Walt offered Miller a job at the studio, which he accepted. Miller started as a second assistant director, but Walt soon promoted him to producer, working on *Old Yeller* and the "Zorro" television series. Soon after Walt's death he was named to the board of directors, and was clearly a rising power in the company.

Like most men of his generation, Walt never seems to have considered his daughter Diane or his adopted daughter Sharon as possible successors. He had, instead, two semiheirs, a son-in-law and a nephew, both of them reasonably competent, neither of them geniuses, both with lots of entertainment experience in the Disney organization and none outside it.

After Walt's death the public and the stockholders gave the company a remarkable grace period. As it slipped bit by bit into a Sleeping Beauty-like torpor, people still responded to the Disney icons and flocked to Disneyland.

The studio continued to churn out Walt's formula, a mixture of cornball comedies, such as *Blackbeard's Ghost* and *The Computer Wore Tennis Shoes*; animated features, such as *The Aristocats*; the odd adventure story, including *The Wild Country* and *Smith!*; and an occasional musical, such as *The One and Only Original Family Band*. Some, like *Blackbeard's Ghost*, were amusing enough for a matinee. Some made money. But none of them had people lining up around the block.

Only once did a Disney movie take off. In 1969, audiences went wild for *The Love Bug*, a comedy about a Volkswagen Beetle with a mind of its own named Herbie. To everyone's surprise, including its producers, it earned $21 million in domestic release, an astronomical sum for its day, which placed it second only to *Mary Poppins* on the all-time Disney hit list. Paradoxically, the success of *The Love Bug* may have been a worse disaster than continued failure would have been for Walt Disney Productions: its surprising returns froze the bland, cornball Disney formula in the minds of the Disney executives for another decade, long after it had run its course in the marketplace.

But if the studio was coasting, the Florida park was moving forward rapidly. By 1970, Walt Disney World and its centerpiece, the Magic Kingdom, was the largest private construction project in the United States, employing over 8,000 construction workers. Some 8 million cubic yards of earth had been moved to create lakes, highways, canals, and berms. Four of the kind of steam trains that Walt so loved were prepared—not scale reproductions, but actual narrow-gauge engines brought from Mexico's Yucatan and renovated for their new task. Submarines—not imitations of military nuclear submarines, as at Anaheim, but reproductions of the fantasy submarine featured in *20,000 Leagues under the Sea*, were built in California, strapped to oversized flatbed trailers, and carried across the continent, causing traffic jams on the highways and gathering gawking crowds at truck stops. A crane lifted the 36-foot gold spire to the top of Cinderella Castle and mated it with the finished tower, and the little bronze statue of Cinderella playing with the birds was installed in the castle courtyard.

By 1971, the Magic Kingdom was finished. Unlike the hastily constructed original, Disney World was complete and pristine the day it opened. The waterways were clear and straight, with long-legged waterbirds poking their beaks about the shallows at their edges. Even the grass along the waterways was carefully mowed.

The opening gala, in October 1971, included a 1,076-piece marching band directed by *Music Man* composer Meredith Wilson, and a 60-nation World Symphony Orchestra directed by Arthur Fiedler, as well as appearances by Julie Andrews, Buddy Hackett, Bob Hope, Glen Campbell, Jonathon Winters, and thousands of Boy Scouts. There were balloons, giant drums with pop-up lids, dancers, cartoon characters, and television cameras.

Roy O. Disney, 78 years old, spoke at the dedication of the Magic Kingdom. But by December he was dead. It was the end of an era. The last of the company's founders was gone. The creative and dynamic tension between the Disney brothers was gone, and nothing would ever replace it.

The two remaining members of the Disney Troika moved quickly to fill the vacuum: Donn Tatum became chairman and Card Walker became president. Walker had first worked for Disney as a messenger boy, earning $15.95 per week, then worked his way up to cameraman on *Fantasia*. A tall man with silver hair swept straight back from his forehead, he was given to leisure suits, polo shirts, and white shoes. Except for a stint in the Navy, he had spent his entire adult life in the service of Walt Disney. An acolyte of the Disney tradition, Walker had eventually found his home in the marketing department. He was an avid enthusiast of films in general and the Disney "family film" in particular, and kept an easel advertising the company's latest production at the entrance to his office. But he had little background in film production. Called by colleagues "an autocrat" and "a strong leader," he could be, like Walt, a tyrant. One man who worked with him closely says, "Card was an enthusiastic, dynamic individual who often let his temper run ahead of reason. Card let it all hang out up front. If he didn't like anything he'd tell you it was dumb and boring right away. You got no coddling from Card." At the same time, Walker was very big on ad hoc committees: "He would always want to have consensus, bring three people in and have them work together on a project."

Walker was a "Walt" man who had the support of Diane Disney Miller and her husband Ron. Tatum was a "Roy" man, an Oxford-trained financial manager with a quiet style. Brusque and energetic, Walker rapidly asserted his control over the firm. Within two years he had added the title "chief executive officer" to his title as "president." In 1976, he appointed Ron Miller head of production. Within a few short years, the "Roy" side of the family, and Roy E. Disney in particular, had been eclipsed.

Throughout the '70s, Walker backed Miller, whom he privately referred to as "a dumb jock," in part to consolidate his own grip on the company. As one insider put it, "Card knew he could control Ron. Ron knew. These guys had a very ambivalent relationship—a love-hate relationship."

The choice of Miller as head of production also bolstered Walker's view of the "Disney film." Whether it improved those films is another matter. One man who worked with Miller put it succinctly: "Ron Miller is a man who's extremely good-hearted and kind and did things for me that I'll never stop being grateful for. He is not a creative genius."

Another colleague called him an "average kind of a guy" with a "low level of drive and ambition. . . . If Ron took an aptitude test, the test would say, 'ski instructor.' He was affable, effective, a bright enough guy doing what he loved to do best, and he didn't have the fire in his belly."

Although Roy E. Disney, with his hawk nose, his moustache, his cigarettes, and his persistent cough, often reminded people of his dead uncle—increasingly so, as he grew older—he was in other ways not at all like his dictatorial, abrasive, and obsessive uncle. He was a quiet, retiring man with even less fire in his belly than Miller. Throughout the early '70s he held a very odd double position. On the one hand, he was a director and producer in the company's increasingly unimportant nature films division. On the other hand, he was on the board of directors and the executive committee of the board, and he was the company's largest shareholder. The ambiguity of his position would eventually lead him into open conflict with Miller.

When the Magic Kingdom opened in October 1971, it was an instant success. Eleven million visitors trooped to Disney World in its first year, more tourists than visited the United Kingdom, West Germany, or Austria. That success emboldened Card Walker to dream about an even riskier project—actually building some version of Walt's dream city, EPCOT. In 1972 he began soliciting ideas on how that could be done.

But while the parks were succeeding, the studio was not. All through the '70s the audience stayed away from Disney movies in droves. Predictably enough, the company tried to repeat its last great success, releasing *The Boatniks*, a wet semisequel to *The Love Bug*, in 1970, then starring Herbie in no fewer than three sequels of his own, in 1974, 1977, and 1980. They were mixed with such innocuous fare as *The Barefoot Executive* (about a chimpanzee who becomes a network programming executive), *The Apple Dumpling Gang* (and *The Apple Dumpling Gang Rides Again*), and the slapstick *Candleshoe*. Nothing worked. The ephemera of public taste eluded the men on Dopey Drive in Burbank. *The Love Bug* proved to be Disney's last genuine hit in over a decade. The company seemed to have lost the knack. The memorable images of the era proved to be not another adorable Disney character but millions marching against the war in Vietnam, the haggard face of a president declaring that he was not a crook, and an overloaded helicopter lifting off the roof of the American embassy in Saigon, dangling bodies. It was not just that Walt had died. The world had shifted. The tectonic plates of the

American psychology had ruptured and cracked, and had not yet reset-
tled. The leading edge of the baby boom was in its 20s. It was an
unsettled, self-involved, unpredictable period. Says one company veteran, "The projects [Disney] had were increasingly out of touch with the
world, often done by people who had lived in that cave for decades."

Hal Vogel, Merrill Lynch's veteran entertainment industry analyst,
says, "They had a mold that they clearly couldn't break out of. They were
deadly afraid of making an adult picture with a dirty word in it, or getting
a R rating. You can imagine the uproar, in the context of the times, if
Disney had a dirty word in a movie, just, 'She's a bitch' or something like
that. They were afraid there would be pickets. And there would be. They
would be flooded with letters." Jim Jimirro says that, at Disney, people
often blamed the company's lack of success on this very insistence on
doing "family films" without sex or a more-than-necessary dash of violence. "People would say, 'You can't do G-rated movies that work. You
can't do Disney-type movies any more. The world is changing; people
want R-rated pictures.' Then some other studio would do *Karate Kid* or
Star Wars, and everyone would say, 'Disney could have made that
movie!' There were all these Spielbergs and Lucases that were doing the
movies that Disney could have done. That was the great cry: 'Why didn't
we make that movie?' "

Throughout the early 1970s, three people conspired to stoke the fire in
Roy E. Disney's belly. Two of them did it consciously, one inadvertently.
The first was his wife, Patty, who had been pushing him ever since his
uncle's death to assert himself. The second was Stan Gold, a partner in
the law firm Gang, Tyre and Brown. In 1974, Roy turned over all his
business affairs to Gold. A vigorous, aggressive, hardball Hollywood
lawyer, Gold had enough ambition for the two of them, and bolstered
Roy's increasing unease about the drift of the company. The third, the one
who stoked that fire inadvertently, was Ron Miller.

By 1977, Roy E. Disney was 47 years old, owner of 3 percent of the
company and a wealthy man. Yet for over a year he had reported directly
to Ron Miller, who had been appointed head of the studio. Roy chafed
under the arrangement. Furthermore, he felt a profound distaste for the
direction in which the company was moving. It had been a dream factory;
it was becoming a real estate development company.

Although Card Walker was a protégé of Walt, he seemed to give almost
all of his attention to the development of the company's real estate—as

Walt had in his last years. He revived the idea of EPCOT, which had lain fallow since Walt's death. He found new designs that tossed out the idea of a residential community (one participant in the discussions said, "You can ask one question: 'Where shall we put the cemetery?' That put a lot of things in perspective.") in favor of an adult-oriented theme park focused on the world and the future. Once the imagineers worked out the idea, Walker hit the pavement personally to sell sponsorships to major corporations and foreign governments.

Walker, by 1977, spoke increasingly of his desire to quit. He had hit 60, and he had lost a kidney. He had a happy marriage, he finally had a grandchild, and he wanted some time to spend playing grandpa. He also loved golf far more than the average weekend duffer, and even served on the board of the Professional Golfers Association. Before retiring, though, he had a goal—to make some version of Walt's EPCOT dream become reality.

While Walker struggled toward EPCOT, the studio continued to languish. It had been eight years since *The Love Bug*, with no other hit in sight. While other studios were producing dazzling blockbusters aimed directly at Disney's old "family" audience—*Star Wars* was released in 1977—Disney was making *The Shaggy D.A.* and losing money. Roy E. Disney felt strongly that the studio should seek new directions. Walker and Miller consistently dismissed Roy's opinions. To Walker especially, the old way was sacrosanct.

Finally Roy, with Stan Gold, met with Card Walker and Donn Tatum to ask for a new relationship—he wanted to work with the company as an independent producer to produce more contemporary films. The company did not use independents, but he was, after all, Roy Disney.

Walker's response was to accuse him of wanting to make *Deep Throat*. Disney, a quiet, conservative, married man with children, was deeply offended. He only wanted to produce movies that had a more contemporary feel than the dim-witted comedies and predictable adventures that had become the company's straitjacketed formula. Nonetheless, his overture was rejected. And Ron Miller took away his parking spot.

In the semiotics of American corporate culture, the reserved parking spot—its exact location and the relative location of other people's spots—who has to walk past whose car on the way in—may be more important than titles or office square footage, and possibly ranks only a step or two behind salary and stock options in establishing who is important and who is not. At Walt Disney Productions, it was certainly more important than who got a corner office, since the eight-winged animation building, which housed the executive offices, had four outside corner offices and twelve inside corner offices on each floor. The parking lot, however, was small, and only some of the spaces were covered. The unmarked spaces sat out in the baking sun of inland southern California.

Roy Disney owned more of the company than anyone else, and he was on the board and the executive committee of the board. Yet Ron Miller had the muscle to take away his parking spot. And Walker refused to give it back to him. The humiliation led to a screaming public fight between Miller and Disney. The fight was reported in the *Los Angeles Times*. Witnesses suggested that it was only Miller's daunting size that kept the spat from degenerating into a street brawl. As a result, Disney quit the company. He kept his stock and remained on the board, but he vowed he would never again work for the company until he could get rid of Ron Miller.

4

Trading Places

Charles Bluhdorn felt stung. An Andy Tobias article in the September 23, 1974 issue of *New York* magazine quoted Frank Yablans, the president of Paramount Pictures, describing the Paramount tough-guy, aggressive trademark as "If you don't like it, fuck you."

It wasn't the language that bothered Bluhdorn. Bluhdorn, the aggressive tough-guy strongman who had assembled and now chaired the Gulf & Western conglomerate, appreciated a man with a tough attitude. The problem was that, in Bluhdorn's judgment, the comment was aimed not only at producers, stars, agents, that whole slime-glitter world of Hollywood—it was directed equally at New York, at Gulf & Western, at Charles Bluhdorn. And that made a difference, because Gulf & Western (and that meant, in practice, Charles Bluhdorn) owned Paramount. In fact, it was his favorite company.

Bluhdorn had been having problems with Yablans for some time, and now it seemed time to replace him. Bluhdorn knew a young man he thought he could get along with much better. He had met him a few years before when he used to go over to ABC to negotiate prices for packages of movies that Paramount wanted to sell to the network. It wasn't necessarily a job for the chairman of the parent company, but Bluhdorn enjoyed it. Leonard Goldberg, the head of ABC, had turned the negotiations over to a smart, tough, savvy young man named Barry Diller. Huddled with Bluhdorn in a small office just down from Goldberg's, Diller would not be intimidated by the powerful conglomerate chairman, by the shouting and table-pounding.

Over the space of two years, Diller had moved up the corporate ladder. He had convinced his superiors to invest in a new, upscale, high-pockets venture: an ABC "movie of the week"—a new theatrical-length film every week, custom-made for the network. He had birthed the idea, had shepherded it through the corporation, had gotten the green light, and had made it work.

His decision made, Bluhdorn got on the phone. He fired Yablans, in the tradition of Hollywood studio heads, whose jobs disappear like smoke in a high wind, and installed Diller in his place as chairman and chief executive officer of Paramount.

At age 32, Diller had never run a company before. He had apprenticed as an agent at William Morris, had worked his way up at ABC, and had pushed dozens of ABC television movies through the grinder, but he had never produced a movie to show in theaters. He had no experience in the arcane world of film distribution, theater chains, and promotion.

He felt lost at first. He rattled around in the huge offices of Paramount in the gleaming G & W skyscraper towering over Central Park, and shuttled back and forth in the spacious first-class cabins between New York and L.A., over and over, wondering if he could really make this thing spin. There was nothing he could put his hands on.

The job began to click for him at a particular moment that he later loved to recall. Searching for something in his desk, he reached into a disused drawer and discovered a script about a hapless baseball team called the Bad News Bears. It was not a star vehicle. It was a story. Diller understood stories. Like Eisner, he had long felt that a good story was the foundation of success in entertainment. "This I understood," he said later. "Three acts. A rotten little team gets better, falls apart, and then prevails. I said, 'My God, a story.' I bought the script in 22 minutes. It was the first time that it seemed possible that things might just work out."

Every great movie has a strong story. *The Godfather*, as Francis Ford Coppola has often said, is not a gangster movie. It's a classic tale of a king and his sons. *Star Wars* is not about spaceships and force beams. It's about men at war, men competing for the love of a beautiful woman, knighthood, and a young man searching for his true self in the secret of his past. Most good films are built on strong stories that spring from clear characters—from *Citizen Kane* and *Casablanca* to *E.T.* and *Raiders of the Lost Ark*. Some feature actors who are already famous; many feature unknowns. Some feature elaborate sets and special effects that consume sums equal to the budgets of small nations. Some, like *Casablanca*, were made inexpensively on back lots and ordinary sound stages. Many fly in the face of the conventional wisdom of their day. *Patton* was made in the middle of the Vietnam War, at a time when Hollywood "knew" that war pictures were doomed. George Lucas peddled *Star Wars* in the face of numerous proclamations that space flicks were passé. *The Godfather* would never have been made if Mario Puzo's novel had not been a surprise best-seller, since everyone knew that nobody wanted to see gangster movies any more. But they all had good stories. The genre, and the stars, were irrelevant.

This is so obviously true that an outsider could begin to wonder why Hollywood spends so much time, money, and effort on star vehicles and the fad of the moment. The history of Hollywood is littered with the wrecks of projects that consumed fortunes and employed the most popular actors of the day—only to garner yawns from the public.

But recognizing a good story is almost as subtle an art as telling a good story. Most studio executives, most agents, far too many producers and directors, indeed many of the people responsible for spending hundreds of millions of dollars of investors' money making movies are not all that good at knowing a good story when they hear one.

Beyond that, film executives expose themselves to less personal risk by making an expensive star vehicle than by gambling on their instinct for stories. The fact is, most film projects fail. Most scripts never get approved for development; most that get developed never end up being produced; many of those that get produced are never aired or distributed; and few of those that are distributed turn out to be hits. No matter how smart Hollywood executives are, they end up pushing a lot of failures. You look smarter after the fact if you can say, "It had Robert Redford and Dolly Parton. How could it miss?" or "People flocked to all the other space epics made in the last five years," than if you are forced to say, "Well, *I* thought it was a good story." It is a curious fact of the jungle that is Hollywood that an executive can prosper in a career for a long time, moving from job to job, up the ladder and sideways, without ever producing a big hit. But the same executive can get fired in a nanosecond for being associated with an expensive failure that provides no excuses.

Hollywood studio executives, producers, and agents alike tend to get excited about projects that feature big-name stars, projects that exploit the latest fad, and projects that are sequels or clones of last year's hit. It's safe: if the project fails, at least they'll have a good excuse. And they often fail to connect with a project that's nothing more than a great original story.

Diller, like Eisner, had made his mark at ABC with a different point of view—the classic point of view that, as Shakespeare put it, "the play's the thing." He would now proceed to rebuild Paramount on that different point of view.

In an early move, Diller turned to his protégé from ABC, the man who owed him his first real job in television a mere eight years before, and who had since then been such a power in turning the ABC network around. Diller had been offering Michael Eisner jobs ever since he had come to Paramount, with no luck. But in 1976, when he offered him the presidency of the studio, Eisner waited "only a few minutes" before accepting. In November 1976, exactly one decade after joining ABC, Eisner left it to become president and chief operating officer of Paramount. Together, for the next eight years, Eisner and Diller would form a tough, dynamic, symbiotic team that dramatically changed Paramount. They formed the nucleus of a ring of executives, including Jeffrey Katzenberg, Don Simpson, Dawn Steel, and Jerry Bruckheimer, who would change the face of Hollywood in the 1980s and 1990s.

The choice of Eisner as second-in-command of Paramount would seem strange to an outsider. Diller was young and inexperienced. Eisner was his clone on both counts: he was 34 years old, and had never produced a theatrical movie. But Eisner also shared Diller's outlook on the importance of stories and real talent over "stars," "bankable" names that were popular at the moment. Years later Eisner summarized their shared point of view for *New York*'s Tony Schwartz: "The one thing you cannot be bad at in this business is choosing material. Yes, it helps to keep your negative costs down, to keep away from the hype, and not to grab for stars and pay ridiculous prices. But you know what? If you pick the right material, all that pales. When Frank Price was at Columbia, he traditionally paid a lot for everything. But when you buy *Tootsie*, so what? It's great to have good marketing, and I think we have the best, but you don't need it to sell *E.T.*, and it won't help if you're selling *The Pirate Movie*. This is a business based on ten to twelve decisions a year. Nothing else is close."

Eisner had made those kinds of decisions over and over again at ABC, and his decisions—for such sitcoms as "Happy Days" and "Welcome Back, Kotter,"—had helped to vault the network past its competition. If what was needed was the ability to make those decisions more often right than wrong, then Eisner was the man.

As the new president of Paramount, Eisner seemed to work harder than everybody. He usually would arrive at his three-room suite of offices on the Paramount lot well before eight, before his two secretaries or most of his colleagues. In between cups of coffee, he would devour three papers (the *New York Times*, the *Los Angeles Times*, and the *Wall Street Journal*) and field the phone himself, talking to New York about the latest casting decisions, script developments, or twists of financing. During the day, he was constantly in motion, running up the aisle at the end of a screening, loping across the lot from one office to another, interrupting meetings with a suggestion, a new statistic, a synopsis of a film he had just seen.

In the evening, he was perpetually going to the theaters to check audiences, dropping in to two, three, or four suburban L.A. theaters in an evening to watch the customers laugh and cry and to talk to them when they came out. Neither Diller nor Eisner went to many parties or openings. But it was Diller who was photographed with Debra Winger, Marlo Thomas, or Diane Von Furstenberg on his arm at the occasional gala or event. His friends included Calvin Klein, David Geffen, Mike Nichols, and Warren Beatty. Eisner tended to shun such events. He had been happily married for nearly a decade, and his favorite topic of conversation was his sons. Even as president of a studio, he had a boyish, floppy charm, like a puppy that's getting too big to hold in your lap any more. Hopelessly frumpy, he wore, it seemed, self-rumpling suits. He was so full of enthusiasm and energy that he seemed to fill doors that he walked through. He pushed the limits of casual in corporate life. Often he would hold meetings in his Malibu beach house, with the California contingent in beach jams and flip-flops, and the New York contingent sweating in their coats and their ties, outclassed by casual.

But he was conscious of his boyish image, and he wielded it at times with all the studied intent of a diamond-cutter. Sue Mengers, the super-agent of the '70s, has said of him, "When he wants something, he won't give up. But just when you are feeling angriest at him, he'll say something funny or charming or self-deprecating that disarms you." A former Paramount executive says, "I remember a meeting with him where he was trying to get a writer to bring a project to us. He was informal and ingenuous and intimate, sloppy in his Saint Bernardish way, telling funny stories about his sons. Then the writer walked out, and he turned to me and said, 'So, do you think I got her?' "

Eisner became known in Hollywood for his rapid decisions. If he was childlike in his energy and enthusiasm, he was also childlike in his greed for immediate action. For instance, Steve Rose, who was then in Paramount's New York-based marketing department, flew to California at one point in 1977 to present Eisner with the marketing concepts for *Heaven Can Wait*. "I thought I had developed one of the best ads that have been in the movie industry—Warren Beatty with wings. Well in advance, the first week the picture was shooting, I took this ad with a report to California and met with both Barry and Michael simultaneously. The first ad did not have Warren in a sweat suit—it had him in a Pierre Cardin suit and hat. Michael instantly recognized the fact that it had great potential, and gave me the approval to go up to Palo Alto to show the ad to Warren. Which was a miracle."

By his own estimate, Eisner heard some 5,000 movie ideas each year. Most he rejected, some he went for on the spot. For instance, one night in 1979 Eisner and his wife were having dinner with his childhood friend and dance-class partner, Susan Baerwald. She was now a script reader at United Artists. Baerwald was in a funk because, as is often the case in Hollywood, she had fought hard for a certain script only to have the studio turn it down. The script had three original writers, who were insisting that they be allowed to direct it. They had made a minor hit with their previous film, a spoof called *Kentucky Fried Movie*. But the new script had been shopped all over town, and no one had bit. She told Eisner the story—a spoof of the *Airport* movie series. Eisner was immediately intrigued. In the middle of dinner, he got up from the table, tossed his napkin on the chair, and found a pay phone in the restaurant. He called Jeff Katzenberg, and told him to get his hands on the script.

Eventually, Eisner struck a deal with the three writers. The film, when it was released, was called *Airplane!* While it didn't win any Oscars or make movie history, it was a major summer success, a big profit-maker for Paramount, and another example of Eisner's creative instincts and his ability to believe in a story even though everyone else in Hollywood had turned it down. In Hollywood, a kingdom of accountants and lawyers, of betting on "proven" material and "bankable" names, the box office proved him right. The film cost only $6 million to produce, and it grossed $83 million.

Eisner could be as tough as anybody in the business, however—sometimes tougher. He was no cuddle toy when it came to negotiating. As he once said, in a quote that follows him around, "I tend to want everything." Mengers found Eisner "the toughest person I negotiate with, and I don't mean that as a compliment. He simply must win."

In 1983 Larry Gordon and Walter Hill had finished a script that they thought would make a hit. Gordon had an office on the Paramount lot at the time. He and Eisner had done good business with the charmingly cartoon-violent gang film *The Warriors* in 1979, and he and Eisner considered each other close friends. Only the year before, Gordon and Hill had made *48 Hours* for Paramount, considered by some to be one of the six best cop films of all time. Made for a paltry $10 million, the film had brought in $77 million, and everyone had gone home happy—almost.

Gordon had been stung by his treatment by Paramount—especially Eisner—during the making of *48 Hours*. There seemed to be endless problems. Eddie Murphy wasn't funny enough. The marketing wasn't right. Hill refused to meet with Eisner. Eisner threatened to shut the film down. Hill didn't want a sneak preview, Eisner did. People played hardball.

Now, with a new script in hand, Hill did not want to be pushed around again. So Gordon didn't show the script to Eisner. He sent it over to Universal first. Eisner heard about the script, got a copy, read it, and hated it. But he hated the fact that Gordon had cheated him of the right to turn it down even more. Two days later Gordon got a call from a friend. Movers were packing his office at Paramount into a moving van—every computer, every movie poster, every telephone wire.

Gordon moved fast, and got a court injunction forcing Eisner to have the movers put his office back. Universal made Gordon's film, and it sank without a ripple. And Gordon and Eisner became friends again.

Eisner could be very hands-on when he felt the need. For example, after viewing a rough cut of *Flashdance* he sat down with the editor and resequenced the film.

On the few occasions when Eisner and Diller picked different horses to ride, it was more often than not Eisner who made it to the winner's circle. Diller, for instance, went to bat for his friend Warren Beatty's massive historical film, *Reds*, even though it was three times as expensive as the average Paramount film of the period. The film was not profitable. On the other hand, although both men liked Steven Spielberg's and George Lucas' *Raiders of the Lost Ark* project, Diller wanted to stay out of it because of its huge cost. The film would have to bring in more than $40 million before the studio made any profit. Eisner fought for the project, feeling that it had the kind of classic story value that makes for great movies. He got his way, and the studio made over $240 million in domestic gross alone on that one decision.

It was an incredible gamble. The fact that it paid off added considerably to Eisner's reputation. If it had failed, it would have been hard to live down. Eisner's own account (in a July 1983 *Vanity Fair* article) of the process by which the deal was made is, typically, straightforward:

> It was the ultimate example of overcoming the odds, and being extremely tenacious, which I would say is one of my assets. Now, after *E.T.*, it would be hard to say whether any executive would consider passing on

Steven Spielberg. . . . I read the script [for *Raiders*], which I thought was fabulous. The problem was, the first scene alone read like it was going to cost $30 million. Spielberg had just done *1941*, which was incredibly over budget and expensive. Lucas had just done the second *Star Wars* [*The Empire Strikes Back*], which we had understood had gone way over budget. The deal that they asked for in a letter to all the studios would have meant that Paramount Pictures would be owned by George Lucas and Steven Spielberg.

Instead of just passing, because I wanted it so badly, I was relentless in coming back, coming back, not letting my management talk me out of it. I kept plodding along, until they both got so sick of me that we made a deal, a very good deal for them, but one we could live with, which we made a fortune from.

Eisner's persistence appeared in one situation after another. For instance, the film *Staying Alive* brought together Sylvester Stallone and John Travolta. The teaming of these two male superstars of the moment was Eisner's idea. For reasons of ego, money, and scheduling, it was nearly impossible to make the film, much less make it in time to hit the screens the following summer. Michael Ovitz, Eisner's longtime friend and Travolta's agent, described the negotiations: "It took an enormous effort, and it all lays at the feet of Eisner. Sly had just made *Rocky III*, which is really a well-made film, and Eisner liked it. So he persisted through weeks of very difficult negotiations. People had other commitments. But he was determined to get the movie made and released by summer. He was very tough."

This level of intelligent risk-taking, deal-making, persistence, and savvy was causing people throughout the industry to begin to track Eisner with a new awareness. In 1983, for instance, Sam Cohn, the superagent at the head of International Creative Management, made a prescient comment: "I can see Eisner as the top executive at a *Fortune 500* corporation. It would have to be entertainment-related somehow, but I could see him as the top man. He's got those kind of skills. I'd hire him in a second." It was an observation that many people in the industry besides Cohn were beginning to make.

The group around Eisner included another figure who would come to fascinate Hollywood—Jeff Katzenberg, a skinny kid in owl-eye glasses that Diller had picked up as an assistant in 1974.

In May 1965, John V. Lindsay had declared himself a candidate for mayor of New York. He mapped out an unorthodox campaign that would eventually use 10,000 active volunteers, many of them kids on vacation, to personally contact over 70 percent of the eligible voters. He impressed his baseline political methods on these volunteers: "Ask and thank, ask and thank, again and again. For money, for support of all kinds. No matter how sophisticated they are, people like to be asked, and they like to be thanked."

Katzenberg, even skinnier then and only 14, was one of the "kids" on the street for Lindsay that grueling political summer. The son of a stockbroker, he had grown up on Park Avenue in the same block as Eisner. He was a miniature entrepreneur, shoveling sidewalks in the winter and selling lemonade from a stand in the summer. He went to the upper-crust Fieldston School. But in the summer of 1965 he was at loose ends. He had gotten busted for gambling at summer camp and was sent home. The Lindsay campaign became his apprenticeship and his finishing school.

Manhattan lawyer Sid Davidoff, then administrative assistant to the mayor and Katzenberg's roommate, years later would give *American Film* a thumbnail sketch of "Squirt," a description that would still encompass his essence decades later: "The guy was four feet, 10 inches, 90 pounds soaking wet, a pit bull, tenacious as hell. He was there when you opened the door in the morning and the last to leave at night. Jeffrey was also a bit of a fire buff and slept with a fire radio by his bed. The fire deputy, responding to an alarm, would pick him up on the way. Jeffrey saw himself as a player . . . even at a young age. He didn't have to be center stage. He just wanted to be in the middle of everything." Ambitious, smart, eager, and energetic, he worked his way toward the center of Lindsay's organization. He swept out the place. He set up campaign stops, and determined whom to see, whom to shake hands with, how to get the press involved. He learned to schmooze, he learned to ask, he learned to find out what there was to know, and he learned to say thank you.

After high school Katzenberg went to NYU "for about 10 minutes," then dropped out to get involved with Lindsay again. When Lindsay hit the streets of the city to walk through Harlem, press the flesh, and try to cool the violence simmering through the long hot summer, Katzenberg helped to organize things, keep it all on track, make it work. He was still learning: Ask and thank. Keep in contact. Be persistent, cool, do what is necessary. Let them know you care. Be organized. Make decisions fast. Don't leave people hanging.

In between campaigns, he helped out at Gracie Mansion, organizing ceremonies inside and working with the gangs in the streets. By 1972, Lindsay was running for president, trying like Gene McCarthy, Bobby Kennedy, and George McGovern to mobilize the baby boomers in his favor. Katzenberg, not quite 21, was an advance man, flying from town to town, driving one rent-a-car after another, staying in chain motels and eating junk food, trying to piece it together for John. In most states he wasn't even of legal drinking age. That didn't matter. He hated the taste of alcohol anyway, and never did get a taste for it, or for drugs.

When Lindsay didn't make it to the White House, Katzenberg quit politics and turned his organizing talents elsewhere. First, with Jimmy Breslin and another Lindsay aide, he opened a restaurant called "Jimmy's." Then there was the business with the card-counting. Davidoff, his roommate, taught him how. In certain games, notably single-deck blackjack, if you keep track of the cards that other players get, you can constantly recalculate the odds and alter your betting strategy. If you do it right, you can, in the long run, beat the house. You have to have exceptional pattern-recognition skills, an ice-clean ease with calculation, and a memory without any visible flaw. And you've got to be able to do it while you look like you're not paying attention. The casinos won't stand still for it. It's not cheating, it's against no law, but if the beefy boys behind the two-way mirrors think you're doing it, they'll take you in for a little discussion, a little wall-to-wall counseling, then show you to the door—or take you on a personal drive to the nearest airport.

Katzenberg—and this is a story that says a lot about his mind, his memory, and his ability to perform under pressure—became very good at blackjack. The gee-whiz, nerdy kid who didn't even look old enough to enter a casino had a mind that was going every second, a quality of attention that didn't waver, and no distracting vices. Katzenberg claims he was never all that good, but he was good enough that a few "investors" he had met in the Lindsay circles handed him and Davidoff a wad of money, and packed them off to Vegas, to Puerto Rico, and finally to the Bahamas to make some money.

In the Bahamas their luck ran out. A delegation of casino security guards collared them. Katzenberg and Davidoff tried to talk their way out of it. Davidoff even did a dance number that involved trying to tumble a roulette table. But inside an hour they were on an outbound plane, and the casino had put out word to other casinos that Katzenberg was unwelcome. The career of Katzenberg the professional blackjack player was over.

With his gambling career shut down, Katzenberg turned to the entertainment business. He became an agent for a while, then was hired as an assistant by producer David V. Picker, helping Picker develop material. In 1975 Picker introduced him to a man who had built a reputation for picking interesting people: Barry Diller.

Diller, only nine years older than Katzenberg, had been lured away from ABC the previous year to become chairman of Paramount. He was looking for an eager young assistant. Katzenberg turned out to be so diligent, so exacting, so able to ask for more without seeming greedy, so able to lead from below, that people noticed him.

After keeping Katzenberg for a year as his assistant, Diller detailed him to the marketing department, sending him down from the 33rd floor of the G & W building in New York to the 29th. On one occasion, Katzenberg had flown west with Gordon Weaver and Steve Rose for a gathering of exhibitors to push the new *King Kong*. When they had arrived at the Beverly Wilshire Hotel, Jeffrey asked, "When are you going to rehearse?"

Rose said, "What do you mean, 'rehearse'? I've done some slides. I'm just going to talk."

Katzenberg said, "That's not good enough. I'll wake you up at 3 o'clock in the morning. We're going over to the Directors Guild Theater and we're going to rehearse." The next morning before the light shone on Sunset Boulevard, they were rehearsing. Rose said later, "He made both Gordon and I put an incredible effort into the presentation—and it came off terrifically. What Jeffrey clearly could do was cut to what the issue was and make it right. And make you understand what was right. It wasn't that he had the power to make us do it. He was just right."

The training was showing. Ask and thank. Do what is necessary. Let them know you care.

Later, at the same convention, Rose, Weaver, and Katzenberg left a meeting and went over to the Palm Restaurant. Katzenberg went to the cashier and paid a bill in advance for an exhibitor who was going to come in to the restaurant. It was one of thousands of small and large gestures that he wove into his professional life. Let them know you care. It might have been tattooed on his palm, he paid such religious homage to it.

But marketing was not the middle of things, and in the middle of things was where Katzenberg liked to be. Before long, Eisner noticed him and sent him to California to try to crank up a fourth network, the Paramount Television Service, exactly as Diller would try years later at Fox. This try didn't work, but Katzenberg ended up as assistant to production chief Don Simpson.

Part of the detritus of the effort to build a new network was a $3 million

Star Trek television movie project. Katzenberg took charge of turning it into *Star Trek—The Motion Picture*. The project was already a near-disaster when he took it on, and Simpson tried to dissuade him. "*Star Trek* is a night-time freight train. It's bearing down on you at 200 miles per hour. Get off the fucking track!"

Katzenberg refused. When the director, Robert Wise, convinced him that the film absolutely had to have the pointy-eared Mr. Spock, Katzenberg set out to convince Leonard Nimoy to play the part he had abandoned for better things almost a decade before. He did what was necessary. He flew to New York, where Nimoy was playing on Broadway. He sat listening to him protest that he had had enough of those stupid ears—for two days. And in the end he signed him.

By the time it debuted in 1979, *Star Trek—The Motion Picture* had cost $42 million. But it made a profit, and it made Katzenberg's reputation. He stayed on as a production executive, working on such hits as *Beverly Hills Cop* and *Flashdance*. After two and a half years, Simpson left to become an independent, and Diller and Eisner picked Katzenberg to replace him. It was 1982, and he was still only 31. He had been at Paramount eight years.

In those eight years, rising through the organization, he never abandoned his hands-on attitude. At one point, Eddie Murphy was filming *Beverly Hills Cop* on a street in downtown Los Angeles. It was a night filming, and a problem came up. There would be a helicopter spraying the area with the insecticide Malathion in the middle of the shooting, hunting down the dread Mediterranean fruit fly.

Murphy walked off the set and went home, announcing that he was not going to endanger his health. The director tried to talk him into staying, but it was no use. It was 1 A.M. The director called Katzenberg at home. Katzenberg called Murphy at his home and talked to him about the details of Malathion and what it would and wouldn't do to his health. When Murphy at last agreed to return, Katzenberg got in his car, drove to Murphy's house, and drove him back to the set. He got home at 5 A.M., plopped into bed, got up again at 6, and was at work by 7.

Katzenberg earned the reputation of a man who would do absolutely anything necessary to get the job done, a man of enormous organization, a man of note cards and lists. Eisner began to dread flying with him. "I would strap myself in, and out would come the 'Michael Eisner' list." In fact, he and Eisner grew so symbiotic that their nearly incessant phone calls had no "hellos" or "goodbyes." The two men would just start talking, and when they were done they would hang up.

The lessons of the Lindsay years for Katzenberg were very simple. Find out what there is to know. Let them know you care. Be organized. Keep in contact. "He's one of the most loyal people you'll ever meet," says producer Ed Feldman. "I made a very bad movie in London called *The Sender* for Paramount [in 1982]. It turned out very poorly, a forgotten movie. I thought that I would never hear from Paramount again. But for the next 18 months I got a call [from Katzenberg] every two or three weeks, just for 30 seconds or a minute, just asking how everything's going. He keeps in touch with me. He keeps in touch with maybe 200 people. He maintains a relationship. Naturally next time you have a project you call him."

Others familiar with his style estimate the number of people getting these quick phone calls at over a thousand.

People who know Katzenberg—which is to say, almost everyone in Hollywood—tend to bubble about him. They use adjectives like "terrific," "unbelievable," "phenomenal," and "astonishing in every way." They call him "the voice of intelligence." And everyone calls him "tenacious."

Rose says, "He was tenacious in his following up and keeping records on everything to do with *King Kong*. You could see the demonstration of delight that he had in it." Feldman says, "Jeffrey is incredibly tenacious about learning everything he can learn about something so that he can make an intelligent decision. He's just so smart. He knows what he wants. He knows what to do all the time. He handles people in a very good manner. He is probably the smartest film executive there is."

The Diller–Eisner team at Paramount in the late '70s and early '80s agreed on the basics. They pushed and shoved the agents, writers, directors, and producers who worked with them into making the movies that Paramount wanted made. Time after time, they went for the jugular. And that time after time they made hit films.

Their team style contained several singular elements, pieces of a house management style that set them apart from the rest of Hollywood. They were fast in making decisions, they fought like cats in a sack, and their judgment was very commercial. They relied on the story more than any other element in making decisions on a script. They developed more projects on the lot, instead of merely bankrolling outsiders. They were obsessed with keeping costs down and spreading financial risk. When possible, they tried to circumvent the power of agents and the twists and

turns of project "packaging" by engaging useful stars in long-term contracts at the right point in their careers.

They were aggressive, and this micromanagement of the budget
and schedules was only a small part of their aggressiveness. Many
film-makers came to feel that they "wanted to make your film for
you." Katzenberg's daily hectoring of James Brooks, when he slipped a
few days behind schedule in filming *Terms of Endearment*, was so
constant and intense that Brooks "felt it threatened the quality of the
work."

They had a formula, described by Tony Schwartz as "simple, access-
ible concepts, mainstream characters, and a dose of melodrama"—nothing arcane, no *Apocalypse Now* or *Big Chill*.

The "concept" in the formula is what Hollywood calls "high concept"—not "high" as in haute, or "high culture," but more like "high"
as in a loose plank on a porch step: "sticking up above the rest, immediately noticeable." A "high concept" film or television show is one whose
plot and characters can be easily and intriguingly encapsulated in a single
line: "A white cop and a black con, forced together to solve a crime, turn
from enemies to allies and friends" (*48 Hours*); or "A rotten little
baseball team gets better, falls apart, and then prevails" (*Bad News
Bears*).

According to Steve Rose, while he was at Paramount Eisner loved
concept movies. "You can talk about all of the things that go into a
movie, but he really wanted to know what the concept was. If you could
tell him the concept very quickly, he would be likely to buy into that
concept. Think of the trouble you're in, on a project that costs millions of
dollars, if you can't make it clear to the public what the concept is. Look
how right he was. Look at the Paramount line-up in those years."

Take Nick Nolte. An artistic actor, but relatively unknown, Eisner and
Katzenberg had cast him in the ABC–Paramount miniseries *Rich Man,
Poor Man* when Eisner was still at ABC and Katzenberg had just joined
Diller at Paramount. Then Nolte did three films, judged by friends as
"artful but uncommercial," for other studios. Then he did *North Dallas
Forty* at Paramount with Katzenberg and Eisner. Then he did three more
"artful, uncommercial" movies elsewhere. Then he did *48 Hours* at
Paramount with Katzenberg and Eisner. Every movie Nolte made with
Eisner and Katzenberg was a commercial success.

They would dredge for those concepts anywhere they could find them,
and Eisner was particularly good at this. He lifted the idea for *Footloose*

("young dance fiend rebels against small town that bans dancing") from Nathaniel Hawthorne's short story "The Maypole of Merrymount" and *The Scarlet Letter*. He thought of *Beverly Hills Cop* when a real Beverly Hills cop gave him a ticket.

When he couldn't come up with ideas himself, he would beat them out of other people, sometimes in marathon think sessions. Don Simpson describes one of the first such sessions, soon after Eisner came to Paramount: "We went into a boardroom at nine in the morning. There were maybe 11 people in the room. At the time, we had absolutely nothing good in development, which is the real estate of this business. Eisner said, 'We're going to come up with 20 projects today even if we have to stay here until midnight. Leave if you want to, but then don't bother coming back.' Several people looked at him like he was crazy. But by 5:30, we had 15 projects."

The Paramount people were skinflints. Most years their average movie budget was about 75 percent of the industry's average. Every year from 1978 through 1983, Paramount was one of the three most profitable studios in Hollywood. It was more consistently profitable than any other studio. Eisner, Diller, and Katzenberg did this partly by keeping a very close watch on budgets and schedules. In the movie business, time on the shooting set translates directly into money: if your schedule gets bloated, so does your budget. Feldman was on the receiving end of this attention: "When we made *Witness* down in the Amish country in Lancaster, Pennsylvania, I spoke to Katzenberg maybe once a week. His executive in charge of the picture was in touch every other day. Because they were on top of everything, they didn't get any surprises."

At the same time that they reduced the risk by keeping the costs down, they would sometimes spread the risk by taking in partners, reducing the potential profits of the film, but covering potential losses, too. They laid off 25 percent of the cost of *Flashdance* on outside investors. And they financed Warren Beatty's expensive and arcane film *Reds*—at $35 million the highest-budget film of the Diller–Eisner era at Paramount—through a complex arrangement with British banks that gave Paramount a virtual guarantee that it would lose no money on the project before the cameras even began shooting.

In some ways, especially in the intrusive management, the signing of creative people to long-term contracts (as they signed Eddie Murphy to a five-movie, $15-million deal after the success of *48 Hours*), the rapid judgments, and the dedication to the strong story with clear-cut, easily identified characters, Eisner and Diller operated more like moguls of an old-line pre-1950 movie studio.

But the effect on the bottom line was very modern. In the late '70s and early '80s Eisner and Diller (along with Katzenberg, Simpson, Steel, and other members of the team) used these old-fashioned ways to churn out a succession of hits. By the end of 1982, Eisner could personally take credit for bringing to the screen six of the 50 highest-grossing films of all time (*Saturday Night Fever*, *Grease*, *Heaven Can Wait*, *Raiders of the Lost Ark*, *An Officer and a Gentleman*, and *Airplane!*). Over the whole period, the team could take credit for a wealth of other films that were popular or critical successes (or both), ranging from the critically hailed *The Elephant Man* and *Ordinary People*, to popular dramas and comedies such as *Footloose*, *Flashdance*, *Trading Places*, *Beverly Hills Cop*, and three *Star Trek* movies, and on into the world of the unredeemed splatter flick with four *Friday the 13th* movies. Just as ABC, with Eisner's help, had moved from last place to first place, Paramount with Diller and Eisner at the helm, moved from last place to first among the six major studios (and never came in at lower than second place during Eisner's tenure). At one point Paramount turned out a string of 20 profitable movies in 18 months. In a decade the studio's profit more than tripled, from $39 million in 1973 to $140 million in 1983. The period from January 1983 to June 1984 was the most profitable 18 months in the studio's history. Tony Schwartz' July 1984 *New York* article on the Paramount team carried the title "Hollywood's Hottest Stars."

But by then things had already begun to fall apart. Diller had a long and tempestuous history with Charles Bluhdorn, the Gulf & Western tycoon who had hired him as president of Paramount, but the two men had a bond. As one insider put it, "Charlie tortured Barry every day, but there was also great love between them." That love came to a tragic end on February 19, 1983, when Bluhdorn's heart suddenly failed on a flight from the Dominican Republic.

When the dust of the succession struggles had settled, Diller found himself working for a very different man. Martin Davis was given to formal hierarchies and distrusted headstrong creative types. Bluhdorn had often been called a "buccaneer." The most colorful label people gave Davis was "manager." But he could be ruthless. He had been supported for the top job by Bluhdorn's widow Yvette, but once in office he wanted to be independent. Despite the fact that she owned 4 million shares in the company, he cut her direct line to corporate headquarters, took away her company limousine, and cut the company's support for her favorite charities. He fired whole cadres of executives who had opposed his rise, and set out to reorganize the company. The clock began to tick on the entire hierarchy at Paramount Pictures.

5

The Fall of the House of Disney

In 1977, Walt Disney Productions was still held together by the energy and vision of its founder. Over the next seven years, the decay of the company would become visible. It would grow shaky, and it would begin to attract people who could profit from its fall.

The management of Roy O. Disney, and of Card Walker after him, had its supporters, especially as the regime that had built Disney World. David Londoner, a stock analyst at Wertheim and Company who has followed Disney since Walt was alive, says of Walker and his team, "They did some extraordinary things. They understood that this was one of the most valuable franchises in the world. They wouldn't really express it that way, but they treated it that way. That awareness caused them to build things with exquisite detail and care. They built an incredible quality into it. And they built, as well, an image of quality. There were only a handful of images that were that good. But it also caused them to husband the resource, and not use effective marketing on it. They really built incredible product, but I don't think they were good managers of it."

Concern for quality abounded; it was an aspect of Walt that became part of the Disney culture. Walker took on Walt's function as the autocratic enforcer of that quality, and became the focus of the hopes and fears of the people who worked for him. A good example is the creation of a show at EPCOT Center called "The American Adventure." In the late '70s, while WED was plunged neck-deep into the torrent of concepts for this vast new theme park, one idea would not seem to float. The center for all the pavilions of the nations at EPCOT would, of course, be the American pavilion. And it had to have a "show"—something both educational and fun, something to entertain the guests with a sense of American history and place. That turned out to be a tall order. One writer after another tackled it, including Marc Davis, who had designed the "Pirates of the Caribbean" ride. None of the scripts worked.

Finally Randy Bright was given the assignment. Walker and Miller loved his idea—the panoply of American history told through the eyes of Benjamin Franklin and Mark Twain, as fellow travelers in time—but it seemed more a television episode than a ride or a Disney robotic "show." His second idea, even Bright agreed, "was awful." His third attempt was a conceptual outline. His boss, Marty Sklar, said, "Great. Now do it." Bright fleshed out the outline, did a storyboard, made a paper model, cut out paper dolls and puppets to represent the historical robots, selected some music, and readied the whole presentation for the day when Walker would review all the developing EPCOT concepts.

Bright was nervous. He had come to feel that his whole career hinged on the acceptance of his idea. He had stayed up all night polishing the presentation and pacing the floor.

When Walker arrived in the presentation room, it was clear that he was in pain. His back was bothering him. The pain made him look angry. He sat down on one of the stools provided for the company brass. Other imagineers hung around the back of the small room or poked their noses in the door. "Usually," according to Bright, "Card was a very good person to present for. He would respond. He would say, 'Yeah, I get that, go on, keep going.' He would get involved." But on this particular morning, as Bright proceeded with his show, "There was nothing, it was just dying. I thought, 'I'm bombing out. This is the end of my career. I'm going back to the training division. It's over.' Finally I said to myself, 'I'm going down with all guns blazing.' So I whipped myself into a frenzy and I acted out every part—Ben Franklin, Thomas Jefferson. I did the whole show."

He finished, standing in the small, suddenly silent room with the sweat rolling down his face. And Card said nothing for a long moment. Then suddenly he said, "It's worth the price of admission to EPCOT." He stood up, bad back and all, and slammed his fist down on the stool he had been sitting on. "Goddamn it, it's worth the fucking price of admission to EPCOT! This show is fantastic!"

Walker was Walt's successor in ways that Walt's brother Roy never had been. He was an autocrat, a one-man show who overshadowed the chairman and the head of the studio, who pushed constantly for the highest quality. Yet he did not have Walt's agile vision. And his concern for quality, for "husbanding the resource," could lead to narrow-minded decisions that contrasted sharply with Walt's bold reach. For instance, as hotel chains continued to build (and overbuild) up to the very edges of

Walt Disney World, and as the hotels within Walt Disney World continued to register occupancy rates far above the industry average, Walker refused to build more hotels on the property to compete with the outsiders. He wanted, he said, to be a "good citizen." In the same vein, he kept the entrance prices at the parks at levels that most analysts felt were artificially low, for fear that the "guests" would not feel they had received good value. At the same time, he refused to advertise the parks for fear they would become overcrowded.

In the early '80s, stock analyst David Londoner was in Los Angeles, visiting various companies that he followed. At Mattel, while talking to Art Spear, the company's chairman, Spear suddenly asked Londoner, "You know the Disney people very well, don't you?"

Londoner said, "Yeah, I'll be going over there in the next day or so."

"Do you think," said Spear, "if you're going to be in touch with Card Walker, would you talk to him and see if we could set up an appointment?"

Londoner said, "I'd be delighted, Art, but you're the chairman of the world's largest toy company. They're seven miles away from you. I'm amazed you can't do it."

"No," said Spear, "we've tried, and we really haven't been able to get in there. What we want to do is have a traveling ice show, using Disney characters. All we want to do is give them money. We don't want them to bear any of the costs. We just want to license the characters."

A few days later Londoner met with Card Walker. In the middle of the meeting he said, "Card, Art Spear at Mattel would like to talk to you. Do you think you could take a meeting with them?"

Card said, "Oh, I know what they want to do. They just want to license our characters."

Londoner asked, "What's wrong with that?"

"Oh," he said, "you know where they have those shows. They're in arenas and things like that. We don't want our characters to hang out in arenas. That isn't the Disney image."

Ultimately Disney did do an ice show. But Walker's gut reaction was protective, rather than expansive. He felt like the physician contemplating the opening line of the Hippocratic oath: "First, do no harm."

There were, as well, deep systemic reasons for Disney's slow failure in the 1970s. One major factor was the closed nature of the Disney organization. "They would not give people any participation," Jim Jimirro remembers. "Card felt that it was a privilege to work at Disney. That was his deep down attitude: you don't have to reach out to other people for talent. The world's going to beat a path to our door. We don't have to give up any [percentage] points [of profit to outsiders]. We're going to own everything, we're going to keep everything, we're not going to share because this is Disney and it's a privilege to work here." Ironically, the only people who did have direct personal percentages of the profits of Disney films were Walker, Tatum, and a few other top officers of the company.

Another Disney veteran commented on the company's insularity. "Even socially, none of those guys was in the loop. They didn't hang out. They weren't eating at Chasen's. There is an infrastructure to this [Hollywood] community. There is something of a club. But they didn't go to the same parties; they didn't go to any parties."

Even down in Malibu, Diane and Ron's neighbors thought of them as a quiet couple. They didn't come to the parties along the water. Sometimes Alan Horn, a neighbor who was an executive first at 20th Century Fox, then at Lorimar, would drop in. But, as one neighbor put it, "You never saw Ron being social along the beach." Diane liked to have company when she swam in the surf, but Ron didn't like to come down on the sand, so she would find neighbors and friends to swim with. He would sit on the deck and watch the ocean.

As Card and Ron kept aloof from the social whirl, Disney held itself aloof from the rest of the industry. It referred to the industry as "Hollywood" or "over the hill," even though many other major studios were located in the San Fernando Valley, near Disney. Disney employees tended to think of Hollywood the way much of the rest of America does, as the stuff of tabloid front pages, awash in drugs, promiscuity, bloated executive egos and salaries, stretch limousines, and car phones. Disney saw itself as being in the "family" entertainment business—a different business from the people "over the hill."

This feeling expressed itself in myriad tiny ways throughout the company. For instance, while all air travel was first-class, all car travel was not. When, in 1977, the company finally decided to spring for company cars for its top 50 executives. It offered only Ford LTD four-door sedans. Color was the only choice you could make—no accessories, no options. You would drive on the lot in the morning and see 50 identical cars in the executive spaces. In 1979, General Motors joined the EPCOT program, and suddenly the 50 Fords became 50 four-door Buick Electras. In 1981 they were replaced by 50 more four-door Buick Electras. In 1983, Jimirro, a single man who wanted a sporty car, wrote an impassioned memo. "Okay, I understand the Buick Electras, but could I have a two-door?" He got his two-door.

But the company would not spring for car phones. They were deemed a luxury. In a town in which it was not at all unusual to spend an hour each way commuting by car, in a business in which communicating with New York, which started three hours earlier, was of utmost importance, even the top executives had to pay for their own car phones.

One executive compared Card Walker's attitude toward expenses of any kind to Nancy Reagan's famous phrase: "Just say no."

The spring of 1977 brought another glimmer of the company's future, and another example of a failure to invest in that future. Two months after Roy Disney's resignation, Jimirro presented Walker and Miller with an idea for a Disney Channel—a separate, satellite-based distribution system for Disney product, either independent or licensed through the then-fledgling HBO. Only 1.2 million people in the entire country then subscribed to cable television. Costs would have been minimal. "Back then," says Jimirro, "we could have done it for 50 cents. Everybody liked the idea, but the truth is, nobody took it seriously. Their reaction was, essentially, 'Jim, go do your 8 millimeter home movies.'"

As one industry observer put it, "When you're running a business it's like pouring a cup of coffee and then putting your sugar in it and then putting your cream in it—certain things you just do. You release product, you get into all the distribution systems that you can." But Walker and Miller were afraid to do anything that might upset the theater owners that showed Disney films. At the urging of Irving Ludwig, the long-time head of Buena Vista Distribution, they put off the satellite channel idea, held back their best product from video distribution, and refused to package any of their material for television syndication.

A year later an extraordinary opportunity offered itself once again, and Walker and Miller shrank from it. Japan's Keisei Electric Railway Company had gotten into debt in the course of some ill-advised real estate speculation, and it wanted to turn some of its railway lands into cash. It owned 201 acres in Urayasu, a suburb of Tokyo—one of the last large open areas left close to the capital. Keisei executives approached Disney, inviting it to build a version of the Magic Kingdom there. The Disney executives had grave doubts about the proposal. Tokyo was considerably colder than California and Florida. The Japanese might not come out to the park in the rain and wind. There were great cultural differences, too. The Japanese were asking for a carbon copy of the American parks. But was their guess correct? Would the Japanese really flock to eat hot dogs, watch mechanical bears play hillbilly music, and ride in flying elephants? Besides that, Disney was pouring funds into EPCOT, and would be for years to come.

In the end, Walker agreed to a deal in which a newly formed Japanese company named Oriental Land (owned by Keisei and Mitsui Real Estate) would build, own, and operate the park; Disney would design it and advise its operators in return for 10 percent of park admission revenues and 5 percent of concessions. In time, the income would turn out to be quite small compared to the park's staggering success and the appreciation of the land—over the next decade, because of the presence of Tokyo Disneyland, Urayasu would experience the most rapid appreciation of land values in all Japan.

While new business opportunities were let slip, the company's old businesses suffered. The slow devolution of the studio was felt especially in its birthplace, the animation department. Increasing tensions began to split the department between the "Nine Old Men" who had grown up in the business with Walt, and the younger animators, many of them recruited from Cal Arts, the arts college founded with money left by Walt. Not that the young ones were agitating for some new, hip, slick way to do things. To the contrary, they saw themselves as upholding the old values. Some of these were technical values, such as the drops of water in *Snow White* that show miniature reflections of their surroundings or the delicate 15-color palette for Jiminy Cricket in *Pinocchio*. Others were creative. The young animators felt the more recent films were bland, that they glossed over the deeper emotions, the fear and longing, the grief and loss that had given the earlier classics such depth. In 1977, *Pete's Dragon* was met with critical yawns and empty seats. *The Fox and the Hound*, which eventually came out in 1981, promised no better.

In 1979, the most prominent of Disney's young Turks, Don Bluth, abruptly left the company in the midst of work on *The Fox and the Hound*. Thirteen others left with him, to form the new studio of Sullivan and Bluth. In time, the new studio, relocated to Ireland, would bring out films that truly competed with Disney animated features, films such as *The Mouse's Tale* and *The Land before Time*. But Disney did not have to wait years to feel the difference. The mass departure was an immediate body blow to Disney animation, another reflection of the severity of the studio's troubles.

As a form, animation was in the doldrums. According to John Pomeroy, who left Disney to become Bluth's partner, "I think '81 or '82 was the low point for the entire industry. There wasn't a lot of money to be made in animated films and there wasn't a lot of interest in them. The animated feature was really close to extinction." Young audiences seemed interested only in the wild special effects of live-action science-fiction films—laser swords, robots, and careening antigravity speeders. Whether Disney, the keeper of the flame, could hold out much longer, was a crucial question.

By 1979, even the conservative Walker–Miller team knew that the Disney studio needed to produce something ambitious and exciting. Their answer was *The Black Hole*, a space-based remake of *20,000 Leagues under the Sea*. The company reached back into its own past to remake a fantasy spectacular, and at the same time reached out to imitate other popular films such as *Star Wars* and *Star Trek*. The growing sense of frustration in the company had focused on this one film. The film had to succeed. At the Royal World Premiere of the film in London, Card Walker sat in the front row, at once hopeful and desperate, softly hitting his fist into his palm and saying, "Gotta go. It's gotta go." But it didn't go. It was an expensive film to make, and a failure. Receipts were modest and the critics unkind. A typical review called it "a sappy science-fiction dud" and "an uninspired collection of space-movie clichés."

In 1980, Walker eased Tatum into retirement, took over the chairman's seat, and named Ron Miller president and chief operating officer. Walker called eight top managers to a meeting at Disney World. In the tight world of Disney, no one had any power but Card, and no one but Card and Ron had added that sixth figure to their income. A typical top manager just under the corporate officers might earn between $70,000 and $85,000 per year. When the eight men gathered around a boardroom table at Disney World, Walker told them, "From now one, you will all be corporate vice presidents. You will comprise the management committee. I'm going to let go. Ron's going to run the company. You're going to be his collective aide-de-camp." Then he walked around the table handing each man a piece of paper with his new salary written on it. As each man unfolded the paper, a series of small gasps rose around the table. The salary increases were dramatic; most of those at the table saw their salaries double. The message for those around the table was clear: Card would make Ron president of the company, but he didn't really think he was capable of handling the job.

But Miller did what he could to change the company. He immediately moved to give the studio a younger bent by appointing Tom Wilhite vice president of creative development for films and television. Wilhite had never produced a foot of film in his life. At 27, he was head of Disney's publicity department. But he was bright, he was eager, and he had ideas; Miller felt he might be just the potion that Disney needed.

Wilhite set to work on films that he hoped would draw in not just children but young adults and adults as well. The results included *The Last Flight of Noah's Ark*, starring Elliot Gould, Genevieve Bujold, and 11-year-old Ricky Schroeder (and a minor scandal when the three stars went skinny-dipping in a pool on the Disney back lot); another Gould vehicle, *The Devil and Max Devlin*; *Never Cry Wolf*; and the $21-million techno-thriller *Tron*.

To the dismay of Disney, none of the films lived up to its hopes. It was a dismal time for the studio. A studio insider of the time now says of the Disney spectaculars of the late '70s and early '80s, "The thing that was missing from those movies was heart. The old Disney movies had enormous heart. And the Disney-type movies our competitors were making had heart. *E.T.* had heart. *Karate Kid* had heart. *The Black Hole* had no heart. *Tron* had no heart. It was one of the great ironies."

But even when the studio did things right, it didn't seem to get rewarded. In 1982, the studio produced *Tex*, a sensitive and well-drawn film, starring a current teen heart-throb, Matt Dillon. The critics liked it, calling it "a superb coming-of-age adventure." Yet it made only $9 million at the box office. The same year, *Porky's*, an aggressively adolescent film that centered on a peep-hole in the wall of the girls' locker-room, made $70 million for 20th Century Fox. The contrast seemed to represent the choice the studio had to make: give in to mindless, tasteless exploitation like the rest of Hollywood, or close down the studio.

It was not just the ideas, the access to talent, and the creative impetus that had been lost. By the late 1970s the studio's technical abilities—its equipment and its attitudes—had ossified. The original sponsorship contracts for EPCOT included a media package, and a promise of a television series on technology and the future, linked to EPCOT the way the Sunday night "Wonderful World of Disney" had always been linked to Disneyland. Yet, despite the efforts of a number of different producers and writers, the series never took form. In the end, Disney renegotiated the contracts and refunded a portion of the sponsors' funds. According to a Disney veteran, "They simply were so immobilized that they never made the shows."

When Elliott Gould filmed *The Last Flight of Noah's Ark* at Disney in 1980, he asked a sound engineer for certain enhancements in the sound track. Gould was a fiddler and tinkerer, eager to be involved in the technical side of films he was in. The engineer looked at him pityingly, then said, "Come here." In the sound booth, he gestured to an ancient-looking array of switches, dials, and meters. "You see this postproduction board we're using? Same one we used for *Fantasia* [made nearly four decades before]. You see these microphones? Ditto."

Gould went to Card Walker and pleaded for more advanced equipment. "I'd like to help you, Elliott," Walker told him, "but we can't afford it. Every penny we have is going into EPCOT."

According to Randy Bright, "The operations head of the studio, Bob Gibeaut, had a mission—not to spend a penny on anything." The Disney studio had built its reputation on technical breakthroughs as much as on creative vision. The string of impressive technical accomplishments— first use of synchronized sound in animation, first use of color in films, first animated features, the invention of the "multiplane" animation camera with its special feeling of depth—accompanied a recurring display of sheer technical virtuosity in such films as *20,000 Leagues under the Sea.* But the technical side, according to Bright, "had grown very old-fashioned—easily last in the industry by a distance."

In 1981, when he was designing shows at EPCOT, one of Bright's responsibilities was to produce "Circle-Vision 360" films about Canada, China, and other countries. In the early 1960s, Disney had pioneered the technique, which involved mounting a number of cameras in a circle and projecting the result on a circle of screens over the heads of the audience. But now those in the studio who knew that technique would not allow it to be changed for the 1980s.

"There was a certain way that Circle-Vision films were made that was not allowed to be improved upon," Bright remembered later, "because that's the way it was done when the first Circle-Vision film was done. There were rules: Thou shalt not pan, thou shalt not tilt the cameras, thou shalt not control the action. You just come in and grab-shoot. I felt that if you want to do a great Circle-Vision shot you don't grab-shoot; you spend days planning and you control all the action for 360 degrees around. None of those things were done. I broke every rule in the book." Bright's films, which run at EPCOT today, include dizzying shots taken from diving airplanes and helicopters, alongside skiers racing down mountainsides, and amid running horses.

"They had these ancient movieolas over there that they cut film on," said Bright. "They told me that when you cut a Circle-Vision film, you have nine panels, so you cut it to the center panel. Everything plays off the center panel. That was the rule." But Bright wanted to direct the audience's attention from one side to the other, from the front to the back, at times putting nine different images on the nine screens, or wiping from one scene to another around the circle. "You couldn't do that with one movieola. I wanted to buy some Eight-Plate KEMs—the flatbed editing systems that any decent movie studio uses today. You can get three images on three different screens. I wanted to string three together to see all nine panels of my show at one time. We'd still be editing right now if we were using a movieola."

Bright went to Ron Miller, explained what the problem was, described an Eight-Plate KEM, and asked for money to buy some. Miller walked with him out of the executive offices in the animation building and down to the studio, where an editor was working on *Tron*. He said, "You mean one of these things?" There sat a KEM, rented for the film that was meant to bring Disney back into contention.

Miller supported Bright, over Gibeaut's objections, and brought in the new editing technology. Even in film production, its own métier, the studio played poor stepson to the parks.

By the early 1980s, Wall Street had begun to sour on Disney. A number of analysts, including Londoner, took it off their "buy" lists. "The stock had done nothing," he says. "They were putting all this money into EPCOT. At the prices they were going to charge, it was going to give them about a 3 percent rate of return. That said to me, this is a great company, but the management doesn't know how to manage it."

The strain showed within the company, as money flowed out to EPCOT, expertise was stretched between Florida and Tokyo, and the studio floundered. Randy Bright prepared a presentation and slide show for Walker, urging him to move the company to catch up with changing public tastes. Walker subjected him to a tongue-lashing, blaming the company's troubles on the imagineers' cost overruns at EPCOT, and threw him out of his office.

People outside the company were really beginning to take notice of

Disney's disarray. For instance, the treasurer of Marriott, a hard-charging young deal-maker named Al Checchi, paid a visit to the West Coast in 1982 that would come to have consequences far beyond anything he could have expected.

Marriott was interested in striking a deal with a local real estate millionaire in Santa Barbara, California, over some hotel properties. The man's name was Fess Parker, and in a former life he had been Disney's Davy Crockett. Checchi and his wife spent a weekend with the Parkers in their sumptuous home above the sea in the exclusive Hope Ranch district of the comfortable old mission town.

The talk went into the night: Marriott might trade Parker a half interest in the Santa Barbara Biltmore for a half-interest in a new hotel. Parker worried Checchi over guarantees against overruns and shortfall, and Checchi pressed Parker to take on the risk without guarantees. Finally the talk turned, as it would, to Disney. The man across from Checchi with that deep velvet drawl was finally not just another deal-maker with property to throw on the table. He was Davy Crockett, American hero, fair-handed Indian fighter and broad-shouldered pioneer, battler at the Alamo for freedom and the American way. At Checchi's urging, Parker talked about Walt and the company. He spoke of the deep "lethargy" the company had fallen into.

"You know, Al," Parker finally said, "I think that Disney is ripe for some positive influence. It's just drifting."

The comment stayed with Checchi. Maybe Marriott could buy Disney. There might be a fit. He and his mentor, Gary Wilson (Marriott's chief financial officer), ordered a detailed study of the company. At the time they concluded that, at least with its present management, Disney stock was fully valued. It was not a bargain that Marriott should scoop up.

But the idea stuck with Checchi even after he left Marriott. He was enticed South later in 1982 by Richard Rainwater, president of the Bass Brothers' far-flung multibillion-dollar network of businesses, investments, and real estate. The job Checchi was offered was, in effect, chief operating officer. The inducement was not just a salary, but participation. Checchi could get rich. The energetic financier guided the Basses' fortunes, gathering the capital to buy a 10 percent stake in Texaco and a leveraged buyout of a Florida-based land-development company called Arvida. But he still had his eye on Disney.

EPCOT finally opened on October 1, 1982. After the speeches, the first paltry crowds spread across the grounds. EPCOT was a carefully groomed landscape of spindly eucalyptus trees, acacia, rubber, and palm set in immaculate lawns, among truncated geodesic glass pyramids and domes and strange dancing fountains with single arcs of water leaping from place to place. "Guests" spiraled up into darkness inside the Buckminster Fuller geodesic-dome "golfball" towering over EPCOT, while Walter Cronkite's friendly video visage told them about "Spaceship Earth" for AT&T and Disney. Boats began to river through the geodesic greenhouses of Kraft's "The Land," full of tourists clicking pictures of cassava and papaya, pointing at the tilapia fish, the pacu, and the channel catfish, listening to the guides carry on about drip irrigation and aeroponic conveyors.

Families in the General Motors "World of Motion" boarded little cars for a ride based on the theme "It's always fun to move." At the end of the ride, only a few were surprised to find themselves in a GM showroom, stocked with the latest models of Pontiac Firebirds and Oldsmobiles, with pride of place given to a Corvette. There were even salespeople armed with brochures. Outside, the monorail ran overhead in its stately pace.

Roy Disney, still a board member and the largest single stockholder, was so shocked at the cost of EPCOT that he refused to come to the opening ceremonies.

The effort to build EPCOT had weakened the company. The original budget of $400 million had tripled to $1.2 billion, but the $350 million of corporate sponsorships had not increased at all. It was an enormous investment in what was essentially an educational institution, in the wild idea that education and inspiration would sell. For the fiscal year that ended the day before EPCOT's opening, net income was down 18 percent from the year before. And the money hemorrhage had not stopped. EPCOT was still being built: the GE "Horizons" pavilion was not due to open until 1983, and United Technologies' "Living Seas" until 1984.

The year that EPCOT opened, Jimirro finally got the green light to go ahead with a Disney Channel—but now it would cost more than his projected "50 cents." In the first year alone the project—one that, like EPCOT, carried a big risk as a pioneer effort—ate up $100 million.

But EPCOT, at least, was bringing in revenue. And Card Walker had finally succeeded in bringing some version of Walt's dream to fruition. Despite the doubters, it turned out that people would pay to walk through the gates.

In a board meeting just after the opening ceremonies, Walker, now 66, announced his intention to retire. In March 1983, he passed the title of chief executive officer to Ron Miller—over the objections of Roy E. Disney. He held onto the title as chairman long enough to fly to Japan and open the new Tokyo Disneyland. On May 1, Walker stepped down as chairman, turning the office over to one of southern California's premier large-scale real-estate developers, Ray Watson.

Watson, another man in a moustache with a passing resemblance to Walt, knew little about films—remarkably little for a man running a major studio. According to Bright, "When he came over to WED (Imagineering) to review our concept for a ride based on *Star Wars*, he sat down and said, 'First, boys, tell me, what is *Star Wars?*'" Watson had trained as an architect, and spent most of his professional life at the Irvine Company, systematically turning some hundred thousand acres of grazing and farm land south of Los Angeles into shopping malls, houses, apartments, and office buildings. His attitude had always been: Find out what the public wants and give it to them. As president of the Irvine Company, he had based many of his decisions on scores of surveys and focus groups that plumbed the thoughts of people of different races, income level, and family size, pulling out which facade they liked the most, which floor plan, how many closets, what colors on the walls.

In 1964, Walt Disney had sought out Watson, on the recommendation of friends, to review his ideas about EPCOT, which was then to be a planned community of 20,000 or more, with churches, schools, and shopping malls, around a central complex whose towers would pierce a great climate-control dome. Watson told Disney the obvious: it looked great, but he'd have to pay people to live there, since Disney intended to control every aspect of the residents' lives, including their clothing, hairstyles, public behavior, and sex lives, at the same time that he forbid representative government.

Disney thought the comments astute and invited Watson back for more discussions. After Walt's death the company continued to ask Watson's advice. By 1973, they had appointed him to the board. Now, Walker invited him to chair the company, to help out Miller, whose competence to run the company Walker—and Miller—doubted.

Watson was a reformer. He and Miller pushed the studio toward more adult themes and formed a new subsidiary, named Touchstone, to carry a series of adult- and teen-oriented films. It was a move that Miller had been urging on Walker for years. The first film under the new name would be *Splash* with Darryl Hannah. The film illustrated neatly the fence on which Miller sat. Because *Splash* was a live-action comedy featuring a beautiful mermaid, part of its attraction was certainly what the industry would call its "jiggle quotient." Mermaids, after all, have breasts. But this was Disney, not Hollywood. Disney veterans were holding prayer meetings against even the suggestion of a topless Disney film.

On the one hand, Miller elected not to cover Hannah's breasts with shells (as Eisner would cover Ariel's several years later in the animated *The Little Mermaid*). On the other hand, Hannah wore a flesh-colored body suit, cleverly camouflaged, and shocks of her long blond hair, methodically glued in place every day, covered her nipples. Maybe the studio needed to wake up to modern entertainment realities, but as Miller had already said in one magazine interview, "The day Disney makes an R-rated film is the day I leave the company."

At the same time, Miller knew that the company desperately needed real expertise at the top of the film division. The studio's income had drifted downward, from $34.6 million in 1981, to $19.6 million in 1982, then to a $33.3 million loss in 1983. The number of films the studio made skidded to three in 1983, and the portion of each film's cost represented by studio overhead climbed to 35 percent, far above the industry average of 20 percent.

The experiment with Tom Wilhite was not working, and in late 1982 Miller began to search for a new studio head. He went "over the hill," to "Hollywood," looking for someone to take on a new position—president of the studio. He considered Dennis Stanfill, former head of 20th Century Fox. He approached Michael Eisner. But Eisner was already president of a studio, one that was larger than Disney—Paramount. If he came to Disney, he told Miller, he wanted to run the parks too. In essence, he wanted Miller's job. But Miller was not willing to replace himself, and in the spring of 1983 he settled on Richard Berger, senior vice president of worldwide productions for 20th Century Fox. Ironically, in that job Berger had passed on the *Splash* project—and had distributed *Porky's*.

It was not a happy marriage. Berger may have had the right skills for the job, but the cultural rub was too grating. He circulated memos on his theories of entertainment, admonishing his fellow Disney executives, "From my conversations, in the short time I have been at the studio, I believe we all have to go to the movies more often." He gave presentations in management committee meetings, with pointer and easel, detailing the failings of Disney films, how bad they were, and how little they grossed—in front of Miller and Wilhite, who had masterminded them. To the horror of Disney veterans, he had an automatic door closer installed in his office—a button under the desk that closes or opens the door by remote control. The device was a common status symbol "over the hill," but few people at Disney had ever seen one. Says one veteran, "Do you think Card, 'Mr. Frugality,' took that lightly?" At a presentation to stock analysts in the studio theater, one analyst asked Berger why he had taken the job, and he answered, "Nobody ever called me 'President' before." Possibly true but flip, the remark was soon the talk of Disney, a company that took itself more seriously than most—even more seriously than necessary.

For myriad small reasons of personality and culture, Berger was sailing against the current almost as soon as he came to Disney. At just the moment when the studio was in crisis, in danger of actually going out of the business it had been in for over a half-century, its management was immobilized by bad chemistry between Berger and Miller.

At the same time, Watson had discovered, to his dismay, that neither the company nor any of its divisions had a business plan. They had no map of what they expected the future to look like, and how they expected to get there. The whole company, with its revenues of over $1 billion per year, just went along from day to day. Watson set about building such plans for the company, and for each division of the company.

But it all began to seem too little and too late. *Splash* would not come out until the spring of 1984. The Disney Channel was still a hole to throw money into. Afraid of competing with its own fledgling cable channel, Disney allowed its contract with NBC for the Sunday evening "Wonderful World of Disney" to lapse. Disney disappeared from the networks for the first time in nearly 30 years, giving up what amounted to a weekly prime-time one-hour advertisement for the Disney parks, films, and characters. After an initial burst of enthusiasm, the crowds at EPCOT were dropping. Wall Street was disenchanted and slipping into restlessness. Analysts had long since throttled back their enthusiasm, as the earnings per share slid to 75¢ in 1982, to 68¢ in 1983, to a projected 68¢ in 1984. For the fiscal year that ended September 30, 1983, net income was off another 7 percent, and analysts thought the coming year would be even worse. The stock price fell by almost half in a single year, from $84 per share in 1983 into the mid-$40s by early 1984.

Yet the company still felt no sense of crisis. There was no terror in Burbank to stoke the creative fires, no adrenaline-feeding panic. In January 1984, for instance, Miller invited the management team to his house in Aspen, Colorado, for a retreat. One person who attended said, "Management retreats are terrific things if you're able to get away and combine recreation and congeniality with planning sessions where you don't have the phone ringing. We went up there for three or four days. It was the perfect venue—ski in the morning, sit around the fireplace later, relax, get to know each other better. The place was so cozy, Ron was such a kindly host—and we did not have one meeting. Not for five minutes. Talk about missed opportunities. Who knows what could have come out of a meeting like that?"

Clearly the company was vulnerable to a takeover, and Watson, more at home in the financial world than Miller, saw it coming. He astutely commissioned a study to find out how much it would take to buy control of Disney—a rough yardstick of how vulnerable the company actually was. The answer: very vulnerable. The value of the outstanding shares at the time was about $2 billion. The parks alone were worth that much.

Watson, Miller, and other top Disney executives then turned to the firm's investment bankers, Morgan Stanley, with a slightly different idea. To stave off a takeover attempt, perhaps they should take the company private. But the Morgan Stanley consultants pointed out two sobering facts. In order to pay off the debt they would create in taking it private, they would have to split the company, selling off major pieces, destroying the very mix that had driven the company's success. And any offer they made for the stock would set off a bidding war, which they were very likely to lose.

Morgan Stanley's advice amounted to this: do everything you can to get the stock price back up. In the meantime, hold your breath.

6

One Hundred Ninety-Seven Days

1984 was the year Geraldine Ferraro ran for vice president, the year Linda Hunt won an Oscar for her role as a photographer in *The Year of Living Dangerously*. 1984 was a year of living dangerously for Walt Disney Productions as well, a year of touching bottom, a year of an end and a new beginning. For Disney, the year started late, almost where the Romans would have started it, in March. It started on March 9, a Friday, and the turn of the new came 197 days later, on September 22, a Saturday.*

It was raining in Manhattan on March 9, on the just and the unjust alike, on the homeless crowding the sidewalks and the executives dashing from their limousines. On Park Avenue, outside the Waldorf, phalanxes of New York City police lined the street in the rain waiting for Barbara Bush. Two blocks north and 29 stories up, the constant horns of the street only faintly penetrated the hush of the corporate offices of Reliance Group Holdings. The art on the walls at Reliance showed a taste at once eclectic and soothing—a giant Revolutionary War flag, ship models of exquisite detail, photos of flamingos, farmland, a building once thought beautiful.

In an L-shaped office lined with management studies and corporate histories, Saul Steinberg, chairman of Reliance, sat with the phone to his ear, cigar smoldering in his mouth, looking out at the rain. A small sign on his desk read, "This too shall pass." Steinberg was a short, robust 45-year-old man with a full head of stiff, thick, dark hair and a cheeky, almost chipmunklike face. As was his custom, he wore a sprightly bow tie with his tailored suit. He was a self-made man with a personal fortune in excess of a half-billion dollars, of which his majority interest in the privately held Reliance insurance conglomerate was only a part. Known in the financial community as one of the earliest and most ferocious of

---

*The source for much of the background on Roy Disney, Stanley Gold, Ray Watson, and the inner workings of the Disney board is John Taylor's groundbreaking book, *Storming the Magic Kingdom,* published in 1987 by Knopf. For a more detailed account of the Disney takeover attempt, I highly recommend the Taylor book.

corporate raiders, Steinberg lived in John D. Rockefeller's former residence—a 34-room, 28,000-square-foot apartment with 15 fireplaces, a gym, a screening room, and two formal dining rooms, large and small. He collected art works by great masters—Rodin, Picasso, Francis Bacon. Rubens' massive *Death of Adonis* hung over the couch.

Starting in 1960 with a $25,000 loan from his father, Steinberg had built an empire worth more than $4 billion by 1984. He had, along the way, helped to pioneer the techniques that came to be known as "greenmail," "leveraged buyouts," "hostile takeovers," and "junk bonds." Arthur Fleischer, a partner of Wall Street's Fried, Frank, Harris, Shriver & Jacobson, says, "Saul Steinberg has been the most prominent figure in the takeover movement for almost 20 years. He has tried every offensive tactic before it became respectable. I can't think of anyone else who has had as much influence."

Neither Ray Watson nor Ron Miller had heard of Steinberg. Nor did Steinberg know much about the entertainment business or California. He thought of both as other worlds, dropping phrases such as, "When you leave California and go back to the real world. . . . " But Steinberg was the stuff of Watson's nightmares. He was exactly the man that Watson's discussions with Morgan Stanley about possible takeover attempts had led him to fear. Despite Steinberg's easy, friendly, open manner, he was an aggressive, uninhibited investor with a lot of liquidity. He had a rapid, fluid mind, and an organization to match, an organization that, because it was privately held, was not restricted by the concerns of stockholders. He had not actually taken over a corporation in a hostile maneuver in 16 years, since he bought Reliance in 1968. But he had "greenmailed" at least a dozen companies, frightening them into buying him out at a premium. Quaker State Oil Refining, for instance, had just bought back his share of the company's stock for $47 million. The stock had only cost him $36 million, but the company's management was so afraid that he was going to take them over that they willingly paid a premium price to get rid of him as a shareholder. His critics thought Steinberg the archvillain of American capitalism, bent on pillage and corporate rapine. *Fortune* had once entitled a Steinberg profile, "Fear and Loathing in the Boardroom." Steinberg was an unusual person. And he had just heard some unusually interesting news.

Steinberg had been following Disney for some time. At lunch one Friday, a broker he knew had suggested that he take a look at Disney; at the time its stock wallowed in the mid-40s, well below the value of its assets. Steinberg had acquired the company's documents—the 10K dec-larations it filed with the Securities and Exchange Commission, its quar-terly financial reports, and its annual reports—and had taken them home for a weekend, as was his habit. He read SEC declarations the way most people read the morning comics—quickly and easily, as much for amusement as anything else. He was fascinated, even obsessed, by the twists and turns of value hidden in their bland numbers and technical terms.

His home reading convinced him that Disney was worth a more de-tailed look. On Monday morning he instructed his staff to find out every-thing possible about Disney—whether printed, heard through contacts, or even extracted from paid moles developed within the company.

What he saw at Disney was a seriously undervalued company, a com-pany with assets worth far more than what it would cost to buy it. The parks, he felt, could earn a lot more money. The land surrounding Disney World in Florida could be developed a lot faster. He realized that, through his subsidiary, Days Inn, he actually owned more hotel rooms in Orlando than Disney did. Disney could, he felt, make more money at licensing, and the studio was clearly floundering. The Disney Channel was not making money, and the company had no clear forecast on when it was going to break even. The studio had no presence on network television. "There was a lot of fuzzy thinking at Disney," according to Steinberg. "They were very confused and financially naive. There was no leadership there. They were a company that was floundering. Walt Disney had the burning vision. Now he was gone and there wasn't anybody to take it the next series of steps. But it was an asset that couldn't be replaced. It could make an incredible amount of money."

Steinberg and his close circle of advisers and fellow investors were not particularly impressed by the Disney management team. "We had heard that this guy Ron Miller was not terribly competent. He was way in over his head. He used to play cards a lot. Maybe his head was into other things, I don't know. He was a football player at one time. He was described to us as a real dope. I don't know him personally, so I can't say. What he had done with the company was dopey and dumb."

Steinberg felt certain that somebody would come along and shake Disney up—buy it, dismember it, have a proxy fight, change the manage-ment, something—and the stock would shoot up in price. When that happened, it would be very profitable to own some Disney stock. Until that happened, it would be foolish to own Disney stock. The shakeup could happen at any moment, or it could happen years in the future—but it would happen. The moment he heard that something was under way, he would buy Disney stock as fast as he could.

This morning, March 9, he had heard the kind of news he was listening for. While most people interested in Disney focused on its annual meeting, which was about to open, or on its new film *Splash*, just about to hit the theaters and perhaps rescue Disney from the doldrums, Steinberg was electrified by another piece of news: Roy E. Disney had resigned from the board of Disney.

From his investigations, he had a few opinions about Roy, most of them unflattering: "Roy Disney was also not considered alive and above room temperature." He was formidably wealthy (with about half Steinberg's net worth). And he was disaffected with the current management. Although he personally was fairly mild-mannered ("He was sort of a nice guy. He wasn't a leader. He couldn't organize anything."), he had an aggressive and savvy financial manager, a lawyer named Stan Gold. And he was the single largest holder of Disney stock.

A man like that, Steinberg reasoned, doesn't quit the board of his family company in a fit of pique. He quits the board because he is about to do something that he legally and ethically cannot do while he is on the board—lead a proxy fight against it, organize a buyout, or even attempt to take the company private. Moments later Steinberg was on the phone, buying Disney stock as fast as anyone would sell to him.

Steinberg's hunch turned out to be right. Roy E. Disney in his 60s was a polite, diffident ghost of his uncle Walt, a man with a mild temperament but with Walt's twinkly eyes, softly lined features and broad moustache, his Midwestern drawl, his cough and the constant curling smoke of Lucky Strikes. Under the guidance of his adviser Stanley Gold, Roy had diversified his inherited fortune, building its value to over $220 million. But the worst investment in his portfolio was the one that bore his own name. Disney's profitability had steadily slowed, and its value had begun to drop precipitously. In jerks and starts, in sudden falls and short climbs, the stock had fallen from 85 in early 1983 to 45, during a year in which the Dow Jones average had climbed more than 200 points. The fall had reduced the value of Roy's 1.1 million shares by $40 million in 15 months.

Watson and Miller felt that they were doing all they could to turn the situation around, by opening the Tokyo site, adding attractions to Disney World, founding the new Touchstone film label, and taking more risks with subject matter. Gold and his client felt they could do much more, and they felt shut out of the process. Early in the year, Gold had formed a group they jokingly called the "Brain Trust" to mull over Roy's alternatives.

One member of this "Brain Trust" was Roy's brother-in-law Peter Dailey. Another was Frank Wells, the man who had brought Roy Disney and Stan Gold together. Back in 1969, Wells cleaned out his desk at Gang, Tyre, and Brown, one of Hollywood's top law firms. Tall, lean, with a tough, chiseled look, Wells was already a man with a remarkable track record. The son of a Navy commander, Wells had graduated Summa Cum Laude from Pomona College in nearby Claremont, and had been elected a member of Phi Beta Kappa. A Rhodes scholar, he had studied jurisprudence at Oxford, then gone on to Stanford University Law School. At 37, after ten years as an entertainment lawyer, he was ready for something new, and he had been offered a vice presidency at Warner Brothers. But before he left, he passed his client Peter Dailey, an advertising executive, over to Stan Gold. Through Peter, Stan met Roy, and came eventually to manage Roy's fortune.

Wells had prospered at Warners, working his way up from vice president for West Coast operations to president and co-chief executive. In 1982, nearing 50, he had made an unusual decision: he would quit the business to go climb mountains. He and a Denver millionaire named Richard Bass had set themselves the goal of climbing the highest mountain on every continent. If possible, they would do it all in one year. Wells had two houses out in Malibu, and now he sold one for about $1 million. Large amounts of money would help in such an enterprise, for assembling equipment, breaking through red tape, and chartering planes. But all the money in the world would not take those steps up the mountain for them, breathe the thin air for them, or make the decisions for them that would save or cost lives.

They climbed them all that year—all except Everest. The Everest expedition was forced to turn back short of the summit. A second expedition to conquer Everest was in the making. But an adventure of a different sort had now arisen, an adventure that might get in the way of Everest. Disney was beginning to intrigue Wells. He was still looking for high adventure, and Roy Disney's enterprise promised every kind of corporate intrigue and daring, every challenge a man like Wells could want. Roy, and Stan Gold, wanted him on board from the start. With his legal mind, his knowledge of the industry, and his experience in running a studio, he would add firepower to Roy Disney's efforts to change Disney. And if Roy were successful, he could add firepower to any new management team to run Disney.

By early March, Roy's "Brain Trust" had become convinced that Roy had to make the break from the company his father and uncle had built. Legally and ethically, he could not serve on the board of Walt Disney Productions while planning moves against it. He had to quit Disney's board and set out to either reform it or take it over.

Roy Disney's March 9 resignation from the Disney board set off reverberations beyond his control or knowledge. Somebody—nobody yet knew who—started buying vast amounts of Disney stock. Rumor had it the buyer was Rupert Murdoch. Watson was convinced it was the start of the takeover attempt that he had feared. On March 27, under Watson's direction, Michael Bagnall, the company's CFO, arranged an emergency $1.3-billion line of credit from the Bank of America (four times the size of their previous credit line). The credit would bankroll any defensive moves Disney might have to make—buying companies to water down the stock, paying greenmail, fighting court battles.

In a matter of weeks after he began scooping up stock, Steinberg owned more of Disney than Roy did. On March 29, he filed a Schedule 13D, required by the SEC to explain any stock purchases that result in one party owning more than 5 percent of a company. Reliance now owned 6.3 percent of Disney—"for investment purposes." Roy Disney had gone on a buying spree earlier in the year (Gold was convinced that if Roy didn't manage to shake up the company, somebody would), but he still owned only 4.7 percent.

Ray Watson was not, officially, CEO of Disney. That was Ron Miller's job. Watson was not even supposed to be working there full-time. He was a part-time chairman without much official power. But Miller was even more at sea than Watson in the fast-moving world of corporate intrigue and high finance beyond the Ventura Freeway. As signs of war grew more frequent, Miller increasingly deferred to Watson, and Watson began to assume the role of *de facto* CEO, working long hours, setting strategy, and looking to Miller for the increasingly perfunctory go-ahead.

Watson had been scanning the horizon for a takeover attempt for months already, and when Saul Steinberg began buying stock like Rommel eating up pieces of Egypt, Watson assumed that he was after the whole company. Watson and Miller hurried to New York for a council of war with their investment bankers, Morgan Stanley. They had the impression that the big guns of Wall Street would know exactly what to do. But the bankers of Morgan Stanley, and Joe Flom, the lawyer from Skadden, Arps, who was in on the discussions, were surprisingly unclear about what to do next. The fact was, there were no truly desirable defenses against a takeover. The only consensus was that Watson should look for acquisitions that would fit well with Disney. Smart acquisitions would eat up some of the company's available cash and possibly put it in debt, making it less attractive to a takeover artist. If Disney traded newly issued stock for the acquisitions, the new issues would dilute the stock held by the takeover artist. And, if the acquisition were good enough, and Wall Street saw the wisdom of it, the price of Disney stock would rise, making it more expensive for the takeover artist to buy and less likely that the other stockholders would sell it to him.

After three days in New York, Watson left, frustrated and more afraid than when he had come. Watson was a developer. He was used to building plans, frame and stucco, bulldozers and permits. He wanted to pin something down, but nothing would sit still for him. Through Flom, he managed to set up a meeting a few days later with Steinberg, who happened to be in Los Angeles. But Steinberg never showed. When Watson finally got him on the phone, he was also surprisingly unclear. When Watson pressed him about his intentions in buying millions of dollars of Disney stock, Steinberg said he didn't know yet. Watson didn't believe him.

According to Steinberg, he did not yet intend to take over Disney. "I thought we would buy some stock and see where it went. Maybe we would get involved with the company. We developed a plan for what we thought the company should do. And we gave the Disney management a copy of our plan."

Steinberg's plan was a series of moves that, to him, made basic business sense. One was to get Disney back on network television. "Even if you lost money, you've got to be back on the air once a week with a show which will remind everybody about Disney. But we didn't think you'd have to lose money. They were talking about a European park. We told them they should go immediately for a European park. If one worked, you may be able to do two in Europe. The first thing they had to do to develop their one big piece of real estate, which was worth an incredible amount of money, in Orlando, was to do a master plan to study where they were going to go. They had never done a master plan."

In an effort to increase the value of his stock, Steinberg began having second-hand discussions with Miller and Watson through intermediaries. "We told them, 'Our instinct tells us that you should have many more hotel rooms.' They said to us, 'If we do that we'll have to spend $50 million on expanding the monorail.' I couldn't say to them, 'Big fucking deal,' because I don't want them to think I want to throw money around, but I said, 'So what?' Should they consider having an office park there? Should they have a research park? Should they have housing? Should they consider having more amusements there? They asked what I had in mind. I said I had nothing in mind, but maybe a 'Sealand' type of thing. That seemed to be successful. Or maybe a movie studio tour. These guys had no such notions.

"We said to them, 'Look, we're a major shareholder, the largest shareholder. You don't have to do what we ask. We understand that. What we would like is your best thinking, so that we can see where you're going, what your thinking is. Maybe we're wrong. It's easy to have these notions, being on the outside.'" But just as Watson felt frustrated in his attempts to divine Steinberg's real intentions, Steinberg was frustrated in his attempts to discuss the future of the company with Disney management: "We never got a decent response to any question from them."

In fact, Watson and Miller had many of the same "notions," but they were different men from Steinberg. Watson was moving in his typically methodical way to expand the company, and he felt that Steinberg was meddling in things he didn't know enough about. Watson felt Disney was moving ahead as fast as he and Miller could move it. They were considering a European park, and had already held discussions with the governments of Spain and France. They were talking to consultants, including Arvida, about drawing up a master plan for Orlando. Under the guidance of Al Checchi, working for Arvida's owners, the Bass brothers, Arvida responded with alacrity. Checchi was still fascinated by the possibility of getting involved with Disney.

In Watson's mind, Steinberg was not a shareholder, a part owner of the company. He was the enemy, a destroyer of worlds, come to shred Walt Disney's dream and glut himself on the carcass. If he did a typical leveraged buyout, Steinberg would use bank loans and short-term debt ("junk bonds") to generate the money to buy the company. Then, to pay back the debt and make a huge profit for himself, he would sell off the company in pieces. So Watson did not want to discuss the company's internal workings with Steinberg. He gave Steinberg no more information than the law required him to give to any shareholder.

This infuriated Steinberg. To him, Watson's assumption that he was bent on taking over Disney was "paranoid." He said later, "My intentions were to invest in the company and make a lot of money. What I hoped that I would find there was that there was a number-three guy, number-two guy, number-four guy who was superb, and these people were sort of in their way, and we would help the board to make the decision to kick out the current management and get things going."

Steinberg continued to buy stock. By April 9, one month after he had started buying, he owned 8.3 percent of the company. In the next two days he bought another one percent. On April 25 he amended his 13D declaration: he intended to buy 25 percent of Disney. "We thought the stock would be worth several times what we paid for it. We would make a ton of money. It was an incredible situation. We talked to people in the industry. I talked to everybody. I talked to Augie Busch about the Anheuser-Busch parks. I talked to real people, businessmen, not stock analysts—Martin Davis, Steve Ross. I asked, 'What are they doing wrong?' And we found the current Disney management was a joke in many ways to their competitors."

At the same time, Roy Disney and Stan Gold plunged head-first into researching the possibility of a buyout of their own. They commissioned Lazard Frères in New York to do a complete study of the company. By late April they were meeting almost daily with Michael Milken at Drexel Burnham Lambert to try to put together the financing.

Before long Steinberg heard through various investment bankers that Watson and Miller, instead of spending their energy expanding the company's operations, were shopping for acquisitions. To Steinberg it looked like a full-scale defensive stance. One of their tactics would be to buy up other companies by trading new issues of Disney stock for the stock of the acquired company—and each new share issued would make Steinberg's shares worth that much less. "What forced our hand was it became clear to us that they were talking out of both sides of their mouths. They were saying to us, 'Yes, we are interested in your ideas, but Walt wouldn't have done this, and that's really our answer. You may not find it constructive, but that's how we've lived our lives.' But what they were really doing by talking to us was trying to buy time to look for acquisitions they could make for stock to dilute our interest."

Other people besides Steinberg heard the word, and soon people began to call Disney with companies for sale, usually at a healthy markup. Irwin Jacobs, a Minneapolis financier who had captured a moving and storage company called Minstar in a hostile takeover, called Disney representatives at Morgan Stanley to let them know that he thought he and his associates could handle Steinberg. The first step would be to get them on the team by merging Disney with the diminutive Minstar. Jacobs bought, sold, and broke up companies, as Steinberg had, but he did it on a somewhat smaller scale. Together with Minneapolis banker Carl Pohlad he had, for instance, bought Grain Belt Breweries, and made $4 million peddling the pieces. He had raided and greenmailed a string of bigger companies, including RCA, Pabst Brewing, and Kaiser Steel. But Jacobs, compared to Steinberg and Roy Disney, was a little fish, and Minstar and the other companies that Jacobs had acquired were minnows. Disney didn't bite.

But the Disney management's shopping spree did turn up something, a company that arguably even had a strategic fit with Disney—Arvida, the Florida land-development firm they had already contacted about working on the Orlando property. It was owned by Bass Brothers Enterprises of Texas, a $4-billion conglomerate run by Sid Richardson Bass. Watson and Miller's advisers were wary of Bass, who had a considerable reputation himself as a takeover artist and greenmailer. A stock swap for Arvida would put Bass second only to Steinberg as a Disney shareholder, bringing a second fox into the henhouse. But on May 15, in the Carlyle Hotel in New York, Watson and Miller had lunch with Bass and Checchi.

Bass was not the brash, aggressive, loud Texan Watson might have expected. He was an educated, cultured man with an almost courtly manner. His education was Stanford, by way of Andover and Yale. His money was oil money, but it was old oil money, at least by Texas standards. It came to him and his brothers by way of a great uncle, Sid Richardson, a wildcatter who was both smart and lucky, and their father, Perry Bass. Perry gave up business to spend the rest of his days sailing when his son Sid was only 27. Sid and his brothers began to use the money to make investments in undervalued assets, buying and reselling when the value had risen, sometimes making plays for companies and getting greenmail money for their trouble. They had made $100 million in a matter of months trying to buy Marathon Oil before U.S. Steel snapped it up. By the early 1980s they had parlayed their father's oil fortune into a vast web of investments, some of them long-term and passive, some of them short-term asset plays.

At the Carlyle, Sid Bass convinced Watson that he harbored no evil intent. He saw a fit between Arvida and Disney. The next day, Disney bought Arvida with a $200 million stock swap that instantly put the Bass brothers among the company's largest shareholders. It also, by the way, brought an immense profit to the Bass brothers, Al Checchi, and other officers of Bass Brothers and Arvida who participated in it: they had bought Arvida only 6 months before for $20 million in cash and $183.6 million in debt. Since the debt would pass to Disney, the $200 million in Disney stock represented a 1,000 percent return on investment in six months.

The Arvida deal brought two contacts to Disney that would make a difference in the long run, a difference that Watson could not have foreseen. One was Sid Bass, a forceful and confident investor and dealmaker. The other was Al Checchi. Checchi became deeply involved in Disney's acquisition of Arvida, and in the attempt to save Disney from hostile raiders. He and his mentor Gary Wilson, CFO of Marriott, would become even more important to Disney in the future.

Wall Street was skeptical about the Arvida acquisition, but willing to be persuaded. Steinberg was not impressed. "Buying Arvida, which they did to dilute our stock, was a total waste. It looked all right financially, but it was not strategic for them. We were telling them to focus their attention, and [instead] they were going into the real estate development business. Disney was not a real estate company. It was an entertainment company that had real estate that should be developed properly."

On May 25, Reliance sued Disney to stop the Arvida swap. The same day, Steinberg filed his intentions with the SEC to buy up to 49.9 percent of Disney. The declaration noted that he had retained Drexel Burnham Lambert, who up until then had been working for Roy Disney, that he had talked to other potential investors, and that he was no longer "merely a passive investor." Four days later he filed a second suit and announced a proxy fight: he would try to get the stockholders to throw out the company's board of directors. Stan Gold promptly flew to New York to try to make a deal with Steinberg: Roy would pay $350 million for the trademarks, the studio, and the merchandising, and leave the parks to Reliance. Steinberg didn't bite: the price was too low. It turned out that Kirk Kerkorian, the secretive financier who owned MGM/UA, would offer Steinberg $447 million for the studio alone.

Within days, Watson and Miller had decided on a second major deal: to acquire Gibson Greeting Cards through a stock swap with former Treasury Secretary William Simon, among others. The swap would greatly increase Simon's already legendary wealth. The terms of the deal would trade one half share of new Disney stock, plus $2.90 in cash, for each share of Gibson. Depending on the current value of Disney stock, that came to between $30 and $40 per share, or between $300 and $400 million—over twice the value that independent estimates by Morgan Stanley and Irwin Jacobs gave to the company. Gibson's book value came to $6.61 per share, its most recent earnings to $2.16 per share. "Bad Bill" Simon and his associates had bought the company only two years before in a leveraged buyout in which their total cash investment came to $1 million. Simon's personal 1982 investment of $300,000 would be turned in 1984 into $70 million worth of Disney stock. The deal would, in effect, make Simon the largest shareholder after Steinberg, give him 15 percent of Disney, and reduce all other shareholders' stakes by the same 15 percent.

The reaction on Wall Street was profoundly negative. Steinberg felt embattled: "Once the Gibson deal was announced, the die was set for us. Shortly after that we decided that strategically we couldn't let ourselves be diluted. We owned 12 or 13 percent of the company and we were going to have to take a heavier hand. So we talked about what we should do. I decided not to waste my time with a proxy fight; we would just go buy the company. We were going to risk our enterprise to buy Disney. It was that good. It was an opportunity to buy one of the premier companies in the country for just a little over book value. And we thought the book value was understated. It's not unlike owning the *New York Times* or the *Wall Street Journal*. These are things where you don't need brilliant management. If you're going to own the Travelers Insurance Company, you need brilliant management, because Travelers is no different from Aetna or Reliance; it's almost a commodity. But if you own the only newspaper in town, if you own Walt Disney, if you own Coca-Cola, it's a franchise, it's not a commodity. You can't replace them easily."

The idea that Steinberg would be the destroyer of Disney was not a fantasy. He would not have the financial muscle to buy the company without cutting it up. "There was nothing emotional about the takeover attempt. It was purely dollars and cents. The way I looked at it was very practical, and maybe that was wrong. I would have had to sell off certain pieces, and it bothered me. It's not that I was a bad guy. I just didn't have enough money to buy the whole thing. Kirk Kerkorian was going to get the movie studio and the vault [Disney's old movies and television shows]. We were getting the parks and the licensing. It bothered me—I couldn't keep the Disney Channel and sell off the vault. I thought I needed the vault for the channel. That bothered me because I believed the channel would be very profitable."

But Steinberg would be the new Disney, and he already had plans for it: "We were going to expand in Europe. We might have gone back into the motion picture business—animated movies and cartoons. I could build another studio in Orlando. We had, on our list of who to run it, guys like Barry Diller and Michael Eisner. I would not have gone into the business without a proven professional."

On June 8, with advice from Michael Milken and backing from Kirk Kerkorian, the Fisher brothers, Irwin Jacobs, and the Financial Corporation of America (a then-high-flying savings and loan), Steinberg made a tender offer for Disney. Disney was trading, at the moment, at $65 per share. Steinberg offered $67.50. If Disney dropped the Gibson deal, he would raise it to $71.50.

Steinberg saw himself as Disney's savior, the man who could rescue a great company from its own incompetent management. But this view was not shared inside the company. As one senior animator put it, "Steinberg was like a vulture looking at an animal that was hurting. The only thing that Saul Steinberg was going to save was himself with the hopes of making as much money as he possibly could. To us in the company, it was very scary. We were afraid of Saul Steinberg. We were afraid for our futures. If the company's being broken up, what becomes of the animation department?" Animator Ron Clements said, "The big fear was that we'd be taken over and [the company] would be dismantled. There would no more Disney animation as we know it. The parks would be sold to someone, and the film library sold to someone else, and someone would make a lot of money. We felt helpless, we felt vulnerable, we kept hearing rumors."

The press went into its own feeding frenzy, portraying Steinberg as the man who would devour Mickey Mouse.

One spring morning in the midst of the controversy, Steinberg stepped out of his apartment building, walking his six-year-old son Julian to school, as he always had. The sidewalk was covered with television cameras labeled "NBC." Steinberg said, "Julian, come with me."

Julian said, "No, daddy, look, they're taking our picture."

Steinberg said, "Okay, then, walk fast with me."

Steinberg and son set off at a pace that was ferocious for a six-year-old, but the cameras trailed along down the sidewalk. A reporter loped alongside the diminutive tycoon, shoving a microphone at him and asking, "Tell us, Mr. Steinberg, what do you intend to do with Disney? The whole world is waiting."

Steinberg said, "I can't comment," and kept walking. The reporter repeated the question, tried a different phrasing, coaxed a bit. Steinberg ignored him.

Finally the frustrated reporter said, "You're not going to say anything? Shall I put away the microphone?"

Steinberg, equally frustrated with the whole business and concerned for the safety of his children, burst out, "Put away the microphone, and stop taking pictures showing my address. That's just terrible! You shouldn't do that. You can't be that irresponsible!"

The reporter said, "Oh, don't worry, we'll cut it out," and put away the microphone.

As soon as the reporter had switched the microphone off Julian turned to him and said, "If my daddy buys Disney, he's going to do it so all the children can go to the parks for free." Steinberg, of course, meant to raise the price at the gates as soon as he was in charge. But the gods had saved him from a controversy he didn't need. The microphone was off.

Underneath the controversy the takeover attempt generated in the country ran a darker stream of anti-Semitism. Steinberg got calls from friends, Jews and non-Jews alike, warning him, saying, as Steinberg later characterized it, "Saul, it's going to be you—and with the name Saul Steinberg it's clear where you are and what you are—taking over another white Anglo-Saxon Protestant company. In all the little towns of America they're going to say, 'That Jew took over Walt Disney. What would Walt say?'" But the warnings did not make Steinberg hesitate. "They just made me angry."

Whether they were right or wrong in the beginning, Watson and Miller were dead right now. Steinberg was indeed going for the whole company. In California, in a conference room on Mickey Avenue, Watson, Miller, and their advisers, Donald Drapkin and Joe Flom from Skadden, Arps, along with Peter Kellner from Morgan Stanley, came to a fateful decision—a two-pronged strategy: to offer to buy out Steinberg, while at the same time making every other course unacceptably risky. Offer him money, and scare him. The scare tactic was a "self-tender": once Steinberg had acquired his intended 49 percent of the company, he intended to offer various notes for the rest. But the company itself would offer cash, at premium prices, for the rest. The management would "burn the company down" by spending huge amounts of the company's debt capacity to buy back everyone else's stock. In the end Steinberg would own the company, but it would be so debt-ridden as to be worthless.

Steinberg spent the long weekend of June 8–11 at his place in the Hamptons with his wife Gayfryd, soaking up sun, walking on the beach, talking on the phone. Gayfryd was dead set against the takeover. She felt that, if it were successful, the quality of their lives would diminish greatly, because they would have to spend a lot of time in California. She didn't want her husband to be in the movie business, a business run by the kind of people she thought of as "not serious people."

At the same time, Steinberg was getting messages from Disney he would later characterize as, "Listen, we're going to do a scorched-earth policy. We're going to make a self-tender at a much higher price, and you'll be left holding control of the company. We won't tender for your shares. You'll own the company and billions of dollars of debt. It financially won't work. We chose a price at a number that won't work."

Steinberg had great difficulty deciding whether the threat was serious. Disney felt rudderless. The board centered around Philip Hawley, CEO of Carter Hawley Hale, who had recently fought off a takeover attempt by The Limited, using techniques that Steinberg and others criticized as self-serving, protecting his own position while diluting the holdings of the shareholders.

Steinberg was convinced that Hawley was going to do it again, at Disney. On Friday night, Larry Tisch (a principal in Loew's, and later chairman of CBS), called Steinberg to say that Joe Flom had called him. Steinberg knew Flom as "a very responsible guy." According to Tisch, Flom was terribly concerned that Steinberg was going to end up owning lots of nothing.

On Saturday Flom called Steinberg directly from the board meeting in Burbank. He said, "I'm going to tell you this now: I cannot control this board. I want you to know—I'm not saying they're going to do the scorched earth. There's an element on that board that wants to do it, but I will tell you, I can't control them. I'm new to them, and I can't control them."

If the threat was meant to frighten Steinberg, it worked admirably. The prospect of "owning lots of nothing" scared him. In the first stage, Steinberg was going to have to borrow approximately $1.5 billion, in addition to putting up $450 million of equity. In Steinberg's estimation, "That's a lot of money. Deals were not done at that level at that time. We were putting almost the whole net worth of Reliance into this deal, plus borrowing a billion and a half dollars, just for the first phase. On the back end we would have to borrow another billion and a half. I was betting Reliance. That was scary.

"At the time it seemed quite real. I felt anxiety. I was very rich anyway. I had a lot of money, and I didn't want to go back to not having a lot of money. I wouldn't end up in The Bowery, but I would go from owning the biggest apartment in New York and being one of the really great old master collectors to collecting lithographs. It was a reasonable feeling. I'm a pretty tough guy. I couldn't believe they would do something so irrational to destroy a great property, but people had done it in the past." To be precise, Philip Hawley, the strongest voice on the board, had done it to Carter Hawley Hale, in Steinberg's view.

So Steinberg walked the beach and played the phones, talking to Tisch, to George Bello, executive vice president of Reliance, to his brother Robert, to Howard Steinberg, corporate counsel of Reliance (not related), to Lowell Freiberg, Reliance's treasurer. Every voice he heard was cautious. "They felt it was not prudent."

And at night, in the warm summer evenings he would walk the edge of the Sound with Gayfryd, the small salt surf hissing around their feet. Listening to her husband voice his concerns, Gayfryd added her own: "Honey, are you crazy? We have everything. There is a chance, a chance that you think is slim, that they'll do something crazy and you'll end up with nothing. Why would you risk everything you have? Besides, we have the greatest marriage. You're going to have to spend some time in California. And it's going to be a considerable amount of time, I know you. That means I'll have to spend a considerable amount of time there. It's going to confuse things for the kids. They have to be with us, and they have to go to school. It's a problem. It doesn't make sense for you to do this. It's a serious lifestyle problem."

She had her say. Then she added, "But in the end, if you decide to do this, I will be 100 percent supportive of you."

Sometime that Saturday night, or in the small hours of Sunday morning, Saul Steinberg said to himself, "It's not worth it." He told Gayfryd that her point of view had won, but only, in the end, because he would have to have split up the company. "Okay, I'm going to let them buy me out. But I want you to know that had I had enough money that I could hold on to everything, I would have gone forward. It just bothered me. And it's not just emotional. It's financial. But it was emotional, because I wanted to do a great thing, and take this company which had been great, fallen on hard times, been leaderless, and I wanted to give it the kind of leadership that it needed."

He phoned his associates, and they agreed with the decision. They were afraid of what the Disney board might do, afraid for Steinberg and for Reliance. Most of them urged him just to walk away from the deal, not even to seek any special payment from Disney. But he had already started the tender offer. He had already promised large commitment fees to such potential investors as Kerkorian and Jacobs. Steinberg felt he had to pull something out of the deal. In the end, the Disney board agreed to pay him a $32-million premium for his stock, plus $28 million for his expenses.

Disney's payoff to Steinberg, however, was far from the end of the story. The company's blood was in the water. Steinberg's attempt had alerted other sharks to the possibilities of the company. A number of the Street's arbitrageurs—short-term investors who buy stock that they expect to be involved in takeovers or other forceful movements—had bought Disney ferociously during Steinberg's move. Ivan Boesky and other high-flying stock speculators had deep positions in Disney stock.

Only the week before, at the beginning of June, Irwin Jacobs had been busily buying options in Disney stock, hoping to cash in if Steinberg were successful in buying the company. Suddenly his secretary told him that Michael Milken of Drexel Burnham Lambert was on the line. Milken told Jacobs, "I'd like to talk to you about Disney."

Jacobs put Milken on hold, called his broker, and cancelled the option orders. He didn't want to be caught on the back side of an ethics problem.

Milken, it turned out, was looking for people to join Steinberg in financing the Disney takeover. "Is this a greenmail situation?" Jacobs asked. "Because if it is, I'm not interested."

Milken assured him that Steinberg truly intended to buy the company. By the end of the conversation Jacobs had promised Milken $35 to $40 million for Steinberg's effort. He hung up and looked at his watch. Time to go home and pack. He was heading for a vacation in Greece.

But Greece is not Mars. It has news stands and brokers' offices. In Greece, Jacob picked up an *International Herald Tribune* and glanced through the business section. There was a story about Steinberg's greenmail. Jacobs found a phone and called his office. "What's this mean to us?" he wanted to know. What it meant, he was told, was that he would receive $500,000 to $700,000 for making the commitment to Steinberg, and that was the end of it.

It was a puzzling turn of events. Jacobs turned it over in his mind, as he walked the steaming streets of Athens, threading through the fumes and screech of the crazed traffic, passing the frantic music blaring from the cafés. Seeing a Merrill Lynch office, he could not resist going inside and punching up Disney on the Quotron. What he saw was even more puzzling. After climbing all spring under the assault of rumors and the buying of the "arbs," Disney's stock had dropped in a matter of days nearly $15 to the $50 level. He was stunned. He thought, My God, what is going on? Why is this company worth so much less today than it was yesterday?

What was happening was quite simple: the arbitrageurs were selling out. But Jacobs knew a stock opportunity when he saw one, and when Disney stock hit 46 he started buying it. In a matter of weeks he owned more than 5 percent of the company. "I didn't plan to," he says now, "but it just kept coming in. The arbitrageurs were just puking it up."

Throughout the summer, rumors of a takeover continued to swirl through Disney: Roy Disney was going to buy the company, Kirk Kerkorian was, Rupert Murdoch was. Morbid humor crept in. Signs popped up reading, "The only difference between this place and the Titanic is they had a band." The signs were surface reflections of the employees' deep fear: that the precious world they knew of as Disney would disappear, and that their jobs would disappear with it.

A curious torpor gripped the company. The energy of the top management was consumed with moves and countermoves, with investment bankers and Wall Street lawyers. They had little strength left to deal with the company's actual products. When Jim Jimirro, with an eye to the circling takeover artists, went to Ron Miller and said, "Let's get some product out on video. Let's figure out the quickest way to earn revenue to show that the pattern has changed," the response was not encouraging. According to Jimirro, "Irving Ludwig was gone, and Chuck Good was the head of theatrical [distribution]. By that time 35 percent of the homes in America had video cassette players, and there's Chuck Good saying he didn't advise that we release the classics. We had meeting after meeting after meeting. Finally we were given the right to release *Robin Hood*, which could be characterized as a third- or fourth-rate classic. It was something. But nobody said, 'Goddamn it, Chuck, forget your provincial concerns, we've got to move quickly.' And it wasn't just that area. Wherever there were other ideas, the management had the same attitude.

"By buying off Steinberg, we had bought ourselves some time, how much, we didn't know. They should have called us all in. Somebody should have said, 'Okay, you guys, I want you back here in two weeks; I want a plan; I want you to show me a way to increase your revenue by 50 percent in the next 12 months. I don't want anybody taking a vacation this summer, I want to see a marshaling of forces.' There were good people around that company. They would have responded to the urgency of that. But through that summer it was business as usual. There was not one organized effort to change, to say, 'We have a challenge here. How are we going to respond to it?' "

A Disney division head who wished to remain anonymous was more scathing: "My memory of the summer of 1984 is that the Olympics were in town, and Ron Miller had great tickets." As for the company's response to the raiders, "Everybody just circled the wagons around the status quo. It was axiomatic that nobody could run the company better than the people that were running it, because they were family. Ron Miller was Walt's son-in-law, Card Walker was Walt's confidante, Diane Disney Miller was Walt's daughter and kind of an aide-de-camp to Ron. I remember Diane saying in no uncertain terms, 'How could anybody from the outside possibly do what we do?' "

But Roy Disney was family, too, and he thought that he and Stan Gold had some answers, some ideas on how to get the company moving again. In April, they had considered buying the company. Like Steinberg, they had come to the conclusion that they would have to split up the company in order to finance the debt incurred in a buyout. They tried to buy everything except the parks from Steinberg, but they couldn't offer enough money. They had tried approaching Watson with a truce offer: the two sides of the family together should tender for the outstanding stock and take the company back under family control. But they got a cold shoulder to the idea. When Watson and Miller had asked Roy to come back on the board, he had asked in return that he be allowed to bring in two other members of the Trust with him, and that Wells be taken into management along with Watson and Miller. Watson and Miller turned that deal down flat.

Still, Phil Hawley was urging Watson to do what was necessary to get Roy back on the board. Hawley felt his disaffection was dangerous for the company. He was an unstable element. He could combine with any of the dissident shareholders in proxy fights, suits, and takeover attempts.

Hawley's fears proved reasonable. On June 17, a Sunday, Gold brought Roy Disney, Frank Wells, and other members of the "Brain Trust" together at the offices of Gang, Tyre and Brown. The time had come to go on the attack. They felt they had no peaceful options left. The

Gibson deal, they felt, was overpriced. The fit was not good, and was intended only to dilute the stock of the rest of the shareholders. Their point of view about the direction of the company was being ignored. Watson and Miller were unable to move the company forward quickly enough. But Roy had continued to buy stock, and on June 12 had hit the 5 percent point at which, under SEC rules, he had to file a formal declaration of his intentions within ten days. Roy and the "Brain Trust" decided that he would declare his intention to launch a proxy fight on the Gibson deal: the shareholders would register their opinions by mail, and the board would be forced to abide by the result. At the same time, Roy would sue the company over the same issue.

On June 21, financial columnist Dan Dorfman leaked the news that Roy Disney was preparing to launch a proxy fight the next day. When he read that in the paper, Watson called Gold and asked him to come to Burbank for a meeting. Over the next 24 hours there was a furious barrage of meetings and telephone calls between the principals. Roy wanted to be back on the board, but with his quiet style, he felt he needed other voices speaking for him on the board in order for his opinions to be considered. On June 22, with an hour left before the SEC filing deadline, they struck a deal: Roy Disney, Stan Gold, and Disney's brother-in-law Peter Dailey would join the board; Roy would become vice chairman; and Roy would drop the suit and proxy fight. In addition, both Card Walker and Donn Tatum would be dropped from the board's powerful and symbolically important executive committee, which rarely met, but could have almost the power of the full board when necessary. These were the men who had run Disney when Roy was sneered at as "Walt's idiot nephew," and their removal (particularly in the case of Walker) was Roy's revenge.

It was not the end of the war, but it was Roy's first major strategic victory. It got him and his forces in the door. There were more battles to fight. Although they had called off their proxy fight and suit, Roy and his men were still eager to defeat the Gibson deal. And although they couldn't admit it openly yet, they wanted Miller's head. The war would not be won until the entire management had been replaced and the company had been launched in a completely new direction.

All through the summer, while Disney ran on automatic pilot, Ray Watson scrambled to defend it against other possible takeover attempts. He went hat in hand to the boards of General Motors, Kodak, and other companies that had invested in EPCOT, asking them to buy substantial portions of Disney stock and pledge to hold it for five years.

But the strategy of getting other companies to invest in Disney was soon overtaken by events, this time in the person of Irwin Jacobs, who by mid-July had spent $10 million on Disney stock. On July 18, he filed a 13D with the SEC declaring that he now owned 5.9 percent of Disney, which made him the largest shareholder—larger than either Roy Disney or the Basses. Like Steinberg, Jacobs at first had no plans to take over Disney. "When I made my investment," he now says, "I never had any intention of even being a major shareholder in Disney." But the management reacted to his stock purchases with the same fear and loathing as it had to Steinberg's, assuming from the start that he was out to uproot the company for his own profit. Jacobs begged Watson to withdraw from the still-pending Gibson deal, which he felt was overpriced and a bad strategic fit, and which he claimed meant "boxcar numbers of dollars to William Simon, the coup of the century, more money than he'll ever see, no matter how successful he is."

On July 30, he filed suit against the company, attempting to force it to scuttle the deal. He began campaigning for changes at Disney. By then, Jacobs no longer just wanted Disney to cancel the Gibson deal. He, like Roy Disney and Sid Bass, wanted a new management team.

Although Jacobs didn't know it, Watson wanted new management, too. He had never thought that he was the right man to be chairman of an entertainment company, and as time went by, he was increasingly convinced that Miller was not the right man to be president and CEO. Watson was troubled by the burden he had taken on at Disney. The job was far more complex and intractable than developing real estate. The pressure made him restless and fatigued. In New York at one point to meet with the board of one company, he asked Jim Jimirro to "take a walk around the block." Watson talked nonstop to Jimirro about his concerns and hopes for Disney, saying, "My job is to find a replacement management for this company." At one point he said, "I'm the guy who has to do it, and I don't want to be the guy." After circling the block, he continued around again, as if unaware of his surroundings. He circled the block again, and again, 15 times in all, buried in intense conversation, worrying the granite walls, the concrete, and the asphalt with his heartache over Disney.

Watson had been acting as CEO all through this turbulent season, making all major decisions and merely seeking Miller's concurrence. It was a situation that could not continue. Gold had been pushing for Frank Wells to be taken into management in some capacity. Now he was pushing for Miller's resignation. Although Watson did not yet know it, even

Phil Hawley, whose wife was a close friend of Diane Miller, had come reluctantly to the same position.

A board meeting was scheduled for Friday, August 17, and the Gibson deal was on the agenda once again. Watson had come to an agonizing conclusion: although he still thought Gibson was a good acquisition, he no longer felt it would fly, for the simple reason that management would lose any proxy fight on the question. He would have to pull the plug on the deal. He had convinced the board through long discussions and presentations that Gibson was right strategically, financially, and tactically. They had trusted his judgment. Now he had to convince them to scrap the deal, even though it would cost them millions to bow out.

On the morning of the board meeting, Watson and Gold had breakfast together. Watson told Gold he was giving up on Gibson, for the sake of the stability of the company, and he wanted Gold to restrain himself during the board meeting. It was no time for grandstanding, or demanding that heads roll. To Watson's chagrin, he discovered that Gold and Sid Bass' man Richard Rainwater had been heavily lobbying the board over the Gibson issue already. Watson did not enjoy chaos; Gold seemed to revel in it. Watson found Gold profoundly unsettling. When Gold mentioned that he was on his way downtown to meet with Hawley before the board meeting, to discuss the Gibson deal and Ron Miller, Watson was even more disturbed. Hawley was the lynchpin of the board, the most forceful outside director, something of a patrician, and Watson was afraid the brash Stan Gold would upset him, back him into a corner defending Miller, and possibly even the Gibson deal. Watson felt he might be needed to referee the meeting. To Gold's surprise, Watson asked if he could tag along.

When the three men met, Hawley reserved judgment on Gibson, but they struck at a deeper issue: Miller. Hawley felt that Walker had imposed Miller on the company without involving the board. And the more he had watched Miller work, the more he felt that, for the good of the company, Miller would have to go. That these three men who had disagreed over so much for so long could come to the same conclusion was astonishing to each of them. They searched for a face-saving way to fire the company's CEO. In the end they agreed to propose a committee of the board to search for wide-ranging solutions to the company's problems.

When the board met, it wrangled with the divisive issue of the Gibson acquisition. Watson urged the board to reverse itself, and in the end it did. Then Watson proposed a committee of outside directors to look at a wide range of possibilities for the future of the company. Miller supported the proposal enthusiastically. He was comfortable with committees, and he failed to see that this proposal was designed to unseat him. After the board meeting, Hawley did the courageous thing: he met with Miller privately and told him that he thought the committee would ask for his resignation. Miller was astonished and furious. While Hawley and Watson watched, he fell apart. He wept. He had given his all to Disney. He felt he had done his best to change it, and now he was being blamed for things far beyond his control.

Early in 1984, when Stan Gold had first sat down with Frank Wells to talk about the future of Disney, Wells had made a flat statement: "I'm going to give you the best advice you ever had on the subject. Whatever else you do, get Michael Eisner. . . . Michael Eisner ought to be running that company. He's hot. He's got a track record. You do everything you can to get him and I'll help." Wells said the same thing to everyone who asked. Roy Disney knew Eisner socially—they both served on the board of Walt's California Arts Institute, north of the valley in Valencia. He knew of Eisner's admiration for Walt. But would Eisner, president of the most successful studio in Hollywood at the peak of its winning streak, want to give up all that to move to also-ran Disney? If Charles Bluhdorn were still alive, Wells, Gold, and Roy Disney might not have given Eisner a second thought—he would have been beyond reach. But Bluhdorn had been dead a year, Martin Davis was firmly in charge of Gulf & Western, and Hollywood was beginning to talk about how things were coming unglued at Paramount. It might well be possible to pry Eisner loose from Paramount, and there were things about Disney that might well entice him.

As Davis consolidated his power at Gulf & Western, relations between the East and West Coast offices quickly grew strained. The man who stood to gain was Frank Mancuso, Paramount's head of marketing. Mancuso was the only top Paramount executive who worked in New York, a few floors away from Davis. His reserved, studied, and careful style matched Davis' and contrasted markedly with what they felt was the buccaneer style of Diller, Eisner, and Katzenberg on the West Coast. Davis and Mancuso understood each other. Yet Mancuso, in New York, did not report to Davis, the chairman of the parent corporation. Officially, he reported to Eisner, in Los Angeles, the president and chief operating officer of the studio. Increasingly, as time went by, Mancuso ignored Eisner and reported to Diller—or ignored both of them and made marketing decisions on his own. Diller and Eisner wanted to move Mancuso to Los Angeles, to get a grip on him. Mancuso didn't want to go.

While the shift from Bluhdorn to Davis had given Mancuso direct access to the chairman of Gulf & Western, it did the opposite for Eisner: his access to the top corporate offices was cut. Bluhdorn had been given to picking up the phone to argue with Eisner about casting, contracts, movie ideas, whatever captured his mind. But Davis didn't want to talk to Eisner. In fact, Davis informed Eisner that, from now on, he would report strictly through Diller, who had been made chief of the new entertainment and communications division, in charge not only of the studio, but also of Simon and Schuster, Madison Square Garden, and a video game company called Sega—all owned by Gulf & Western. Eisner was clearly not one of the big boys in Davis' eyes. His style—irreverent, shirt-sleeve, fast, and intuitive—was a continuing rebuke to Davis. Eisner felt discounted and left out. He began to think about his options.

The isolation made Eisner restless, as did the pepper of criticism coming out of New York in the face of Paramount's ongoing phenomenal success. Katzenberg had told Eisner of going to see Davis in New York in October 1983. Davis had excoriated the team at Paramount, claimed that they were conspiring against him, and called Katzenberg "a little Sammy Glick," referring to the shallow, grasping main character of Bud Schulberg's *What Makes Sammy Run?* Davis had accused him, Eisner, and Diller of conspiring to get the board to fire him.

The previous few years had been the most successful in the studio's history. For fiscal 1984, Paramount eventually showed a record $150 million profit before taxes, up from $40 million in 1977 (the first year after Eisner had come on board). For three years running, Paramount had won a higher share of box-office revenues and a higher return on equity than any studio in Hollywood. But Eisner and Diller's enormous success did not seem to impress Davis. He dismissed it as insufficient, and said at one point, "What worked in the past won't necessarily work in the future," a statement that was cryptic at best, and rang strange in the world of business, where a bottom line solidly in the black usually brooks no comeback.

The pressure also drove a wedge between Diller and Eisner. Contentious and difficult as their relationship had been, it had always been tight, like a family that likes to shout and throw things. Now Diller seemed to be siding with New York. When Eisner complained that Davis didn't even know him, Diller told Eisner he was "too sensitive. . . . Just let me handle it."

Diller was keenly aware that his contract expired on September 30, 1984. Eisner felt just as keenly the fact that his could be cancelled by either side with two months' notice. Hollywood, the biggest of all small towns, could smell the dissatisfaction, and both men began to get offers. By the turn of 1984, the Denver-based billionaire Marvin Davis (not to be confused with Gulf & Western's *Martin* Davis) started dropping hints in Diller's ear about coming over to his money-losing 20th Century Fox to replace chairman Alan Hirschfield. He promised Diller a piece of the company for his trouble—5 percent, perhaps as much as 10 percent. Eisner, too, began to receive offers. ABC began wooing him back. Leonard Goldenson would give him and Katzenberg a $300-million stake to start their own studio. And in late July Roy Disney tracked him down by phone at his sons' summer camp in Middlebury, Vermont, to talk to him about Disney. The rush of time began to tear at both Diller and Eisner as never before. Both were men of extreme ambition and unusual accomplishments. Both were in their early 40s, an age at which more than one man had decided to stop working for somebody else and start running the show himself.

The battle of nerves at Paramount took a peculiar turn during the spring and summer. *Terms of Endearment* scored big in the Oscar race, and the media began to notice the studio that could do no wrong. In April, *Newsweek* ran a big article praising the Paramount team and declaring the studio the "best all-around movie studio" in the business. In June, *Business Week* raised its trumpets to praise the Paramount team and show "How Paramount Keeps Churning Out Winners." Both articles focused on Diller, Eisner, and Katzenberg. As if in a counterpunch from the New York end, Mancuso showed up as the focus of a *Wall Street Journal* article on June 27.

On July 30, *New York* came out with an article by Tony Schwartz called "Hollywood's Hottest Stars." According to Schwartz, Hollywood's hottest stars were Eisner and Diller. The press drumbeat did not go over well in the white tower at the edge of Central Park that housed Gulf & Western. Schwartz' article did not mention Davis at all, and Eisner seemed to have taken a deliberate swipe at New York, and Mancuso in particular, when he said the business was based on 10 to 12 decisions a year, and that great marketing of a bad film couldn't help sell it, while the marketing of a great movie, like *E.T.*, didn't matter. In other words, it was Eisner's decisions, not Mancuso's, that made the difference. Mancuso made copies of that page of the article, circled the quote, and sent the copies, with a cutting note attached, to Eisner, Diller, and Katzenberg. Ironically, the article ended with a pagewide photo of the three with Mancuso. The caption quoted an anonymous producer: "Paramount's great strength is that its executives know they'll be there tomorrow." It was a line that would turn out to be embarrassingly unprophetic.

The unrest at Paramount and Disney turned into a dizzying sequence of corporate pirouettes when Gold and Wells holed up at Gold's house to talk strategy the evening of August 17, the day Ron Miller had learned that he was about to be fired. Suddenly there was a hole in Disney management, and Wells and Gold were determined to have a hand in filling it with either Eisner or Wells. Wells suggested that Gold call Eisner, right then. Gold did. And Eisner said he would come right over, as soon as he completed another important task—taking his kids out for ice cream.

That night, drinking grappa in Gold's study, Eisner and Disney began to click. It was not a new idea to Eisner. In fact, he had said yes to Disney two years before, when Miller had approached him—but only if he could have Miller's job. Now, Eisner was getting whispers and outright offers from all over town. But he saw something in Disney that he could not find elsewhere. Despite the wretched state of Disney's growth, despite its nearly unnoticeable pulse as a major studio, the company had profound strengths and great potential. More than any other studio, it was a name, a franchise, an American institution. For himself personally, Eisner saw the chance to once again start with a last-place finisher and turn it around, as he had helped to do at ABC and at Paramount, but this time to do it as the guy in charge, the CEO. And he saw a chance to play: Disney had the theme parks and a rich tradition of imagination. He had long been a fan of Disney ever since his days at ABC, where he had steeped himself in programming for children. He liked animation, he liked family entertainment, he wanted to be the man in charge, and he wanted to move to a place where he could really make a difference. It all fit. Eisner wanted Disney.

But which way would Watson go? He was under great pressure. Miller was suddenly gone from the lot, before anything had been made official. The company swirled with rumors about Miller, and Roy Disney, and Irwin Jacobs. On August 28, Jacobs flew to Burbank to meet with Watson, and they ate lunch in the commissary, where all the employees could see them. He had dropped his suit and proxy fight when Watson had dropped the Gibson deal, but Watson still feared him. He was still the biggest shareholder, and he seemed dangerously unpredictable. According to Jacobs, he told Watson, "Look, I've got no problem holding the stock of this company. I'll be real patient, if that's what it is, because I think this is a great company here. But you stop this nonsense! Don't you go doing these stupid deals to fend off your own shareholders." And he pressed Watson to come up with new management of the highest caliber.

Watson felt he was already doing just that without advice from shareholders. Gold had convinced him to meet separately with both Eisner and Wells. When he met Eisner, he was profoundly impressed. When he met with the lawyerly, intense Wells on September 2, he recognized his executive ability and grasp of Disney and the entertainment industry, but he didn't see the creative dynamism that he saw in Eisner. When he told Wells that there was only one job open at Disney, Wells replied, "Then get Eisner. You need creativity more than anything else."

Watson agreed. When Watson left, Wells called Eisner to tell him that he thought Eisner had the job. Eisner was elated. He had begun to hunger to run Disney, and now it seemed only a matter of some formalities before it was his. He started to think of it as a done deal before, it turned out, it was actually done.

On Labor Day, September 3, Martin Davis flew into Los Angeles International Airport for his first visit to the West Coast since taking over Gulf & Western. He was determined to resolve what he saw as the situation at Paramount: he wanted to renew Diller's contract, but he wanted to reduce the bonuses that Diller and Eisner were receiving—$1.8 million and $1.5 million, respectively, for the recent record-breaking year—and he wanted to reorganize the company, making Mancuso, as head of marketing, coequal with Eisner. At the moment Davis' jet was touching concrete, Watson was putting the final touches on a memo to the committee of outside directors considering management changes, recommending that Eisner replace Miller as president and CEO of Walt Disney Productions. Watson would stay on as chairman to look after the firm's vast real estate developments—but he made it clear that he was willing to step aside in favor of a new chairman, if the board thought that was best.

When the members of the committee saw the memo, however, they were not encouraging. Hawley, Robert Baldwin (the retired head of Morgan Stanley), and Caroline Ahmanson (of the Ahmanson family, prominent fixtures of the Los Angeles establishment) told Watson of their reservations: they feared that Eisner lacked corporate experience. Eisner, after all, had never run a company by himself. He had never dealt with a board, or shareholders, or subsidiaries, or investment bankers. He had been the number-two man at a division of a conglomerate. Hawley, with his experience with takeovers, and Baldwin, with his background in investment banking, were strongly convinced that, especially with Disney still "in play" on Wall Street, managing the company's interactions with the press, stockholders, and analysts would prove to be as crucial to Disney's survival as managing the company itself.

On September 4, Davis and Eisner met at Paramount. Their conversation was cool to the point of abrasiveness, with Davis arguing that Eisner was being paid too much. Eisner felt glad he would soon be free of this difficult relationship. Davis later met with Jeff Katzenberg, apologized for his earlier criticisms, and showered him with praise.

On September 5, Ray Watson drove to Eisner's Bel Air home for a second meeting. He now wanted Eisner to replace Miller as CEO, but after hearing from the outside directors, he had begun to fear that he would not get what he wanted. So he was looking for a compromise, some way to lure Eisner to Disney if the directors wouldn't give him the whole show. He asked Eisner whether he would be willing to take the number-two spot, as chief operating officer. But Eisner could not be swayed. He told Watson what he had told Miller two years before: he wanted to be the top guy. That was what Watson wanted, too, and they went on to discuss salary. That evening, Watson called Eisner to tell him he was going to recommend to the board that they hire him as CEO—but he could not guarantee that they would.

The day of the board meeting, September 7, Eisner was scheduled to meet with Davis again. Unfortunately, the meeting was scheduled for 10 o'clock. The Disney board would not meet until 11. How could he negotiate the details of a new contract with Paramount, and perhaps a reorganization of the company, an hour before he would be named CEO of another company? Eisner couldn't do it. He didn't have that level of bald guile. Besides, deep down he was tired of Marty Davis, and eager to move on to Disney. So he told Davis that he was about to be appointed head of Disney. Davis' response was polite. He would not, he said, stand in the way.

An hour later the Disney board met, approved the recommendation of the outside directors, and formally fired Miller, as expected. But, to Gold's astonishment, they did not vote on Watson's memo suggesting Eisner as a successor. Instead, Philip Hawley proposed a search committee of outside directors. Miller, after all, had been imposed on the board by Card Walker. This time they should be more active in the selection. The board approved that idea, and a committee was formed: Hawley,

Gold, and Watson (the three whose morning meeting a month before had led to Miller's demise), plus outside director Sam Williams, a lawyer.

Eisner, at Paramount, grew more and more apprehensive as the hours dragged by with no news from Disney. What could be going on? In mid-afternoon Wells finally called Eisner to tell him that he had not been chosen, and that the board in fact had spoken of looking for someone with more corporate experience. Hawley had been talking about a candidate he liked: Dennis Stanfill, former head of 20th Century Fox.

The call was a terrible shock. Eisner drove immediately to Roy Disney's Shamrock Enterprises to demand that Gold tell him what was going on. Gold was nearly as upset as Eisner was. It looked like his and Roy's grasp on the top slots at Disney was slipping away. Eisner was furious and embarrassed. He felt that he had made a foolish move of major proportions. He drove back to Paramount for one of the more difficult discussions of his life: telling Davis that maybe he wouldn't quit after all. But the ordeal of his embarrassment didn't end there. That night, at a party for the top 20 Paramount executives and some of the Gulf & Western board at Barry Diller's house, Eisner felt like a skydiver looking for the ripcord that was there a second ago. Others must know by now of his conversation with Davis, but he had to pretend that it had never happened, that his loyalty was unswerving. Davis chatted amiably, mentioning prominently and favorably in almost every conversation the one top Paramount executive who had not come to the party: Frank Mancuso.

The next morning, Eisner still felt like he was looking for the ripcord. Nevertheless, he had family obligations: his son had a tennis tournament, his first, in Santa Barbara. Despite anxieties about his future, Eisner drove him the 90 miles up the coast, his agitation and confusion contrasting oddly with the crumbling sandstone bluffs and the leafy, palm-decked mission town. He was in no mood to appreciate Santa Barbara's fog-and-sand beach resort atmosphere. In between sets, he called Barry Diller, who he knew was pondering his own future. At mid-day, standing at a pay phone at the edge of the sunlit tennis courts, Eisner heard more surprising news: Diller was resigning to go to 20th Century Fox as chairman and CEO. For eight years Eisner had been the number-two man at Paramount. With Diller gone, he would have been a natural choice for the top job—maybe—if he had not jumped the gun the day before. He even had a clause in his contract, written when Bluhdorn was still alive, stating that if Gulf & Western offered the chairmanship of Paramount to anyone else, they owed Eisner a hefty bonus, and forgiveness of all his debts to

Paramount, which had helped him buy his $1.25-million home. More and more it began to look as if he had made a major career mistake. In trying to grab Disney, he had lost both Disney and Paramount.

Although it was a Saturday, financial analyst David Londoner was working, as he sometimes did, at Wertheim, in its midtown offices on Park Avenue. So, too, was Bud Morton, the firm's director of research. Londoner walked into Morton's office with the business section from that morning's September 8th *New York Times*, tapping the headline of the lead story. It read, "Disney's Chief Is Forced Out." Londoner said, "Bud, put Disney on the recommended list now."

Morton looked at Londoner as if he were searching for signs of insanity. Disney had been off the company's buy list since 1981. He said, "David, you've been telling me to sell the stock every time it reaches 60 for three years. It's fairly close to 60 now. What, are you becoming a short-term trader?"

Londoner said, "No."

Morton said, "What's changed?"

Londoner said, "Control. The family no longer controls Disney."

On Monday, September 10, Hawley and Watson met with Dennis Stanfill at Stanfill's office in downtown Los Angeles. Stanfill was an Annapolis grad and a Rhodes scholar in economics at Oxford. He had been an investment banker at Lehman Brothers and the chief financial officer at the Times Mirror Company. Stanfill was the man Lehman Brothers tapped to head 20th Century Fox in 1971 when it appeared about to go under from the extravagant failure of *Cleopatra*. He was a conservative financial disciplinarian who had stayed away from the creative side of the company. Like Hawley, he had a reserved, patrician air. Those who liked him thought this impressive. He struck Hawley as just the kind of disciplinarian the company needed. Those who disliked him found him prissy and distant, and recoiled from the thought of such a man running the familial, shirt-sleeve Disney organization. He struck Watson as too formal for such a casual, close-knit company.

Watson drove from that meeting back to the Disney lot to face that close-knit company in person. Over 1,000 of the employees who worked on the lot or nearby came to a mass meeting. They heard Watson "trying," as animator Ron Clements put it, "to explain what was happening." The employees had heard nothing but what they read in the paper, along with the official pronouncements from Erwin Okun, the vice president of communications, that the company was looking for a completely new management team, and that Watson was not a candidate. Rumored candidates for the jobs included Eisner, Wells, Stanfill, and Alan Hirschfield, whom Diller had just bumped from Fox. "People asked a lot of questions," says Clements. "They were a little bit panicked. Nobody knew what was going to happen. It wasn't an optimistic feeling." Watson could make no promises in the name of the new management, but he tried to cheer the employees, telling them, "This is for you. It'll be over soon. Hang in there."

At 6 that evening Davis called Eisner: Diller had just told him, over the phone, that he was resigning. Davis wanted Eisner to fly to New York immediately to discuss the matter. It couldn't wait for a morning flight. Eisner refused to take the "redeye." He never flew at night, because he was never at his best for the next day's meetings. He wanted to talk it out over the phone. He was convinced that Davis had already made up his mind to replace Diller with Mancuso, and his trip would be for nothing. Besides, in the morning he was making another try at Disney. Davis told him he had not made up his mind, and he wanted Eisner to come to New York. Eisner said he would be there the next day.

Eisner met Tuesday morning with Hawley and Watson, to present his case again, then flew to New York Tuesday afternoon with Katzenberg. On the way, going over the details with the ever-orderly and quick-thinking Katzenberg, Eisner became convinced that there was no chance that Davis would offer him the job of chairman. Yet if Mancuso became chairman, his career at Paramount would be seriously compromised, and he should consider other offers. His strategy, he decided, should revolve around the details of the contract. He couldn't be sure that Davis knew about the clause that gave him a windfall if he were not named chairman. Eisner would not resign, because it would cost him too much money. He had to wait for Davis to breach the contract by offering the chairmanship to someone else. Then he would see what he could do about getting the Disney job.

At midnight on Tuesday, at the Gulf & Western headquarters at the edge of Central Park, Davis met first with Eisner, then with Katzenberg. Davis told Eisner that he had not made up his mind about who would replace Diller. After Eisner left, Davis tried to get Katzenberg to agree to stay on past December, when his contract expired. But Katzenberg felt confused by Davis' swift shifts of mood about him, and he was uncertain about the future of Eisner, one of his two mentors, so he put Davis off.

As Katzenberg was returning to the Regency Hotel at three in the morning, he picked a *Wall Street Journal* up from a stack in the lobby. It was the Wednesday edition, fresh off the press. On the front page of the second section he found an article quoting "G & W executives" saying that the next day Frank Mancuso would be named chairman of Paramount. The quotes and discussions behind the article must have taken place well before Eisner and Katzenberg had arrived in New York, yet the article spoke of Eisner in the past tense, as if he had already resigned. The article quoted Davis directly: he was harshly critical of Eisner and Diller. Using an accounting procedure that credited much of Paramount's profits to the balance sheet of the parent corporation, the *Journal's* anonymous Gulf & Western sources claimed that Paramount's operating profits had actually been declining since 1979. Katzenberg called Eisner at the nearby Mayfair Regent and read him the article. Eisner called Diller in California, where it was by now one in the morning.

To Eisner, the article itself breached his contract. The next afternoon he met with Davis, asked that a $1.55-million bonus check be delivered immediately to his office, and resigned from Paramount. His resignation statement was restrained, but it managed not even to mention Gulf & Western, let alone Martin Davis: "The untimely death of Charles Bluhdorn and this week's resignation of Barry Diller marked a period in my life to move on. I will always be indebted to both men."

Eisner stayed in New York Wednesday night and Thursday, juggling the phone. Thursday night he put off returning to California to have dinner with Arthur Krim, head of Orion. Six years before, Krim had been the chairman of United Artists, which was owned by Transamerica, just as Paramount was owned by Gulf & Western. The corporate meddling from Transamerica had reached such a pitch at United Artists that the entire management team had resigned to form Orion. The opportunity to compare notes was a great lure for Eisner at that particular moment. But late in the dinner, the conversation took a different turn when Krim described the work his wife, a medical researcher, was doing on AIDS. The far-reaching consequences of this grim destroyer were just beginning to make an impact on the national consciousness. Hearing of Mathilde Krim's efforts in AIDS research, it suddenly seemed to Eisner that his preoccupations were small indeed.

There was no need, in any event, for career panic on Eisner's part: by the end of the week—September 14—he had four firm job offers. Diller wanted him to complete the act at Fox. His alma mater, ABC, wanted

Eisner to build a feature films division, and two other studios were eager for his services. But Eisner put off his suitors. He had been president of a studio. He had been second in command. And he had been a great success at it. He wanted more. He wanted to be CEO, and he wanted to be CEO of Disney, the company he had admired since he had first worked in television.

That same Friday, September 14, Irwin Jacobs, who by this time owned 7.7 percent of the company—over 2.6 million shares—announced that he would attempt to take over Disney. As Watson and the Disney board feared, Jacobs, like Steinberg, would dismember it. Like Steinberg, it was rumored, he counted Kirk Kerkorian among his financial backers, and would spin off the studio and the vaults to him. Once again, at the very moment that it was searching for new management, Disney was fighting for its existence.

Phil Hawley, who had been appointed by the board to head the committee searching for a new CEO, saw things through the lens of his own experience. He had recently had experience at Carter Hawley Hale fighting off a hostile takeover attempt by The Limited. He felt deeply the precariousness of management in the '80s—how a company could find itself fighting for its life on short notice. For CEO at Disney, Hawley wanted someone with a reputation for financial discipline, someone with what he called "corporate experience." The person he favored for the job was Dennis Stanfill.

At a crucial meeting of the search committee, Hawley pushed Stanfill. Creative talent, Hawley argued, you can buy by the project; financial discipline and corporate know-how have to run the show.

Stan Gold argued strenuously with Hawley in a now famous speech reported in *Storming the Magic Kingdom*: "You think creative talent can be bought as a commodity. You see guys like Eisner as a little crazy or a little off the wall. But every great studio in this business has been run by crazies. What do you think Walt Disney was? The guy was off the god-dammed wall. His brother Roy kept him in check. This is a creative institution. What's been wrong with this institution over the past 20 years is that it hasn't been run by the crazies. It needs to be run by crazies again. Clean out your image of crazies. We're talking about creative crazies. That's what we ought to have. We can always buy MBA talent."

With the bitter feuds that had divided Disney over the preceding months, Ray Watson's lens showed him a profound need for unity. It began to matter less to him which management was best. What was most important was finding management that would please, or at least calm, the two sides of the family, the dissident shareholders, the rest of the shareholders, Wall Street, and the Disney employees. He began to back off from either Eisner or Wells. If Eisner, or Wells, only had the support of the Roy side, they would be poison. If Hawley pushed hard enough for Stanfill, maybe Watson could get agreement for Stanfill from the board as a whole.

For himself, he didn't care. He could stay on as chairman, or go. He wasn't like Ron Miller. Miller had come of age in the company. He was married to Walt's daughter. His identity as an adult was here on this lot, and it had been devastating to him to have that taken away. Watson, in contrast, had built his identity at the Irvine Company. He was the man who had transformed Irvine, California, from orange groves and onion fields into a city. If it was time to be done with Disney, he could happily turn it over to someone else, as long as he felt that he left the company united, strong, and prepared to fight its way back.

By mid-September, with a week remaining before the crucial board meeting that would decide the matter of the new CEO, Gold could only count on his own vote, Roy's, and Peter Dailey's, out of 13 on the board. He needed four more to install a management that he and Roy would like, to win the decade-long war against Walker and Miller. He had been suggesting Frank Wells for various spots in management for months, and had gotten nowhere. He had suggested Eisner, and Eisner had been caught in a pitch-out. There was just room enough and time enough, he thought, for one more try. The problem was that Eisner lacked experience running a company, while Wells lacked the creative talent and imagination so necessary for Disney. Why not pitch the two to the board as a team, Gold thought. It would take two things: an all-out lobbying campaign among the directors, with Eisner and Wells actively asking for the jobs; and rounding up support among the other top shareholders.

The first task was to get the team together. It would be the dream team: Eisner as the creative force, Wells with the "corporate experience," the financial discipline, the perceived rigorousness. Eisner and Wells had met several times, but could they work with each other? Who would be the top man? On Sunday the 16th, after attending one of his kids' baseball games, Eisner came to a meeting at Gold's house to work out a strategy. But first they had to settle exactly what kind of package they were proposing to the board: who would be the CEO, who would report to whom, how the power would be divided. Wells proposed that they split it down the middle, as co-CEOs, the way he had been co-chief executive of Warner Brothers. As he had at every contact with Disney since Miller had first approached him two years before, Eisner ferociously stuck to his insistence that he alone be CEO. He wanted to be the man in charge. Wells finally conceded: Eisner could be chairman and chief executive officer. Wells would accept the number-two title as president and chief operating officer, on one condition: that he report not to Eisner but directly to the board. That turned out to be agreeable to Eisner.

Next Gold convinced the two men to campaign actively for the jobs, to get on the telephone to board members, to visit them personally. The two of them, in the space of a few days, managed to visit almost every member of the board, except for Caroline Ahmanson, who was in China, and Card Walker, who was out of town on a fishing trip in Arizona. Going door-to-door, selling himself, was new territory for Eisner. He was telling people not just what he saw as a good film idea or casting combination, but who he was, what his talents were, where his heart was. He had never had to sell himself in quite this way since he had sent out résumés 18 years before when he was a lowly commercial-shuffler at CBS.

Gold knew his ace in the hole was the dissident shareholders. Jacobs and a number of his backers in the Gibson suit and proxy fight favored Stanfill, for the same reasons that Hawley did. They were businessmen; they understood a man like Stanfill. But when Gold called Jacobs with a strong pitch for Eisner and Wells, Jacobs made a few calls of his own around the industry, and got the word on them: "Some very high marks came back both on their abilities as well as them as people. They were considered very special as individuals, as people of their word, and not insecure." Jacobs was finally convinced, and he brought in other dissident shareholders with him.

Another major shareholder, Sid Bass, didn't tip so easily. Bass had been leaning toward Stanfill, or at least Wells; he knew next to nothing about Eisner. Only when Wells told him that he supported the choice of Eisner as CEO did Bass go along. He respected Wells' judgment. Bass promptly called Watson to inform him of his support. In a typically direct Sid Bass phone call, he leaned heavily on Watson. He had just bought another million shares of Disney at $60 a share, and had told the Disney specialist on the floor of the exchange to buy him all Disney stock that came up. By the end of the week he had increased his stake from 5.5 to 8.6 percent of the company. Bass, Boesky, Jacobs, Roy Disney, and other dissident shareholders together owned over 40 percent of the company. When Stanfill called Bass, asking for his support, Bass told him he had promised his support to Eisner and Wells, and he would back up his promise: "If you win on Saturday, we'll start a proxy fight on Monday. We'll replace the board and appoint new officers." Bass conveyed the same forceful message to Watson, and it rocked Watson's thinking. Perhaps Dennis Stanfill was not a horse that could be ridden to unity.

Gold's other trump was Card Walker. Gold counted him as three votes on the board, since he had great influence over Donn Tatum, the retired president, and Dick Nunis, the head of the parks. Frank Wells flew to Arizona in a corporate jet belonging to Shamrock, Roy Disney's holding company, to pitch the Eisner–Wells team. He knew Walker would be a tough sell. Walker had been unceremoniously tossed off the board's executive committee at the insistence of Roy Disney and Gold. The whole campaign for a new CEO was directed, in a sense, at him and Ron Miller. But it wasn't Roy or Stan Gold who showed up at his fishing camp. It was Frank Wells, a man everyone respected. Furthermore, Frank Wells and his wife Luanne were friends of Ron and Diane Miller. They were neighbors at their beach houses in Malibu. Diane and Ron had bought Keith Moon's house on Victoria Point, just down from Broad Beach. Frank and Luanne had an old 1960s ranch-style double-lot home right on the water on Broad Beach Road off Trancas. Now Frank Wells came to Arizona carrying a peace offer: Gold would be willing to resign from the board in favor of a candidate from the Walt side of the family—Ron or Diane, or Sharon Disney Lund, or one of their lawyers—if Walker would vote for Wells and Eisner. It would help unify the family and the company once again. Walker went for it.

On Friday, the *Los Angeles Times* reported that a majority of the board favored Stanfill. But Watson had begun to see that Eisner and Wells could indeed be the unifying management he sought, especially if Walker and his allies would go along with them. He began calling board members, convincing them that the Eisner–Wells team was a done deal—that most of the active shareholders were for it, the two sides of the family were for it, and most of the other directors were for it. By the time he was finished calling, what he had argued was true: it was a done deal. The board meeting opened at 11:05 Saturday morning. Card Walker, talking by speakerphone from Arizona, nominated Michael Eisner as chairman and chief executive officer of Walt Disney Productions, and Frank Wells as president and chief operating officer. Every director, even Philip Hawley, voted in favor. The meeting adjourned at 11:40 and Stan Gold called Eisner's house to tell him and Wells the news.

It was September 22, 1984. Michael Eisner had what he had wanted for a long time. And the Magic Kingdom had a new prince.

7

Prince of the Mouseworks

Michael Eisner once described his feelings on becoming CEO of Disney as equivalent to being asked to spend all his time in a toystore: "I don't know which toy to take home because they're all fabulous and they all work and I'm so excited I can't sleep at night."

Eisner couldn't wait until Monday morning, his first day on the job, to visit Disney. As soon as he was elected, Eisner and Wells went to lunch with the Disney board at the Lakeside Country Club near the studio, then drove to the lot to meet with Flom and other attorneys about the state of the company. The next morning Wells came to Eisner's house again, and the two of them took their families over to the Disney lot to look over their new corporate home. It was a quiet little family tour. They looked the place over. They walked the lot.

By 1984, Disney had 30,000 employees worldwide, and was represented on every continent except Antarctica. But the heart of it was here, in this quiet 44 acres just off the Ventura Freeway in Burbank. It was humble for a kingdom, small even for a movie lot. Its entrance sported nothing like Paramount Pictures Corporation's grand faux-Roman double stucco arch. There was just a kiosk for the guard, and low sheds to cover the VIPs' cars. There was nothing like the hurly-burly of Paramount. Here, according to Hollywood legend, even the birds sang on cue and in harmony. The main buildings, now 45 years old, with their minimalist curves, glass brick, and circular cutouts, showed Walt's futurist mood. Across from them glowered the newer, massive, modern, and undecorated Roy O. Disney building, as if the serious, practical "Roy men" were still trying to cow those creative goof-offs next door.

No cars poked in among the buildings. Festooned with trees, bushes, and flowers—palms, poppies, and rhododendrons, like some Northeasterner's dream of California—the Disney lot held the softness of a campus. And Mickey showed up everywhere: on the mailboxes, on the street signs. In front of the commissary, a topiary had been trained in the shape of Mickey. Even the double doors of the huge sound stages sported Mickey, peeking through a fence, with the legend, "No Looky-Loos."

The commissary was in its own time warp. The sign still advertised chili dogs for 35¢. Tom Hanks, who had eaten there when he worked on *Splash*, his break into the big time, compared it to "a Greyhound bus station in the '50s."

Beyond the neat offices and the sound stages, the usual back-lot industrial jumble had grown: the electrical department, the carpenters, the plumbers. Around one corner stood a quiet Midwest town of false-front buildings with verandas and cupolas, a run-down curling-shingle version of Disneyland's Main Street, held up from behind by half-rotten two-by-fours. A brick building carried a sign reading, "Kansas City Star Gazette"; a window read, "Mary's Barber Shop." It had been built for *Pollyanna* and used over and over. Down the way stood another main street, this one a western set. Next to it was the set for "Zorro," out of production for nearly three decades. A 20-foot satellite dish pointed high and to the south, out along the back fence. The silver water tower stood over it all, emblazoned with Walt's famous signature.

That first day, wandering the Sunday-quiet lot, might have seemed a moment for celebration for Eisner. A great victory had been won. He had been appointed head of the company he most wanted to run. But the state of the Magic Kingdom was not good. Even now there were barbarians massed at the borders. No sooner had one corporate raider been repulsed, bought off with massive tribute, than another appeared at the gates. The movie studios lay fallow. And the employees of the old guard were in revolt, raising the banner of the great and sainted King Walt, now long dead.

The company was emotionally exhausted from months of attacks. It was financially exhausted as well. Already deeply in debt when the year began, Disney had more than doubled its debt, to $900 million, after paying off Steinberg and muddling through another year of less-than-sizzling operations. And now it faced yet another threat in Irwin Jacobs, who had pledged to take the company over and dismantle it.

The Disney Channel was still hemorrhaging money; it had slowly been gaining subscribers, but it still had not broken into the black. The movie studio was moribund. It had one great success under its belt—*Splash* had grossed over $70 million. The Touchstone label had begun to break through the prejudice against Disney among Hollywood "names," but only in dribs and drabs. The old Hollywood saw still held: "Disney gets you on the way up, or on the way down." It was not the studio of choice. In fact, it was not even a major studio. *Daily Variety*, as a matter of course, counted six: Columbia, MGM/UA, Paramount, 20th Century Fox, Universal, and Warner Brothers. As one animator put it, "Disney was absolutely bottom of the barrel, the laughing stock of the motion picture industry. There was no one who was going to dispute that."

Attendance at the parks, too, had been declining for years. The number of people coming through the doors at Disney World had peaked with the opening of Epcot Center in 1983, and had fallen the following year by nearly 10 percent. Attendance at Disneyland had peaked at 11.5 million in 1980, and had drifted steadily lower, to less than 9.5 million. Under parks chief Dick Nunis, the parks management had decided to handle that problem by cutting wages. The union contracts at Disney World in Florida were coming up soon. They had always been semi-sweetheart deals, with the unions just glad to have the members in such a union-poor state. But those members wouldn't stand for much more. In Anaheim, the old contract for a third of Disneyland's workers had expired a week before, and Nunis had asked them to take wage cuts of 17 percent over the next three years, plus some hefty cuts in benefits. There were 1,800 people on this contract—ride operators, ticket sellers, sales clerks, candy-makers, blacksmiths—hard-labor, front-line employees. The most any of them made was $11.60 an hour, and some of them put in full shifts at $3.74 an hour. They had said no to the wage cuts, and the self-proclaimed "Happiest Place on Earth" drifted toward picket lines, arrests, and violence.

And now the problems of Disney had been thrust into the hands of Michael Eisner, who had never run a whole company before. Eisner had to do a number of things quickly. First, he had to stabilize the company. He had to slow down, if possible, the wave of attacks—suits, proxy fights, and takeover attempts—from dissident shareholders. He had to gain control of this massive, old, inbred dinosaur of an organization. Most of all, he had to gain the appearance of control, since the appearance of control and the reality are so often the same. If he wanted to scare away the vultures, he had to get the company moving. Just as important, he had to appear to get the company moving. He had to impress people both inside and outside the company that things were different, that Disney was once more a great place to work, a creative and expansive organization, a locus of excitement and growth. Finally, he had to raise revenues. He had to get more money in the door in every division.

All this had to start soon. His honeymoon was bound to be short, perhaps just a few months, and some people were not likely to give him any honeymoon at all. The very people who had put him in office— especially Irwin Jacobs and the Basses—were likely to dismember the company from under him.

Moments this fertile are hard to come by.

On Monday, September 24, his first official day at work, Eisner took a tour of the studio with Frank Wells and Roy Disney. It was a get-to-know-each-other tour. Eisner smiled, shook hands, asked questions. Within the company, the mix of emotions was palpable, and at times confusing. Most employees could only vaguely track what was going on, and few knew much about Eisner or Wells.

The departure of Ron Miller had been an occasion for relief, but also for sadness, since he was almost universally liked as a human being, even among those who derided his abilities as a chairman. But the sudden reappearance of Roy Disney had an effect that was at once reassuring and eerie. It had been Roy whose actions had precipitated the 197 days of traumatic change. It had been Roy who had sponsored Eisner and Wells. He was still a fabulously wealthy man, he was now vice chairman of the company, and he had asked Eisner for one favor: fearing that the new management he had installed might decide to end Disney's root business, Roy had asked to be head of the animation department. In the words of one senior animator, Roy Disney's reappearance on the lot was "intriguing . . . Initially we thought he was in charge of everything. All we knew was that the Bass brothers and Roy Disney had taken over the studio. The name Michael Eisner never came up in conversation. We had, frankly, no idea who Eisner and Wells were. Not a clue. We had heard that Eisner had a lot to do with *Raiders of the Lost Ark*, and the *Star Trek* films. We thought the live film department would get a big shot in the arm. These guys would put them back on the map."

A number of animators had gathered in a screening room in the animation building when Roy Disney came visiting. As one animator put it later, "This man walked in that looked like Walt. It was scary, in a good way. You look at pictures of Walt in the 30s and the resemblance is uncanny. And he smokes like a chimney, and coughs, and has a very casual manner about him. He came in, the vice chairman of the company, a man worth hundreds of millions, and he put me completely at ease. Roy was a real Disney."

At ten in the morning, the employees gathered on the back lot, just beyond the old town. Eisner stood under a gazebo and made a short speech. So did Wells. They said, as one who was present remembers it, "all the right things"—what a great company it was, how they were all going to grow together. The employees listened politely and cheered at the right moments. But, in fact, they were still in shock. They didn't know how long this new bunch would last. They didn't know how long they themselves would last—the new people would probably want to clean house.

Afterwards Eisner ate lunch with the top eight or nine people in the company. Again he said "all the right things." Then he got to work. He had a typewriter brought to his office, and started pouring out his customary torrent of memos that he typed himself, the same memos that he would pour out wherever he was, typed, scribbled on yellow pads or even on the backs of envelopes, menus, receipts, whatever came to hand.

That afternoon Eisner announced that by the following fall he wanted to have at least one animated show for kids on Saturday morning television. He put out a call for "the six most creative people at Disney," and ordered them to attend a brainstorming session, at his house, at 8 o'clock on the next available Sunday morning. Eisner clearly had the kind of energy—and the lack of tradition-bound restraint—that the company sorely needed.

That night, at a meeting hall in Anaheim, the Disneyland workers gathered to consider Dick Nunis' latest offer to the union: a two-year wage freeze for present employees, along with a cut in pay and benefits for future employees. This offer would, in effect, create two classes of union workers at the parks. The workers turned the contract down, and voted, by a margin of 69 percent, to go on strike.

The next morning picketers showed up at the Disneyland ticket booths, passing out pamphlets to the park's guests. "Caution: Disneyland employees are on strike," the fliers read. "If you are planning on going into Disneyland and riding one of the many attractions, you should be cautioned that inexperienced and unqualified personnel may be operating the attraction. This could cause a safety hazard to the public. Supervisors and temporary employees, without full training, may be operating the attraction you and your family are planning to ride."

Some of the picketers wore T-shirts emblazoned with Mickey behind the international "no" symbol—a circle with a diagonal line through it.

One striker, a cashier named Ray Haller, carried a sign with a drawing of Walt Disney, and a quote from Walt: "Disneyland is a work of love. We didn't go into it with just the idea of making money." Beneath it Haller had written the message, "We miss you, Walt."

The officials and members of the union did not know the salary and benefits terms Disney had given Eisner to convince him to come to Disney. For weeks the company negotiators had been pleading with the union members to be loyal "citizens" of Disney. They had cited their bottom line, telling the union that the company needed to improve that bottom line quickly if it wanted to save itself from the vultures who were descending from Wall Street.

At the same moment, unknown to the union or anyone outside the top management itself, the board had agreed to pay Eisner a salary of $750,000 (half again as much as Ron Miller had received after a recent substantial raise), plus a $750,000 bonus for signing on, plus options on a half-million shares of Disney stock, plus—and this was the kicker, and the reason the numbers had to be kept secret from the union—an annual bonus calculated at 2 percent of the dollar amount by which the company's net income exceeded a 9 percent return on shareholders' equity.

This was not a number that would make headlines, even when it was eventually confirmed, because it was so abstract. But it was the big number. Shareholders' equity in the just-ended fiscal 1984 came to $1.15 billion. Nine percent of that would be $103.7 million. The fiscal year's net income would eventually work out to $108.2 million, a difference of $4.5 million. Two percent of that came to $90,000—which would have been Eisner's bonus if the deal had been in place for the past year. A $90,000 bonus will buy a lot of ice cream at Baskin-Robbins. But if, with the same equity, Eisner was able to squeeze a 15 percent return out of the company, his bonus would jump to $1.4 million, almost double his base pay. If he could rev it up to 20 percent, he would get over $2.5 million in bonus, over three times a base pay that was already equal to the highest in Hollywood.

In addition, the board awarded Eisner options on 510,000 shares of Disney. He could buy them from the company at any time over the five years that the contract would run—but the price would always be what it was the day he signed the contract: $57.43 a share. And the company would even loan him the money to buy those shares. If the value of the stock was more than that, he would make a tidy profit.

Wells had a similar incentive deal. His salary was $400,000, his signing bonus $250,000, his annual bonus half the size of Eisner's, and he had options on 460,000 shares.

The bonuses meant that if Wells and Eisner increased the company's total revenues, or decreased its expenses, by 9 percent, they would share $3.75 million a year in bonuses. And if Wall Street liked what it saw and bid up the stock, they stood to make tens of millions each. To the unions, the key phrase in all this would be "or decreased its expenses." In time the unionized workers at Disney would come to feel that this was the key, that this new management had a deep personal stake in squeezing the unions.

But Eisner, who has been called "more hands-on than Mother Theresa," didn't show up at the negotiations or at the picket line. He didn't just want to squeeze more out of the company. He wanted to change it. He wanted to turn its crank. Among people that he knew, the word associated with Disney was "dusty." In his first week, for example, he attended an employee recognition dinner at which people sang Disney songs. And it struck Eisner that the newest song they sang was from *Mary Poppins*, already two decades old. He had been out to the parks a number of times as a guest with his children, and Tomorrowland had always seemed to him more like Yesterdayland, a monument to the 1950s image of the future. He wanted to be the person who brought Disney into the future.

Eisner aimed not merely to improve the Disney studio's position, but to make it a power in the industry. And the massive cash flow of the parks, between 66 and 80 percent of the company's revenues in recent years, could give him the flexibility to do it. But he needed help. He needed a crack mind that he knew he could work with—no experiments, no hip shots. And he knew just where to get such a mind. By the end of the week, he was able to announce that, within a few months, Jeffrey Katzenberg would follow him from Paramount to replace Richard Berger as Disney's head of production.

After two days at the helm of Disney, Eisner got on a plane for Fort Worth with Frank Wells and Michael Bagnall, Disney's chief financial officer, to take care of task two: calming the "arbs." It was time to meet Sid Bass.

Disney was in the business of creating miniature worlds. The Bass brothers had done something similar at their compound in Fort Worth. They weren't ready to leave Fort Worth for the glass towers of Manhattan or Century City. But neither were they willing to throw themselves on the mercy of Fort Worth. So they had their own black-glass towers built, one 32 stories, one 38, connected by a glass-enclosed walkway. Not that they needed two. Fort Worth wags would tell you that the Basses had so much money, they could afford a spare. They hired a security force and a catering service, built a gym and stocked it with the best equipment, and added a quiet, elegant restaurant and club. Then, anticipating that a few friends might visit, they bought the Worthington Hotel next door and made it over. The rich of Texas tend to do things on a certain scale.

For this meeting with the new Disney management team, Sid Bass had sent his private Gulfstream jet to Minneapolis to fly down Irwin Jacobs. Jacobs and his partner Carl Pohlad wanted to buy more of the company. They were still intending to take it over. In fact, Jacobs was considering buying out the Basses' holdings. Jacobs' appetite had been further whetted by what he had learned about Disney. He saw, as Steinberg had before him, how deeply undervalued the company was, and he had begun to crave it.

Eisner and Wells had an agenda, too. They needed space. They needed time. The Bass brothers, Irwin Jacobs, and other large Disney shareholders such as Ivan Boesky had the financial muscle and the ferocity, separately or together, to launch proxy fights, shareholder suits, and even takeover attempts. Jacobs had already announced that he would try for the whole company. It was rumored that he had already cut a deal to sell the Disney catalogue of old films to Kerkorian, the same deal that Steinberg had made earlier.

Bass and Jacobs had battled to have Eisner installed in office, but they had done so on second-hand information. They had never met Eisner. Eisner needed to convince them that they would make more money with a little patience and trust than by continuing to fight.

Jacobs would later call their meeting a "touch-and-feel." Sid and Bob Bass were there, and the Basses' strategist Rich Rainwater, Chuck Cobb, chairman of Arvida, and Al Checchi, and Eisner and Wells, and Jacobs and an assistant.

At the beginning, the Basses seemed to be looking for the right moment to unload their stock. They told Eisner and Wells that they were short-term players. "You're coming in to run this company," Sid Bass told Eisner, "but don't assume that the same ownership is going to be there that there is today."

Jacobs reiterated his intentions to get in for more of the stock, even for all of it, if he could swing it.

Eisner and Wells told the group they had no feelings one way or the other. "Basically," said Eisner, "our job is to run the business, without worrying too much about who owns it."

"This is a great opportunity for everyone concerned," added Wells. "We intend to make it a great company no matter who owns it."

"We're not locked into our stock," Sid Bass told them. "If Irwin wants to make an offer for the company, we might seriously think of selling out to him."

Bass and Rainwater, who had as much experience in real estate as Eisner did in film, presented the potential that they saw in developing Disney's Florida properties and expanding elsewhere. Eisner presented his five-year vision for Disney, describing for the meeting the value of video and cable, the new opportunities available in syndicated television, and more than anything else, the extraordinary opportunities in a re-vitalized Disney studio. It was not the usual top-level corporate presentation. He had no slides or charts, no handouts or photos. He only had his notes, which he had prepared on the plane the day before in conversation with Wells and Bagnall, and a green felt marker to write on the white laminate presentation boards that lined the walls. But it didn't matter that he had no slick presentation, since everyone present had already studied the corporation carefully. What they were studying now was Michael Eisner and Frank Wells.

As the group broke for lunch, Sid Bass turned to Jacobs and said, "Why don't you come with me? We'll go into my office, and we'll let everybody else sit here and talk."

Once in his office, Bass began to think aloud, and his thinking reflected a key new fact: he had been powerfully impressed by the conversation with Eisner and Wells. "These guys know what they want to do," he told Jacobs. "It's not often that you see management so open, someone who will talk like that to shareholders." He went on, "You know, maybe we won't sell our stock. I don't know. Maybe we'd have an interest in buying more stock in this thing. But we probably should not go against one another. We should probably pool our resources and have a long-term investment here, together."

Jacobs was surprised by the sea change in Bass' thinking, but he said, "I have no problem with that. Look, you let me go back to Minneapolis and I will have a conversation with my people, Carl Pohlad and myself, and we'll let you know what our interest level is as far as increasing our holdings together with you or individually."

Bass was still cautious. "My mind's not made up. I'll let you know."

They left his office, and Bass gathered a few of his own people in a side room for a discussion that lasted, he guessed, "thirty seconds." When the whole group sat down again in the conference room, he announced, "We're not selling any of our stock. We're staying in the deal. In fact, we're with you for the next five years."

The decision was quick, but its long-term meaning was far from clear. Bass was wary of his new accidental partner, Jacobs. After the meeting, Jacobs flew back to Minneapolis, and he was excited—it looked to him like he and the Bass brothers were going to buy Disney together. It was High Holy Days, the turn of the Jewish New Year that begins each fall with Rosh Hoshanah and ends nine days later with Yom Kippur. There were services to go to. As soon as Rosh Hoshanah was past, he would meet with Pohlad.

Back in Anaheim, the Disneyland employees' strike was getting worse, generating un-Disney-like images on the evening news. A park employee had been arrested and charged with assault with a deadly weapon. According to the police report, he had tried to run down a pregnant picketer with his car, missing her "by less than a foot." The next day, the park management ordered the pickets off the property. Now a judge had backed up the management's order, and the unions were debating whether to obey it.

When Irwin Jacobs met with his major partner, Carl Pohlad, after Rosh Hoshanah, Pohlad was pleased at the prospect of buying Disney in tandem with the Basses. Jacobs immediately called Sid Bass: "Pohlad and I will be pooling our additional resources, and we will match your investment in Disney, dollar for dollar. We might be prepared to buy as much as $300 to 400 million dollars more stock. We aren't trying a one-upsman game. We'll be prepared. We're getting our ducks in order to do this."

Bass sounded thoughtful on the long land lines from Texas. "Three, four hundred million dollars?"

"Yeah."

"That's a lot of money."

"Yeah, it's a lot of money. We'll get back to you and confirm this."

But Jacobs noticed something curious: two days after he had left the meeting, and he thought the conclave was over, Eisner and Wells were still in Fort Worth, still talking to Bass, to his right-hand man Rich

Rainwater, and to his chief financial officer, Al Checchi. It didn't seem like a time, or a place, for soaking up the sun. They must have had a lot to discuss.

The next day, October 3, a big piece of the puzzle came in over Jacobs' Quotron: two major blocks of Disney shares had "gone up." The word was that Ivan Boesky had sold his shares, and the Basses had bought them—over 2.5 million shares altogether, for over $150 million. This would nearly double the Basses' share of the company, bringing it to almost 16 percent. And Bass had not mentioned it to Jacobs. Was Bass trying to cut him out?

The UPI wires carried a quote from the Disney management interpreting the buy as "a vote of confidence," saying it was "enormously pleased with this development." And there was something else on the UPI wires. A new group called the Walt Disney Employees Association had formed to fight Jacobs. They had sent a letter to all 30,000 employees inviting them to join a campaign to "save our jobs."

"Are you tired of the 'sharks' deciding your future for you?" the letter asked. "Are you sick of seeing the raiders fill their coffers with gold from our company's funds that you helped earn with your talents, your creativity, your inventiveness and your plain, old fashioned hard work?"

Instantly Jacobs was back on the line to Sid Bass. "Sid, I'm sure it isn't true, but the word is that you bought this stock."

"Yeah, we bought it."

"We'll take half," Jacobs said.

"We're not selling you half."

"What happened to this arrangement that we had?"

"We don't have any arrangement."

Jacobs was shocked and resentful. Bass was trying to cut him out. He said, "I'm not real comfortable with this situation, after we just got through with this meeting. I'm not very pleased with what took place."

Bass said, "Well, I'm not selling you half."

"Okay," Jacobs said, turning bitter. He decided, on the spot, to give up on Disney. "I understand. But I no longer have any interest in being in this relationship. We're getting out. You can have it all to yourself. A dollar more or a dollar less won't make any difference. You call me tomorrow morning. You tell me what you want to pay me for the stock. I'm selling out."

The next day, Sid Bass bought $182.5 million in Disney stock from Irwin Jacobs, and settled in for a long growing season. Now the Basses owned nearly 25 percent of the company, a percentage large enough to give the Basses the ability to dictate its future. And, for the present at least, they were willing to bet that future on Eisner.

Jacobs felt burned by the twists and turns of dealing with the Basses; nevertheless he was well compensated for his troubles. "I made over $30 million on the investment," he says. A $30-million profit for a three-month investment was apparently a big disappointment to Jacobs, but even so, he allows that "it was substantial to me at that time. I was rewarded." And he feels in retrospect that it was better for Disney that he never came to control the company, because he would have needed to soak the company for cash to pay off the huge debts he incurred to buy it: "I doubt in all honesty it would have been the company it is today had I been there. Because of the leverage I would have needed to buy it, I don't think I could have given Eisner and Wells the flexibility and the resources that they needed to do the things they ultimately did. Clearly it was better off without me."

Sid Bass' purchase of Jacobs' shares was the final act of the takeover drama. What had started as an uncertain but desperate move by Roy Disney to preserve his assets and his pride, had been taken up by Steinberg, and then by Jacobs, as a straight corporate raid, and had ended as a friendly takeover directed by Roy Disney and sponsored by the Bass brothers.

With Jacobs out of the picture and Bass pledged for the long term, Eisner had some of the stability he needed. And he had something equally important: financial expertise. Sid Bass had asked his own financial wizard, Al Checchi, to go to California and help Eisner turn the company around. Checchi was more than happy to help. He had a good deal of his own money in Disney stock by now. He and Rainwater together owned some 1.5 percent of the company. If Disney turned around, he would be independently wealthy for the first time. John D. Rockefeller had advised would-be capitalists to "put all your eggs in one basket and watch the basket." In December 1984 Checchi came West to watch the basket for himself and for the Basses. He had come for brief visits before; this time he would stay for six months. In those six months of brainstorming and advising, he would begin to explore with Eisner and Wells a new global vision of Disney.

By Thursday, October 4, Eisner and Wells were in Florida touring Disney World. Jane Eisner and Luanne Wells were with them, and so were

Jeff and Marilyn Katzenberg. For three days, they toured every nook and cranny of every park and hotel from nine in the morning until far into the night. Dick Nunis, who expected like all top Disney executives to lose his job soon, acted as tour guide. He showed his guests possible plans for the future, including a new ride for EPCOT that would take visitors through the history of the movies, with "Audio-Animatronic" characters reenacting moments from *Casablanca, The Wizard of Oz, Gone with the Wind,* and other great films. Nunis also told Eisner of a long-developing idea that was far more vast in scope. As early as 1976, Card Walker had suggested that Disney build a park in Europe. All the company's money was pouring into EPCOT at the time, so the idea was set aside. In 1983, seeing the success of the Tokyo park, Watson and Miller had felt that the time had come, but they were too busy with the takeover to do more than send out a few feelers and commission Nunis to do a study of potential European sites. Eisner immediately told Nunis to expand his studies. The idea felt right—it had the global reach that he was seeking.

In the parks, Eisner and Wells made speeches and shook hands with some of the 16,000 park workers. Two thousand four hundred of them—plumbers, electricians, and other maintenance personnel—were working under a contract that had expired four days before. As in California, Nunis was looking for a wage freeze, this one for three years.

Saturday morning, October 6, Nunis sent a letter to the Disneyland strikers in Anaheim, telling them they would be fired if they didn't come back to work by the 10th, only four days away. Saturday night found several thousand strikers and their supporters on the dark sidewalk outside the closed "Happiest Place on Earth," silent, burning candles to the memory of Walt Disney. Some held signs that read, "Disneyland, Walt's Dying Dream." Some sang "It's a Small, Small World." In spite of Walt's own bitter history with unions, strikers told reporters they were confident that Walt "would not have let this happen." The union spokesman, Michael O'Rourke, told reporters, "We are saluting the memory of Walt Disney's ideals and reminding the present management of Mr. Disney's belief that his people are his greatest asset."

Early the next morning, as the strikers were still sleeping off their midnight vigil for Walt, six people arrived at Eisner's house in Beverly Hills to brainstorm about children's television, and to cook up new assets for the company. Disney had been off network television completely for almost a year and a half. But television was Eisner's home territory. They had to come up with some television ideas. Someone asked, "Why not just throw some old cartoons on television?" But that idea lacked one important element, an element that would become a mark of Eisner at Disney. That element was synergy. Eisner didn't want to make anything he could sell only once. If he put the old cartoons on television, yes, they could make money from advertisers with minimal expense. But if they put new cartoons on television, they could make money from advertisers. And they could sell dolls of the new characters. And endorsements. And games. And books. And rides at the parks. In fact, the whole business cycle could be repeated with every new character they created. It would be more expensive to create new characters, but in the long run it would be more profitable, because Disney knew how to do it, and the Disney name had the trust of children and parents alike.

As the small group tossed out ideas for new animated shows, Gary Krisel, head of the merchandising group, came up with a story line based on an uncharted island called "Wuz" populated with weird hybrids, including the Bumblelion (half bee, half lion), the Rinokey (a rhinoceros and a monkey), and the Eleroo (an elephant and a kangaroo). The stuffed animals would make great merchandising toys. Why not build a show, "The Wuzzles," around them?

Eisner threw out an idea that had been rolling around in his head for a while. His seven-year-old had pulled him into a neighborhood store recently to buy some candy—but he did not want just any brand. He wanted "Gummi Bears." Eisner was captivated by his son's fascination with the little, chewy, translucent, colored candy bears. He began playing with ways to make the candies into a show featuring magical animals in medieval garb. It was another idea that was ready to fly. The final show, however, had nothing in particular to do with the candy. Disney's only contact with the candy company was to pay for the use of the name.

But how could Disney compete with other animation companies if Disney made the cartoons the old-fashioned Disney way? Everyone else in children's television worked in "limited animation"—flat characters against a flat background, their movements minimalized and jerky to save drawing costs. Each "half-hour" show was actually 22 minutes long. Twenty-two minutes of classic Disney animation would call for about 25,000 individual drawings. Twenty-two minutes of "limited animation" would call for only about 12,000 drawings. And in many of those drawings only one small part was changed from the drawing before it. Often the characters stood still while only their mouths or hands moved. So one

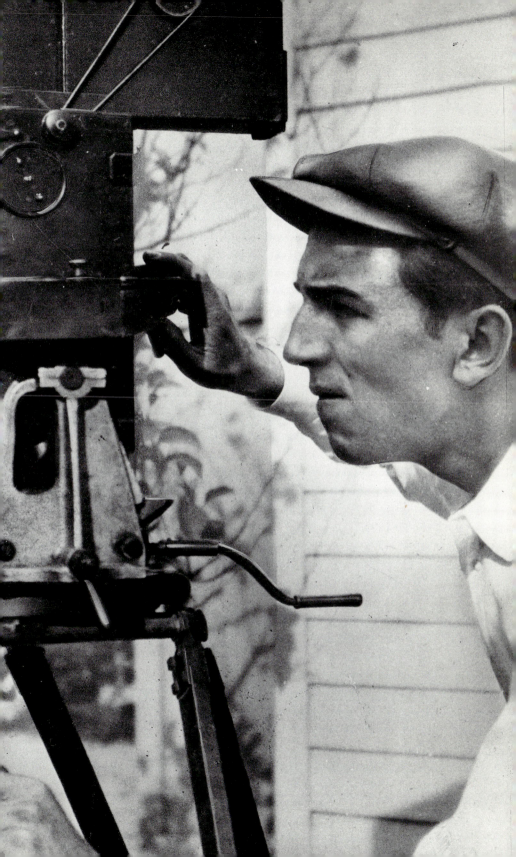

Walt Disney at the opening of Disneyland, July 17, 1955.
(Bettmann Archives)

Preceding Page: *The young Walt Disney in 1927, poised to launch an empire.*
(Wide World Photos)

Sid Bass (above, left); Roy E. Disney,
Walt Disney's nephew (above, right);
and Saul Steinberg (left). Following
Saul Steinberg's attempt to take over
Disney, Roy Disney teamed up with
Sid Bass to install Michael Eisner as
chairman and chief executive officer.
(Wide World Photos)

After taking Paramount from seventh to first among major studios, Michael Eisner faced his biggest challenge yet—turning Disney around. (Wide World Photos)

Frank Wells, an entertainment lawyer and former president of Warner Brothers, was lured by Roy Disney to join "Team Disney" as president. (Wide World Photos)

Jeffrey Katzenberg, who had earned his reputation at Paramount as Eisner's "golden retriever," moved with Eisner to become president, and later chairman, of Disney Studios. (Wide World Photos)

Michael Eisner, with French Prime Minister Jacques Chirac, after signing the agreement that would allow Disney to build EuroDisneyland outside Paris. (Wide World Photos)

Eisner's contacts and savvy brought some of the biggest names in entertainment to the company, including Michael Jackson, Francis Ford Coppola, and (pictured here with Eisner) George Lucas. (Wide World Photos)

Julia Roberts (below) and Bette Midler (right) were but two of the stars whose careers were reestablished by Disney. (Wide World Photos)

basic drawing would suffice for a number of seconds of action, with mouths or hands drawn on clear overlays that changed more often. It was far less expensive, but the characters looked far less real.

It was a tough question. On the one hand, they had to uphold the Disney "mark"—the cartoons had to look better-crafted than the competition's. On the other hand, they couldn't do three hours of *Snow White* every Saturday morning. In the end, they compromised. They would do limited "limited animation," using about 18,000 to 20,000 drawings for each 22 minutes. They would design the characters in California and ship them to Japan for animation. With the yen running at 250 to the dollar, Japanese animators could be hired very inexpensively.

The traditionalists at Disney would never have allowed any kind of "limited animation," or sent work out of the country. Already Eisner was transforming the way the company worked.

Back at the lot the next day, Eisner, Wells, and Katzenberg rolled up their sleeves and set to work on Disney's movies, watching whatever was available of what was already in production, reviewing scripts. They found some promising projects for the future, including a pile of 11 scripts for a live/animated film called *Who Framed Roger Rabbit?* that had been kicking around the lot since 1980. They tossed aside dozens of scripts, and even stopped projects already in production. Eventually, including the costs of abandoned Epcot pavilion projects for Israel and Spain, and the costs of the change in managment (legal fees and settled contracts) Disney would write off $166 million of costs in the first quarter.

But even the projects that they allowed to go forward—including *Country, Baby, Return to Oz, The Black Cauldron*, and *My Science Project*—held little promise of a repeat of the *Splash* success, and several of them were fast becoming extremely expensive. *Return to Oz*, a send-up of the great classic, and *The Black Cauldron* were running budgets that would top at an un-Disney-like $25 million each. *The Black Cauldron* lavished years of beautiful animation work on a dark sword-and-sorcery epic with a difficult and wandering story. *Country*, which starred Jessica Lange and Sam Shephard, was a strong, touching drama, real critic's stuff, but not great box office. None of them seemed to be a ready source for new cash. Disney had the parks and other businesses to help finance films, but it is rarely a good idea for one division of a corporation to be a "cash cow" for the other divisions for very long. The studio would have to find some other source of money to fund productions.

Within the week, Wells set off for New York to size up one idea. He went to see Roland Betts at Silver Screen Partners. Betts had offered Wells a revolutionary new way to finance films by allowing the average Wall Street investor to buy a piece of the action. Betts' first Silver Screen Partners deal had financed the cable channel HBO's attempt to produce its own films—an attempt that didn't make the partners any money. Now he desperately needed a deal that would work, and he hoped that Disney would be it. It was only the start of long and difficult negotiations.

If there was one thing Eisner did know, it was stories, scripts, film production. In mid-October, Eisner gave the green light to his first Disney script. It was a script that he had heard was "in turnaround" (on the toss pile) at Universal: *Down and Out in Beverly Hills*. The package included Nick Nolte (by this time he had done his quota of three non-commercial but artistic films since *48 Hours*). It was time for another successful film with Eisner. It also included Bette Midler and Richard Dreyfuss, and eventually even a cameo by Little Richard, with Paul Mazursky directing. It was a very un-Disney-like set of actors, a prominent and even avant-garde outside director, and a script headed for an "R" rating. It was a choice designed to say that there were new people on the premises.

It said something else as well. Disney had always been reluctant to go "outside." Eisner made it clear that he would not hesitate to go outside the company to sign up the best creative people, wherever they were in the industry.

Out in Anaheim, the strike was dragging on, and growing more bitter. Throughout the week, the picketers, along with a handful of national union leaders, paraded in front of Disneyland. Many of them wore "No Mickey Mouse" T-shirts. Some booed and hissed park officials, some yelled obscenities. Others carried signs with big pictures of Walt, and chanted, "We want Walt. We want Walt." One toddler marched with his parents, carrying a picket sign that said, "I miss Mickey, but I love my mommy." On Friday pickets showed up at the Disney studios, and Teamster truck drivers refused to enter the studio. National union leaders announced a boycott of all Disney facilities and movies. It all made great television, but not the kind that Eisner and Disney wanted to make.

On Saturday, union officials bought tickets to gain entrance to the parks as paying visitors, then passed out leaflets along Main Street and in front of Sleeping Beauty's Castle. The leaflets asked the guests to boycott the park, claiming, "The current corporate management has betrayed the intentions of Walt Disney, who always was concerned with the welfare of his employees." Some guests sympathized with the strikers, feeling, as one put it, "I guess they have a right to be mad." Other guests were as shocked as if a worship service had been invaded. One 78-year-old grandmother from Pennsylvania, who had brought her seven grandchildren to the Magic Kingdom, said, "They should be ashamed to do this inside Disneyland. They belong on the sidewalk."

Then something changed. Despite the leaflet invasion, the tone of the company's public statements took a turn for the better. Suddenly the company began going out of its way to sound conciliatory. One official statement read, "We regret any implication that we are antiunion. We have enjoyed a long history of excellent working relationships with a large number of unions and Disneyland continues to have a collective bargaining agreement with more than 20 different unions." The next day, federal mediator Bonnie Castrey called both sides back to the table. The company came up with a new, slightly improved, offer, and the strike was settled. Castrey had acted, she said, on a "gut feeling." The unions said the breakthrough had happened because they had intensified their efforts. The company didn't say why it had softened its stand. But it was the first sign that Eisner was turning the company's attention away from stringent cost-cutting alone toward other ways of deepening the black ink on the bottom line. The East Coast unions settled without a strike. For the first time, Eisner's influence was felt on the strike lines, and it had not taken the direction the union members had feared.

Frank Wells took on the business side of the parks, and set Nunis to work preparing a comprehensive report on the state they were in. Eisner and Wells quickly discovered that while the theme parks, the company's biggest money-makers, were being run magnificently, they needed major new attractions and improvements to help them maintain their appeal. But big new stuff, Disney-style, takes time, money, and inventiveness. Eisner wanted something for the parks now.

The parks' designers were already hard at work on a number of ideas that could move the parks to a new level. One idea was flight simulation technology that would in time become an industry standard and spawn several new Disney attractions. Randy Bright had discovered it over the summer at a British company, Rediffusion Simulation Ltd. Originally used to train jumbo jet pilots, it featured a capsule set on a network of hydraulic rams. Driven by a computer program, the capsule could simulate acceleration by leaning backward, deceleration by leaning forward.

When synced to the actions of a robot crew and the movements of a film rear-projected onto what seemed to be the spacecraft's "windshield," the result was a jarringly realistic and rapid ride in a twisting, turning, plunging space vehicle.

George Lucas had already been working on a similar idea. Ron Miller had even proposed that Lucas build a ride based on it two years before, but Lucas had not been interested. So in mid-October, when Eisner invited Lucas to come to Glendale for a tour of the imagineers' projects, Lucas focused immediately on the simulator. Now he was ready for it. Bright and the other imagineers set to work melding the simulator with Lucas' *Star Wars* characters. By early December 1984, Eisner at least had something he could announce about the future of the parks, something that sounded like movement, like excitement, like something very different from the old Disney. The imagineers were working with George Lucas to come up with attractions based on *Star Wars* and *Raiders of the Lost Ark*. It was all still vapor, but vapor was better than nothing. And it was another sign that Disney was reaching out.

By late December the imagineers had another unusual visitor: Michael Jackson. Just coming off his *Thriller* album, Jackson was one of the most famous stars in the world, at the height of his popularity. He was also one of Disneyland's biggest fans, often visiting the park several times a month. Katzenberg had no sooner settled into his animation building offices than he received a phone call from David Geffen, the recording executive who was closest to Jackson. Jackson wanted to make a movie for Disney. But Katzenberg and Eisner had other thoughts: Jackson was just the kind of draw the parks needed. So here was Katzenberg personally leading Michael Jackson on a tour of the imagineers' strange laboratory and studio. What Jackson focused on was the state-of-the-art 3-D camera the imagineers had put together. Before he left, Jackson and Katzenberg had begun bouncing around ideas for a 3-D movie, filmed specially for the parks. But Jackson said he would only do it with somebody big—somebody like Stephen Spielberg or George Lucas.

At the turn of the year the company announced another drum-beater for Disneyland: to entice more people through the front gate, they would give away prizes—right there at the front gate. Starting New Year's Day, the park's 30th anniversary would be celebrated by a giant electronic lights-and-buzzers-and-bells counter. Everybody going through the turnstiles would be numbered. Every 30th guest would get a free pass, every 300th a stuffed toy, every 3,000th a watch, every 30,000th a Chevy, every

300,000th a Cadillac. The 250 millionth guest in Disneyland's history, due sometime in midsummer, would get a Cadillac, 30,000 miles of air travel, and 30 free visits to Disney parks. In the hot months it would work out to a prize every two seconds and two cars a day. It would cost the company about a dollar a visitor, but they hoped to push the attendance up to a record 12 million.

And by the end of 1984, Arvida-Disney had announced plans to develop some of the Orlando pine woods, building an array of houses, highrise condos, shops, and hotels. It was called the "Core" concept. Set near EPCOT, it would include not only permanent housing—reaching back to the original EPCOT idea of a prototype city—but also manufacturing facilities that would include tours. It was, at the moment, more vaporware, but it was another sign of life on the Disney planet.

All over Disney, the natives felt like they were being shaken awake. They were used to a management team that spent its afternoons playing golf and its evenings at home with the kids. These guys arrived at 7 in the morning and didn't go home until far into the evening. Katzenberg, who had moved into an office down the hall from Eisner's and set up his by-now trademarked operation, was the biggest shock of all.

Eisner's energy, which was already far different than what Disney expected of its executives, was amplified in his sidekick. Katzenberg was known in the business as the "golden retriever": whatever was needed, he could get it—the star, the script, the writer. This was a man who said of himself that he and his wife Marilyn had twins in order to save time, a man who stop-watched the lights between his home and his work to figure out the most efficient route. He claimed that he "did Paris in a day, including Versailles." He traded in his white Porsche Carerra for a more pedestrian five-liter black-on-gray Mustang convertible with an automatic transmission because, in the hideous morass of Los Angeles traffic, it was hard to shift and work the car phone at the same time. The man who bought the Porsche from him confessed that he had nightmares that the car would start itself up at 4:30 in the morning and head to the studio.

The car may not have started at 4:30, but Katzenberg usually did. A personal trainer would come to his home to work out with him before the sun rose. Katzenberg would hang by his ankles, all 5' 7½" and 128 pounds of him. He would lift dumbbells, do 60 sit-ups, 75 knee-raises, and myriad other exercises, while devouring four newspapers. He was usually at his desk, sipping the first of interminable Diet Pepsies on ice, by 6:15, often even on Sundays, working the phones, starting on the East Coast, where people were already awake. He would often call just to say, "I was thinking about you today. I wanted to say hi, what's going on in your life, how's the family," looking for the next thread of information, the next nuance of tone, rumor of a script, smell of a deal, that might make a difference. According to attorney Steve Sauer, "Jeffrey gets back to you within three hours every day. He just runs through that call sheet." It was the same practice he had honed ever since he had learned it working for Lindsay's political campaigns in the '60s and early '70s: ask and thank, ask and thank. Keep in touch. Know about it first. A Paramount VP who had worked with him said, "He has this compulsion to be on top of everything. A screenplay, a pitch, he wants it all, even if it's just to pass on it."

He constantly worked his "cards," 3 × 5 note cards lined up on his desk in perfectly perpendicular lines, the notes in bright blue felt ink: a line of cards for phone calls, a line for projects, a line for schedules, a line for weekend plans—his own and anyone else's that he might want to stay in touch with.

As head of the studio, he not only read all the scripts that he considered, he read every draft of every script. He not only monitored productions, he sat in on the rushes, the "dailies." He wrote agendas for every meeting he attended. Most Saturday nights found him at theaters in Westwood, watching two or three of the opposition's films in ordinary theater seats with other patrons. Mike Simpson, an agent with William Morris, called Katzenberg "a gladiator with a mission. . . . The man is possessed." David Geffen said, "Compared to Jeffrey, everyone else in this town is on vacation."

Katzenberg asked the same obsessive energy of the people who worked for him (whom he dubbed "Disnoids"), and most of them gave it. One famous quote attributed to Katzenberg, said with only half his tongue in his cheek, was, "If I don't see you in here on Saturday, don't even bother coming in on Sunday." He would often schedule meetings for 7:30 in the morning, script conferences at 10 P.M., and marketing meetings on Sunday mornings, with attendance mandatory. One veteran Disney executive, surprised to hear Katzenberg ask him to drop by the next day for a meeting, reminded Katzenberg that the next day was Thanksgiving. Katzenberg replied, with a straight face, "Why, do you have something planned?" His welcoming jibe to 28-year-old Jane Rosenthal, whom he had just hired as a vice president, was, "Put on your crash helmet."

Randy Bright said of Katzenberg and his people, "The work ethic is off the chart completely. It is absolute and total fanaticism." It was a work ethic that had not been seen at Disney since Walt was young and struggling.

The flavor of Eisner's first few months at Disney was one of frantic exploration. It was as if he had moved to Oz. Watching Disney from the outside, and discussing its possibilities with Roy Disney, he had long suspected that the company held great potential. But the wealth of possibilities he discovered once he got inside the company dwarfed anything he could have imagined. The relationship between the new team and the old hands was one of constant culture shock. In the first weeks after joining Disney, Frank Wells commented to Jim Jimirro, "Jim, I can't believe it. Every time I open a door at this company there's money behind it."

"[Eisner and Wells] would ask me questions 15 times," says Jimirro, "because they couldn't believe the answers. 'You mean you've got all this library,' they'd say, '500 Mickey Mouse cartoons, and they've never been syndicated to television? Are you serious? Wait a minute. You mean to tell me that you've never released any of the animated classics on video, never? You've never advertised Disneyland or Disney World?' "

Wells expressed his astonishment: "Every single day there is a new matching up of the assets, the characters, the history of this company that Walt Disney and our predecessors built with the modern-day business world. . . . No one should be this lucky. It's absolutely incredible. . . . You could spend a lifetime in the core businesses we've got. You could build a movie and television company, you could build the Disney Channel, you can put new characters into consumer products, you can find new assets for Arvida to run, and most of all you can develop Walt Disney World and build another park in Europe. You're talking five lifetimes. . . . My only wish is that I was 30 to do this instead of 53, not for any other reason than that it would be fun to keep doing this for the rest of my life."

Although Eisner's appointment had in large measure been a rejection of Card Walker's leadership of the company, he walked down the hall to Walker's office almost daily for a chat about this or that aspect of the company. He also kept on Ron Miller's lead secretary, Lucille Martin, to help him discover how this complex and far-flung company functioned.

"It was a big leap for a guy as smart as Eisner to come to a company with this much scope and breadth," says Jimirro. "Eisner came into the company as a guy with an enormous curiosity, an incredible thirst for knowledge. He was smart enough to realize how much he didn't know about the company and its 60 years of history, the movies, the library, the parks. He was like a sponge. Whether you liked him or not, at first all you saw was this very genuine curiosity. He was interested. He wanted to know. He was like a little kid. Michael would ask questions and let other people do a lot of the talking. So there was a little bit of a honeymoon period, where everybody got along very well."

Eisner was the curious outsider peeking in the store window. At first he could barely find the men's room, he had no idea how the company's financing was arranged, he had only a vague notion of how many businesses the company was in. Yet, as always, under the slightly loony expression, the rumpled suit, and frizzy hair, Michael Eisner had a deep and flexible mind, and an unwillingness to settle for less than the best.

He understood a few key concepts with profound clarity. He understood that Hollywood was changing. Forty years before, there had only been one distribution system, one market—dark theaters with popcorn machines and ticket booths—and the studios controlled it. The studios lost control of that market through government action, and were forced to compete with a second market—television. By the 1980s and increasingly in the 1990s, studios had multiple markets, multiple media, into which they could sell their creations—theaters, television, cable networks, home videos, computer games, books, toys, and myriad other forms of merchandising based on their characters. Most studios also owned considerable real estate, could indulge in a wide array of unusual ways of financing their projects, and held the rights to decades of old productions. The future of the business belonged to the company that could combine all these profit centers in the most powerful way. And in every one of these areas, Disney held greater potential than any of its rivals.

Eisner also understood the power of creative leadership. A company lived off the drive and direction provided at the top. It couldn't come from the past; it had to come from the present.

Eisner understood intuitively two long-recognized properties of large systems like Disney, properties so common that they are rules of thumb to systems thinkers. First, if you have a systemic problem, anything you do to fix the symptoms just makes the problem worse. All of the tinkering that had taken place under Miller—the new Touchstone label, new production chiefs, a few outside directors and stars—had only played with the symptoms of the problem. And the problem was in the system.

The problem was not anybody's fault, exactly. It was rooted in the second rule of thumb about systems: in any new system, the available choices for action are essentially infinite. As the system ages, it forms itself around the choices taken in the early phases, and the chances of a truly new choice being taken diminish rapidly. Before long, it becomes nearly impossible to make a truly new choice. Buildings, equipment, people's jobs and skills, work rules, relationships with suppliers, social status—all these are connected to the choices taken earlier in the game. To come up with real changes, you have to change the system totally, from the top down. Evolution no longer works. If you want change, it's time to become revolutionary. By the turn of 1985, Michael Eisner was set to do just that. The honeymoon was over.

8

1985—The Year of Starting Over

Late in January 1985, on a podium at the Academy of Television Arts and Sciences, Michael Eisner told the academy the story of Bongo the Bear. Among the audience were Barry Diller, the chairman of 20th Century Fox, and just four months before Eisner's boss; Bob Daly, head of Warner Brothers; Lew Wasserman, head of MCA, owner of Universal Studios; Brandon Tartikoff, head of NBC; Bud Grant, head of CBS; Lew Erlicht and Tony Thomopoulos, who together ran his alma mater ABC. In fact, Eisner pointed out, it could have been one of the most prestigious gatherings in Hollywood history with one exception: there was no one there from Paramount.

In 1930, Sinclair Lewis wrote a short story about Bongo the circus bear running away to the wild life of the forest, suffering from the unexpected rain and frost and battling against the big bad bear of the wilderness, Lumpjaw. In 1947, Disney made an animated film called *Fun and Fancy Free* based on the story. In the Disney version, Bongo of course vanquished Lumpjaw, discovered the biggest honey tree in the forest, and lived happily ever after.

To Eisner, retelling the story with all its color and detail, this was not just a Disney story—it was the story of Disney. Like Bongo, Disney had to end its isolation. Like the "smart and lively" Bongo, Disney "can no longer be content alone in Burbank, caged by its previous success. We must climb over the Santa Monica mountains to Century City."

Bongo, he said, must "go to lunch with Lew Erlicht, breakfast with Brandon Tartikoff and dinner with Bud Grant. Bongo must ally himself with Lew Wasserman, Barry Diller and Bob Daly to protect his woods against a Tony Thomopoulos who wants a bigger share of the honey. Frankly, Bongo must go Hollywood."

Los Angeles Times writer Michael London curtly noted in his report on the speech, "One thing seems clear: If Disney's new film slate is as corny as Eisner's speech, it could be bedtime for Bongo." The industry assumptions about corny-dusty-cheap Disney were alive and well, and Eisner's speech did nothing to kill them off. He had only been on the job about a hundred days and, except for an unusual flurry of pronouncements, nothing startlingly new had come out of the Disney lot. Hollywood still did not know what to make of the new team on Mickey Avenue. But, although his listeners could not tell yet, Eisner was, in fact, turning the crank, starting up a powerful engine—1985 would be the year he would build a new Disney on the chassis of the old.

His first asset was his relationship with Frank Wells. They worked well together, it turned out. "There's no more fun in this world than this company," Wells said. "Michael and I are still like two little kids. We call each other up and say, 'Listen to this!' "

Wells was the perfect complement to Eisner's lightning intelligence and unfettered imagination. He was quick, too, but his was a practical and thorough intelligence. While Eisner played the visionary, Wells became the operations man. He rolled up his sleeves and began digging into the company, going over the books, questioning assumptions, getting into the details. "When he came to imagineering to go over the books," Randy Bright later recalled, "we had a line for new filters for the air conditioners. He went out to see them. He wanted to be sure they were dirty."

He was, at the same time, more conservative than Eisner in many ways, a stronger voice for tradition. He would even go out of his way to vigorously defend the old management, calling them bold risk-takers: "There's much less risk-taking today than there was in the 15 years or so since Walt's death. There isn't a modern practitioner of the somewhat arcane art of business-school management that would have ever built EPCOT. There probably aren't very many people who fall in that category who would have started the Disney Channel. . . . The people who went before us put in place assets that I don't think we would ever have the guts to do, I really don't. And we're the inheritors of those. You would never build EPCOT if you sat there and brooded over a pro forma [projection of future financial expectations]. You probably wouldn't have started the Disney Channel if you knew you were going to spend over $100 million to put it into place before you ever broke even, let alone earned back the investment. And if you were really wedded to the past you wouldn't have invented a new name and logo for a new movie division, so to speak, called Touchstone. They did all those things. We're just here to build on them."

Eisner was careful never to denigrate Disney's old management, and even praised them publicly. But in fact their complacency set Eisner's teeth on edge. "They were still making Don Knotts movies," was the way he put it. After three months getting his bearings, he now set about renewing the company from the top down, sometimes by setting people free from their assumptions, sometimes by setting them free from their jobs.

Eisner and Wells began cleaning house, weeding out dead and useless projects that consumed capital and energy (Wells called them "black holes"), and people who they felt were not going to contribute. They went through the company "with a strong rake," according to Wells. Eisner's chief housecleaner was Jeff Rochlis, hired by Eisner with the title of senior vice president of finance and administration. Behind his back he was called Eisner's "hatchet man," as he did the dirty work, going from department to department, reorganizing and inviting resignations. It was work the chairman needed done, and didn't have to do himself. By mid-1985, an estimated 1,000 Disney employees had been shown the door.

At the same time, Eisner brought more than 60 new executives into the company, most of them from Paramount. He had the western set and the "Zorro" set ripped out of the back lot and replaced with quick clapboard office buildings and trailers to house all the new executive offices. People began calling Disney "Paramount in the Valley." Eisner referred to himself as Disney's personnel director, and said that his most challenging task was "putting together a crack executive team." His most valuable talent, he said, was "pretty good judgment in finding people that are talented. . . . One of the keys to success is having people who are all better than you."

Eisner dubbed the growing crew brought in to run the company "Team Disney." The once sleepy and chummy company headquarters acquired an entire night-shift secretarial team to cope with the 18-hour-a-day outpouring of memos, letters, contracts, and proposals from the cheerfully fevered executives. The executive parking lot filled most days by 8 A.M.; at 8 P.M. half the cars were still there. In the first nine months after he took charge the company issued 40 press releases—more than one a week—announcing contract signings, new personnel, film projects, and coming attractions.

Eisner was doing more than making a lot of motion for motion's sake. He was also doing more than exploiting the assets that were already in place, as he claimed to be doing. In fact, Eisner was laying the basis for a grand vision of Disney as an international entertainment conglomerate built, paradoxically, on the values of a close family. He gave the clearest evidence for this in a personnel move that provoked little notice at the time. Eisner was running a company that, until recently, had no business plan. It still had no strategic planners on the staff, and few people with the necessary business school training to run financial analyses of potential new businesses, acquisitions, or cash flow problems. Eisner needed a strategic planning department, headed by a chief financial officer with extraordinarily wide vision. He found one through Al Checchi.

Working out of a second-floor office in the animation building, Checchi spun out ideas for Eisner and tried to put together what he saw as advantageous deals. Among other ideas, Checchi led Eisner and Wells into thinking about selling and leasing back some of the company's hotels, and entering into agreements with companies that knew hotel management. This led to first to a February 1985 conference of futurists at Disney World's vast A-frame Contemporary Resort, where such writers and thinkers as urban planner James Rouse and author John Naisbitt (*Megatrends*) discussed ideas for the future use of the Disney World property. Checchi then took Eisner to the Maryland suburbs of Washington, D.C., to meet his old boss, Bill Marriott.

There were possible synergies to explore between Disney, a mismanaged entertainment franchise that happened to own tens of thousands of hotel rooms and hundreds of thousands of restaurant seats, and Marriott, whose expertise lay in hotel and restaurant management. Prompted by its chief financial officer, Gary Wilson, Marriott had in fact approached Steinberg the year before to explore the possibility of participating in the takeover—to the tune of $200 million—and buying Disney's Orlando hotels. Checchi now focused on hotels because of his background at Marriott, but also because of the clear opportunity at Disney World—at a time when hotels nationwide usually sold about 45 percent of their rooms and hotels in Orlando managed to sell 68 percent, the Disney World hotels usually sold about 98 percent. And resort hotel rooms traditionally had a profit margin that hovered somewhere above 60 percent, three times the profit margin of most other Disney operations.

Checchi already had a plan cooking that would make Marriott and Disney joint venture partners in a vast complex at Disney World that would include 20,000 hotel rooms and a convention center. But Eisner had another interest: for months already, he had sent headhunters scouring the country for a crack chief financial officer. After several near misses, and after hearing the headhunters and Checchi repeatedly say, "You need someone like Gary Wilson," Eisner was more than eager to meet the Marriott CFO.

When they met, Eisner saw what he needed: a crack financial mind that could lay the groundwork for a company with global reach, many times the size of the company he was trying to resuscitate. He soon offered Wilson Michael Bagnall's job as Disney's chief financial officer, with a $500,000 salary and a stock option plan that would in time make him the highest-paid CFO in American corporate history and an independently wealthy man. By August, Bagnall was gone and Wilson was on board at Disney.

Wilson presented himself as the unflappable deal-maker, cool and cerebral. Like Eisner and Wells, Wilson was a tall, thin man. Aloof, the stoic Spock to Eisner's happy child, he moved with his wife Susan into a home in Beverly Hills and bought a $1.6-million beach house in Malibu, just down the road from Frank Wells and Ron Miller, where he could take his recreation jogging by the surf line or reading on the porch. One man who worked for him called Wilson "the ultimate rational man. He's like a laser beam." Another compared presenting a proposal to his merciless logical scrutiny with "going up against a shotgun blast." He complemented Eisner and Wells: Eisner the visionary—creative, warm, energetic, upbeat; Wells the manager, overseeing budgets and real estate and riding herd on the company; Wilson the hard edge, crisp and cynical, questioning, patrician. Eisner, who dressed as often as not like someone out of a J. Crew catalogue, contrasted oddly to Wilson, who was given to tailored suits and silk ties that matched the hankie poofing out of his coat pocket.

Wilson brought a particular rigor and ferocity to the process, which sprang not only from his knowledge and experience, but from his personality. Wilson had read Machiavelli's *The Prince* three times, and it often seemed like it had not been idle reading. Like Katzenberg, he wanted to know everything, and he usually managed to. He planned far in advance. He had a poker player's sense of timing. An avid card player in high school, Wilson liked to say, "Business is very much like a poker game. Luck is part of it. But it's more how you play your cards. A good poker player will tend to win every time he plays."

According to one person who bargained with him, "He's one of the toughest negotiators I've ever encountered. He's sort of relentless." As Wells put it, "He doesn't wear down." Checchi said of him, "In every sense of the word he was my mentor. . . . He's the guy you want to be in a foxhole with. You know he wouldn't ever give up." According to Checchi, Wilson begins negotiations by presuming that "he deserves it all. He'll get the other guy to agree to things you'd blush to ask for."

He was well schooled, a graduate of Duke and Wharton, the West Point of the business set. But his real education as a deal-maker may have come from two more earthy sources: those high-school poker games and, more important, the sugar traders of the Philippines. Hired out of Wharton by a Washington-based business consulting firm owned by Al Checchi's father and uncle, he was packed off to Manila to manage the finances of the Trans-Philippine Investment Company during the early years of the Marcos regime. There, the wet-behind-the-ears businessman from one of the world's best business schools was astonished by the skill of the Chinese sugar traders he dealt with. He quickly discovered why they were so good: they had information. They knew where every *pical* (sack) of sugar in the island nation was located—how many, in which warehouse, from which refinery, what the supply was, what the demand was.

In this rough-and-tumble school, he learned first-hand about leveraged buyouts. He joined a group of local businessmen in buying a small agribusiness conglomerate on borrowed money. "Our goal," he has said, "was to improve operations, sell assets, and pay down the debt. We sold a cement plant, a jute bag factory, and a small sugar mill. We used the cash flow from one large sugar mill to repay debts and buy the biggest construction company in Southeast Asia. Today the company is one of the best managed and most profitable in the Philippines."

After his stint in the Philippines, Wilson joined Marriott in 1974, and eventually became its chief financial officer. At Marriott, Wilson was one of the leaders of a movement in the 1980s that shifted the role of America's corporate financial officers away from mere accounting into more strategic concerns.

Wilson made an important strategic distinction: Marriott knew how to run hotels. That was its strength. Yet much of its cash and its debt capacity were tied up not in running hotels, but in owning them. Wilson's plan was to sell off the properties to tax-sheltered limited partnerships, and take back a management fee for running them. The plan freed up cash and debt capacity for unparalleled growth, and set a major new pattern for the industry. As a result, Marriott's earnings tripled and its return on equity nearly tripled between 1975 to 1980. In a capital-intensive, capital-hungry industry, Marriott grew rapidly, at a pace greater than 20 percent per year for the decade Wilson worked there, increasing its market value from $200 million to $5 billion.

Because of his background at Marriott, the financial press speculated that Wilson's chief role at Disney would be the development of investor-financed hotels on the Florida property. But Eisner's hopes for him, and his eventual role, proved to be far more important than that. He eventually brought a dozen people with him from Marriott to form the core of a financial management and strategic planning team that was nimble, aggressive, and capable of powerful, multilevel analysis. This ability would prove crucial to Eisner in the years to come.

The eyes of Hollywood, however, were not on Wilson, but on Jeff Katzenberg. Still only 34 years old, Katzenberg was a ten-year veteran of the Hollywood wars. His instructions were simple. Referring to such blockbuster heartwarmers and adventure stories from other studios as *Raiders of the Lost Ark*, *Star Wars*, *Karate Kid*, and *E.T.*, Eisner told Katzenberg, "Everyone else has been making Disney films except Disney. Bring them in." Over time, Eisner expected Katzenberg to expand production from the four or five feature films per year that Disney had been doing, to the level of the major studios—15 or more per year. At the same time, Team Disney planned to speed up the schedule of rereleasing classics, crank up animation, shorten schedules, reduce budgets, fill the pipeline with new projects, plunge into the video market, and expand in the cable television markets. Katzenberg would be the power driver of all this expansion.

If Katzenberg's frenetic energy mirrored and even outpaced that of his boss, in another way they were opposites: Katzenberg, at the core, had a methodical calm, an anchoring. He played everything by rules, and reduced the variables to a minimum.

For instance, on May 20, 1985, principal photography began on the new regime's first film, *Down and Out in Beverly Hills*. The principals were talented people, but Katzenberg could get them cheap because their careers were going nowhere at the moment. The town joke had Katzenberg waiting outside the doors of the Betty Ford substance abuse clinic to catch stars on the way out. After appearing in three of the highest-grossing films of all time (*American Graffiti*, *Jaws*, and *Close Encounters of the Third Kind*) and winning an Oscar for his part in *The Goodbye Girl*, Richard Dreyfuss had hit the skids, becoming addicted to cocaine and at one point smashing up his car in a one-sided argument with a tree. Midler, after an Oscar nomination for *The Rose*, had bombed in *Jinxed* and gotten a reputation as someone who was impossible to work with. Her career needed resuscitation. Midler, who became a mainstay of the new Disney, said, "Even when I was down on my luck they felt I could make a good picture." But they also knew a deal when they saw one. Katzenberg got her to sign for only $600,000, with no percentage of the profits. Dreyfuss got paid a mere $300,000, one-quarter of his asking price. Katzenberg was controlling the variables—in this case, costs.

Ruthless People followed a similar pattern. The film's first announcement shocked Disney-watchers, not so much because of its potential "R" rating as its announced star: Madonna was already known as a shock-and-schlock Marilyn Monroe wanna-be. Robert and Marlene Hughes of Woodland Hills wrote to the *Los Angeles Times*: "Oh, give us a break, already!!! Madonna??? In a Disney film??? Isn't that a little, um, shall we say, uh, inappropriate, perhaps? How about downright stupid????? A little like Fritz the Cat co-starring with Mickey?" Madonna, however, stuck by her demand for $1 million, a fee Eisner and Katzenberg would not pay. They turned again to Midler, whose first Disney film was still in production, and signed her for a second one at the same price. By that time, though, *Ruthless People* had already accomplished its first purpose—working a powerful symbolic shift on Disney's image in the industry.

"Controlling the variables" also applied to financing. Wells' negotiations with Roland Betts at Silver Screen Partners had provided Eisner and Katzenberg with a new way to spread the risks of film-making—or "rationalize" them, as they say on Wall Street. In the spring of 1985, Silver Screen created its first limited partnership for Disney, called "Silver Screen Partners II," to be sold through the E. F. Hutton brokerage houses. Starting on May 1, Eisner dispatched traveling Disney shows, complete with dancing characters and video clips, to E. F. Hutton brokers' meetings across the country.

The terms of the offering were unusual. In effect, investors gave five-year interest-free loans to Disney through the partnership for financing particular films. In return, the investors got a share of the profits, but only after everyone else had been paid off. If the films were not profitable, in five years Disney would simply give them their money back and say goodbye. The partners' money was safe as long as Disney remained solvent, and their potential profit was enormous. At the same time Disney got a pool of cash with which to produce films, at no cost except a share in potential profits.

Eventually Silver Screen Partners II brought Disney $193 million; Silver Screen Partners III brought in $300 million; and Silver Screen Partners IV brought $400 million—a total of nearly $1 billion in interest-free loans to underwrite Disney's costs of production.

Keeping the costs down and spreading the risks were important, but Eisner and Katzenberg were willing to stretch the formula to get the kind of occasional blockbuster film that would make them heavy hitters in Hollywood. Early in 1985, for instance, they responded to a suggestion from Michael Ovitz, Eisner's close friend and, as head of Creative Artists Agency, one of the most powerful agents in Hollywood. The project Ovitz suggested, called *The Color of Money*, was a "package." Packages were not in Disney's style, but this was a particularly attractive one. The hook was Paul Newman, in a sequel to his stellar 1961 performance in *The Hustler*, teamed with Tom Cruise, a current major heartthrob. Eisner and Katzenberg would have to pay high salaries and percentages to both of the stars, but they went for the package anyway in the hopes of creating the new Disney's first major hit.

In the summer of 1985, Katzenberg also went after what seemed at the time a less promising idea: a comedy/drama about the Vietnam War, starring Robin Williams, to be called *Good Morning, Vietnam.* Americans had still not quite gotten settled about the Vietnam War; the subject was a kind of quicksand into which entire films had sunk. And Williams, a manic standup comic whom audiences had loved as an extraterrestrial in the late-1970s television series *Mork and Mindy*, had made seven films with no real hit and some embarrassing bombs. The whole package was a serious risk, but Eisner and Katzenberg went for it, paying Williams half of his $2-million asking price, plus 10 percent of profits. Like Dreyfuss and Midler, Williams was another great talent who was not doing so well at the moment. If he was given the right backing, he might turn a corner.

"I think what motivates [Katzenberg and his people] is the opportunity to grow very quickly," said Randy Bright. "If you strut your stuff and you do well, you can move awfully quickly. You can get film deals with Katzenberg. He'll take more chances on new talent in Hollywood than anybody that I know of. He even takes chances on people that haven't done anything." One of his hard-driving new creative affairs executives, Lou Camer, was all of 19. Phil Joanou, 24, was fresh out of USC film school. Katzenberg and Spielberg saw his thesis film, a short called *Last*

Chance Dance. Katzenberg thought it showed "a lot of skill and real spark." Spielberg hired him to direct a segment of his "Amazing Stories" television series. Katzenberg gave him a contract, an office, and money to write three screenplays, with clauses in the contract that allowed him to direct if Disney picked up the films. According to Joanou, who had until recently been eating at Taco Bell and writing at the La Cañada Library, Katzenberg also took the time to teach him the nuts and bolts of Hollywood: "How development works, who makes decisions, what makes this business tick."

To Katzenberg, his job was about relationships. He'll call when he needs you. He'll also call when you need him. When screenwriter Joe Ezterhas noisily split with powerful agent Michael Ovitz, with Ovitz allegedly threatening that Ezterhas would never get work again, Katzenberg called and asked to make a deal with him right then for whatever his next project might be. When director Jim Abrahams' Malibu home was wrecked by a storm and began sliding into the Pacific, Katzenberg called unasked and offered to advance him the money to buy another house.

"It's as important for him to be friends with you as it is to make that deal," says lawyer-manager Steve Sauer. "He'll crack you up, just the way this guy has so much enthusiasm for it. It's not done with any type of negativity. He's not a screamer. There are never any threats. There is never any of this pounding of a fist on a table. It is pure enthusiasm with a boyish grin that comes attached with him. But he'll find you, you know. He'll call you, send you baskets, he'll do whatever he has to do to make sure he's in front of you to have an honest shot at having your services, whether you're an actor, a writer, a director, or a producer."

It was just another level of "Ask and thank. Ask and thank. Make connections. Do what needs to be done." When the Creative Artists Agency went to the desert for a weekend retreat, Katzenberg sent them a pickup truck loaded with cake and ice cream. When he was after director Martin Brest, who had done *Beverly Hills Cop* for Eisner at Paramount, he heard that Brest had complained to a friend that he gains weight between projects. The next morning Brest came to the door to find a bathtub-sized collection of cakes and muffins. Attached to it was a note saying that he would get another such pile of bakery goodies every day until he committed to directing a Disney movie. As Sauer puts it, Katzenberg is capable of "calling you 16 times during the day. If you don't return the call he'll probably end up walking in your door. He'll find out what restaurant you're in and make sure a bottle of wine is sent over there with a note on it that is on his stationery. He gets things done immediately."

Katzenberg also amplified Eisner's willingness to go off the lot for talent. Veteran Disney producers and writers were let go right and left, and Katzenberg began to make quick deals with outside talent, long-term deals that brought instant credibility to Disney as a new emerging studio. By mid-year he had signed Lauren Schuler, Bette Midler, Cindy Williams, writer Dan Petrie, Jr. (*Beverly Hills Cop*), and Paul Mazursky, as well as Jim Abrahams and the Zucker brothers, Jerry and David, the trio who had made *Airplane!* for Eisner at Paramount. "The contract requires us to make 23 pictures about lost dogs in 24 months," Abrahams joked to the *Los Angeles Times*. Katzenberg also signed production deals with Interscope Communications and Sam Goldwyn, Jr.

Pursuing talented people and persuading them to enter long-term but flexible contracts with Disney were essential to Katzenberg and Eisner's strategy. It was unusual, almost a throwback to another era, to put actors and writers under long-term contract. They hired more than 30 script writers in the first year alone, paying them $75,000 salaries to help develop the studio's own ideas.

Putting producers under exclusive or semiexclusive contract, on the other hand, was right in the Hollywood mainstream, and within the first year Eisner and Katzenberg signed on more than a dozen producers. One of them, David Bombyk, commented on the arrangement: "Because you can only take projects to them, you are almost a part of the staff. It's to their advantage to use your talents, and in this case they made me feel like part of the family. . . . By making this kind of deal, there is a basic understanding of taste and the way you do business. You are forming a pact." He contrasted it with working independently: "Inevitably, what happens is you wind up spending 20 percent of your time in meetings and 80 percent of your time driving between the various lots."

But such arrangements guaranteed nothing to either side. Nothing Bombyk worked on was produced while he was at Disney, and after a year and a half he was gone, partly because Katzenberg and the other Disnoids liked to come up with their own ideas and get people working on them. According to one former Disney executive, "These producers go in and pitch [ideas] over and over again, and they [Disney executives] don't say yes to anything. There is one producer there who has literally pitched about 30 times and never gotten a yes. They brought these producers on the lot but they don't always trust their judgment. The philosophy is,

'You're going to do what we want to do.' " So many veteran producers shied away from Katzenberg's carrots, and did business with Disney one project at a time.

When they wanted people, Eisner and Katzenberg went after them with ferocity. Katzenberg once called top agent Sam Cohn. Cohn wouldn't take his call. Katzenberg had his secretary dial Cohn every ten minutes all day long until Cohn got on the line. Steve Tisch, who had produced *Risky Business*, got on a flight to Dallas and discovered that his seatmates in first class were Eisner and Katzenberg, who were going to see Sid Bass. All through the flight they pummeled him with their vision of what was possible at Disney. "Their enthusiasm was really contagious," Tisch said later. "I got off that plane feeling like the eighth dwarf. If they had asked me to put on a mouse suit and go work at Disneyland, I probably would have done it." He did sign, to produce *Big Business*.

Katzenberg's management style was so hands-on, it has been variously described as a "choke-hold" and a "walking straitjacket." His production executives would report by cellular phone right from the set, and Katzenberg would call the directors with ideas, scribble additions and changes in the scripts he constantly read, and send writers as many as 30 single-spaced pages of notes on a script— "more than any other studio in town," according to one writer. "Sometimes they take it to the point of idiocy."

Katzenberg consulted Eisner on every project, and deferred to his ideas. They had honed their instincts together at Paramount. At Paramount, both Eisner and his boss Barry Diller had been disparaged originally as "TV guys," and their ability to pick good films had been questioned. But they turned out to have the hottest hands in the business at picking commercial films. "The truth is," Eisner claimed, "all that television training was a big help to me. That's because of the voracious appetite of the TV schedule: You have to produce good ideas, and lots of them."

Eisner's method of picking a hit was, as he confessed, a bit hard to describe, "but you know when it's there. It's the script you put on top of the pile at your bedside, the one which confirms that the grass is greener on the other side. To me, the familiar is boring, excessive violence is antisocial, and stupid is just stupid." He jovially admits to stealing ideas. He calls himself "a complete thief. If my wife has an idea, if my son has an idea. . . ."

He would grab ideas anywhere. "I've gotten ideas from everyone—

from taxi cab drivers on the way to the airport to a checker at Ralph's. My mother's hairdresser has even given us ideas." He grabbed Jim ("Hey, Vern!") Varney in Indianapolis. Memorial Day 1986 found Eisner in the stands for the Indianapolis 500: "There was a parade . . . 500,000 people there. The governor went by—applause. The mayor—applause. Mickey Mouse went by—more applause. All of a sudden, Jim Varney went by, and 500,000 people went berserk. So I said, 'We ought to do something about that.' " The moment turned into a contract and, eventually, a movie: *Ernest Goes to Camp*.

The speed of Eisner and Katzenberg's decisions became legendary in Hollywood. Brian Grazer came over the hill to Burbank to talk to Eisner and Katzenberg. He had directed *Splash*, Disney's most successful film since Walt died, and they were interested in a sequel. They pulled him into one of the still-empty offices in the animation building to knock it around. In the middle of the conversation he brought up another idea, which he called *The Last Secret*. According to Grazer, "Five minutes into the pitch, they said, 'That sounds great. That's fantastic. Let's do it.' The next day the papers were drawn up. It was like magic." Screenwriter-producer-director Dan Petrie, Jr., who ended up with a $1.5-million, three-picture deal with Disney, said, "If you turn in a script on a Friday, by Monday they have suggestions for the rewrite. At other studios, they'll pay you $200,000 to write a script and then wait six months after you deliver it to let you know what they thought of it." As Brest put it, "The intention [at Disney] is to make movies, and not overponder them. The important thing is to get out and do it."

By mid-1985, while the last grand projects of the ancien régime (*Baby*, *Return to Oz*, and *The Black Cauldron*) were disappearing into a cinematic black hole, Katzenberg and company had 75 new projects in development. Eager to make a mark on prime time, Disney had also bankrolled a television series called "The Golden Girls" for Witt–Thomas–Harris. But in order to bring such a prime production team to sign, Katzenberg had been forced to break one of his dearest rules: he gave up all creative control. For this production, Disney acted as little more than a specialized bank. By October, "The Golden Girls," with a story line at once steamy and geriatric featuring the antics of four older women roommates in a Miami apartment, had proven an instant hit on NBC—the only new hit series that fall.

By November, under former Paramount syndication guru Robert Jacquemin, Disney salesmen had hit the road with television syndication packages under their arms. They were offering a careful selection of the contents of the vault, which the old management had guarded like the crown jewels. The packages included such Disney classics as *Dumbo*, *Splash*, *20,000 Leagues under the Sea* and *Mary Poppins*, plus 29 years of "The Wonderful World of Disney." And a new version of that Sunday-night series would be on ABC early in the new year. Eisner and Katzenberg had taken Eisner's old boss at ABC, Leonard Goldenson, to lunch, and pitched it to him. Goldenson offered Eisner $20 million for the series. This "flagship" show was part of the overall strategy to sell Disney to the consumers and to Wall Street, to give Disney, once more, a living face.

A most special challenge for the new Disney lay in animation, Disney's métier, its key to the hearts of the world, the soul of the company. The animation department had been floundering. It had not produced a hit movie—what the company liked to call a "classic"—in decades. Animators at Disney and elsewhere were convinced that the golden age of animated story-telling was well behind them. There had been a boom in 1980 and 1981, when more animated features had been in production throughout the industry than ever before in the history of the medium, including Disney's *The Fox and the Hound* and *The Black Cauldron*; Hanna Barbera's *Heidi's Song*; and Sullivan Bluth's *The Secret of NIMH*. But that had faded under the pressure of the 1982 Screen Cartoonists Guild strike and a series of box-office bombs, including *Twice upon a Time*; *Hey Good Lookin'*; *Fire and Ice*; *Bon Voyage, Charlie Brown (and Don't Come Back)*; *1001 Rabbit Tales*; and *Daffy Duck's Movie: Fantastic Island*—all of them from other studios than Disney.

By early 1985, many of the young animators at Disney were pinning their hopes on the studio's movie *The Black Cauldron*. In production since 1980 and in development for six years before that, the $25-million sword-and-sorcery epic—the most expensive animated feature ever—represented their hope for a *Snow White* that would launch their careers and revive their industry. Producer Joe Hale said of it, "My fantasy has always been to do a picture that's as good as anything Walt ever did."

Eisner and Katzenberg were not yet convinced that Disney animation could survive. The studio executives actively debated whether to keep it alive or sell it off. It was an expensive and slow way to make films, and maybe it was a way whose time had passed, even at Disney. Roy Disney was determined to keep the tradition alive, and he made that determination known.

Keeping the animation workshop going as a museum to Walt might have been sweet and noble. But the arguments for reviving animation went way beyond the mere sentimental. They were pure box office: only 50-odd animated features had ever been produced in the United States, but 22 of them had found places on *Variety's* list of the top 100 grosses of all time. Furthermore, animated classics have a staying power enjoyed by few live films. *Pinocchio*, for instance, had actually lost money in its opening run in 1940. But over the years it had garnered $40 million at the box office in five releases, and when the company put it out in rerelease for Christmas of 1984, it added another $15 million in its first 12 days and $24 million for the whole run. Besides what it could reap at the box office, animation provided much greater opportunities than live action for creating characters that could be sold a hundred different ways, from videos to lunchpails to rides at the parks.

For the present, Eisner and Katzenberg were willing to give it a try. If animation was to succeed, though, costs would have to be brought down and the speed of production would have to be stepped up from one feature every three or four years to one every year and a half, then one every year, if it was possible. Since it took at least three years—and often four or five—to produce just one film, this meant both gearing up to produce several at once, and using new techniques, some of them computer-based, to cut the production time.

Katzenberg had never dealt with animation, but he had a strong story sense, according to animator David Block. "That's basic film-making. You haven't got diddly squat without a good story." Disney had been founded by a master storyteller, and the studio's animation system had been built around him. There had been no scripts for the animated films, just sketches pinned up on a board for Walt to act out—and he was a vivid actor. That tradition had continued after Walt's death, but without the master storyteller. Eisner and Katzenberg were appalled. How could you spend millions of dollars on a movie and never see a script? They wanted scripts.

"I didn't understand it," Eisner said. "The story boards were not particularly interesting, and didn't hold together. All the things I learned in English 101 about beginning, middle, denouement, and structure were not there. And then the more I've been here, the more I hear what a fantastic storyteller Walt Disney was. He could mesmerize a room with his storytelling. He could mesmerize children. I finally realized that there was a script, but it was an oral script. Walt Disney would tell a story, and they wrote it down. The process was great. But we don't have anybody here now who can tell a story the way Walt Disney could. So we are going to go outside and hire a writer. If we had Walt Disney, we wouldn't need anybody else. If I could do what Walt Disney could do, we could save a fortune in scripts."

But at the first meetings they went with what they had, which was story boards, the more succinct outline boards, and story reels, which are films of sketches and a rough sound track, with the animators filling in the voices.

While *The Black Cauldron* had ground forward, Ron Clements, a young strawberry-bearded animator with a decade of Disney experience, had been working away with a few other young animators, including John Musker, on *Basil of Baker Street*, an animated sendup of Sherlock Holmes scheduled for release in 1987. They had been working on it for nearly three years already, in between other projects. They had created outlines; they had done some casting, a little animation, and lots of story boards. They had met with Roy Disney soon after the takeover, and he had made encouraging noises about the project. But now suddenly they had to meet with Eisner and Katzenberg ("We'd never heard of Jeffrey Katzenberg," said Clements) and pitch the show as if it were a brand new idea. It was frightening. It is common in a studio shakeup for the new management to toss out everything the old management has initiated to make way for the new guy's projects, and for fear the old guy's projects could be embarrassingly successful. They could easily have said, "Forget it," and tossed aside years of planning and drawing.

Roy Disney was at the meeting to discuss *Basil*, as were Eisner and Katzenberg. Clements, Musker, and animation producer Burny Mattinson had been asked to present the project. Mattinson paced the executives through the outline board (actually three or four story boards, typically four by eight feet, pinned with drawings and scraps of dialogue), then showed a story reel.

Neither Eisner nor Katzenberg had ever judged an animated feature film before. For Eisner it was a 15-year trip back to his days at ABC; but holding a sleepy five-year-old's attention for 22 minutes on television on a Saturday morning is completely different from holding the attention of a mixed audience, at $5 a person, for 90 minutes in a theater. But Eisner watched it like any other film—he looked for the story.

Katzenberg asked questions. Why are they doing it this way, what if you broke up that long scene, how would they handle the relationship of the Sherlock-like mouse detective with the human Sherlock? The animators began to feel relieved. At least these men spoke the language of storytelling. They seemed to understand.

Eisner said, "That part with the song. You know, we're working with Michael Jackson on this thing at the parks. I'll bet we could get him to do the song." There was an uncomfortable silence as the animators looked at each other. Eisner laughed, and said, "If you think it stinks, say so. Your job is to talk us out of bad ideas."

The animators left the meeting with a go-ahead for *Basil*, and something more startling: the intimation that their new bosses, far from reining in their creativity, would be likely to outrun them. As another animator, George Scribner, would later put it, "I'm really stimulated by the powers that be. There's a lot more in development, there's a lot more ideas being tossed around."

One Saturday in the early months of 1985, everybody involved with animation gathered in a conference room on the lot for a "gong show" on animation. The format had become the favored means to jump-start a division or a project that needed new life. If the Disney animation department were to survive, it would need a lot of ideas that had box-office potential. Wells was a fervent admirer of Eisner's gong shows, saying, "I have never seen such an interchange and interplay of ideas. Good ideas rise to the surface, and you must not ever feel inhibited to do that. . . . One of the things we've stood for is a good idea. . . . If it's there, you know it, you feel it, you do it, no matter where it comes from."

Eisner came to the animation "gong show," and Katzenberg, and Roy Disney, and the top animators. Everyone was told to bring five ideas to the table. Ron Clements brought five ideas, each neatly typed up in a two-page treatment. He had rooted around in old books of fairy tales, as was his habit. In Hildebrandt's *Fairy Tales* he had found Hans Christian Andersen's story, "The Little Mermaid." Andersen's visual, cinematic writing excited Clements as he flipped the pages. He began to imagine what could be done with underwater animation scenes. But "The Little Mermaid" was such a dour story. "It starts out sad, and then it gets sadder and sadder and sadder, then she dies," he thought. So he had put his feet up on the desk, doodled a bit, made some notes, and began to work out a more upbeat story. He was getting excited, and he was wondering whether these new guys would go for it.

Clements was used to the leisurely way ideas were treated under the old regime: you submitted them and you waited. Weeks would go by, sometimes months, while the idea got tossed from desk to desk, from one committee to another. And often as not, when the answer came back, it was "maybe."

So when he got to the gong show he was surprised at the rapid-fire tossing and batting of ideas around the table. It was like batting practice: toss 'em up there, strike, ball, out of the park, foul—fairy tales, classic stories, comic characters, even "Li'l Abner." In the midst of the gongs, the rejects, the ideas that Katzenberg would sometimes refer to as "anteaters" or "bow-wows," some flew up that stuck: a sequel to *The Rescuers*, for instance, and *Oliver Twist* as a musical, starring dogs and cats (an idea Katzenberg suggested himself). Suddenly all eyes were on Clements and Eisner was asking, "All right, you brought five ideas, what's your best one?"

Clements said, " 'The Little Mermaid.' "

Eisner said, "Nope. Too close to *Splash*."

Clements was disappointed. It was a mermaid story, but it was completely different from *Splash*. "But I wrote a treatment. Two pages. Would you. . . ."

Eisner said, "Sure, we'll take a look at your ideas, but I think we're going to pass on the mermaid."

As the meeting broke up, Eisner and Katzenberg left with an armful of ideas. Monday morning the phone rang in Clements' office. It was Katzenberg, going rapid-fire down the list of his ideas, tossing them aside, boom-boom-boom—except the mermaid. After reading the treatment, he and Eisner both liked the mermaid.

Clements put the phone down, stunned at the speed of these guys.

Clements' next surprise was not such a pleasant one: Eisner and Katzenberg expected the same speed of everyone else, as well. The new orders for *Basil* were to cut the budget and move the release date up to the summer of 1986—a little over a year away. *Black Cauldron* was going to cost over $25 million, but *Basil* would have to come in at less than half that. "It felt real scary," Clements said. "The first reaction was, 'That's impossible!' We were used to working a certain way. There's a certain amount of footage that has to be done." But at the same time the animators felt they had to show Eisner that they could produce animated films for a reasonable amount of money. And, after all, they reasoned, *Basil* wasn't *Cauldron*. It was "animals with clothes on," the easiest kind of animation, easier than the realistic animals of *Bambi* or *Lady and the Tramp*, and far easier than the realistic humans that had been required for *Snow White* and would be required for *The Little Mermaid*. Nonetheless, the pressure was on.

More dismaying yet was the news that on the first of February, the animation department was being moved off the studio lot, out of the Disney temple, four miles across town to some nondescript tilt-slab warehouses hard by the freeway in Glendale. This was almost as unsettling as the news that the new television animation work was going to be sent overseas. Animator Jane Baer expressed the fears of many Disney artists when she said, "[The new management] are stressing the live action more so than the animation. The animators have been made to feel like second-class citizens."

In July 1985 *The Black Cauldron* came out and turned belly up. It could not carry the animators' dreams, because it did not excite the audience. The critics admitted that it was beautiful. Charles Champlin, the *Los Angeles Times* redoubtable critic, celebrated the film's "shimmering reflections, its flocks of birds in flight, its play of light and shadow and its full-figure motion," its "effects even richer and subtler" than earlier Disney work. But the story lacked "the simplicity and the clarity" or "the child-sized wonder" such a film needed. Apparently the audience agreed with the critics, and stayed away. At the same moment, the *Care Bears* movie was released by a rival studio. It made the same amount of money at the box offices as *Cauldron* but cost very little to make. "Everyone was kind of scared about the future of Disney animation," said Clements. "It wasn't a good time. It was really a terrible time."

Eisner's strategy for animated television series was equally challenging: first, he wanted to get one or two shows going against the competition on Saturday morning. Later, he wanted to expand into the weekday afternoons. Eventually this would become "The Disney Afternoon," a two-hour block of four half-hour shows, sold as a package. And every year, just to keep them fresh, one of the four series would be replaced with a new one.

By January 1985, Eisner had already personally sold "The Tales of the Gummi Bears" to NBC (where it would eventually become the number-one show on Saturday morning, year after year); "The Wuzzles" had been sold to CBS. Ironically, they would compete against each other in the same time slot. Animator David Block found himself on a plane to Japan, with an order to start up and oversee the work of a Japanese animation company that would ink the shows. According to Block, "It was without a doubt the most ambitious thing I had ever laid my eyes on for a Saturday morning project."

Animators back home grumbled about shipping work overseas, and were deeply concerned about the quality of the work. Baer, who was involved in the preliminary designs for "The Gummi Bears," said, "In a way, Eisner and Wells are very good for the studio because they're doing so much more now. But the Disney quality has always been so unique, and it's what set the studio apart. To see it deteriorate would just be a tragedy." Yet there was little doubt that the Disney animators couldn't have done it themselves. They were busy enough. According to Block, "In one year, during the time we made "Duck Tales," "Rescue Rangers," "Winnie the Pooh," and "Gummi Bears," we produced more animated footage for television than Disney features has in 50 years."

And there was little doubt that no one, not even Disney, could turn out classic, Disney-quality animation that fast. Even doing "limited limited" animation, even having most of the actual animation done in Japan, "The Wuzzles," for instance, cost $285,000 per episode to make—$35,000 more than the network was paying for it.

The cost of such quality was a highly conscious choice, one that was debated long after the series were sold. In July 1985, Eisner summoned the top Disney executives to a "corporate creative seminar"—another gong show of a sort—at the Ritz-Carlton in Laguna Niguel, not far from Disneyland. The weekend at a luxurious resort hotel for 50 executives and their spouses dug deep into the corporate pocket, but, said Eisner, it "cost less than one bad script one executive decides to have written for no apparent reason."

The two animated series were already deep in production, and their debut was only weeks away, but here in the shirt-sleeves atmosphere, on couches and big soft chairs, the top executives of Disney were still asking themselves about their intent and their strategy. Richard Frank (a former Paramount executive who had just become the Disney studio's president, while Katzenberg took the title of chairman), asked the obvious question: why not do it cheaper? "Does it pay to spend twice as much as Hanna-Barbera? Do the kids know the difference? Should we not be in the business?" Like almost everyone in the room, he wore Disney attire—a black satin jacket sporting Mickey as the Sorcerer's Apprentice. Frank Wells, the exception to the rule in un-Disneyed blue denim work shirt and white cords, took the same line: "If you had the same great stories and the same marketing and characters, why not do it cheaper? Perhaps we should put on a different label, call ourselves 'Joe Blow' for Saturday morning."

Eisner, in a Mickey Mouse T-shirt and a Mickey Mouse sweatshirt, his long frame draped on a couch, said, "No upside." Putting a different name on the product would block the possibility of using the characters elsewhere in the Disney empire.

Katzenberg, wearing a pink golf shirt with a mouse in place of the Izod crocodile, amplified Eisner's point: synergy was tied to quality. "That would mean no characters for the parks. We need new characters for the parks."

Eisner, in the end, gave a pronouncement that put him on the side of the preservationists: "We can't go on television and look like trash."

Eisner wanted to make money, but in the long run, Disney's possibilities for revenues rested on the quality of its product. It was one of those occasions that caused Frank Wells to comment, "There are any number of times we have come down on the side of remembering we're the Disney company, and making a decision that you might not make were you in any other company. . . .You really do have a larger responsibility when you carry that name around."

In the video market, Disney took a cautious first step. Back in 1980 and 1981, Card Walker had released 13 Disney films on videocassette: ten live-action films that were not its best, box-office champion *Mary Poppins*, and its two weakest animated features, *Dumbo* and *Alice in Wonderland*. Since then, except for a few cartoons, the company had withdrawn from the market, as Ron Miller closed down every avenue to the Disney films except the Disney Channel. Now, although Eisner had promised the Basses that he was going to exploit the great video potential of the Disney archives, a ferocious debate developed within the company. Katzenberg was concerned, as the old management had been, that videocassettes would compete with theatrical releases. Why would anyone go to the theater to see a rerelease when they could see it at home? Others, such as Rich Frank, argued just as strongly that the videos, staggered with rereleases, would make money as they whetted the consumers' appetite for more.

In May, Eisner broke the logjam by ordering Bill Mechanic, another Paramount arriviste who had taken over home video, to release the first of its great classics on tape: *Pinocchio*. The movie had been in the theaters just five months before, creating a huge market for a videocassette, and it wouldn't be back in the theaters for a long time. As a concession to Katzenberg's concerns, Eisner determined that the cassette would only be on the market for a limited period of time. When it came time to release the film to theaters again, most of those cassettes, it was hoped, would have gone the way of all good things—worn out, lost, or destroyed by overinquisitive toddlers' fingers. With sales of VCRs soaring—over 25 million were expected to be in American homes by the end of the year—the company hoped to sell 100,000 to video rental stores at $79.95. *Pinocchio* sold over 100,000 copies in the first week, and by December had sold over 400,000. Even with a price that dropped to $29.95 for Christmas, the sale turned the studio an $11-million profit.

The Christmas price drop was a tactical gamble thought up by the new head of home video, Bill Mechanic: price the product for consumers to buy, not just video stores. It was an important marketing coup, especially for Disney, who owned the kind of timeless classics that people would like to buy and watch repeatedly.

Eisner's overall strategy was to expand in all directions at once. The old team had a horror of competing with themselves. The new team was determined to use every avenue of distribution open to them. On January 16, 1985, for instance, Disney licensed seven recent films, including *Splash*, to Showtime and Home Box Office, cable services that competed directly with the Disney Channel. Already, in January 1985, far ahead of projections, the Disney Channel had broken into the black, with over 2 million subscribers. By the end of the year, there were 2.5 million. In a flat cable market, it was the only rapidly growing system. But its "churn rate"—the rate at which new subscribers cancel—was close to 80 percent, far above the industry average. By June, Jim Jimirro had unexpectedly resigned, to be replaced by John Cooke, a former Times-Mirror executive. Cooke moved aggressively to capture more contemporary programs, such as Garrison Keillor's "Prairie Home Companion," to get the churn rate down, at the same time that he dropped the channel's price to local cable companies and hotel chains. The channel's growth continued, but now with a more solid base.

In all this ferocious activity, Eisner and Katzenberg were, in effect, building an entire new studio on the bones of an old one, using the name, the cash flow, and the credit of an existing business. It was an existing business that carried with it some unique opportunities. For Christmas of 1985, for instance, the studio rereleased *101 Dalmations*—not exactly *Casablanca*—and brought in nearly $34 million for an investment that was near zero. Rereleases, video, and cable outlets, as well as the cash flow of the parks promised the new Disney studio a base of funds with which to work, a luxury no other film-makers in Hollywood could claim.

"The basic fabric of the company hopefully will remain," said Eisner, "and on that fabric we will build a different company."

The new studio they were building in many ways resembled a cross between the old studio system and the techniques of television production that Eisner and Katzenberg had learned at ABC and Paramount: fast, definite, "high-concept." Like Warners in the '40s with its *film-noir* detective flicks, or MGM with its lavish spectacles, Disney had a brand identity. The Disney name signified family-oriented comedies and adventures. Yet Disney could release adult comedies and dramas under its new Touchstone label. By signing writers, directors, and actors to long-term contracts and searching out the projects most suited to them, Eisner and Katzenberg were forming something not unlike a repertory company, a creative, rich environment for creating films. According to producer David Bombyk, "When you enter the studio, you have the feeling of a midwestern college campus. They will use that atmosphere to get a lot of people working together creatively." Lauren Schuler talked about a "spirit of creative camaraderie."

They didn't offer huge amounts of money in these contracts. As Steve Sauer puts it, "In making a deal with Disney, many times you have to sacrifice certain quotations that you've had in the past, have to sacrifice certain dollars." What they offered in return was a percentage of the box-office gross ("points"), plus something equally important to creative people: the sense that they had some input in the process, that they could help choose projects, that they could expand creatively, that the studio would back them up, and that they would get the chance, if they wanted it, to produce and direct their own films. In the process, Disney took some of the studios' power back from the agents and "packagers" who in recent years had become the muscle boys of Hollywood, brokering every creative interaction.

They also, not accidentally, saved themselves money. It made a big difference at a time when Hollywood seemed to be modeling its economy on the hyperinflation of Brazil rather than Japan's stable growth. The average production cost of a feature film in 1983 was under $12 million. Only two years later it was approaching $16 million. Eisner hoped to repeat his performance at Paramount, keeping the studio's average film cost well below the industry average. As Katzenberg said, "We watch every single solitary nickel." Richard Frank, president of the studio, echoed him: "We have the money, but we won't pay retail."

In this, the new Disney was not so different from the old Disney.

Disney under Eisner was tightfisted, so tightfisted that it left a bad taste in some people's mouths. One agent complained to the *Los Angeles Times*, the industry's hometown paper, "They are so tight on deals, they really think you should consider it an honor to do business with them, that they know how to make pictures better than anyone else. . . . Money is not everything, but it is something. They are not the only ones making pictures, and sometimes they do come off penny-wise and pound-foolish."

Yet Disney's most revolutionary moves may have been its least-noticed. For one, it quietly let its film executives know that they wouldn't get fired for one mistake, that they could afford to stand on the strength of their convictions. For another, it merged its television, cable, video, and theatrical film divisions into a "filmed entertainment" unit. No studio had ever done that. The aim was to allow directors and writers to move more easily among media, and to search for synergies between film and television. In this merger, Disney acknowledged the increasing power of television and other media. And finally it let producers, directors, and writers know that, as Lauren Schuler put it, "If they determined they wanted to make a movie, they didn't hinge it on finding a big box-office star. If they believed in the material, and in the director, if they felt that you could find the appropriate actor, it didn't have to be Tom Cruise. They go with the good material."

As Eisner himself put it, "In this business, the script is the base of the pyramid. I'd rather hire ten good writers than one big-name star. It's self-defeating to be obsessed with any one star or director. If you can't get Steven Spielberg—well, there's another Spielberg coming of age in Columbus, Ohio, or someplace."

Unlike many other studio heads, Eisner tried to resist the temptation to make the blockbuster. "My theory," he told one reporter, "is, don't try to second-guess the audience. In basketball, you don't throw the ball all the way down the court or shoot for three-pointers all night. The trick is simply to take quality shots from close in. That's what we're doing here—taking quality shots, over and over again, and not worrying about the audience. If we make good pictures, they'll find us."

Frank Wells neatly defined the new Disney: "We've never sat around and looked at each other and said, 'What would Walt have done?' What we have rather done is say, 'What will work? What will be successful? What will please? What will draw people? What will attract people?'" That judgment—the audience plunking down money—would not begin to be made until the turn of 1986.

9

Awakening Sleeping Beauty

The studio was the glamorous part of Disney—movie stars, Hollywood, gala premiers, *People Magazine* covers. But the parks were the engine of Disney, in revenues and profits, in numbers of employees, in uniqueness. There were other studios in Hollywood. There were plenty of theme parks in the world. But there were no theme parks that approached Disneyland, Tokyo Disneyland, or the Magic Kingdom in Florida in style, in clarity of execution, or in reputation. Nothing else remotely like EPCOT had ever been built. The market share of the theme park industry held by the Disney parks operation was IBM-like in its dominance—one-fifth of all visits to theme parks in the country were to a Disney park, far ahead of any rival. And most important, the parks supplied fully 66 percent of the company's revenue. It was this enormous revenue base that gave Eisner and Katzenberg the freedom to build the studio.

Yet the parks had not been doing well. Attendance, and revenues, had flattened out after the leap provided by the opening of EPCOT in 1983, and fallen by 10 percent in 1984. Attendance at Disneyland, especially, had dropped from a peak of 11.5 million to barely more than 9.5 million. The parks needed Eisner's jumper cables as much the studio did. The health of the whole Disney operation depended upon sustaining and increasing the revenues of the parks.

The task was enormous. "Our eternal frustration," said Wells, "is and always will be that we can't move fast enough. . . . The basic restrictive fact of this company is that we just don't have enough time to do all the things that clearly and obviously should be done." The things that needed to be done in the parks were both short-term and long-term at the same time. The immediate goal was to get more people in the gates. The parks couldn't be made new overnight—new attractions and new parks would take years. All that could be done in the short term was to advertise them, and promote them through giveaways and tie-ins.

Wells was convinced that the parks were underutilized, and began to pan for ideas. Soon after he became president of Disney, he held a gong show brainstorming session much like the one a few months earlier that had produced so many ideas for children's animated television shows for Eisner. This one was designed for the 15 people who had in their hands the sales and marketing for the parks. The parks had never been actively advertised by the company. Wells asked for ideas around the table, and got none. He was met with what he called "a stony silence." He was not happy and he let the group know it. He said, "This is not a satisfactory meeting. We're going to come back tomorrow, you 15 people, and I want each of you to have at least one idea." And he walked out of the room. The next day he reconvened the same group, and went around the table. Idea after idea (43 in all) popped up, "every one of them . . . new and fresh and different," according to Wells. Many of the ideas were put in practice as soon as possible, including an "800" information number and itinerant free road shows of Disney characters.

The major idea—simply to advertise the parks as any other company would—had already been suggested repeatedly to the previous management by Jack Lindquist, now the executive vice president for marketing. Card Walker had always felt that there was no sense in advertising the parks when America's television networks would always give Disney what was, in effect, free advertising by showing yet another Disney special. But after Walker retired, Lindquist had done some tests in a few markets, comparing the efficiency of print and broadcast ads, and following up with questionnaires at the parks to discover who had come to the parks because of those ads. The results were startling: on average, each $6.50 spent on advertising the parks resulted in a visitor who spent around $40 on admission, food, and souvenirs. Advertising was clearly worth it.

Eisner called up his one-time Paramount colleagues Gordon Weaver and Steve Rose, now ensconced as a public relations subsidiary of the advertising firm Young and Rubicam. After failing to talk them into coming over to Disney, he gave them the Disney account. The result was a media push in 51 markets for Disney World, and bookings in 120 cities for character road shows celebrating Disneyland's 30th birthday. Although one Disney executive admitted, "We are making something out of nothing—nobody celebrates 30th birthdays," the Disneyland birthday hype worked. As early as February 1985, Anaheim hotels were reporting record reservations tied to Disneyland's 30th anniversary.

But Eisner also laid out longer-term goals. At EPCOT Center, the

"Living Seas" pavilion, begun by the old management, was nearing completion. But otherwise the new team had to start from scratch. At the annual Disney stockholders' meeting in February, the confident new chairman announced the deal with George Lucas for a "Star Tours" ride, and said they were considering a "major studio tour" in Orlando, and looking at sites in Spain and France for a new park. Frank Wells talked about preparing a master plan to develop 10,000 acres of Disney World property. This was heady new stuff for the minor shareholders—often families that had bought Disney stock for their children—that typically made up the crowd at such meetings. Many of them knew little of the internal struggles of the company the previous summer, but the idea that their new chairman could reach out and touch a man like George Lucas spoke powerfully about the changes Disney was going through. So did the subtle change in the company's name: "Walt Disney Productions" would be known from now on as "The Walt Disney Company."

The same month, Eisner called together four imagineers and gave them a challenge: take four days to brainstorm and come up with some concepts that will go with three elements—George Lucas, Michael Jackson, and 3-D. On Valentine's day imagineer Rick Rothschild met with Eisner, Lucas, and Jackson to pitch them three concepts. They went for one called *The Intergalactic Music Man*, a 15-minute space thriller film featuring 3-D, Lucas' famous special effects from his Industrial Light and Magic Company, and physical effects in the theater that would include explosive sounds, lasers, strobes, and fog.

Frank Wells soon had put together a deal with Metropolitan Life to sponsor an entirely new $90-million pavilion at EPCOT dedicated to personal health. This pavilion, although educational, would be far from boring. It would utilize every bit of technological dazzle that Disney could pull together.

In April, the company announced a stopgap project that would be ready for the summer crowds—a teen open-air dance club called Videopolis, featuring live bands and taped music, huge video monitors, lights and lasers, seating for 1,500, and 5,000 square feet of dance floor. Faced with the need to have something in place while the Lucas projects matured, the imagineers designed and completed it in a record 104 days. "Michael's strategy was to use all the with-it icons of entertainment, whether Disney or not, make it a hip place for teenagers to go again," said imagineer Randy Bright.

The company announced the Michael Jackson project in July. Francis Ford Coppola had agreed to direct, and the title had been changed to

Captain Eo. Once again, the announcement spoke powerfully about the changing face of Disney. Coppola was a director of Promethean reputation, not the sort who would have worked on a little Disney film for the parks in the old days. And Jackson was the biggest-selling recording star in history, then at the peak of his popularity. And his hip, androgynous, sexy, glittery image was as far from Mickey Mouse as you could get and still be in the same business. Disney was clearly stretching.

The changes at Disney rippled through every part of the company. Old resistances were broken, old ideas overturned. New ideas that provoked great interest from the public often provoked resistance from many of the old guard, especially among the park operators. According to Randy Bright, "We [veteran Disney employees] had a certain arrogance that said we can do it better; we'll design our own show. We don't need Diana Ross or Michael Jackson or Bobby Darin or Johnny Mathis. When we were trying to get the 'Star Tours' ride in, it was very difficult for people [at Disney] to think that there would be any value in having the name George Lucas at Disneyland. Michael saw the value immediately."

The Michael Jackson *Captain Eo* project came up against the same barrier of insularity as "Star Tours" with, this time, the added negative of prejudice. The imagineers heard from the park operators that "Michael Jackson is a wimp, he's a fag, he's gay. He dances terribly. He's just a fad. He's going to go away." The old guard thought that adding the Michael Jackson movie was a terrible idea.

But 1985 was not 1984. *Captain Eo* went forward. The rules of the game had changed, and the idea people could feel their influence within the company growing. A year before, Ray Watson had been preparing to scale down the imagineers, folding the designers into park operations and farming out the engineering to outside firms. Since building EPCOT and Tokyo Disneyland, the imagineers had been reduced from a 2,000-member team to a team of 450. Frank Wells had undertaken a study of the operation, which included compiling a listing of over 60 highly specialized talents—from robotics to making imitation rocks—that would be dispersed if the operation were cut back to just design. Eisner looked over the list, visited the imagineers, and decided to keep them independent. In fact, Eisner came to see them in a much wider role, as "the backbone" of the company, commenting that they were the essence of what made Disney different: "We are the only studio with a research and development team."

Eisner looked on the parks as an extension of his sense of story: "It's basically the same business. An attraction in one of our parks is like a film, in that it has to have a theme and tell a story. And I know a good story always has a beginning, middle, and end."

He applied this point of view not only to the attractions, but to the parks themselves, the hotels in them, even the restaurants and stores: "We ask, 'What is the story we want to tell when people walk into one of our new buildings? What are they going to feel? What is going to happen next? And how will it end?'"

At the beginning of 1985, Eisner asked the imagineers to start work on a pavilion of the arts at EPCOT Center. The idea rapidly skewed toward the motion picture arts, and came together with the "movie ride" idea that Nunis had already shown Eisner. The pavilion would be about Hollywood as a whole, rather than just about Disney. The idea grew, until there was more planned for it than one pavilion could possibly hold. "It was spilling out everywhere," said Bright.

When Eisner dropped in for a presentation, his reaction was instant: "It's a new park, a new gate." It was an idea that, in fact, had its roots in Disney's history. When Walt built the Burbank studio in 1940, he had wanted to find a way to bring the public in, to create a studio tour, but his production people and the city fathers of Burbank had dissuaded him. When he originally imagined a theme park, his first plan was to build it on land across the street from the studio, land that later became part of the Ventura Freeway. His backup plan for Disneyland, if it should fail, was to turn it into a studio lot. And the various stages of plans for the Florida land had always included the idea of a movie production facility. Now Walt's ideas meshed with the new ideas for an arts pavilion at EPCOT, and became a new "gate"—a tour of a working studio, wrapped around a Hollywood-style theme park.

By April 1985, Disney formally announced its intention to build a new $300-million Hollywood theme park. But it was critical that Disney be able to reach beyond its own characters and films if it wanted to create a sense of the excitement of Hollywood. The one studio that had the greatest trove of such titles, MGM/UA, happened to be the one studio most in need of cash. It was owned by Kirk Kerkorian, a man reputedly willing to sell anything for the right price. By June 27, Disney had signed an agreement with MGM/UA executives giving Disney the right to use hundreds of films and characters for the park, including such classics as *Gone with the Wind*, and *The Wizard of Oz*, plus the "MGM" name and the roaring-lion MGM trademark—for a pittance. The price started at $100,000 per year, and slowly rose to $1 million over 20 years.

Kerkorian, usually a mild man, became infuriated at his executives, and eventually filed a still-pending suit against Disney to break the agreement. But the company went forward, and gambled the future of its theme park that the contract would stick.

Across the freeway and down two miles at Universal, the announcement was also greeted with fury, but for a different reason: Universal had been planning just such a theme park in Orlando since 1981, and had been struggling with financing. In fact, they charged that, years before, when Eisner was still at Paramount, and Universal was looking for partners in their project, they had showed him the plans. They claimed that many of the ideas mentioned in the announcement came straight from those plans.

Eisner and Disney vehemently denied any plagiarism. Eisner, they claimed, had never seen Universal's plans. Furthermore, they pledged that they would beat Universal to opening day. Industry analysts thought the announcement would stop Universal's planned theme park. Opening their own park next to Disney's would not make financial sense, and potential partners would be scared away. Disney clearly hoped that was true, fearing the impact of a thrills-and-spills movie theme park nearby on attendance at the relatively tame EPCOT.

The 30th anniversary of Disneyland's opening day fell on July 17, 1985. Eisner was determined to make the most of it. The Anaheim park stayed open around the clock, with celebrations from midnight to midnight that included special television shows, prizes, parades, 30,000 balloons released, and planes skywriting "Happy 30th Birthday." Michael and Jane Eisner arrived just after midnight. He did two television shows in the small hours of the morning, and walked the quiet streets in a tan suit, one hand holding a box of popcorn, the other holding Jane's hand. NBC's Willard Scott was there, doing the weather for the "Today Show." Mexico, Canada and Great Britain had sent television crews for live shows. By the end of the day the old one-day record of 82,000 visitors was shattered. In fact, all year long, records were broken not only at Disneyland, but at nearby Knott's Berry Farm and at tourist attractions and hotels all through the area. People in the industry attributed it all to Disney's birthday celebration. One industry consultant called it "the most successful promotion in the history of the theme park business."

On August 25, when Brooks Arthur Charles Burr stepped through a turnstile at Disneyland, lights flashed and bells started clanging. Somebody stepped up and handed him the keys to a new car, a lifetime pass to Disney parks, a card good for 30,000 miles of air travel. He was the park's 250 millionth visitor. People clapped and cheered, but Brooks didn't know what to say. He just put his arms around his father's neck and stared. After all, he was only three. Finally Mickey Mouse himself picked him up and hugged him, and Brooks smiled.

Eisner and Wells pushed steadily for expansion and profit in the parks. Studies showed that, even if price increases convinced five percent of the visitors not to come to the park, every extra dollar Disney charged at the gates would add $26 million per year to the company's bottom line. Nunis had pushed for price increases for years, only to be vetoed by Card Walker. Checchi advised raising it $5 right away. Eisner agreed, but he was afraid of the bad publicity that the price rise would bring if it happened all at once. So Eisner decided on a stepped rise in prices, spread out over two years. Backed by focus group studies run by Young and Rubicam, they began to raise the prices at the gate: from $15, for instance, for an adult day at Disneyland to $16.50. In September 1985, the company announced that starting in 1986, Disneyland would be open every day, instead of closing Mondays and Tuesdays in the off-season. They also toyed with bringing back the ticket books for attractions, which had spawned astronaut Sally Ride's famous comment describing the space shuttle as "an E-ticket ride."

In December, Eisner flew to Paris to ink an agreement with Laurent Fabius, the prime minister of France, for a billion-dollar theme park near Paris, which the company expected to open by 1990 or 1991. Eisner had kept other governments guessing about his intentions. He informed the Spanish government that he would not build a park in Spain only one day before he signed the agreement to build one in France. He had held talks not only with France, but with Spain and with Portugal (through Prime Minister Mario Soares), both of whom had also vigorously campaigned for the park. Nunis' team had scoured Europe, considering hundreds of sites from England to Italy; Marne-la-Vallée, just east of Paris, had won Eisner's approval. It would be the Disney parks' biggest expansion since the beginning of Disney World nearly two decades before.

By the end of its first year under new management, Disney showed surprising new energy. Even relatively small areas of the company, such as publishing, records, and direct mail, hit new highs. Disney comic books hit the racks once again; Disney released a record number of books and magazines around the world, including magazines in China, Italy, and France, about Mickey and Winnie the Pooh; easy-reading children's books; and an Italian book series about nature. "Mickey Mouse Disco" records sold more than 2 million copies, the first multiplatinum children's album in the history of the industry.

In Eisner's first September-to-September fiscal year, revenue broke $2 billion for the first time, up 22 percent. Operating income was up 44 percent. Net profit was up 77 percent. Despite the box-office fades that the old management's movie projects suffered, operating income in filmed entertainment went from 1984's $2.2 million to $33.6 million, riding on the strength of the Disney Channel and video sales. Attendance at Disneyland, buoyed by the giveaways and the birthday hype, had shot up from 9.5 million to 11.3 million. Vigorous advertising and marketing had pushed attendance at all the parks up 8 percent, despite higher prices. Combined with rising ticket prices, the higher attendance had pushed up the parks' profit by 38 percent in one year.

The composition of the company's revenue stream was changing shape as well. When Eisner took office, filmed entertainment was contributing only 13 percent of the company's profits—despite the success of *Splash*—down from 60 percent a decade before. Now, the contribution of movies, television shows, videos, and cable was once again increasing. Eisner commented, with typical understatement, "We've got a lot of things going on. It's become a very active company." At the same time that he seemed to outsiders to be expanding the company with reckless abandon, Eisner felt a certain caution: "I want to keep my foot on the throttle, but I'm real quick to move from the throttle to the brake." He didn't even feel that he was the change-maker, the risk-taker, saying, "The change was coming. I don't think I brought the change. It was inevitable."

Not everyone was happy with the "inevitable" change. Letters to the *Los Angeles Times*, hometown newspaper to the company and the entertainment industry, ran heavily negative, complaining of the compromise in quality in Disney's Saturday morning cartoons, the "commercialism" of the new management's projects and the dilution of the Disney name.

Bob Burman of Glendale wrote: "It appears that the Eisner/Wells team at Disney is striving to increase Disney profits. It is a shame that many of their decisions bode ill for the long-term health of Disney, as the unique entity that it has always been. . . . They will do so at the expense of any cohesive long-term concept. Eisner's direction seems more focused on the bonus clause of his five-year contract with Disney. . . . [It's a] pretty good reason to only be concerned with short-term gains. Five years from now, Eisner may be gone, with bonus money in his pocket, perhaps working for another studio for which Disney is just another competitor."

Wall Street had no such qualms. As early as February 1985, the stock had hit $75 a share. By the end of May, it had doubled from the previous year's bottom of $45 (a doubling that helped kick the five Bass brothers' fortunes each past the $600-million mark, and Roy Disney to $255 million). Eisner could do no wrong. *Forbes* dubbed the cheering on Wall Street "The Tinker Bell Principle," recalling the final scene in *Peter Pan*: Tinker Bell lies dying, and the children in the audience are told that little Tink will live if only the children in the audience clap their hands and truly believe. Wall Street loves a good story as much as Hollywood does. It revels in true belief.

Eisner turned into a major curiosity. The *New York Times Magazine* described him as having a "squashed nose and excited grin" that "give him a resemblance to the television puppet Howdy Doody." Magazine writers profiling him and Disney could not seem to resist starting their pieces with "once upon a time." Taking its cue from his "Bongo the Bear" speech, his "kid in a toy store" comment, his self-effacing manner and ready smile, the press often treated him as if he were an overgrown child who had somehow lucked his way into the most fun job a kid could ever have.

But there was more to Eisner than met the eye. Agent Jerry Berg called him "a more complex thinker than he appears to be, and very seductive with talent." The temptation to underestimate him was increased by an unusual trait: he seemed to live on the surface. Just as people who liked him called him "disarmingly childlike," there were people who said he had the attention span of a three-year-old. To those who didn't like him, he had no depth. To his admirers, as one associate put it, "What you see is what you get with Michael. He has no hidden agenda. He's one of the few people I know who has no guile. Therefore he doesn't allow it in people around him."

When Barry Diller, his onetime mentor, would get cornered by a determined journalist, he would steadfastly and pointedly refuse to be introspective, to look within himself for complex motives, for twists and turns of feeling. In contrast, Eisner, in interviews and speeches, cheerfully offered up emotion after emotion—his joy on getting the job at Disney, his hopes for the future, his pride in his children, his appreciation for his wife—but they were simple emotions, unshadowed by doubts, contradictions, or hidden impulses. In interviews, he would flit constantly from one subject to another, spending 30 seconds on this exciting possibility and 40 seconds on that new project.

Nor was this simplicity deceptive. Eisner did live on the surface. His career as a builder of stories, and a maker of coalitions that provided entertainment to millions, allowed him to become rich, respected, and powerful without ever abandoning the wonder and adventure of childhood. At the same time that he appeared ambitious, hard-working, even driven, he also appeared more settled and happy in that ambition than most other driven men.

The lack of the usual flashy Hollywood ego made it possible for him to work well in a team atmosphere. "When we're both in town," Eisner said of Wells, "we're in and out of each other's offices 20 times a day. . . . We do many of the same things, and yet we have many different interests. Frank is a real full-time lawyer, and I am a gentleman lawyer. I'm a real full-time creative executive, and he's a gentleman creative executive. He corrects my legal blunders, and I take his creative thoughts and steal them for my own."

Wherever he got his new ideas, Eisner fairly exploded with them in his first years at Disney. Some, like bringing the Sunday night "flagship" show back to the air, were traditional, common-sense ideas that perhaps any competent executive would have seen. In fact, most of the Wall Street analysts had been urging such a move in their reports on the company since Disney left Sunday night television in 1983, as had Saul Steinberg and other outsiders. Even if it lost money, the Sunday series acted as a massive weekly advertisement for the parks and the movies—and in fact for all Disney products. Other ideas, like signing Bette Midler, Michael Jackson and George Lucas, and pursuing Madonna, broke the "Disney" mold.

Some ideas, however, were off the charts completely, as Eisner would often recognize himself. For instance, he proposed, for Disney World, a 43-story hotel in the shape of Mickey Mouse, an idea of which others quickly dissuaded him. He wanted to get in a Winnebago and drive across the country with his family to get closer to his Disney World customers. At one point he proposed a Disney car. His oldest son had just come of driving age. Wouldn't it be wonderful, he thought, if Disney could design, for General Motors, the world's safest car? He asked imagineers to come up with design suggestions, and they did: Velcro-like styling with easily changeable roofs and fenders. Then he asked Steve Rose and Gordon Weaver at Young and Rubicam to do focus studies, and see what people thought of the idea. According to Rose, people thought it was a terrible idea. "When you say, 'a Disney car,' immediately you think of Goofy on the hood, and a Mickey Mouse steering wheel. The public was not interested." Eisner discovered that he was the only one who was excited about the idea. So he shelved it.

Sid Bass tells the story of a walk at EPCOT with Eisner. Eisner realized that there were no boats on the lake in the middle of the "Many Lands." He found a board and a marker and made a sign reading "Boat Rides" with a price on it. Within hours, according to Bass, the lake was full of kids in boats.

But according to Eisner, the story has gotten simpler and happier in the telling. He did come up with the idea, and the park employees tested it out, but the wakes bouncing off the concrete walls of the lake made the boats wobble and bounce. "Our people who were testing were all capsizing and getting sick and everything." In fact, Eisner uses the story to make a different point—the limitations of wild ideas: "Not all my ideas are practical. For every idea I have that we go forward with, ten others, people yell me down on. Most of the dumb ones I try to get rid of before they come to fruition."

After a while, Eisner found that he had to watch what he said. "If I say, 'Why don't we try putting a lamp here that goes sideways,' the next day there will be 12 new lamps there. My problem is not too few ideas; my problem is too many bad ideas. I have got to control myself. When I hear a bad idea come out of my mouth, I've got to stop before it gets to somebody who's going to spend some money on it."

In fact, according to Dennis Holt, head of Western International, Disney's media buyer, separating the good ideas from the bad ideas is one of Eisner's great strengths: "He's also willing to hear you say, 'Michael, that stinks.' He has no false pride."

Running a corporation that finds its roots in family values, it is not surprising that Eisner gets a lot of his ideas at home, and screens them with his wife Jane. "Ninety-eight point five percent of my ideas revolve around things that we are both involved in. With the stuff that is really on the edge, I will ask her if I'm crazy. Of course she usually thinks I am."

He will take ideas from anywhere: "You just have to be receptive. You have to have respect for the creative process, not denigrate people's desire to be creative. Then the ideas are there. Everyone has them. There is not a person who is walking that doesn't have ideas. Even people who are boring have ideas."

His love of new ideas was not mere whim. It was also shrewd business.

According to Eisner, "My primary interest is ideas. The rest is kind of housekeeping to me. I understand business, but it's the product that has traditionally gotten me out of economic trouble." He complained that "every CEO has to spend an enormous amount of time shuffling papers. The question is, how much of your time can you leave free to think about ideas? To me the pursuit of ideas is the only thing that matters. You can always find capable people to do almost everything else."

One expression of Eisner's love of creative ideas was the attention he lavished on the imagineers. Another was his quirky hatred for the proliferation of "vice presidents." To him, the title smacked of creeping bureaucracy. It was even worse for creative people to carry such titles. A VP was a creature of spread sheets and committees, not a fountain of wild new ideas. He gave the creative people throughout the organization titles that sounded like Hollywood. For instance, Randy Bright, who had been "vice president of concept development" became "executive producer for Disneyland and Disney World."

Eisner walked with Bright through EPCOT Center on one trip early in 1985, through Future World and the World Showcase. Unlike almost every other part of Disney World, Future World held no gingerbread, nothing quaint, no whiff of nostalgia. The hard, curving surfaces and massive, beetling structures, unfriendly and corporate at the street level, the central plan obvious and overpowering in its symmetry, surmounted by the massive golf-ball Bucky dome of "Spaceship Earth," all spoke of a 1960s image of a clean and utterly ordered future, George Orwell's *1984* with sun and flowers and fountains. As they walked, Eisner and Bright poked through a book of ideas that Bright had for making the vast three-year-old park friendlier—little things, interstitials, "in-betweens," as the animators would have called them—a bench with a back on it here, a magician there, a suggestion for a storyteller or a kiosk, little bits of life and color that would add to the overall effect. Eisner loved it, saw the point instantly, and ordered most of it done.

Bright was the kind of person who made Disney work for Eisner. Although Eisner had brought in many outside executives, the changes at the executive level fell far short of a clean sweep. The company seemed close to bursting with talent and energy. It seemed to him that "a lot of people here were waiting to do something, to get going."

At the same time that Eisner worked to expand Disney as rapidly as possible, he knew that its growth depended on preserving its culture: "We have to act like a giant company. We can't act like a small company. The question is whether or not we can evolve into a giant company without losing that family feeling."

Family feeling Eisner had in spades. For all his corporate energy, he was the kind of man who kept his calendar clear on Tuesday evenings, because that was the night one of his boys had Indian Guides meetings; who almost missed a breakfast meeting once because he had been helping his older boy study for a Latin exam. "My priorities," he said, "are simple. My family comes first and Disney second. When I have to choose between them, I'll always choose the family, whether it's a school play or a hockey game, or whatever." The Disney culture—upbeat, family-oriented, imaginative—not only matched his own leanings, it reinforced them. If Eisner was energizing Disney, Disney had infected Eisner and released him. As he put it, "The culture is catching. Even if you've been inoculated against it, you can get it."

For Eisner, it was the perfect job. He was, as people said, "happy as a pig in shit." His position had all the power, all the scope, and all the fun, of any job he could imagine. He told one reporter, "This is it for me—for life. If I have a choice I'll be doing this until I'm 95. If they kick me out because they think I'm senile, well, then maybe I'll go back to Paramount."

At the end of 1985, no one thought Michael Eisner was senile. He and the people he brought to Disney were laying the long-term strategies that, over the next five years, would not only expand Disney tremendously, but actually change the nature of the company.

10

Laying the Foundations

In 1985 and 1986, Michael Eisner was not merely making Disney bigger. He was laying the groundwork for turning Disney into a global entertainment conglomerate of unprecedented size and breadth. Team Disney had to lay this strategy not in a time of cool repose, but in the middle of ferocious attempts to get the company moving again.

The media had begun to rave about Eisner and company well before any of the new movies had hit the screen, before any of the new major attractions had been built. The attention just amused Eisner. "I wish I had all those articles about how great we are when I was in school," he told *Forbes*. "In school you had to take the test and then be graded. We're being graded, and we haven't taken the test. All those periodicals and newspapers are waiting for our first movie and may say, 'Ah ha! These men are only mortal.' We may go two years before we have a hit. We may have one at Christmastime. I have no idea. . . . It takes time, it takes development, and we could fail."

The first clear indication that Eisner and his team might succeed came in early 1986, 15 months into the job, when the first of the new crop of Eisner–Katzenberg films hit the neighborhood cineplexes, and people liked them.

Down and Out in Beverly Hills was Eisner's first Disney film to hit the marketplace, and the first R-rated film in Disney's history (the "R" garnered not by graphic sex, but by the inclusion of a single "bad" word). It featured Richard Dreyfuss and Bette Midler as a blasé Beverly Hills couple, with a Scottish Collie named Mike as their neurotic dog Matisse (complete with his own psychiatrist), and Nick Nolte as the bum whom they rescue from drowning in their swimming pool—and who, of course, turns their lives upside down. It was a big risk for both Dreyfuss and Midler, the first big movie in years for each of them, as well as director Paul Mazursky's first venture into broad comedy. It was a risk for Eisner as well: the Disney board could have ordered him not to show the film, or to sanitize it. The board had played just such a censor's role during the Watson–Miller regime, restraining Miller even in the mild forays that he wished to make into contemporary material. Eisner had shown the finished *Down and Out* to the board in November 1985, and had laid out to them the risks of censoring the film: the Hollywood community would get the message that Disney was not serious about its new way of operating. To censor the film would seriously slow the studio's momentum. He showed the film, and fielded some questions, but in the end the board gave in to the market savvy of their new, young chairman. The risk paid off for everyone: *Down and Out* opened in January 1986, and by May it had pulled in $57 million.

Ruthless People, Team Disney's second film, followed *Down and Out* by a season. In another wacky, cartoonlike comedy, Bette Midler plays a loud-mouthed shop-a-holic married to a millionaire (Danny DeVito) with an equally disgusting personality. When she is kidnapped for ransom, he is delighted and refuses to take her back. In the rush of the summer of 1986, aided by a promotion campaign that involved mailing thousands of seven-inch brass screws to media people around the country, *People* brought in a healthy $60 million—again, not a blockbuster, but the second profitable, popular film in a row.

Basil of Baker Street went through an embarrassment early in the year, when the Disney marketing department decided the name was "too British" and asked the animators to suggest new titles. In the end, all their suggestions were ignored, and the marketing department renamed it *The Great Mouse Detective*. The incensed animators lampooned what they considered the unimaginative, generic sound of the new name in a bogus memo that "announced" that all the Disney classics would be renamed— a memo that showed up in the *Los Angeles Times*. The new names included *Seven Little Men Help a Girl* (for *Snow White and the Seven Dwarfs*), *Color and Music* (for *Fantasia*), and *The Girl with the See-Through Shoes* (for *Cinderella*). Yet, generic title and all, the critics raved, calling it "an animators' picture" and "first [animated classic] completed since Walt Disney's death in 1966 that the artists could show to him without apologies or explanations." In the same summer that George Lucas' $35-million animated *Howard the Duck* brought in only $15 million at the box office, *The Great Mouse Detective* brought in a respectable $24 million.

The Color of Money turned out to be one of the better films of the '80's, featuring a marvelously maturing 61-year-old Paul Newman in a reprise of his "Fast Eddie" Felson role from the classic 1961 pool-hall film *The Hustler*—a role that many consider Newman's best. But now, in a sequel directed by Martin Scorsese, Eddie is 25 years older, and Tom Cruise is the young upstart pool shark. Katzenberg personally jawboned the usually reticent Newman into involving himself in a full-bore media campaign that eventually netted cover spreads in the *New York Times Magazine*, *Life*, and *USA Today*, a five-part series on "The Today Show," a series on "Entertainment Tonight," and major stories in *Vanity Fair* and *Newsweek*. *The Color of Money* did $6.4 million in its first weekend alone, and eventually brought Newman his first best-actor Academy Award. With an eventual domestic theatrical take of $52 million, it was not, in the end, the blockbuster hit Eisner and Katzenberg had hoped for—that would have to wait another year—but it was profitable, and it added to Disney's prestige.

Even without a blockbuster, though, the studio had clearly turned a corner. Suddenly, after Eisner had been at the helm for only two years, the studio that had been the local joke had the highest average box-office gross in the industry. It was a heady experience for Disney veterans.

As for the hoped-for blockbuster: early in 1986, Eisner personally led the fight to buy the foreign-language rights to a small French film, made for little more than $1 million, which had made a surprising coup in the French film market and would soon pick up the César (the French Oscar) for Best Film. *Trois Hommes et un Couffin* (*Three Men and a Cradle*), a light-hearted story of three carefree bachelors who suddenly find themselves rearing a baby girl left on their doorstep, had been directed by Colline Serreau, and produced by a company so tiny that its phone was cut off for nonpayment soon after the movie was finished. Eisner was determined that his old rival Mancuso at Paramount not get the rights, and eventually paid $750,000 (a record for rights to a foreign film), plus 7.5 percent of the profits to the French film's producer, Jean Francois Lepetit, and 3.5 percent to Serreau, along with a guarantee that she could direct the film.

Katzenberg went to work assembling what he saw as the prime cast. Typically, none of them were big-screen idols. One, Steve Gutenberg, had been in *Cocoon* and *Police Academy*, but was not a major star. The other two, Tom Selleck and Ted Danson, were well known television stars who had not really gotten a break on the big screen yet. Katzenberg hounded both Selleck and Danson with call after call, offer after offer, until they agreed to the parts.

In fact, Katzenberg's handling of Ted Danson was typical of his ferociously gentle persistence. Danson picked up the phone one day and found Katzenberg on the other end. He was calling about a script he had sent, to be called *Three Men and a Baby*. Danson said no, he wouldn't take the part. "It doesn't turn me on. Besides, I want to spend more time with my wife Casey. The series ["Cheers"] only gives me three and a half months vacation time, to either be with my family or do a movie. This doesn't add up to being worth it."

Katzenberg said, "I'd like you to give it a second look. We really think it's going to be a big hit, and it would be good for you. With the three of you it will be really wonderful and charming. It's going to be a very big hit. We're very excited about it."

As Danson would later put it, "Jeff is very good at giving you lots of space to see his point of view." So Danson read the script again. He talked to Casey again. And when Katzenberg called again, full of intensity and certainty ("Boy, does he give you certainty!"), Danson said no again. When Katzenberg called a third time ("He's relentless."), Danson said no a third time.

"'No' doesn't really mean too much to him," Danson reflected later. "It's almost become a Hollywood joke. He's a model in how to get what you want. He doesn't bully, he doesn't threaten. He doesn't do any of those things. He just gets your considerations and keeps putting out his point of view."

Katzenberg upped the ante. He put more money on the table, "a lot more money, hugely a lot more, almost four times as much as they offered to begin with," said Danson. And Katzenberg tied the project in with everything else Danson wanted to do. "It got to the point where it would have been absurd to say no, where if I had said no I would have been saying no not just to this film, but to you and your studio and the horses you rode in on. I have a production company, and we were coming to them with certain projects. They were offering me a relationship, not just a film. It became larger than just one film in my mind. Whether or not that's true, I don't know. At the time it felt like it."

But if he felt love-bombed, sweetly strong-armed into doing the project, in the end Danson felt cared for. Katzenberg—and Disney—did exactly what they said they would. They gave the film all the energy and attention and hype that Katzenberg had promised. "It's attractive to work for someone who is very bright, smart, and highly intended," said Danson. All through the filming Danson would get phone calls from him, brief but constant, making sure things were going well. Katzenberg was interested and aware. Blurbs showed up in *Time* and *Newsweek*. "They were declaring the movie an event before they'd finished shooting it. They started declaring it an event when we were just beginning to shoot it. So it was an event. I was being interviewed by the world, while I was making this film. They didn't wait around to see whether people would respond to their film in the way they predicted. They started creating that response while we were shooting it."

Katzenberg not only tolerated crisis, he loved it. He seemed to revel in it. Crisis would provoke not scowls and tirades but giggles and maniacal cackles. There was, for instance, the matter of the guarantee that Serreau could direct the *Three Men*. The studio was into it deep–big stars hired, millions out for sets, the media alerted. Five weeks away from filming, Katzenberg didn't like the script; it was too "Frenchified" for him. Serreau disagreed, things got intense, and Serreau got on a plane for Paris. And the Director's Guild was set to strike. Soon there would be no replacement directors available at any price. That night Katzenberg called James Orr, the cowriter of the script, to discuss the situation. And he kept giggling. Orr said, "You're enjoying yourself, aren't you?"

Katzenberg said, "I'm having the time of my life."

In the end, Katzenberg brought in Leonard Nimoy to direct, and the film was saved.

At the same moment that Eisner was dickering for the rights to *Trois Hommes*, he and Katzenberg invited Stephen Spielberg to try his hand at *Who Framed Roger Rabbit?* Ron Miller had bought the rights to the story in 1980, but no one had been able to make it work, and the mix of animation and live action throughout an entire feature film had made the film seem both technically challenging and very expensive. Both guesses turned out to be right. But Eisner was pushing for synergy: a film could cost a lot of money and still make the company a profit, he reasoned, if it created characters that could be used in toys, rides, other movies, television shows, and promotions. So far, he had not succeeded in creating or finding a character that fit the bill.

Spielberg took on the project, and hired director Robert Zemeckis, with whom he had made *Back to the Future*. Spielberg doubted whether the Disney animators could handle *Roger*. Disney very much wanted the prestige, and the shot of energy to its animation department, that would come from doing the film in-house. The two sides compromised: Disney and Spielberg created a special animation unit in London, under Richard Williams, the widely admired Canadian brought in by Zemeckis. Half of the unit was staffed with Disney animators, half with outsiders.

Spielberg also managed another chore that was critical to the film: the script required that a great many animated characters from different studios appear together—including Bugs Bunny, Porky Pig, Daffy Duck, Woody Woodpecker, and Betty Boop. Miller had tried it earlier, and had the doors slammed in his face. Spielberg, though, had made hit movies for every one of the studios involved—Warner Brothers, Universal, and MGM/UA–and got the rights for a mere $5,000 per character.

At the same time that Disney was building itself into a major film studio, it made a ferocious run at capturing a piece of the small screen. "The Golden Girls" television sitcom became the hit of the '85/'86 season, garnered nominations for 15 Emmy awards, and took home two. "The Wuzzles" and "The Adventures of the Gummi Bears" made their debut on Saturday mornings on competing networks, and pulled good ratings. The studio also contracted with NBC to produce eight prime-time specials. And on February 2, 1986, Eisner went on the air as host of the "Disney Sunday Movie," saying his first words on television: "Good evening. I'm Michael Eisner." After searching high and low for an actor with the right voice, the right credibility, the right sense of sincerity to be the television "face" of Disney, Rich Frank and Jeff Katzenberg had pressured Eisner into taking the job. They had three conditions, however: he needed a voice coach, he needed to lose 30 pounds, and Jane had to buy him a few new suits—tailored. Chairman Michael met their demands, and got the job. Disney's flagship show had been missing from the airwaves for nearly three years, after a previous run of 29 years. The new show was an enormous effort: the first season alone promised 23 original one- and two-hour films.

In hopes of rapidly becoming a force in mainstream network television, the studio had five pilots ready for the fall season—and, in addition, was flogging some of the weekly Sunday night movies as pilots for possible series. The "flagship" series also provided Katzenberg with the opportunity to try out a lot of new talent quickly. Steve Sauer, a lawyer and manager for a number of actors, picked up the phone one day to find Katzenberg on the other end, nearly breathless. One of Sauer's clients, blond former beauty queen Nancy Stafford, had signed on to do a Disney Sunday Movie, *The Last Electric Knight*. "I've just seen the dailies," said Katzenberg. "They're great. I have to have this girl. I want to put her in on an overall deal over here. Make this thing happen."

The phone call began negotiations that stretched over eight months. Stafford and Sauer "took a meeting" at Disney with Katzenberg and Frank. At one point in the meeting, Eisner popped down the hall to say,

"Hello, I hope you'll come aboard." Stafford was a little nervous about the deal. She had just spent three and a half years on "St. Elsewhere" and wasn't sure she wanted to tie herself down.

Katzenberg "hammered away" at them to make a long-term deal with Disney. He talked fast; he was excited and positive, "like a little tornado." He talked about what a wonderful thing it would be for her career, how she wouldn't want to let this go, what a great studio Disney was going to be, what a wonderful actress Stafford was, what wonderful things they could do together, what great care the studio would take with her.

According to Stafford, "Katzenberg doesn't let go until you've said yes." At last Stafford said yes. She left the meeting feeling secure, "like I had a home, I would be cared for. I felt great."

They had "a handshake," says Sauer, "and a handshake with Jeffrey is all you need. The man stands by what he says. If I make a deal with Jeffrey I don't have to worry about it."

The theme parks had always been the dog that wagged the Disney tail. In the early 1980s the parks had generated 85 percent or more of the operating income of the company. By the last third of the decade that had dropped to 65 to 70 percent, but the parks were still the engine of the Disney prosperity.

The parks now joined in the company's upward spiral of revenue, in part because ticket prices continued what had already begun to seem an inexorable climb—from $16.50 to $17.95 at Disneyland (and from $11.50 to $12.95 for kids). The climb was a basic part of the emerging strategy: the new men in town had found the money spigot that would fund everything else.

To show that they were giving something back, Team Disney turned up the pace of change in the parks. In 1985, Eisner had to rely on quick fixes: the nearly-instant Videopolis teen nightclub, and the giveaways at the gate. Eisner declared 1986 "Minnie's Year" at the parks, and put the 60-year-old screen idol through a makeover, complete with disco outfits and records to match. Disneyland kept the giveaways going and added a "Circus Fantasy" promotion.

In January 1986, at EPCOT, the first visitors began streaming into Seabase Alpha in the "Living Seas" pavilion, riding "sea cabs" under water into the center of the world's largest man-made ocean environment, complete with coral reefs, sharks, and octopuses. Actual undersea scientists descended through a column of water right into the "Seabase" to talk to visitors and answer questions. Visitors could pick up and feel live anemones and crabs in a working tide-pools—or eat seafood below the sea in the underwater Coral Reef restaurant.

"Big Thunder Ranch," a re-creation of a nineteenth-century horse ranch, opened at Disneyland in June of the same year. Like parts of "Living Seas," it offered some hands-on experiences for urban children, including the opportunity to pet barnyard animals, spin a little wool, or watch a horse-shoeing. But it was a temporary place-holder, due to give way in time to another theme area.

On September 19, on both coasts, the Michael Jackson–George Lucas–Francis Ford Coppola extravaganza *Captain Eo* opened. It had become a symbol of the reach of the new Disney team. The array of talent from "outside" went far beyond its three principals. Special effects were by Lucas' Industrial Light and Magic Company. The set designer, John Napier, had designed the Broadway shows *Cats* and *Nicholas Nickleby*. Choreographer Jeffrey Hornaday had choreographed *A Chorus Line*. The opening was boosted by ads on ABC, MTV, and the Disney Channel, and in print and radio spots across the country. The premiers turned into "A-list" parties on both coasts. Once again, the American public had to readjust their image of "dusty" Disney.

At Disney World work began on the MGM/Disney Studio Tour; on a pavilion for Norway in EPCOT Center's World Showcase; and on "Pleasure Island," a collection of nightclubs, teen spots, theaters, and restaurants near the borders of Disney World. And on the West Coast Eisner and Nunis announced that the company was planning vast new expansions of Disneyland, including as many as four new "theme" areas (including "Edison Square," a second Main Street that had appeared on Walt's original renderings), or even a whole second park—possibly a scaled-down EPCOT. Disney had begun to look toward high-tech, software-driven, repeatable, and reprogrammable experiences on the model of *Captain Eo* as the wave of the future, replacing "big iron" thrill rides. As Nunis said, "You don't have to spend all your money on bricks and mortar."

The greatest expansion, and the biggest leap for the company, would be the new park outside Paris. The old management had cautiously explored the idea, but Eisner made it happen in short order. Disney had more experience with theme parks than any other company in the world, and this time it was determined to make good use of that experience. Each Disney project in turn had become the anchor of large real estate booms beyond its control. Anaheim, California, once a wide, quiet expanse of orange groves, where the loudest noise was the cranked-up war-surplus DC-3 engines used to drive the frost off the trees on cold winter mornings, had gone wall-to-wall with motels, coffee shops, bedrooms, rival "attractions," freeways, a baseball stadium and, in nearby Garden Grove, the Crystal Cathedral. Anaheim's land values shot up 25 percent compounded every year for a quarter-century after Disneyland opened— well above the average even for growth-happy southern California. But beyond the borders of its parking lot, Disney owned little land, did not control or profit from the development, and did not benefit from the appreciation in land values.

Orlando had seen its land values jump 30 percent every year since the first spade of dirt was turned over at Disney World. Once a sleepy lake-dotted central Florida town known for its quiet life among the Spanish moss, Orlando had turned into a sprawling scrub-jungle metropolis, where vast hotels towered over the undergrowth, as if wandering Mayan pyramids had found new lives in Florida as temples to commerce. By the turn of the '90s it was the fastest-growing metropolitan area in the country, a sprawl of 70,000 hotel rooms, the mother lode of cheap rental cars, the most popular honeymoon destination in the world, the largest convention town east of the Rockies, and home to the country's fastest-growing international airport. But most of this development had taken place beyond the borders of Disney World, where by far the majority of the land remained wilderness.

In Tokyo, the story was even more magnified. Tokyo Disneyland, a 3-D photocopy of Disney World's Magic Kingdom, right down to the racks of mouse-ear hats and the parade down Main Street, had been filled to capacity almost every day since its opening in 1983. But not only did Disney own none of the land around the park, it did not even own the park. Since the announcement of the project, the land near the park had appreciated faster than any other land in Japan, a market notorious for high appreciation. But the company had no control over the development, and no share in the growing equity in the park or outside it.

Paris would be different. In fact, it would be easiest not even to think of Euro Disneyland as a theme park, but as a massive real estate development anchored by a theme park. The park would come first, but piece by piece it would be surrounded by nearly eight square miles of development—all designed and controlled by Disney. Euro Disneyland, in Marne-la-Vallée 32 kilometers east of Paris, would be a $4-billion developer's dream a fifth the size of Paris itself. Eventually it would boast several theme parks, over 18,000 hotel rooms, 3,000 apartments, 2,400 houses and condos, 2,400 time-share apartments, 1.4 million square feet of commercial space, 6.3 million square feet of office space, and a 6.7-million-square-foot corporate park. France's proud new TGV, its 230-mile-per-hour rail line, would disgorge its passengers right across the street from the Magic Kingdom's main gate, through which would pour an estimated 11 million visitors in the first year.

All through 1986, and into 1987, Disney's chief counsel Joe Shapiro spent much of his time in Paris, negotiating an extremely complex agreement with the French government, with its multiple layers of bureacracy and competing interests. Until the French agreed on a single negotiator to represent their side, he sat with 36 negotiators from federal, provincial, and metropolitan governments, transit districts, and redevelopment agencies. Gary Wilson and Frank Wells would call him (often in the middle of the night Paris time), urging him to hang tough and get the best deal he could. It didn't help that Laurent Fabius' Socialist government had fallen soon after it had signed the original letter of intent, and was now on the sidelines complaining that the new prime minister, conservative Jacque Chirac, was selling the country down the river.

Eventually, Shapiro did wring remarkable concessions from the French. The land was artificially valued at $5,000 per acre, its value as agricultural land in 1971, and that value was guaranteed for 20 years, no matter how long Disney took to buy the land. Everyone else in France pays a "value-added" tax of 18.6 percent on every franc of goods sold; Disney would pay only 7 percent. The French would improve the highways to the site and extend the TGV express train at their own expense. And the French government would loan Disney as much as $770 million for the project at an artificially low interest rate of 7.85 percent, with no repayments for the first five years. These were concessions that would eventually make the project extremely profitable for Disney.

In part, Eisner's and Team Disney's explosion of energy in its first two years was aimed at the investment community. If Disney were to survive and prosper, it needed to be safe from takeover attempts. That security could only be grounded in the collective mind of Wall Street. Disney not only needed a new master, it needed to be seen to have a new master, a sure hand that could take the company where it needed to go.

By early 1986, Wall Street had fallen in love with the man with the Howdy Doody face and the million-dollar gut. In January, the company announced a four-for-one stock split, and on the day the new shares were to be distributed in March, the stock hit 143, over three times its price 18 months earlier.

To Wall Street and to the public, Disney was coming alive, and Eisner had become the new face on a company that had been faceless since the death of its founder. But behind that face, something deeper was going on. Eisner was building a grand strategy aimed at making the company dominant in all its fields—and this was the real significance of the hiring of big gun Gary Wilson as chief financial officer.

One of Wilson's most important functions was helping create the company's strategic vision. Eisner, with the help of Wilson and Wells, began to devise a long-term strategy for Disney. They operated as a team— Eisner spun visions; Wells played with practicalities, business realities, politics, macroeconomics; Wilson was the mechanic, the financial wizard.

The basic strategy was simple: Eisner wanted to exploit Disney's assets more fully, and develop new businesses that fit with the old ones. But the strategy had to be different from the way Disney had done business before—and in fact different from the ways Hollywood had done business in the last few decades. By the middle of the 1980s, Hollywood operated in a profoundly changed environment. The ground on which it was built had shifted as thoroughly as it had in the early 1950s, when the studio system had been destroyed by government antitrust action and the growth of television. In the 1980s the forces were even larger, less manageable, and less predictable. Three main forces came together at once, entertwined like a three-stranded braid.

The first had to do with world markets. The world wanted American entertainment. Unlike the demand for American steel, cars, shoes, or wheat, the demand around the world for American entertainment grew like a new hunger in the '80s. For reasons both simple and complex, American movies, television shows, music, and the fads of fashion and consumer products that flowed from them, became widely considered the best, the style to be emulated everywhere—even as many regions of the world experienced a renascence of their own cultures.

For example, the new Michael Jackson tour in 1985 opened not in New York but in Tokyo; Michael Douglas would film his highly considered *Black Rain* in Tokyo, with much of the dialogue in Japanese; Paul Simon filmed his *Graceland* concert video in Zimbabwe with South African musicians; and Madonna began to consider Germany a prime market for her music videos. In film, television, recording, animation, theme parks, and other related industries, the ability to market and distribute beyond the borders of the United States rapidly became essential to survival.

The second force acting on Hollywood was more complex. Demography, that deep driving force behind so many trends, was shifting in multiple layers around the world. In many areas, including Western Europe, major parts of Africa, South America, and the Middle East, Japan, and the smaller nations of Asia (including Singapore, Taiwan, and South Korea), the ability of the middle and working classes to pay for entertainment was increasing at a rapid rate.

The United States was aging rapidly, and its middle-aged and older populations were playing increasing roles in the marketplace. The increasing median age was pushing up the demand for more sophisticated types of entertainment. The percentage of the population under 30—especially those under 25, the market for grunt-and-giggle films like *Porky's* and splatter films like *Nightmare on Elm Street*—was falling, and the earning power of the younger age groups, when adjusted for inflation, was dropping. At the same time the crest of the baby boom generation was approaching 40, reaching the period of its highest earning power—and these baby boom parents were rearing families of their own and looking for entertainment for their children.

Throughout the '80s, industry pundits repeatedly expressed amazement at the continued vitality of the "family" film. With the exception of *Jaws* and *Beverly Hills Cop,* the top ten films on the industry's list of the all-time highest-grossing productions (including *E.T.*, *Star Wars* and its two sequels, three "Indiana Jones" films, *Batman, Ghostbusters,* and *Back to the Future*) were all films to which one might take a child or young adult.

At the same time that the global demand for American entertainment was rising and the demographics of that globe were shifting dramatically in favor of entertainment and leisure industries, the ways the world received its entertainment were changing drastically. In the 1970s, most commercial entertainment in the world arrived in the form of live concerts, theatrical films, records, audiocassettes, local radio and television, and radio and television networks distributed by land lines and microwave. In the 1980s, all those systems were still in place, but they had been augmented by videocassettes, cable radio and television, satellite broadcasting, compact discs, video games, and computer programs.

In 1980, few people in the United States had a VCR. In the early

1980s, Disney helped lead the fight to keep them out of the country, suing Sony and taking the fight to the Supreme Court. Similarly, in 1980 people in and out of the industry still doubted whether cable would ever hook up enough of the country to amount to much of anything. MCA and several other majors launched their own cable system to try to cut in on the growing reach of Time Inc.'s Home Box Office. Hollywood lost both fights, but won the war. By mid-decade some 57 percent of Hollywood's profit came from video and cable, and only 30 percent from the domestic box office.

With so many different ways to package a star like Madonna, the trick was to market her in as many packages as possible. The company that controlled those myriad distribution methods, and had products that would sell in all of them, held the key to the future. Studios moved toward "vertical integration," toward combining distribution channels under one umbrella. Disney already owned its own theatrical film distributor and cable channel. While Fox bought the old Metromedia system and started the Fox Network, Warner combined with Time, which owned HBO, MCA beat out Disney to buy WWOR in New York, and Paramount bought the TVX broadcasting group's five stations.

These new methods of distribution began to have a profound effect on Hollywood strategy, and Eisner helped to lead the change.

Hollywood film-making had always been risky, an old West high-stakes dice game. After the the demise of the studio system in the late '40s, the cost of film-making skyrocketed; both stars and theater owners could pick and choose which film they wanted to be associated with; and every film became a multimillion-dollar crap shoot. Since the early 1970s Hollywood had increasingly looked to "blockbuster" hits to make up for the duds. Then endless sequels of the hits could reduce the risk to the studio—or at least the risk to the job of the person who ordered the sequel ("Hey, the first six did great business. How was I to know the seventh one would bomb?"). It was not a risk-free strategy, and it was boring—sequels have to be virtual copies of the original in order to have a chance of succeeding. Eisner acknowledged this in a 1982 private strategy memo at Paramount: "Most of the sequels that have succeeded have been mirror images of the originals. They involve the same kind of attitudes, feelings and morals. When you take the sequel and try to do something revolutionary with it, you tend to fail."

In the traditional strategy the big risk, the risk that gives everyone in the business cold sweats, is creating that original model, the one the studio can make sequels and copies of. Studios repeatedly tried to create blockbusters by large applications of money, talent, and hype. But spending a lot of money cannot guarantee even a reasonable return on investment. It is difficult, if not impossible, for a studio or a producer, let alone an outside investor, or an executive of a corporation that owns the studio, to tell how a film is going to do in the marketplace before it hits that first weekend up on the marquee. The descriptions given out beforehand, the reputations associated with it, the originality or familiarity of the concept—none of these, in the end, are truly "bankable."

Analyst Chris Dixon of Kidder, Peabody puts it this way: "Imagine that I'm going to give you the opportunity to invest in a picture that we will distribute. It will be produced by either Steven Spielberg or George Lucas, both well known, talented individuals. They are going to use the best special effects people in the world to do this project. It involves a cartoon character and some live action, a combination of both. They have an idea that they presented to us, an idea that we like. You have to make a $25- to $50-million decision right now. That's all the information that's presented to you as a businessman, as an investor, as a producer, as a studio executive. You don't have any way of knowing, 18 months before this thing actually is going to be shown on the screen, how it will come out. I could be describing *Roger Rabbit* or *Howard the Duck*."

Lucas' *Howard the Duck* came out in 1986 with tremendous fanfare, and within two weeks was playing second on double bills. It was a disaster. Yet its concept was virtually indistinguishable from Disney and Spielberg's *Who Framed Roger Rabbit?* "From a business point of view," says Dixon, "the only decision that you have is how you manage your risk of failure."

Satellite, cable, video, and other new delivery methods helped do just that. They made new products more profitable. They also made the studios' libraries of old films worth much more. And the Disney company, starting with Walt, had never let a single film out of its grasp. No one in Hollywood had firmer control of their old films than Disney, and few could compete with the sales value of the Disney classics. Disney was perfectly poised to take advantage of the new environment.

The new outlets for movies also reduced the risk of producing films by giving movies a shelf-life, a second chance to build a following. A movie that did so-so at the box office could (and surprisingly often does) do very well in video, or on cable, or in spin-off CDs and music videos. Hollywood, which had always been America's twentieth-century equivalent of a gold rush, began to look more like a manufacturer of a commodity. The way to play the game was to get out as much product as possible, packaged as many ways as possible, spreading the risk and increasing the chance of profit. By late in the decade, the typical Hollywood movie could pay most or all of its production costs from video sales alone. This came close to "no-fault" movie-making—if you could avoid big-budget, make-or-break projects.

If films that were no better than average could make a profit, then it made little sense to risk large amounts of money on one film in hopes that it would be a "blockbuster." The better strategy was to spread the risk through a "diversified portfolio" of films appealing to different age groups and interests. Movie-making became, as one Wall Street analyst put it, "a game of singles and doubles and bunts, not of home runs." The smart executives brought more of the movie-making process in-house, where they could control the concepts, the process, and the costs. Instead of looking for the big breakthrough, the next giant sleigh-ride, they looked for solidly constructed, familiar scripts with roles built for the people they had on contract.

Eisner and Katzenberg followed exactly that formula, and they further spread the risks by looking for outside partners. Oddly, Wall Street's initial reaction to the Silver Screen partnerships was cool, despite the fact that each one was rapidly oversubscribed. As a 1987 Kidder, Peabody analysis put it, "We believe Disney has given up the high returns associated with hit films by using Silver Screen Partners to finance company pictures. As the product mix moves from highly profitable animation classics to Silver Screen and Touchstone Pictures offerings, operating margins for the [film] division are expected to shrink."

But profits did not shrink. By raising the prices at the parks and keeping up attendance through marketing, by selling limited partnerships, by making profitable movies, rereleasing the classics in theaters and putting them out in video, Disney quickly began to pull in large amounts of profit. Revenues, which stood at $1.7 billion in 1984, hit almost $3 billion in 1987. Net income rose from 1984's $98 million to $445 million in 1987. Annual increases in net income after 1984 averaged over 50 percent per year, and in 1987 reached 80 percent. The company's return on equity rose from the 8 percent it had been when Eisner walked on the lot, to 15 percent in 1985, 19 percent in 1986, and a phenomenal 27 percent in 1987.

Eisner claimed a certain ambivalence about growth, saying at one point, "Sometimes bigger is better, sometimes not," but his company showed no ambivalence at all. By the beginning of 1987, the company had paid off the huge debt it had when Eisner arrived, and was sitting on a $340-million pile of cash. But buried in this success was a "problem" that drove Disney's growth as much as the new risk environment, global changes, and sheer ambition: Disney actually had too much cash.

Suppose you are running a company that can borrow money at 10 percent. Suppose further that investments that are liquid enough to be considered cash reserves are returning 12, 15, or even 20 percent, while the money you invest in your own enterprise returns 25 to 27 percent. Then your fiduciary responsibility to your stockholders demands that you keep your cash reserves low, reinvest that extra cash in the company, and borrow more cash to expand your business as fast as possible. Every dollar of extra debt capacity (an estimated $2 billion by 1987), every dollar of cash sitting around in reserves, represents a drag on the value of the stock, since it is not bringing in the return it could bring in if it were working for the company. And, especially in the mid-1980s, a big, successful, media company, awash in cash and low on debt, could quickly become a prime takeover candidate despite the high price of its stock.

So Disney's success and growth were, in part, self-driving. Because of the superb assets built by the Disney brothers and their successors, it had a tremendous capacity to grow. Because of the ambition of Eisner, Wells, Katzenberg, Wilson, and the other top managers of Disney, it was managed toward growth. But, once they had made the decisions that began bringing more money in the door, the company's tremendous cash flow and high return on investment forced it to grow rapidly. The alternative would have been stagnation as a cash cow, and the ultimate threat of takeover.

Both the speed and the character of that growth owed a fair amount to Gary Wilson. At Disney, Wilson played with variations of the idea that he had used so profitably at Marriott—put your capital into the things you do best, and let other people's capital take up the slack. At Marriott, that meant putting the company's capital into developing and running hotels, without tying it up in actually owning the buildings and land. At Disney, the idea was similar: use Disney's capital on its creative ideas; use other people's capital to pay for the bricks and mortar.

Wilson even investigated the idea of selling EPCOT, or all of the parks, to outside investors, while retaining control through general partnerships or leases. But Disney had no need for the cash such a mammoth deal could generate. Besides, says Wilson, "after analyzing Disney, it apparent to us that the parks themselves were very high-return assets with a relatively low tax basis."

Overseas, working this theme of owning only the high-return assets while retaining control over the enterprise, Wilson worked out deals so complex that one observer commented, "Some people will make you an offer you can't refuse; Gary will make you an offer you can't even understand." Perhaps the iconic example of Wilson's financial wizardry was his handling of the profits from Tokyo Disneyland, an essentially fixed percentage of gross receipts—in yen.

In Wilson's eyes, this was an unacceptably uncertain and uncontrollable source of cash, subject to the whims of the Japanese public and to the vagaries of the yen and the dollar. Although expansion of the park would bring in some profit in the long run, it did not seem a quick or easy way to make more money, unless the ownership structure could be changed. The park had been packed from the day it had opened its doors, and the percentage of revenue was fixed. The cash came in year after year, steady as an annuity. It was a nice revenue stream but, to someone like Wilson, boring. He wanted some way to crank it up—to find a way he could invest it at higher rates of return. So he sold it.

Wilson projected the revenue stream from Tokyo Disneyland for 20 years into the future, discounted it 6 percent, and sold it to Japanese investors for about $750 million. He held onto the more than ¥90 billion this produced until the yen strengthened to 124 to the dollar, then converted it to dollars and reinvested it at 10 percent until it could be reinvested in more profitable Disney businesses. He gained control of the future revenue stream, made four percent more on the cash transaction, and hedged the revenue stream against foreign exchange fluctuations.

The financial structure of Euro Disneyland, which Wilson created in his first 18 months at Disney, is Byzantine in the extreme, an interlocking set of companies that gives Disney effective control of the entire enterprise, although it owns only a small fraction. Wilson's complex piece of corporate sculpture served several ends: to provide incentives to see that the project met its goals, to rationalize the risk, and to bring in low-cost funds for the capital-intensive development phase of the project. The whole enterprise is being developed and built by Euro Disneyland SCA (*Société en Commandité par Actions*), similar to an American limited partnership. Disney can own up to 49 percent of the SCA; Europeans own the rest. Euro Disneyland SCA, in turn, is controlled by its *gérant*, or managing agent, a company called Euro Disneyland S.A.

Euro Disneyland S.A. is wholly owned by Disney, and can only be removed by the general partner, which is another Disney subsidiary. Through Euro Disneyland S.A., Disney controls the entire enterprise.

But control and ownership are kept separate. Euro Disneyland SCA, who is building the project, will sell the Magic Kingdom (the theme park itself, centerpiece of the project) to Euro Disneyland SNC (*Société de Nom Collectif*), in which Disney has a 17 percent stake, then lease it back. After 20 years, when the financing and tax benefits of this arrangement are used up, the SCA will buy the park back from the SNC, and the SNC, whose only function is to finance the park through the leaseback arrangement, will disappear like a dipped "toon" out of *Who Framed Roger Rabbit?*

This complex structure is a prime example of Wilson's aggressive asset management. The entire $4.2-billion project cost the company only $160 million in equity. In return for that investment, Disney would receive 10 percent of all admissions, 5 percent of all concessions, and 49 percent of all profits, an estimated take of $1.12 billion in the first year alone. Wilson's legerdemain gave Disney high returns on investment, but left it in complete control of the project.

Within the company, Wilson instilled a high measure of discipline once he had his team in place. Starting in the 1986 fiscal year, he laid down certain requirements for the company: every division would build a five-year business plan demonstrating 20 percent growth in each year. Every acquisition would have to pay for itself in five years. These firm guidelines were called the "20-20" plan.

He began to look over possible acquisitions that would meet those guidelines and fit Disney. Among other possible buys, his team did deep analyses of the libraries of television shows at Lorimar and MCA; Kerkorian's MGM/UA Communications; CBS Records; A&M Records; Geffen Records; the Cineplex Odeon theater chain; and the Sea World theme parks. In most cases, Eisner, Wells, and Wilson decided the price was simply too high—they would do just as well, for less money, building their own company. Throughout the late '80s Disney remained poised to buy companies that fit, but bought only a few small enterprises.

Wilson further fashioned a way to meld Disney's creativity with the necessary financial controls. He gave each Disney project a "financial box" that described a range of assumptions within which the project would work. A new project could have a budget of a certain amount if it could handle a certain number of people and generate a certain amount of revenue. If the designers could find ways to attract more people, move them through faster, or make more money from them, then the "box" would allow the budget to grow. This "box" was much more useful than a simple budget would have been. It allowed a flexible interaction between the creative designers and the financial management people under Wilson. The creative people could build things wilder and bigger if they could show that the improvements would pay for themselves. "We're very disciplined about budgets," according to Wilson. "We swear at each other a lot in the process. But if the company had financial guys that were pushovers, we'd lose financial discipline." Describing himself as a puppy, Eisner added, "I put a leash on myself and give the leash to Frank Wells and Gary Wilson."

Wilson added, "We give our creative people and operators a big box within which they can exercise their prerogative. In films, we recognize that the script is the most important creative decision, so our creative people make those decisions. But when it comes to producing and marketing the films, it's got to be economic." The discipline for the parks was even more stringent. Referring to the budget for the Studio Tour then under construction in Florida, Wilson commented, "There's no change in that budget—unless Michael Eisner himself goes in and says we need to do this or that to improve the show."

Making this interplay work was essential to making Disney work, and the box allowed for creative movement. The building of Typhoon Lagoon, the new water park at Walt Disney World, provides the perfect example. The park operators had observed the success of nearby competitors with cheap plastic-and-steel water parks. It made sense. Florida is hot, and inland Orlando is even hotter. The operators prepared a proposal, complete with pro formas, to build just such an attraction on the property. They intended to just go out and buy a complete water park from the people who made their competitors'.

Eisner rejected the idea. It had no "show," it had no "theme." It wasn't Disney. He said, "I want to be sure that imagineering's involved, and I don't want it to be a typical plastic park." So the operators did involve the imagineers—but they required them to stick with the original budget. They also suggested several themes. One was a rather nonaquatic space theme, complete with aliens. The imagineers struggled with it, but they couldn't make it work. With Eisner's approval, they tossed aside the aliens and designed a logging camp.

In mid-1986 Eisner came to Florida and stood with Randy Bright in the middle of the swamp, looking at the drawings Bright had brought. He handed them back. "It's okay," he said, "but it's got to have something with greater snap to it; it's just not Disney. Give me something more outrageous."

Back at imagineering, Bright told his designers, "Forget the budget. The main mission here is to design something that's outrageous and Disney, and then we'll worry about the dollars later."

Walking through the imagineers' studio one afternoon, Bright happened to see a sketch on the board of a younger designer—a cockeyed paddlewheel steamer stuck on top of a mountain. "That's it!" Bright cried. "That's our theme! A typhoon has come through this island, throwing everything topsy-turvy. That's our story." The steamer became a shrimp boat. The park became an island full of all kinds of nautical flotsam and jetsam deposited there by the typhoon—which the people on the island used to build a tourist attraction.

Eisner loved it. It wound up costing over $62 million—twice what the other budget was—but the financial "box" showed that it could be priced high enough, and attract enough visitors, to make money. And the actual operation has repeatedly beat the projections. As Bright said, "It's wacky, it's creative, it's incredibly and radically different. It's what you'd expect from Disney."

"What you'd expect from Disney" was given another twist by a rapidly developing love-hate affair between Eisner and the world of architecture.

Soon after he took over the company, Eisner realized that, with all his expansion plans, he would be commissioning scores of buildings. It would ultimately be his decision to say "yes" or "no" to plans for facades that millions of people would see and use—hotels, office buildings, convention centers, condominiums, golf courses, shopping centers, even private homes—practically the entire range of domestic and public buildings. When the previous management had ventured beyond the gates of their parks (for the hotels built in the Disney Village, within the boundaries of Disney World, for instance), they had not expressed anything distinctive in the architecture. Disney Village could have been any collection of hotels with palm trees.

Eisner felt sensitive about the impact all those buildings would have, and about his own relative ignorance about architecture. And much of what passed for modern architecture outraged his sensibilities. "It's not so much that you want to do good architecture, it's just so offensive to do bad architecture. It's like doing a bad movie," he said. "You have to be careful, because unlike the movies, if the building is a dog, if it's terrible, you can't hide it. You have to go on looking at it every day, reminding yourself of your own bad taste." So he turned to the man who had hung a Picasso on his bedroom wall as a child—Victor Ganz. Ganz recommended that he talk to Philip Johnson and Michael Graves, two giants of postmodernism. Johnson had designed, among many others, the AT&T Building in Manhattan with its furniturelike pediment. Graves, a Princeton architectural professor, was gaining renown for his designs for the Humana building in Louisville and the high-rise addition to Frank Lloyd Wright's Whitney Museum in New York. Soon after, Eisner happened upon both of them at a Metropolitan Opera intermission. Johnson did not catch the significance of the loose-limbed, enthusiastic man he was introduced to, and wandered off in search of some spring water. Graves stayed to talk, and a long-term relationship began to take shape.

Eisner schooled himself in architecture, reading dozens of books and arranging his travels to allow him to see and walk through specific buildings. It helped that, in late 1984, he had hired as his personal assistant 27-year-old Arthur Levitt, III, son of the chief of the New York Stock Exchange. Levitt was an architecture maven, and Eisner charged him with guiding his architectural studies. Before long, Eisner began giving commissions to Graves and a series of other well-known architects—and began to push them just as he would push a screenwriter or an imagineer. He commissioned Graves to design a new headquarters building for the company on the lot in Burbank. When Graves produced sketches full of porticoes, columns, domes and pediments reminiscent of Tuscan villas and midwestern banks, Eisner suggested that he lighten it up—by supporting the main pediment not on columns but on caryatids of the Seven Dwarfs, done in stucco, 19 feet tall. Graves agreed. "The fact is," said Eisner, "we're the only company that could get away with it. If you saw seven dwarfs holding up a building anywhere else in the world, you'd think it was like plastic reindeers or something. We're not about safe-deposit boxes. We're in the entertainment business."

That was the key: Eisner felt that, because Disney was in the entertainment business, everything it did should be entertaining, from its movies right down to the doorknobs on its office buildings.

Within the first year Eisner announced the Grand Floridian, a massive new hotel to be set on a lagoon near the Magic Kingdom in Disney World. A white-clapboard and gingerbread wedding cake of Victorian furbelows and cascading red-tiled roofs modeled on such great turn-of-the-century resorts as San Diego's Del Coronado and Oakland's Claremont, the Grand Floridian would be complete with bellboys wearing plus fours, golf caps or straw boaters, and (in cool weather) cable knit sweaters. The hotel's theme was spun out by the imagineers, and the execution turned over to an outside firm. At the same time the imagineers re-created Hollywood Boulevard, right down to the lamp posts, the palm trees, the neon, and the diners, for the newly announced Studio Tour.

Disney also announced it would build two huge luxury hotels, complete with an attached convention center, which would eventually be named the Swan and the Dolphin. This originally had been Checchi's 20,000-room deal with Marriott. But that deal had fallen apart when Eisner and Wells began to feel that they didn't need Marriott, and when Tishman Realty & Construction Co. of New York had sued: the old management had signed a deal with Tishman that made them the sole developer of hotels on the Disney property. The Swan and the Dolphin also replaced Arvida's "Core" concept of home and factory/theme parks, leaving only the original thought: Disney World did indeed need a core, a center of gravity. And the right place for it would be near the physical center of the property, between Epcot and the emerging Studio Tour.

Michael Graves got this commission, too, and produced two extraordinary buildings of Babylonian proportions with Cecil B. deMille's sense of decoration, sporting six-story-tall statues of swans and dolphins on their "shoulders."

In the same vein, Eisner commissioned Robert Stern to design a Florida "casting center" (hiring hall) that ended up with Peter Pan murals on the ceiling and doorknobs like the one that says, "Ouch!" in *Alice in Wonderland*. Stern also whipped up a pair of hotels to sit next to the Swan and Dolphin, the Beach and Yacht Club Hotels, each frothy imitations of their namesakes.

Eisner was an extremely active patron, treating the architects the way he would treat film directors. He involved himself directly in picking the architects, going over ideas, debating colors and motifs, and sitting through the endless presentations, even picking materials for bedspreads and curtains. He pushed the architects whom he commissioned to take greater visual risks, to go farther than they had gone before. And in so doing, he occasioned a tempest of debate in architectural circles about the nature and purpose of architecture, whether an architect could properly be used to market a corporation, and whether a building with ten-story blue banana leaves painted on the side (Graves' Dolphin) could be considered "serious." Some architects turned down Eisner's commissions and snidely called Michael Graves "Mickey," while others came to see Eisner as a modern Medici. Not that Eisner pays big fees, or allows buildings to become expensive. He argued openly that, after their Disney buildings have helped make them famous, the architects can charge their next clients big fees, and brags that the Dolphin and the Swan cost no more than the average Sheraton.

And, in another sense, the Swan and the Dolphin signaled the new Disney: the company did not own them or pay to build them. Disney retained only a 10 percent stake in the hotels' ownership, along with Tishman, Metropolitan Life, and Japan's Aoki Corp. The Swan would be run by Westin, the Dolphin by Sheraton.

Eisner's unfolding strategy aimed at turning exactly this combination of creativity, risk-taking, financial wizardry, and strong financial controls into a recipe for dominance of the global market for family entertainment. Because of Eisner's strong leadership, the talented ferocity of the Team Disney he put together, and the latent assets of the Walt Disney Company, the strategy rapidly began to show results.

11

Masters of the Universe

By 1987, Disney was already a far different, and far larger, company than it had been only three years before. The strategy mapped out by Eisner and Wells in Fort Worth in 1984, elaborated with Checchi's help in the spring of 1985 and given teeth by Wilson in 1985 and 1986, had already begun to show clear results.

Before 1984, "what you would expect from Disney" had meant, for the public, inoffensive cartoon characters, spotless theme parks, and "family" movies, including classic tales retold in beautiful animation with upbeat endings. For Wall Street, Disney had come to mean a declining, lackluster stock. For Hollywood, Disney had become a "niche" studio with a rapidly shrinking niche, and without the talent, imagination, contacts, or access to capital to climb out of it.

By 1987, most of these perceptions had changed. The public had begun to associate the Disney parks with such popular, creative people as George Lucas and Michael Jackson. In films, the effect was less direct: although the public paid little attention to the Touchstone label on movie posters, and few people associated it with Disney, movie-goers had bought plenty of tickets to see the screwball comedies coming out of Disney. But at the same time, the public eye began to see another side to Disney: tough, greedy, and far more "commercial" than they had considered the old company. To Wall Street, Disney was a rapidly rising star. To the rest of Hollywood, Disney was a new, tough competitor. Between 1984 and 1987, Disney had rapidly come to stand for creativity melded with financial discipline, rapid expansion based on high cash flow, hard bargaining from a position of strength, and ferocious global ambitions.

The company had responded rapidly to Eisner's frenzied cranking of its corporate machine. In 1986 it beat its 1985 net income—its profit—by 42 percent. In 1987 Disney turned around and beat 1986 by another 59 percent. Disney's cash flow had passed the billion-dollar mark, double what it had been only two years before. The stock price, after splitting four-for-one the year before, had climbed once again from $35 a share into the $80 range. By the turn of the decade, the stock would climb as high as $136 per share, a dozen times its level at mid-decade.

Eisner and Katzenberg had built Touchstone, which had been nothing more than an alternative label for the release of *Splash* under the old management, into a complete second studio capable of producing a dozen movies per year. This rapid growth meant broadening the Disney portfolio to include adult comedies, such as *Down and Out in Beverly Hills* and *Three Men and a Baby*, dramas like *Good Morning, Vietnam*, and movies designed to sell to all ages, such as *Roger Rabbit*.

The strategies Eisner and his Team Disney developed worked more rapidly than even an optimist like Eisner could have hoped for. If 1986 found Disney in the odd position of pulling in the industry's highest average box office, 1987 found it in an even more surprising position: third in the industry in total box-office. As recently as 1984, despite the success of *Splash*, it had been a distant 12th, in a field that only counted six or seven major studios. With *Stakeout* pulling in $64 million and *Snow White* becoming the highest-grossing reissue in history with $46 million in domestic ticket sales, suddenly Disney was earning 13 percent of all the dollars shoved through movie ticket windows in America.

At the same time that Disney suddenly turned into a power in the theaters, the company also became a heavyweight in the video industry. Disney had fought videocassette recorders in an attempt to protect the market value of movies it might show on the Disney Channel. As in many other instances, the initial reaction of the ancien régime to technological challenge was not to exploit it but to hide from it.

But when Sony prevailed and the black machines began to flood the country, Disney turned to the new field with gusto and market savvy. Its archive of classic children's films, its strong connection with the baby boomers (who now had their hands full with babies of their own), and its reputation for quality gave Disney a tremendous edge. In 1986, Disney sold 1.2 million units of *Sleeping Beauty*; in 1987 it sold 3.2 million of *Lady and the Tramp*. By 1987, of the 20 best-selling children's videos in the country, 18 were released by Disney.

Early 1987, though, marked the beginning of the making of a major mistake for the studio: *Dick Tracy*. Still looking for those blockbusters whose prestige and cash flow could shelter many lesser films (what the industry called "tent poles") and eager for characters to spin off into other media, Eisner and Katzenberg began talking to their long-time friend Warren Beatty about his pet project. The *Dick Tracy* project was already familiar to them. In fact, Beatty's interest in the film dated back to Eisner and Katzenberg's first run at it a decade before at Paramount. They had enlisted Universal to carry some of the costs, and Universal had enlisted director John Landis. Landis, when he couldn't get Clint Eastwood, enlisted Beatty.

Beatty eventually bought the rights to the project for $1 million and listed himself as director. That made the film even harder to make, since Beatty had a reputation as a perfectionist—reshooting scene after scene, recutting and editing for months beyond deadlines—and as fiercely protective of his creative work. He was also reclusive: as star and Oscar-winning director of *Reds*, he had refused to do any publicity at all, and the film barely made back its then-extraordinary $35-million costs.

Friend though he might be, the way Beatty worked was the polar opposite of the way Eisner and Katzenberg worked. They went at filmmaking hands-on, watching the budget and hitting the media with everything they had. But Beatty and Team Disney continued to waltz closer throughout 1987, and in 1988 got down to serious talking.

For the studio, 1987 was a great year. By the beginning of 1988 Eisner and Katzenberg had turned out 20 films at Disney, 18 of which had turned a profit—a phenomenal .900 batting average. But 1988 was even more phenomenal: Disney became the top studio in the industry, with four of the top ten films, 19 percent of all domestic box office, and over $1 billion in revenues for the studio alone. In the same year Disney sold 7.5 million videocasettes of *Cinderella* and became number one in the entire home video industry.

In the theaters, *Three Men and a Baby* opened in late November 1987 (in the 1988 fiscal year) and took in $10 million in the first weekend. Even after the film was out, the calls to Ted Danson from Katzenberg kept coming, every week, sometimes every three days. Not infrequently Katzenberg would be on a speaker phone with a room full of people in a financial meeting, giggling and joking—and telling him the phenomenal numbers the film was racking up.

Good Morning, Vietnam, released two months later, did even better, pulling in $12 million in its first weekend alone. The unusual story of the wise-cracking motormouth Armed Forces Radio deejay Adrian Cronauer bucking the brass and heartening the soldiers in the field seemed to strike just the right chord for Americans, whatever their memories of that war.

After the first weekend of *Three Men*, Katzenberg had danced on the conference table in the animation building. After the first weekend of *Good Morning* he flopped on his back on the table, shouting, "I've died and gone to heaven!"

Robin Williams, who played Cronauer, called the film's producer, Larry Brezner, to see how the film had done. When he heard that it had done very well, Williams asked him, "So we could make money on the back end?" Brezner didn't encourage him. Back-end profits are notoriously scarce in Hollywood. Many films that have made fortunes for the studios have never returned a dime to people who had percentages of the profits. Later, Williams did an interview on the "Good Morning, America" television show, in which he joked that he would never see those profits. Katzenberg, interested in the PR that Williams was giving the film, happened to be tuned in. The next day Williams received a note from Katzenberg. The note read: "Here's the beginning of the back end." It was wrapped around a check for $1 million.

In June 1988, *Who Framed Roger Rabbit?* hit the malls. One of the strangest films anyone has ever produced, *Roger Rabbit* combined a *film-noir* detective story with wacky Warner Brothers-style cartoon antics. Set in the late 1940s in Los Angeles, the film was built on the idea that cartoon characters ("toons") are real, and live in a place called "Toon Town." But evil Judge Doom, who hates the toons and covets the land on which Toon Town is built for his beloved freeways, is out to destroy all toons, starting with Roger. The film's real and toon characters constantly interact. This interaction required a new level of realism in the toons, created with the help of computers that tracked the modeling and shadows of the animated characters as they moved. In one remarkable scene, for example, Roger bumps a hanging lamp in the middle of a tussle. Throughout the rest of the rough-and-tumble scene, not only does the shadowing on Roger's puffy face change each time he moves, but it changes with each swing of the lamp. The film also required elaborate puppeteer work, since toons often smoked real cigars or brandished real guns. The costs rapidly climbed past the $30-million budget, and the slipping schedule threatened the opening date and all the elaborate promotional tie-ins that the studio's marketers had cooked up. In February 1988, Katzenberg personally took control of production. Within two months it was back on schedule, although the costs topped out at over $50 million, plus $32 million for promotion. But all the risks and promotion paid off: *Roger Rabbit* hit blockbuster status.

With *Three Men and a Baby* ($167 million), *Good Morning, Vietnam* ($124 million), and *Who Framed Roger Rabbit?* ($152 million), Disney became the first studio in history to release two films back-to-back—not to mention three in one year—which grossed over $100 million domestically. In the same year the Tom Cruise showcase *Cocktail* grossed $75 million, *Big Business* (pairing Bette Midler and Lili Tomlin) brought in $40 million, and the rerelease of *Bambi* generated another $38 million. As one admiring *Los Angeles Times* writer put it, "If this keeps up they're going to have to change the name of Dopey Drive."

In the summer of 1988, Eisner convened the company's usual mid-year planning session in Aspen, Colorado. Topic A was the studio's growth. In fiscal 1988, Disney would end up making a dozen films, and marketing 14 (counting two rereleases) under the Disney and Touchstone labels. Given the way Disney liked to handle films—with lots of executive oversight, plenty of poking and prodding and budget-watching—the number of films was straining the capacity of the studio to oversee them. Yet Eisner, Katzenberg, and the rest of Team Disney wanted to continue expanding the company as fast as possible. And the opportunities were there: while many of the smaller production companies that had sprung up in the 1970s were folding, unable to finance the rapidly rising costs of producing and marketing films, the number of theater screens in America was rising, not to mention the new fields of opportunity opened up by video, cable, and other forms of marketing.

The studio also had a personnel problem in its top ranks: two of the company's best production executives—David Hoberman, a 34-year-old former agent, and Ricardo Mestres, recently named as president of Touchstone—were becoming intense rivals in their ambition to expand the company and rise with it. If they were not given space to grow, one or both of them might leave Disney.

The solution to the two problems, Eisner decided, was to start a new studio under the Disney umbrella. He would put Hoberman in charge of the Touchstone and Disney labels, and give the new studio, Hollywood Pictures, to Mestres. Eisner joked, "We're paying Katzenberg like he's running two studios, so why not let him do it?"

In the fall of 1988, the studio signed Katzenberg to a highly lucrative new contract. At the same time, Katzenberg signed with Beatty for *Dick Tracy*. Beatty would get $9 million plus 15 percent of profits. While Disney could not control the picture as they normally did, the company created a safety net: production costs beyond $25 million would be charged to Beatty's percentage. Beatty agreed to cooperate in besieging the media. By this time Disney already had three "tent poles," but the experience had made Eisner and Katzenberg hungry for more, and had given them the cash to pay for it.

In 1989, the studio dropped to number three in the theaters of America, but studio revenues rose to $1.6 billion—another sign of the increasing importance of so-called subsidiary income from cable, video, and foreign sales. Disney videos led the market for a second year as *Roger Rabbit* sold 8.5 million copies, and *Bambi* a record 10.5 million, giving Disney three of the top five best-selling videos ever. The Disney Channel, for five years the fastest-growing cable service, reached 5 million subscribers.

Early in 1989, Ricardo Mestres moved across the street from the animation building to the Roy O. Disney building, set up an office, and started signing projects for Hollywood Pictures. Mestres slated *Pros and Cons*, about a con man who discovers a businessman's pocket scheduler and takes on his identity, to be Hollywood Pictures' first film. But it was overtaken by a Stephen Spielberg spider horror film, *Arachnophobia*. Disney had not dipped into the horror genre before. It was somehow even farther from Disney's "family film" background than were R-rated films. And the film would have a lot of expensive special effects. But it had Spielberg's name on it, and it carried the whiff of a blockbuster, so Katzenberg let Mestres sign for it. By the end of 1989 Mestres had 85 projects signed, and a dozen moving toward production.

Katzenberg hired Garry Marshall, who long before had created such television shows as "Laverne and Shirley" and "Happy Days" for Eisner, to work on another idea, a script called *3,000* that involved prostitution and a drug overdose. It wasn't Touchstone material, but Katzenberg gave Marshall a peculiar charge: he was to take this dark, heavy, mean-streets script and make it into a light-hearted comedy. If anyone could, it would be Marshall. He went to work and produced a new script, called *Off the Boulevard*. Katzenberg, meanwhile, had seen a beautiful young actress named Julia Roberts in *Mystic Pizza*. He signed her for a bargain-basement $350,000 to play the prostitute who is picked up by a businessman as an escort for a week, only to change both their lives. Katzenberg signed Richard Gere to play the businessman, paying his going rate of $2 million. At the last minute, as the film was being mixed, Roy Orbison's "Pretty Woman" was added to the soundtrack, and it seemed to click. Katzenberg renamed the slight but sexy Pygmalion-on-Hollywood-Boulevard tale *Pretty Woman*, and scheduled it to hit the theaters in the spring of 1990.

Meanwhile, in a summertime dominated by *Batman*, the highest-grossing film in history, Disney managed to place two very odd films into the year's top ten, both of which carried an unusually low count of breasts, blood, and car crashes. *Honey, I Shrunk the Kids*, a silly mad-scientist tale of the "Flubber" genre, brought in $130 million, while *Dead Poets Society*, a gentle and loving paen to the courage and vision that can be found in literature, made $95 million.

In the same year *Oliver and Company*, the animated musical dogs-and-cats version of *Oliver Twist* that had survived the 1985 gong show, featured the voices and singing of Billy Joel, Cheech Marin (of "Cheech and Chong"), Huey Lewis, Bette Midler, and Ruth Pointer (of the Pointer Sisters). More lively than *The Great Mouse Detective*, the $18-million film did $53 million in the most successful initial release in the history of animated film. But less than 12 months later *The Little Mermaid* took that record away with a $76-million gross. Katzenberg had immersed himself in the making of *Mermaid*, signing Broadway songwriters Alan Menken and Howard Ashman to do the music, and allowing the budget to climb past $23 million. But it was worth it. Critics solidly applauded it as the first true "classic" since Walt Disney was alive, the best animated film in 30 years.

But 1989, for the Disney studio, was the year of filming *Dick Tracy*. As Warner Brothers' *Batman* racked up record numbers on its way to becoming the highest-grossing film of all time, Katzenberg and Eisner became determined that *Tracy* would beat it. Beatty enlisted old friends in the project. Stephen Sondheim agreed to write the music. Dustin Hoffman and Al Pacino both agreed to appear in the film for union scale—$1,440 per week. Madonna, who had starred in two duds since turning down *Ruthless People*, personally begged Beatty for the part of Tess Trueheart. She finally landed it—but at union scale, instead of the $1 million she had demanded four years earlier. The look of the "dailies" was gorgeous, and Disney executives began to bet that they could turn the film into a gold mine of characters, from Tracy and Tess Trueheart to the scabrous lineup of villains—Lips Manley, Flattop, and Pruneface.

For all the excitement on the lot, 1989 had its share of bombs—so many, in fact, that once the summer had passed the studio seemed to have hit a slump in live films. Three bombs closed the year—*An Innocent Man*, *Gross Anatomy* (Matt Modine goes to medical school), and *Blaze*, a wonderfully fun little docudrama that had Paul Newman playing Louisiana Governor Earl Long having a prolonged affair with a stripper. The new year opened with *Where the Heart Is*, which grossed an embarrassing $1 million, and *Stella*, a four-handkerchief Bette Midler remake (done as a favor to Midler) that *Premier* called "so embarrassingly smarmy that company executives were said to be referring to it privately as 'Smella.'"

But in the spring of 1990 *Pretty Woman* pulled in a surprising $180 million, making it the second highest-grossing film in the industry for the year (behind *Ghost*), as well as the top-grossing film in all of Disney's history. *Pretty Woman* helped pull the studio to the top of the industry with nearly 20 percent of the summer's domestic box office.

Pretty Woman was the first of two box-office surprises for Disney in 1990, the first half of a "good news-bad news" joke. The *Dick Tracy* production budget had climbed to $47 million, and the promotion effort cost another $55 million. Beatty did everything the Disney publicists told him to do, met every reporter, sat through every talk show, posed for every picture. Disney pushed the big film hard, smothering America in a yard-thick layer of Beatty interviews, T-shirt giveaways, cereal-box coupons and trench-coat "fashion statements." Yet for all the Herculean effort, the new Disney's first big-budget film turned in only $102 million at the box office—ironically, just equal to the costs of the effort.

The performance of *Dick Tracy* ate into the confidence of Wall Street. The project represented a sudden break with Disney's "get-'em-cheap" philosophy, their announced love of "singles and doubles." After giving away big chunks of the gross to its star, *Tracy* would have had to pay off in Carl Sagan numbers to return anything soon to the studio's bottom line. *Tracy* did not outperform *Batman*. Instead, it failed even to outperform *Honey, I Shrunk the Kids*. Another film with high expectations, *Betsy's Wedding* (starring Alan Alda and Molly Ringwold), brought in only $19 million. *Arachnophobia*, the first film out of Hollywood Pictures, returned $52 million—a profit, but far below the expectations that Disney had built up. Hollywood Pictures' second film, *Filofax* (the renamed *Pros and Cons*), took in only $19 million. Wall Street began looking carefully at other cracks in the Disney success story.

It did not have to look far for further signs of gloom. Disney's efforts in television had met with a surprising lack of success. After all, Eisner and many of the people who made up his team had cut their teeth on television. They did well with "Golden Girls" early on; yet "Golden Girls" was not home-grown, but had been bought from Witt–Thomas–Harris.

The Sunday night flagship show was to be the most visible symbol of the rebirth of the company, and Eisner had pushed it hard, telling reporters at the introductory press conference, "It is the No. 1 priority in the entire corporation. We have put all of our resources, all our manpower, all our creative impetus into this show." But the weekly one- and two-hour movies limped from one format to another, from one network to another, from one night to another. Called "The Sunday Movie" at first, it debuted opposite the popular news magazine "Sixty Minutes." The premiere ranked 41st out of the week's 68 network programs. It showcased new films with the trademark Disney "family" stamp. By 1988, running 59th out of 85 series on the networks, the company reworked it and transported it to NBC as "The Magical World of Disney," but it did no better there.

Nothing seemed to work for Disney forays into television. One Disney series after another magically disappeared from the air, including the "Ellen Burstyn Show" (ABC, 1986), "Harry" (ABC, 1987), "The Oldest Rookie" (CBS, 1987), and "Down and Out in Beverly Hills" (Fox, 1987).

In late 1988, Katzenberg launched a major push to carve out more market share in television. The push led to long-term contracts with such major traditional television stars as Carol Burnett, and such top writer-producers as Bill Blinn and Terry Louise Fisher, some with salaries in excess of $1 million ("in the low seven figures," was the way Blinn casually put it). Disney lured Garth Ancier, a top programmer who had developed "In Living Color" and "Married . . . With Children," from Fox. Still, "Hard Times on Planet Earth" (CBS, 1989) crashed and burned. Even "Nutt House" (NBC, 1989), created by genius screwball Mel Brooks, lasted a mere five weeks. And the company's continued attempts to create series in the hothouse of "The Magical World of Disney" all flopped, including revivals of *Davy Crockett, The Absent-Minded Professor, Pollyanna* (in a black musical version called "Polly!") and *Parent Trap*. By the 1989/90 season, "The Magical World" had dropped to 76th out of 96 series on the air. It languished in part because people just didn't warm to anthology series, in part because the "Disney" tag still seemed to mean "excessively G-rated and boring." Early in 1990, NBC cancelled the flagship show. By then the studio was once again reorienting its efforts in the medium that its top executives considered home. Later in the year Disney announced that it would no longer make one-hour television shows.

What kept Disney from being a power in television? Everything that seemed to break Disney's way in movies broke the other way in television—partly because Disney made them break that way. Several writers and producers who worked on television projects with Disney, speaking anonymously, pointed out the combination of ingredients that have made Disney a failure in television.

One ingredient, oddly enough, was conceptual, a simple creative failure. For example, in 1986, Eisner and Katzenberg went directly to their one-time boss Barry Diller at Fox, without a pilot or a script, and sold him on the idea of doing a television series based on their hit movie *Down and Out in Beverly Hills.* Only afterwards did they consult their creative staffs, who quickly discovered that the story of a bum taking over the lives of a rich couple makes a great movie, but does not lend itself to spinning out comedy bits week after week.

Another surprising ingredient is complacency, an emotion that one would not expect in a division plagued by a singular lack of success. Disney's success in other fields infected the executives that dealt with television. As one Disney producer put it, "There ought to be a place for healthy rebellion. The success Disney has had lately tends to put a muffler on that. It makes people play safe." Disney did remakes of decades-old Disney stories while other studios did "Twin Peaks," "Cop Rock," "The Wonder Years," "L.A. Law," and "In Living Color." Another producer commented, "They're simply too corporately shy, excessively timid. They have been unable to shake the Disney reputation in television, as they have in features."

Some felt Disney had an inability to feel the market: "They're a decade behind in television. They have a better pulse with features than they do in television, a better feeling for what the audience is going to get into."

A major ingredient, many felt, was arrogance. As Warren Littlefield, executive vice president of prime-time programs at NBC, put it, "[Disney] comes to its projects with a point of view. They come at it with a stamp. Sometimes we go to war with them." Former staffers on "Nutt House," conceived as a Mel Brooks-style bit of crazy comedy, complained that Disney repeatedly tried to "sugar-coat" the series, slathering it with "heart and poignancy." One writer commented, "Because of their incredible success in features and in theme parks, they bring into a network meeting a certain arrogance. That arrogance is frankly resented because they haven't earned it in television. When someone from Lorimar who has eight hours on the air walks in, you're going to listen. Disney walks in, with one hour on the air, and still behaves like a 400-pound gorilla."

Another writer recounted a network meeting with "two actors involved with a projected series we were pitching. The producer was there, and I was there as writer and executive producer, as were a couple of Disney executives. The network people were there, three or four on their side of the table. There was the obligatory couple of minutes of chatting and schmoozing and gossiping about nothing in particular, just sort of gentling up the mood of the room. One of the Disney executives made a joke, saying, 'If you guys don't like what we're going to pitch to you it doesn't really matter because we'll just sell it to the Disney Channel.' He was making a joke, but I could see the eyes of all concerned on the network side just glaze over. You could just hear them go click click click click click. We were not going to make a sale, and it had nothing to do with the merits of the idea. He seemed to be saying, 'We don't need you.' And when you say that it's very tempting to respond, 'Okay pal, you don't need us. Take a hike.' I think that's happened more than once."

In the opinion of a producer, "The arrogance comes from the top. And if you can pull it off it's not arrogance, it's just honesty. If I walk into a room and say, 'I can lift that desk,' and I then proceed to lift the desk, well, that's just a fact of life. If I walk into the room and say, 'I can lift that desk,' and then walk on out of the room, then you'll say, 'What's he about?' In television, Disney has continued to walk out of the room while still maintaining they could lift the desk."

Bill Blinn was willing to take a guess about the future of Disney in television: "It goes one of two ways. Either they throw up their hands and say, 'To hell with it, we can't make money in this racket, we can make money elsewhere,' or they bring someone in to run the TV department, someone who has enough confidence in himself or herself to say, 'Just leave me the hell alone here and I'm gonna do what I do,' and is able to generate great, exciting programming. Somebody who's like a young Michael Eisner. Somebody to say to Michael, take a vacation for about six months in regard to television, and let Sam or Alice or Mary run it with an iron hand. You might not like what happens, or you might like it a lot. But Michael can't do it all. He's only doing part of the job and the person he hires to do it is only doing part."

The "arrogance at the top" came directly from Eisner and Katzenberg, both of whom believed in themselves and their abilities. Yet Eisner's arrogance was mixed with a professed fear of failure. When asked for his feelings about the future, he would offer one: "Panic." "You always have to believe you're in last place," he would say, and he worked as if he was, with a frenetic energy that sometimes energized and sometimes worried his staff. He avoided bravado, and often made such remarks as "today's hottest company is tomorrow's struggling, helpless giant."

Katzenberg, on the other hand, would not know a doubt if it left tread marks on his face. After coproducing *Stella* with Disney, Sam Goldwyn, Jr., told *American Film*: "No doubt about it, everybody at Disney works for one man. There aren't a lot of guys running in every direction jockeying for power, no faceless executives polled by a studio chief who then turns to God for advice. Jeffrey is one of the few who has the courage to say, 'I believe.' " A former colleague from Paramount said, "I like Jeffrey but I wouldn't want to work for him. By stressing 'the company' or 'the family,' he doesn't recognize or allow for idiosyncracies—those things that make people special and creative. Though he's a great motivator, he doesn't always get the best out of everyone."

Writers and directors often squirmed under Katzenberg's micromanagement at the same time that they reveled in Disney's skill in marketing. In 1986, Leslie Dixon wrote *Outrageous Fortune* for Interscope, which sold it to Disney. She firmly resisted Katzenberg's desire to get her under long-term contract—only to discover that Interscope, with whom she already had a contract, could rent her out to Disney like an indentured servant. So, in 1987, she rewrote *Big Business* under duress. And when she was done, she changed her phone message so that it ended: "And if this is anybody from Disney, fuck off forever!" It didn't matter. It only took three weeks for the studio to call her with another offer. Little things like screaming hatred didn't seem to bother Katzenberg.

Producer Mark Johnson told *American Film* that "Disney is very specific about what it wants and hires people to deliver on its terms. Certain film-makers won't work there. Others are prepared to bite their tongues. In the end, it's a tradeoff. You may not enjoy making a film at Disney, but they'll help you make it better and sell it better than anyone else."

That reality showed up most clearly in the studio's phenomenal track record under Katzenberg. By mid-1990, he had produced 44 films, of which 70 percent returned a profit. The industry average is 30 percent. Richard Schickel, author of a highly critical Walt Disney biography, told *American Film*: "The battery was dead, and it was 30 degrees below zero. Not only did they manage to start the car . . . but the damn thing turned out to be a Mercedes."

Not everything was running smoothly, however. Although Silver Screen Partners had raised nearly $1 billion in production money for Disney, the relationship was not working out. Roland Betts, the head of Silver Screen, withheld funds from movie deals that, in his estimation, gave away too much profit. Woody Allen's *New York Stories*, for instance, had three directors, Allen, Martin Scorsese, and Francis Ford Coppola, and gave cuts of the profit to all three; and Betts refused to finance it. The same was true with *Arachnophobia*, which gave Spielberg a large percentage, and Bette Midler's *Stella*. The Disney executives felt that Betts was constantly second-guessing their judgment. In the fall of 1989, Gary Wilson met with Betts to renegotiate Disney's relationship with Silver Screen. Disney needed another $600 million in production money. When that didn't work out, Eisner got on a plane for Japan. Japanese money was already flooding Hollywood, and Eisner was determined to get some of it—but on his terms.

Eisner also moved the company into a part of the entertainment world into which it had never moved before: owning and operating individual television stations, which can be a highly lucrative business. For Disney, owning stations in important media markets would provide the company direct access to audiences to which it could sell its vast array of other products, from movies to theme parks. The strategy was sound, but the market refused to cooperate with Disney, whose avowed policy was, "We won't pay retail." FCC rules and the nature of the medium limit the number of broadcast stations in a given area. This natural and enforced scarcity drives up prices and makes it nearly impossible to start a station from scratch. By the mid-1980s, the price of television stations in major markets was routinely hitting the $500-million mark.

Nonetheless, Eisner encouraged Wells and Wilson to make offers. In 1986, he tried and failed to buy WWOR in New York. The next year, he and Wells succeeded in buying Los Angeles' last-place KHJ-TV. Disney promptly changed the station's call letters to KCAL and set about rejuvenating it. By 1990, KCAL was up and running with a daringly different format: three hours of prime-time news every night, featuring 67-year-old Jerry Dunphy, a locally famous anchor lured to the station from KABC by the traditional "offer you can't refuse"—in this case a five-year, $5-million contract. That offer was just a piece of the $30 million the company had poured into the news operation for trucks, a helicopter, over 100 new employees, and 21 editing sites. It was a gamble in a highly competitive, news-saturated market that didn't even begin to pay off until the war in the Persian Gulf began to whet the public's appetite for a steady diet of news.

But before the "news evening" even hit the air, Disney was in the market for more stations. Richard Frank, president of the studio, who had himself graduated from local television, said, "We are not looking to develop another network, but television stations purchased at the right price are good investments. The price of stations has stabilized. Now we need them to do a click or two down. We look at every (station) group that comes up for sale, and I believe that the time will come when we will buy a group."

In late 1986, Steve Burke, a young Harvard MBA on Wilson's team at Disney, brought Eisner and Wells a proposal for a "Disney Store" that would bring Disney's hundreds of consumer products straight to the consumer. Eisner was lukewarm to the thought, but gave Burke $400,000 to try it out. When Burke opened the store in the nearby Glendale Galleria on March 28, 1987, Eisner was there. He was amazed to find that hundreds of other people were there, too, patiently waiting for the new store to open. The store quickly began to rack up figures of $1,000 in sales per square foot—very large for a retail business.

The response excited Eisner, and he asked Burke for a five-year plan. Burke proposed opening 100 stores by 1992, and Eisner gave him the green light. By the turn of 1988, two were open, by 1989 a dozen, by 1990 41 in malls across the country. The stores have proven profitable, and they have also proven to be powerful marketing tools for the parks, the films, and everything else Disney does—a clear example of the synergy that Eisner preaches.

A visit to a Disney Store reveals extraordinary attention to design and atmosphere. It is more than just a series of racks filled with merchandise. Disney music wafts out of the store, attracting children's ears and eyes. In most stores the back wall is reserved for displaying high-value stock. In a Disney Store the whole wall is a movie screen showing a constant loop of Disney cartoon clips, the Mickey Mouse Club, clips from Disney classics, and short trips to the parks. The images on the screen pull people from the mall in through all the racks of merchandise to the back of the store, and rivets them there, particularly if they have children with them. The screen surmounts not a neat rack of toys but a massive pile of stuffed Mickeys, Donalds, Tiggers, and other characters, all begging to be climbed on, hugged, and bought. On all sides, pastel racks and alcoves frame bright-colored games, backpacks, toys, and videos. Above the displays, the walls overhead burst and overflow with movie sets, complete with klieg lights, ropes, extension cords, trunks, giant movie reels, and strips of film—all the paraphenalia of movie-making—with Clara the

Cow playing *Clarapatra*, Mickey and Minnie in *The Mouse Family Robinson*, and Goofy starring in *Goofenstein*. Up in one corner, a frazzled-looking "Mr. Producer" (a huge bulldoglike character) clutches four phones at once behind a desk piled high with scripts, a Rolodex, an Oscar in the shape of Mickey, and a five-gallon bottle of aspirin. The staff of the store have all gone to Disney University, the company's training center, and they act that way—unflappably smiling, helpful, and sweet. The store, like much of the company, combines cuteness with Hollywood glitz and glamor, plus a strong whiff of nostalgia for a simpler, more beguiling time.

After the success of the stores, Eisner soon became excited about another possibility: creating a Disney healthy-but-fast-food restaurant to be called "Mickey's Kitchen." This time it was Burke that was lukewarm. Fast food is a notoriously risky business, and in the late 1980s it was going through a shakeout. But Eisner persisted, and by late 1989, Burke opened one next door to a Disney Store in Orange County, California. Decorated much like the store it was connected to, it broke even in its first year—but the Disney Store doubled its sales from the increased foot traffic that the restaurant brought in. By mid-1991, the second restaurant was ready to open, and more were planned.

At the same time that Disney was getting into broadcasting, fast food, and retailing, it was getting out of the land-development business. By the beginning of 1987 Disney had sold Arvida for $400 million to JMB Realty, a Chicago-based firm.

The sale was both personal and strategic. Chuck Cobb, the onetime chief operating officer of Penn Central who ran Arvida, was an ambitious man. In 1984 he had flown to see first Ray Watson, then Sid Bass, with the suggestion that he, not Eisner, be brought in to run Disney. He chafed against the rule of Frank Wells and Gary Wilson, a "hands-on" rule that felt oppressive and demeaning. Wells liked to come to Florida and open the books. He and Wilson liked to negotiate the big deals. When Disney decided to work out (with Tishman, Metropolitan Life, Westin, Aoki, and Sheraton) the deal to build the huge Swan and Dolphin Hotels at Disney World, it was Wells and Wilson, not Cobb, who sat at the table.

But the differences represented more than mere executive personality clashes. The management that had bought Arvida in 1984 had seen Disney as a land-development company with some entertainment components. The new management reversed that argument. It saw Disney as an entertainment company that played out some of its stories in real estate rather than on celluloid. Arvida was in the business of developing vast chunks of land into planned cities that, from the Disney point of view, had no "story."

Eisner wanted "story," and he wanted it big. He intended the parks, like the studio, to expand. Geographically, he would expand them by opening new parks in Europe and southern California. Demographically, he would expand them by offering nightime attractions for teenagers and adults; mid-level accommodations for families; high-priced accommodations for the well-heeled; as well as convention facilities to attract business groups, corporate seminars, and association meetings during the slack parts of the year.

But the older parks would not suffer from lack of attention, as they had during the building of EPCOT. They were engulfed in the same Eisner-generated storm of activity as the rest of the company. Team Disney made sure that a steady stream of events, promotions, and new attractions kept the people coming through the gate.

Eisner picked up one of his major inspirations for promoting the Disney parks from his wife during a social evening with friends. After Jeannie Yeager and Burt Rutan returned from their flight around the world without stopping or refueling—a first—they had dinner with Michael and Jane Eisner. Michael asked the obvious question after such an achievement: "What are you doing next?"

Their reply was surprising: "We're going to Disneyland."

Jane turned to her husband and said, "Michael, you've got to use that."

As a result, in 1987 Disney began featuring ads after great sports events like the Super Bowl and the World Series. The hero of the hour would be caught walking off the field. An off-screen narrator would pop the question, "Now that you've won, what are you going to do next?" The hero of the hour would reply, "I'm going to Disneyland!"

The same year "Star Tours" opened at Disneyland. The ambitious ride, featuring new technology, had taken two years to complete, months longer than planned, because of numerous difficulties synchronizing the movements of the ride to the movie playing on the screen. Fine-tuning had been necessary to give visitors a great ride without giving them motion sickness. But finally it was open, and the waiting lines snaked through the Ewoks' redwood forest.

At all the parks Disney began one of the strangest promotions imaginable: it announced that, when you bought something at a Disney park, you could take your change either in regular currency, or in "Disney Dollars," which could only be spent on the Disney property. Surprisingly, people loved this funny money. In fact, most of it never was redeemed—it found its way home as another souvenir.

In 1988, since anniversaries seemed to work so well at home, Tokyo Disneyland began a year-long celebration of its fifth anniversary, and all the parks celebrated Mickey's 60th birthday.

At Disney World the new Grand Floridian Hotel opened for business across the lake from the Magic Kingdom. Speedboats, sailboats, and outriggers sprinkled the white coral-sand beach, and Cinderella Castle rose across the water. Just outside EPCOT, the first section of the Caribbean Beach Resort opened. Cheaper than most of the other Disney World hotels ("mid-priced"), it carried the stamp of Eisner's obsession with "story," with "what you would expect from Disney." The two-story buildings were determinedly picturesque in a style that might be called Island Victorian: verandahed, deep-eaved, gingerbreaded, with brightly colored metal roofs. Each group of buildings sported different colors and details. The massiveness of the development was softened by the sense of clustered buildings, and the cacophony of dormers and cupolas, half-columns and arches in whimsical, light hues, clustered around a man-made lagoon. The pool at "Old Port Royale" bent around carefully man-made ruins and battlements with cannons sticking out of the towers, spewing not smoke but a fine mist.

Bright yellow, blue, and red inflatable rental boats zoomed about the lagoon. Guests strolled across wooden foot-bridges to a bamboo-dotted, palm-furred central island called Parrot Cay, decked with slides, climbing structures, picnic tables, battlements, and cannons for playing pirates. Ten-foot-high cages filled the trees with the sounds of Monk parakeets and other exotic birds. Lovely white coral-sand beaches wound along the lagoon, marred only by signs that read, "No swimming allowed" and "Please notice: For health reasons people swimming in any Florida lake should use nose plugs. And avoid underwater swimming, especially near the lake bottom."

The same year in Anaheim, Disney bought the Disneyland Hotel (which it had never owned) from the Wrather Corporation. In the same package it obtained the contracts and leases for the *Queen Mary* (the classic passenger liner, now retired as a hotel and tourist attraction at a dock in Long Beach), the *Spruce Goose* (the world's largest airplane, a vast seaplane built and flown once by Howard Hughes, now under a geodesic dome next to the *Queen Mary*) and quaint shops and restaurants called London Village, set between the airplane and the ship. Eisner wanted the Disneyland Hotel partly because the Wrather Corporation was down on its luck, and the hotel, with Disney's name on it, was getting ratty. He also coveted the acreage that Wrather owned around the hotel, for future expansions of Disneyland. And finally, he wanted to retrieve something important that Walt had given three decades before to his friend Jack Wrather—the right to use the Disney name, not only on the Disneyland Hotel, but on any hotel built anywhere in southern California.

In 1989, like trimmings around the edges of the main attractions, Team Disney added more low-key fun designed to entice visitors to stay another day or two at Disney World. Typhoon Lagoon opened, offering surfing, water-sliding, snorkeling, swimming, and almost every other water sport in one grand swimming hole. Up near the Magic Kingdom, a launch took guests to Discovery Island, a certified zoological park featuring rare species in seminatural environments. In a postindustrial imitation of con- verted warehouses and factories, Pleasure Island featured nightclubs, eight of them in all, with music from rock and roll to country, dining and dancing, and even alcohol (except at Videopolis East, aimed at teens). The clubs competed for the night dollar with a ten-marquee Pleasure Island movie complex.

But the biggest news at Disney World was the Disney-MGM Studio Tour, which in the end had cost not $300 million but $500 million. The tour was small, and possibly overpriced, but there was little doubt that it was a triumph for the imagineers—the public loved it from opening day. The design had a purposeful hodge-podginess, a charming un-Disney-like clutter. Every fantasy of old Hollywood was crammed and jumbled into one tiny area, from the Brown Derby to old Hollywood Boulevard, in- cluding the Chinese Theater with its acres of fake chinoiserie and its handprints and signatures pressed into the concrete of the courtyard: Kate Jackson, Bob Hope, Alan Alda, Phyllis Diller, Bette Midler, Carol Burnett, Jackie Cooper, Pat Boone.

The architecture, like old Hollywood, mashed together Main Street, with its cast-iron and wooden park benches and old-fashioned streetlights, and the streamlined '30s art deco of the Fox and Paramount Theaters. Actors and actresses dressed like Carol Lombard, Clark Gable, Mickey Rooney, and lost waifs off the bus trying to make it big in Tinseltown chatted up the visitors and signed autographs. It was the way we would like to picture the old Hollywood, a Hollywood that never really existed.

A '50s Prime Time Cafe offered a television at every table—black and white Automotronic 400 television sets running set pieces from "I Love Lucy," "My Three Sons," and a seemingly endless train of generation-old situation comedies. Porcelain gew-gaws sat on knick-knack shelves, ruffled curtains framed the windows, and a basket of knitting crowned an end table, as if Mom had just set it down. The soft-drink "bar" was a living room out of the 1950s—Naugahyde couches, tract-home open-beam ceilings, formica table tops with oil patterns and stars, and venetian blinds in the front windows. Suddenly one's own childhood had become a nostalgia piece for tourists.

Outside, an SFX studio invited guests to create their own sound effects. A music video made them the stars of their own lip-sync tapes. The television studio nearby picked its cast right out of the crowd. To one side, the Indiana Jones stunt show featured machine gun fire, fist fights, chases, explosions, flames, Nazis, and a brave hero rescuing a beautiful woman live before the visitors' very eyes. Across from it Dinosaur Gertie's Ice Cream Stand of Extinction dispensed snacks from the belly of a towering apatasorous that intermittently jetted steam from its nostrils.

The back lot areas, like real back lots, favored corrugated tin, old industrial piping, and streets of facades. Behind one facade lay a scatter of props and set dressings: Pacific Electric Railway signs, old British telephone booths, Maya *chacmool* statues, klieg lights, an overturned plastic tree. The "dip" spraying machine from *Roger Rabbit* emerged from a warehouse, tilting threateningly toward the tourists' videocameras. One street of painted facades used "forced perspective" to give an illusion of depth: although only about 40 feet deep, it looked like a mile or more of Broadway, disappearing into a congeries of New York skyscrapers, with the Chrysler Building and the Empire State Building towering in the distance.

The rest of the street conveyed New York perfectly: construction fences carefully covered with graffiti, New York Bell trucks, Empire cabs with New York plates, a New York city cop car, a Metro transit authority bus, a hot dog cart, even a subway entrance that proved to be only about three feet deep, with graffiti scratched in the railing and grime on the walls, half washed off. Only a New Yorker would not be fooled: none of the graffiti was obscene, all of it was readable, and the air did not stink of urine. After all, this was still Disney.

On the studio tour itself, volunteers from the audience commanded submarines under attack, or a tug in a storm. Children from the audience climbed aboard a giant bee and recreated a scene from *Honey, I Shrunk the Kids*—and instantly got reviewed by Siskel and Ebert: one thumb up, one down on the bee, two thumbs up for the kids.

Guests peered into actual sound stages, some of them in use, while videos starring the Cosby family, Mel Gibson and Pee-Wee Herman, and Warren Beatty, explained what was going on. They watched a five-minute film in which Bette Midler wins the lottery, then loses the ticket; afterwards they saw all the tricks that went into making those five minutes—the front of the subway car, the turnstiles, the newstand, the sets, the angles, the visual twists and turns. Then came a new twist in theme parks: paying visitors filed through behind glass to watch other people actually working—editors and sound men toiling in postproduction services, while George Lucas, on the monitor, explained editing.

The tour opened on May 1, 1989. With Wells riding herd on construction, Disney had beaten Universal to opening day by more than a year. The park proved so popular that by July Eisner had decided to double its size, by November had decided to add it as the second "gate" in Paris by 1996, and by the next year was considering plans to add it both to Disneyland in Anaheim and to Tokyo Disneyland.

Metropolitan Life's $90-million "Wonders of Life" pavilion, which opened at EPCOT in November 1989, turned everything from dieting and exercise to the workings of the hypothalmus into entertainment. Under another vast geodesic dome with a Calder-like mobile hanging from the ceiling, exercise machines took the puffing guests on video rides through the Magic Kingdom. Cartoons showed guests how to be healthy "the Goofy way." The "Cranium Command," following a typical 12-year-old through a typical day, led by Buzzy the Cranium Commando, taught guests to avoid stress by staying balanced. Every Disney entertainment trick—from thrill rides to cartoons to folk singers—was turned to the task of educating the public about health. In "Coaches Corner," guests received tips on their golf, tennis, and baseball swings from actual coaches, then got advice (through the magic of computerized videoclips) from experts like Chris Evert. Guests could review their lifestyles on interactive computer screens, explore a sensory funhouse, or watch the Anacomical Players in live comedy sketches, singing and dancing about being "Flossed in Space." One top draw was a thrill ride through the circulatory system called "Body Wars" (another *Star Wars* knockoff), and a film that might have made Walt shake his head in disbelief. The film, *The Beginning of Me*, explored "the mysterious, wonderful and often funny process of pregnancy and birth." Warning signs at the entrance to the film theater advised viewer discretion, but it was not a how-to. The hilarious script, narrated by Martin Short of "Saturday Night Live," managed to lay out the whole process without ever saying, "penis," "vagina," or "breast." If young or virginal guests didn't know how to do it beforehand, they still wouldn't afterward.

By the close of 1989, Disney World definitely bore Eisner's stamp.

Eisner's imprint on Europe was also beginning to become real and visible. Early in 1989, working out of the offices of S. G. Warburg, a merchant bank on Finsbury Street in London, Gary Wilson began piecing together the elaborate team of banks that would sell the Euro Disneyland stock offering in the fall. As with everything else, Disney paid special attention to public relations. Wilson gave some 200 European bankers and their spouses free trips to Disney World in Orlando, so that they could see for themselves what kind of operation they would be selling. Once again, careful preparation paid off. When the offering opened on October 8 at $14 per share, it sold all 43 million shares within days.

Even as Wilson was putting together this massive financial edifice, the planning for the park itself was moving into high gear. Early in 1989, Eisner brought together some of the country's—and the world's—most highly-regarded architects for an unusual brainstorming session, arranged by Arthur Levitt, III, at the imagineering works in Glendale, California. Through a long afternoon and into the night, over Peking duck and rice wine, the architects threw out ideas, sketched, and argued. The discussion got so heated that at one point Eisner had to separate two of the men to keep them from settling their aesthetic argument physically. Gradually, though, the outlines of a plan began to emerge. The design of the Euro Disneyland theme park itself was largely left to the imagineers. For the most part a copy of the Magic Kingdoms in Tokyo, Anaheim, and Orlando, it would substitute a "Discoveryland" with a Jules Verne ride for "Tomorrowland." Each themed area would be signed and narrated in the language the original story came from—the "Pinnocchio" ride in Italian, for instance, and "Snow White" in German. To accommodate Paris' colder climate, all waiting areas would be covered. To accommodate the French distaste for waiting in lines, the waiting areas themselves would be sprinkled with live and mechanized entertainments.

In Anaheim, Walt had never been able to buy enough land to stave off a forest of hotels sitting right outside the property line, taking business he felt should have been his. In Orlando, the company had the land, but had built hotels so slowly that competition had grown up anyway. In Paris, Eisner wanted to build five large hotels with 4,688 rooms right at the start, to steal the march on potential competitors.

Grouped around Lake America, the five major hotels that the architects were assigned all had an American mythic theme. Robert Stern designed a 1,100-room colonnaded Newport Bay Club, shingle-style, with gambrel roofs. Antoine Predock's Santa Fe Hotel would represent New Mexico, complete with low-rise motel-like bungalows and a drive-in movie theater in the parking lot. Stern's Cheyenne Hotel looked like a set for the town in *High Noon* or "Ponderosa." In Hotel New York, Michael Graves strove to bring visitors a bit of New York's tall, narrow buildings, with one great hallway painted to resemble a subway, and an ice-skating rink outside duplicating Rockefeller Center's famous rink. French architect Antoine Grumbach designed the Sequoia Lodge to evoke the massive rustic resorts of America's national parks.

In between these five hotels and the park itself, the guests passed through an Entertainment Center, a midway of stores, restaurants, and a Wild West show designed by Frank Gehry, a wild hodge-podge mall of buildings with an open, gridded cover hung with klieg lights and supported by twisting, dancing columns. All of these buildings, as they emerged from the architects' drafting boards and computer plotters, had in common with Walt's Disneyland the evocation of other times and places, the studied re-creation of experience. But they differed sharply from Walt's creations: where Walt Disney's architecture was over-sweetened and simplified, but sincere, these projects seemed to offer ironic commentary on the America they professed to copy. It was fun architecture, architecture as entertainment, but it was not innocent.

By the beginning of 1990, as the infrastructure, the roads, sewers, and drainage ditches, the landforms and the lakes, of Euro Disneyland were taking shape outside Paris, Michael Graves' flamboyances in Orlando were ready to open. All through 1989, the forest next to the Studio Tour reeked of resin and fiberglass. Towering figures peaked through the trees, gradually taking shape as giant swans and leaping dolphins—the decorations meant to sit on the shoulders of the architecture-as-entertainment Swan and Dolphin Hotels going up between the Studio Tour and EPCOT Center. The swans on the epaulets of the hotel were so large they had navigation warning lights on the tips of their wings.

At the beginning of 1990, the Swan and Dolphin opened their doors, showing their first guests a light-hearted decorational splendor that made them unique. Inside the Swan, the carpet displayed a massive floral pattern, with flowers and butterflies a yard wide. The walls were decked with prints of Rousseau, Van Gogh, Dufy, Matisse, Picasso, Hockney, Oldenburg, and Lichtenstein—all modern, bright, and upbeat. The wall decorations in the bar carried flowers six feet wide, along with plywood cutouts of cockatiels and toucans sitting on perches holding lotus lamp chandeliers from their beaks. Overhead, seahorses held the bowls of huge chandeliers.

The opening of these two grand hostelries gave the company over 10,000 rooms in Disney World itself. Within a few months, Disney World added even more rooms in Robert Stern's mid-priced Beach Club and Yacht Club Hotels just around the corner from the Swan and the Dolphin.

In spite of all this razzle-dazzle and the millions invested in new hardware, attendance at the parks had climbed only fitfully over the years. From 9.5 million at Disneyland in 1984, the great giveaway and Videopolis helped boost the numbers to nearly 12 million in 1985. Mickey's 60th birthday made 1987 a record year, bringing 13.5 million into Disneyland, and breaking 50 million for all the parks combined. But the next three years limped along without any significant increases.

Yet revenues soared. This riotous expansion, and much of the growth of the whole company, had been nurtured through a very simple funding device: jacking up the prices at the gate. Ten price increases boosted the adult price at Disneyland to $21.50 by 1988, and to $25.50 by 1990. Epcot hit $28 by 1988 and $31 plus tax by 1990. Taking a family of four to Disney World for four days at the three major parks in 1990 would cost—with the special $102 ($112 with tax) four-day passes (only slightly less for the kids)—about $450 for tickets alone. Add an average of $30 per day per person for snacks, mouse-eared hats, pennants, autograph books, film, and stuffed animals, and that's another $480. Throw in airfare, hotel, meals, and a rent-a-car, and the figure begins to approach the annual budget of a small Third World country.

Then there is the multiplier effect. Disney marketing studies had picked up a peculiar phenomenon—the more people spend at the gate, the more they spend inside the park. The new attractions convinced people to stay longer, eat more, and spend more in the shops and hotels. And, while the promotions encouraged people to come to the parks, the higher prices discouraged the less affluent. By 1990, the median household income of the households coming through those gates had reached $44,500, 38 percent above the national average. Nor were most of those people in the funny hats little kids. Although 62 percent of the people through the park gates came with their families, teenagers and adults outnumbered children four to one.

The struggle over pricing struck at the heart of what Disney was about. The Studio Tour gave the clearest example of the new thinking. It had grown out an idea for a pavilion at EPCOT, and its designers had always seen it as a small thing. Randy Bright commented, "I was on the project at the beginning, and we said, 'We want to do a little half-day park and prove to ourselves that we can do something that doesn't have to cost a billion dollars, like EPCOT Center or the Magic Kingdom.' Then we began to add and add and add. We did keep it under $500 million. But then we looked at it with a different mindset, with the Hollywood mindset, and said, 'Isn't this great?' We began to believe our own publicity. There were knock-down drag-out fights in the financial circles here at Disney. Finally they determined that this is worth the price of admission to EPCOT or the Magic Kingdom. So we opened at $30.65. At the opening, I turned around and said to somebody in the top management, 'I don't understand it. This is still a little half-day park.' And this person looked at me and said, 'Oh, no, no. I totally agree with this pricing strategy, because if we didn't do that we would imply that this park is less than EPCOT.' But it is less than EPCOT. It's a third of EPCOT. And the public tells us that in letters."

"There were even suggestions made," said Bright, "in meetings I attended, that we use higher prices as a way to keep the crowds down. It's classic supply-and-demand economics. But I'll bet if anyone had made such a suggestion to Walt he would have been fired on the spot."

The rapid price rise did make a difference. It began to bite. Like many other things about Disney, it began to appear that the "Disney magic" could grow thin, that it might even have a dark side. People had a vested interest in keeping it alive. Nobody wants to kill off their own feelings of innocence and wonder, but at times it seemed that Disney was making it hard for them. Patti Sauber and Rene Berger and their mother Sylvia Berger, down from Chicago for a "girls' week out" at Disney World in late 1989, called it "kind of neat," and "fun," but "real touristy." Marian and Joe Strachman, visiting with their two kids from Norwalk, Connecticut, figured that their vacation set them back about $3,000. According to Marian, "The ticket prices are too high. . . . I paid it, but I might not come back so soon next time. Or I might only spend a day here. It's become very, very commercial."

It was an interesting phrase, a phrase one would hear over and over from "guests" at the parks: Disney had become "too commercial." It was a phrase that rang more than a little strange. No one would accuse General Motors, or RCA, or Marriott, of being "too commercial." "Commercial" is exactly what people expect an American corporation to be. But Americans clearly expected Disney to be something more than a profit-making, growth-oriented American corporation, and increasingly the public began to wonder about the emperor's clothes.

Ken Zimmerman of Cypress, California, put it this way in a letter to the Los Angeles Times: "Disney, an organization whose mission was once to make children happy, has become a self-centered, intimidating bully whose main goal is to reap steadily rising profits at the expense of everything else. Rather than a symbol for the fulfillment of children's dreams, Disney is becoming better known as a training ground for tough, greedy, heartless executives."

12

Chairman Michael and the Dark Side of the Force

As Michael's Disney grew, a dichotomy also grew within the company, a split in the seed, between Disney as a dream-weaver and purveyor of myth and magic, and Disney as a global corporate juggernaut that at times seemed capable of crushing anything in its way.

The split between fantasy and commerce ran all through the organization, but it didn't start at the bottom. It started at the top, in the personalities of the two men who had most shaped it: Walt Disney and Michael Eisner.

Walt had always had the split in his heart. To the outside, he was the world's sweet storytelling uncle; but out of the public eye he could be irascible, harsh, even at times vicious. His fights with his brother were legendary in Hollywood. His dealings with unions were bitter and personal. When forced by the National Labor Relations Board to hire back people he had fired for union activities, he hired them back, then refused to acknowledge their presence for years on end, until they quit the company in disgust. When other people quit the company for personal reasons, he often considered it an act of personal disloyalty, and never spoke to them again.

Michael Eisner, too, had both elements in his personality: he was both the ebullient, creative idea man, and the able, hard-nosed negotiator behind some of the best deals in Hollywood. A man of enormous energy and enthusiasm, he also had the capacity to "want everything," and at times he could turn personally vindictive. As his corporate sophistication grew, he increasingly realized that he could distance himself from the dirty work of corporate ambition. But that only gave his ambition greater scope. He could, in effect, run rough-shod over those who stood in his way without (as he had in dismantling Larry Gordon's office at Paramount) getting personally involved, without showing his hand.

Walt's Disney had been a tightly run patriarchal organization. The company had always been tough on unions, quick with a lawsuit, and, especially on the parks side, regimented right down to strict dress codes and drill-sergeant scheduling.

But Michael's Disney has come to be bigger, tougher, richer, faster, meaner. When the strict patriarchy of the old Disney merged with Eisner's ambition to build a global company, Katzenberg's drive to build the studio, and Wilson's icy discipline and harsh standards of negotiation, the result was a corporate ferocity that went beyond the standards even of Hollywood. This ferocity complicated Disney's relationships with the cities in which it operated, as well as with both its competitors and its collaborators.

As the company grew, so did the "face" of its chairman, as the Chinese would say. He grew in power, and in perceived power (which often comes to the same thing). In 1990, *Premier* published a list of the 100 most powerful people in Hollywood. Eisner was number three, behind Michael Ovitz, the superagent at the head of Creative Artists, and Lew Wasserman, the head of MCA (owner of Universal). The same year, *Us* ranked all the studio heads—and Eisner was number two, behind Barry Diller. *Entertainment Weekly* looked at it from a broader perspective: it listed the 101 most powerful people not just in Hollywood but in the entire entertainment industry. They listed Eisner as number one. Hollywood observers began to feel that, as one put it, he had started to believe "everything that's written about him and his bank account."

Disney had always seemed the Teflon company, able to shrug off even the most egregious public relations gaffes, but by the turn of the '90s the Teflon seemed to be wearing thin, and Disney's image with the public it depended on was in danger.

What could destroy Disney? What could damage it? One of Wall Street's top analysts thought about the question, and said, "This 'Masters of the Universe' syndrome." Eisner said it himself. Flying across the country in the company's Gulfstream III jet, talking to a reporter, he gestured at the opulent, private surroundings and said, "Flying on this kind of plane is exactly what leads to your financial demise."

In fact, with Eisner at the helm, Disney often seemed pestered by some evil public relations gnome bent on mocking its alleged magical status. Sometimes it seemed as if the company were doing itself in on purpose. In the summer of 1989, when the world was outraged by the bloody

Chinese crackdown on prodemocracy demonstrators in Tienanmen Square, the *Los Angeles Times* called companies that did business in China to ask them their plans. Would they pull out, cancel contracts, curtail their business? Disney, which ran "Mickey and Donald" cartoons in Mandarin over the national television network, made the most extreme comment of any company surveyed. Erwin Okun, vice president for corporate communications, told the *Times*, "Frankly, it's nothing to concern ourselves with."

Sometimes the public-relations gaffes grew out of Disney's strict, generations-old, puritanical standards of dress and behavior. For example, a Florida woman and her granddaughter sued Disney—and won—when they were denied entrance to EPCOT because of the granddaughter's green hair and halter top. Disney, the judge ruled, had not applied uniform standards. The gay community of Los Angeles sued because park security at Disneyland had repeatedly broken up same-sex couples dancing at Videopolis (the company changed its policy as a result of this suit). Late in 1989 Disney began to enforce its dress code on the employees of the former Wrather Company properties, which it had bought the year before. The code called for "no facial hair." The employees included a man playing the part of the captain of the *Queen Mary*; he stood on the bridge in captain's regalia, answering tourists' questions. He was perfect for the part. He was a retired British sea captain, with the requisite knowledge, the requisite bearing, the requisite accent—and the moustache common to the British maritime tradition. He had sported the moustache for over 40 years, including all his years at sea, and he refused to part with it in favor of a regulation.

On Christmas Day, 1989, Disney fired him, along with six other *Queen Mary* miscreants. The firing prompted a storm of letters to the Long Beach and Los Angeles papers, and didn't help Disney's image.

Other problems stemmed from the company's ferocious defense of its copyrights and trademarks. The tiny Canadian town of White River asked permission to erect a giant statue to Winnie the Pooh. Pooh, it turned out, was styled after a real bear of that name that A. A. Milne and his son Christopher Robin saw in the London Zoo. The black bear had been caught in White River, sold to a soldier for $17, and carried to London as the mascot of a Canadian brigade going to fight the Great War. Disney refused White River permission for what would be, in effect, free advertising for one of its characters, and persisted in its refusal until the issue arose in the press.

Disney has always had genuine copyright concerns. Its most important corporate assets—far more important than its real estate or even its vault—have always been the rights it holds to certain images, characters, and stories, which are among the most popular in the world. They are also among the most easily copied. After all, Mickey Mouse is only a little more than an agglomeration of circles. The cartoon characters have been liberally pirated around the world since their beginnings over 60 years ago.

According to American copyright and trademark law, the owner of such rights cannot simply wink and shrug at piracy. If you don't defend your rights, you can lose them to the public domain. So Disney sues hundreds of T-shirt manufacturers, poster-makers, and video distributors around the world every year. In 1987 alone it filed more than 1,000 such suits.

Occasionally such suits turn into public embarrassments. The 1989 Academy Awards, for instance, featured a dance satirizing Snow White. The dance had been performed on and off for years in San Francisco's "Beach Blanket Babylon." As satire, it was legally protected from copyright concerns. But Disney sued the Academy of Motion Picture Arts and Sciences and the impersonating dancer anyway, and dropped the suit only when the academy publicly apologized. That prompted the *New York Times* to give Disney a "Can't Take a Joke" award. Garry Trudeau drew a "Doonesbury" strip that showed a Disney lawyer dragging Snow White away, singing, "Hi ho, hi ho, it's off to court we go!"

In Hallandale, Florida, near Orlando, three day-care centers wanted to put Mickey, Donald, and friends on their outside walls. But instead of pinning up legally produced posters, they decided to paint the characters. Disney lawyers sent the day-care centers snarling "cease and desist" letters, alleging copyright violation and threatening suit. The story appeared in newspapers across the country. MCA, about to open its own Universal Studios Tour just down the road from Disney's, couldn't resist the PR opportunity. The next morning a team of artists from Universal showed up at the day-care centers, painted over the offending ducks and mice, replaced them with the Flintstones, Deputy Dawg, Yogi Bear, and Boo-Boo, then threw a party for the children. The mayor of Hallandale said he'd "like to ban Mickey Mouse from the city limits."

In the same six-month period, the company was first forced to pay a $500,000 EPA fine (because a subcontractor had been polluting Reedy Creek at Disney World with toxic substances for eight years), and then got caught beating endangered birds to death. An endangered species of vultures, it seemed, were making it difficult for other species at Disney World's Discovery Island, as well as roosting ominously atop Space Mountain in the Magic Kingdom (which was not surprising since, at 176 feet, it was the third highest hill in Florida). Overenthusiastic gamekeepers trapped 42 of them and beat them to death. Disney first denied it, then said that they had a permit (they did, but only for trapping). Later Disney apologized and hired a professional zoologist to oversee all the company's animal-handling.

Disney's reputation in Florida has grown tarnished for a number of reasons. The company has come to be known as "the mouse that ate Orlando." In early 1990, when local authorities in southern California were considering several Disney theme park proposals, Orange County, Florida, commissioner Bill Donegan cautioned his California colleagues to "look long and hard at Disney. Those people are powerful and dangerous around here. The roads are jammed, everything is clogged and now we have to raise taxes to pay for Disney's business. . . . It's just plain greed." Commissioner Linda Chapin added, "Don't get carried away with the pixie dust. I, like most everybody else in Orange County, have a love-hate relationship with Disney."

Disney's fall from grace in Florida was rather sudden. In 1967, just after Walt's death, Disney convinced the Florida legislature to do its part for Disney World in memory of Walt by creating the Reedy Creek Improvement District for Disney's 28,000 acres. The district was theoretically self-governing and independent from the company—and Disney insisted with a straight face that it was—but only residents could be commissioners or vote for them, and only a few picked Disney employees would be allowed to live on the land. In effect, the legislature created a company-run local government. The company wouldn't have to go before local planning commissions or zoning boards, or seek any local variances. It could create its own sewage systems, roads, and fire and police forces at will. And it could use the state's full faith and credit on tax-free development bonds to build the infrastructure of its private, profit-making enterprise. It was, to say the least, an unusual arrangement.

When Card Walker ran Disney, he was always careful not to irritate the company's neighbors in Orlando, but after 1984 the new management seemed at times strikingly cavalier about these neighborly relations. For instance, in the summer of 1989 Disney reached an agreement with Orange County. It would give the county $14 million to help pay for the widening of the overburdened roads that feed Disney World. In return, the county agreed not to challenge the legality of the Reedy Creek District for seven years.

It seemed like Disney had made peace with its neighbors—until a few weeks later when, without even a courtesy call to local officials, it announced its expansion plans for the '90s—plans that called for a fourth major park, 19,000 extra employees, seven new hotels, and 29 more attractions. The expansion promised to once again overburden the area's roads and housing. Some in Orlando felt they had been conned.

Disney's ferocity in its own interests emerged again and again in the company's dealings with the state of Florida. For example, Disney had been talking for two years to a German-Japanese consortium that wanted to build a demonstration model of their 300-mile-per-hour magnetic-levitation train. Disney loved the idea. It would be very EPCOT, very future-oriented, the first commercial mag-lev in the world. Just as important, the train would whisk visitors straight from the Orlando Airport to EPCOT in a hair-curling seven minutes, without any need to rent a car or drive past any of Disney's competitors, such as Sea World, Wet & Wild, or Universal Studios. One Universal executive described the project as "just another E-ticket ride for Disney."

Universal, and the owners of other local attractions, lobbied the governor and his Rail Commission for a stop half-way, where most of their attractions are congregated, or for spur lines, complete with access to the Disney property. Tourists who had, say, "done" the MGM/Disney Studio Tour could be whisked off to Universal for a comparison. As these ideas gained support, Disney backed off of the project. Finally Disney announced that it didn't even want the train on the property at all, seriously reducing the possibility of it ever becoming a reality.

In January 1990, Disney went a step further, hogging all the development bonds available for a six-county area. The bonds were made available by the state on a first-come, first-serve basis. Reedy Creek Improvement District, in typically thorough Disney fashion, made sure its representatives were at the door, forms filled out, when the offices opened on the first day of the year. They bagged $57 million in tax-free state-backed bonds, leaving high and dry every other agency that had hoped to win some of the bonds, including one that had planned to use them to develop housing for the poor.

It did not escape the local politicians that the two highest-compensated executives in America during 1989 had been Frank Wells and Gary Wilson. Counting stock options they had exercised, they had taken home

$50 million each. Disney had once been sacrosanct in Florida, a touchstone of all that was wonderful in life. Now a Republican running for governor filed suit to force Disney to give back the development bond money (the suit was later thrown out), and a state legislator introduced a bill that would limit Disney's access to more state bonds. On its editorial page the *Orlando Sentinel* asked, "How did such a smelly problem develop, especially one that pits families of modest means against a resort giant? . . . Unless Reedy Creek turns back the bonds, Disney will become the grinch that stole affordable housing." It didn't help when Eisner let slip that he considered local officials "incompetent" for not having gotten to the bonds first, a statement for which he soon apologized.

Orlando, once a quiet farming town, was desperate to manage its growth, and Disney was completely outside its control. But its experience with Disney was not unique.

Early in 1987, officials of the city of Burbank came to Eisner with an unusual request. Forty acres of its downtown had been sitting empty, waiting for redevelopment, for over a decade. One developer after another had failed to put together a project that would renovate "beautiful downtown Burbank." Could Disney do something special? Eisner had a few city officials to lunch in his office to discuss the project, and in the course of lunch became quite excited about it. He talked of the possibilities of rebuilding the city's center. When his secretary came in to tell him of other appointments waiting, he put them off. The lunch stretched to two hours as he talked, paced, drew on napkins, and pulled ideas out of the air. Cities across the country had been inviting Disney to develop various projects, so far to no avail. Dallas had even sent a lavish videotape pleading with Eisner to visit. Imagineering had already been exploring ways to build Disney projects into cities. Would Burbank be the first? Burbank, after all, was the company's home base.

The Burbank officials were dazzled. The city gave Disney an exclusive option to develop their ideas. Eisner's sketchy ideas grew into a $300-million project. Town meetings about the project were packed. A few citizens had concerns about traffic, but the only serious objections came from Disney's rival MCA, whose original Universal Studios Tour sat just a couple of offramps down the freeway. MCA quickly sued the city twice in succession, claiming they had been cut out of the deal through secret meetings and sweetheart machinations, and papered the city with unsigned "concerned citizens" flyers calling the project a waste of taxpayers' money.

The project evolved into an "MGM/Disney Studio Back Lot" complex that would surround mall-style retail spaces with theaters, restaurants, a moatlike "Burbank Ocean," full-scale waterfalls, a ferris wheel, wandering performers, a "Hollywood Fantasy" hotel, and a ride taking guests through famous movie scenes. The price tag continued to grow, as well, to $611 million. Unfortunately, the "financial box" that Gary Wilson's wizards worked out gave a return on investment of only 8 or 9 percent. That wasn't enough for Disney, and after a year of study Eisner abruptly dropped the project and turned his attention elsewhere. The city officials who had spent a year defending the project in public and in court complained that Disney had shown little interest in scaling back the project, and had never sat down with them to discuss ways of cutting its costs.

Troubles with neighbors tend to snowball, for companies as well as for people. In Long Beach, California, Disney encountered a first—true local opposition to a Disney project. Disney took a hard look at several Wrather properties that had no sensible relation to each other—the *Queen Mary*, the *Spruce Goose*, and some assorted shops and restaurants, taking up a few hundred yards of otherwise empty shoreline in the port of Long Beach.

All through 1989, Disney dangled the possibility of an ocean-front theme park before the city officials of Long Beach. Then, in January 1990, Eisner abruptly announced that Disney would indeed build a $1 billion theme park in southern California. The company would locate it either in Long Beach or in Anaheim. "It depends a lot on which community wants us more," he said.

The mayor of Anaheim said what Anaheim had always said to Disney: "Yes, yes, yes." What Disney wanted, it soon became clear, was not a show of love, but tax breaks, roads, zoning changes—all the things a city can do to make a company feel truly welcome. An Anaheim city council member said, "Anaheim is prepared to cut any deal we'll have to."

But as the imagineers released the details of their designs—a new version of EPCOT for Anaheim; a "Port Disney" for Long Beach that would include a maritime theme park, docking facilities for a half-dozen cruise ships, marinas, shops, and restaurants—grumbling began to surface in Long Beach. The vice mayor of Long Beach said, "The mayor of Anaheim can say 'yes, yes, yes' to Disney, but he can't say 'yes, yes, yes' to an open checkbook." The city of Long Beach was interested, but it had its concerns—traffic, access, landfill, jobs that would be created and who would get them, and, it turned out, Disney's corporate character, which once would have been considered unassailable. Disney's new reputation had preceded it, and for once that was not an unmixed blessing. "We've read what they did in Orlando and we know what they did to employees with moustaches when they took over the *Queen Mary*," said one neighborhood association leader. "Walt, bless his heart, is dead. And this is not the corporation it once was," said another. Another asked, "Why in the world would we want to give money to a company that has more money than they know what to do with?" Others wondered whether local minorities would benefit at all. As one put it, "Importing blonds from Huntington Beach is not our idea of providing local jobs. And dreadlocks don't exactly fit into the Disney dress code."

The dress code was just one example of Disney's attitude toward labor. The company's bald aggressiveness with its own employees might be cheered by the stockholders and other corporate executives, but it didn't help its cuddly image with the public. For instance, in early 1987, Disney announced a 159 percent increase in its quarterly profits, and a $2.6-million yearly bonus for Eisner—and at the same time doubled the deductibles and out-of-pocket expenses on its employees' health insurance.

In 1988, Disney World was hit by several strikes. Eisner's reaction was to tell parks chief Dick Nunis to threaten to fire the strikers. The same year, a 154-day writers' strike split Hollywood, a town in which "labor" (writers) and "management" (producers and studios) are almost always friends, often lovers, occasionally married to each other, and not uncommonly are actually the same person. The writers sought more money from the reuse of their work in other forms, such as video and cable, which were rapidly becoming a majority of all profits. The studios sought to limit the writers' share of the profit from the new media. In this volatile and difficult atmosphere, Disney and MCA stood out as the hard-liners against the writers.

Disney's relations with other companies could be just as bad. Struggles between the Hollywood giants heated up during the '80s to the point of genuine rancor, causing one film producer to call the current group of studio executives "some of the most aggressive guys on earth." But Disney, according to many observers, seemed to lead the pack. Katzenberg's business affairs chief, Paramount veteran Helene Hahn, and her two assistants, came to be known in Hollywood as "Mickey's Angels," with a sense of their nearly preternatural toughness.

"They don't try to work out a deal that is good for everyone," said one executive who had dealt with other Disney negotiators. "They leave nothing on the table." He echoed others who say that Disney takes extreme positions on every issue and can be unyielding.

One subcontractor, after going through extensive oral contract negotiations, was thoroughly rattled when the contract came back from Disney in written form. Not only had the Disney lawyer changed several things that had been agreed to in oral negotiations, but the new version of the contract allowed Disney to take his business gratis if it proved successful. The subcontractor complained to the lawyer's boss—who called back and apologized. The negotiatior turned out to be a new hire on his first case. Apparently, he was trying to fit into what he saw as the corporate culture.

He could be forgiven for the misperception, for the corporate culture had its dark, grasping, bullying side. He could look back, for example, to the circumstances surrounding Disney's acquisition of the assets of the Wrather Corporation. Wilson's negotiations with Wrather exemplified the new Disney's emerging style. After the death of Walt's friend Jack Wrather in November 1984, the Wrather Corporation was eager to sell its assets to Disney—including its major asset, the Disneyland Hotel. Wrather had built the hotel at Walt's request in 1954, after Sheraton and Hilton had turned up their noses at the strange project in the orange groves. Wrather had never built a hotel, but Walt couldn't afford to do it himself. He enticed his friend with an interesting fringe benefit. He planned to build a monorail, and he would make sure that the monorail went straight to Wrather's hotel, and no other. Wrather could license the monorail rights from Disney for a nominal fee.

When the Wrather and Disney negotiators finally sat down at a table in Beverly Hills on a sunny morning in March 1987, Wrather stock was selling at about $20. Wrather had about a dozen people in the room—principals, bankers from Drexel Burnham Lambert, real estate consultants, lawyers. Disney had three, led by Wilson. Wrather asked $28 a share for the company. Wilson, for Disney, offered $14. The Wrather side was shocked, and negotiations almost broke off. But they dragged on for nine more months, while Wilson kept an eye on the calendar—Wrather's rights to the monorail were about to expire. He informed the other side that if Wrather did not come to an agreement, Disney could jack up the rates, or cut off the access entirely, and the value of the hotel would fall. Wrather finally caved in, and sold for $21.50. Such strong-arm tactics were fast becoming common at Disney.

Actors and personal managers like Steve Sauer may feel comfortable making "handshake deals" with Katzenberg, but contracts with other corporations are another matter. Critics claim that Disney regularly goes back on its word, repeatedly changing the terms of "handshake deals" and preliminary written agreements, and even attempting to back out of signed contracts if circumstances change. For instance, Disney had a contract with Fox and its parent, Rupert Murdoch's News Corp., to provide programming for the European "Sky Channel." When the channel did not get the subscription base that Disney would have liked to see, Disney walked out of the deal, alleging that Murdoch had failed to promote Disney's programming properly. In May 1989, Fox and Murdoch sued Disney for $1.5 billion, claiming fraud. They eventually settled out of court, but Fox executives privately called Disney "hyperaggressive" and "arrogant." A month later, Disney walked out of another deal with Lorimar, its partner in Metrocolor Laboratories, a film-processing company. Disney claimed that Lorimar had breached an agreement to bring the business of processing films for Warner, its parent company, to Metrocolor. Lorimar, too, sued.

In fact, most of the corporate fights in Hollywood in the late 1980s involved Disney. Fox's Barry Diller—Eisner's former mentor and partner—was baffled and enraged by Eisner's behavior: "The way you resolve things is sitting down and trying to solve the problem, not unilaterally, suddenly, repudiating the deal."

In 1989, Jim Henson agreed to sell his Muppet menagerie, including Fozzie Bear, Miss Piggy, and Kermit the Frog, to Disney for over $150 million. Eisner and Henson had long been personal friends. They held a joint press conference at the entrance to the Studio Tour to announce the deal. Both parties to the handshake deal said publicly that it did not include Big Bird, Oscar the Grouch, Grover, Cookie Monster, and other "Sesame Street" characters that had for years been licensed to the Children's Television Workshop, and represented CTW's major source of income. But when they got to the table, Disney negotiators fought ferociously for point after point. The Henson side was appalled, and almost called the deal off. Henson was personally chagrined that Disney pressed hard to change the deal to include the CTW characters.

Joan Ganz Cooney, head of CTW, said that the differences between Henson's free-flowing corporate culture and Disney's tight control had left her "shocked." She said, "The Henson people were never really happy with the Disney situation and are probably less so after working with them. It's clear they've been having a severe culture clash."

In May 1990, Henson suddenly succumbed to pneumonia, and by

December 1990, the deal had come completely unraveled, with the two sides announcing that they "could not come to terms." The publicly announced reason was that estate taxes of 55 percent made it impossible for the Henson children to get a price that made sense for them. But at the same time Disney insiders privately blamed Henson's children for holding out for "more and more" until Eisner got irritated and pulled the plug on the deal. In the long run, it seemed that a partner that made a lot of long-term corporate sense had been chased off the mat by Disney's corporate hard line and its chairman's unwillingness to settle for less than everything he could get.

Then there was the small matter of who owned Peter Pan. Despite the persistent marketing of "Walt Disney's Peter Pan," the story, and all the characters in it, were created in 1911 by the Scot playwright James M. Barrie. Disney bought the rights to the name, story, and characters, but copyrights don't last forever, and these ran out at the beginning of 1987. So CBS considered making its own version, an animated series. Katzenberg called up Kim LeMasters, the network's programming chief, and Howard Stringer, head of CBS' broadcast division. Katzenberg later claimed he asked politely if they would drop the idea, "if it isn't of the essence to you." Other sources say he promised "all-out corporate war" if CBS didn't drop the idea. CBS did.

Later Barry Diller, at Fox, decided to make a Peter Pan series. Fox Broadcasting president Jamie Kellner quickly received a visit from a Disney delegation that included Roy E. Disney. Disney claimed specifically that the original Tinkerbell was just a point of light—the tiny winged female fairy was Walt's creation. Fox executives countered with quotes from the Barrie work referring to Tinkerbell as a girl "gowned in a skeleton leaf, through which her figure could be seen to best advantage." Fox went forward with its plans, despite Disney's objections. Diller had repeatedly clashed with Disney and later called its tactics an "odd, self-destructive thing . . . that isn't needed from a company that's succeeded as brilliantly as this one has."

Disney shows a tendency to reach for its biggest weapon first. In the middle of a struggle with Disney over children's television, Fox told some of its affiliate stations that it would drop them if they didn't carry Fox programming instead of the "Disney Afternoon" cartoon package. Disney could have responded by sweetening the deals with the affiliates, or suing Fox for interfering with a contract. Instead, it filed a heavy-gauge antitrust suit against Fox.

At times the squabbling has turned into name-calling. Universal Studios and its parent, MCA Inc., have repeatedly clashed with Disney over the Burbank theme park proposals and the Orlando Studio Tours. In the furor over the announcement of the MGM/Disney tour, Sidney J. Sheinberg, president of MCA, referred to Mickey Mouse as "a ravenous rat," and later said that Disney "isn't just aggressive. They have crossed the line." Eisner later called Sheinberg "the Manuel Noriega of MCA."

Part of the aggressiveness at Disney came from Eisner and Katzenberg's determination to keep their costs in line. During his time at Paramount, Eisner had said, "You've got to get hysterical and pretend you're playing with your own money." That attitude informed much of Disney's business dealings. By 1989, when the average Hollywood movie cost $23.5 million, Disney was still making them for $15 million—at least in part because they got the talent for less money.

After Barry Levinson directed the hit *Good Morning, Vietnam*, he asked for $4 million to direct his next Disney film. Eisner and Katzenberg turned him down, and he left Disney. Zucker, Abrahams, and Zucker, who had made *Ruthless People* for Disney in the early days for a total three-person salary of $1 million, now wanted $1 million apiece. Disney's answer was no, and they left, too, to make the hits *Naked Gun* and *Ghost* for Paramount.

In negotiations with talent, Disney bargained so hard that some Hollywood lawyers and agents openly advised their clients to stay away. Disney retaliated against two of them, Barry Hirsch and Bertram Fields, by cutting them off, refusing to take their calls, even returning their letters unopened, and telling their clients that maybe they should have someone else represent them. In both cases, the fences were later mended, but Disney's actions seemed extreme even for Hollywood. As one former Disney executive put it, "Mickey Mouse may be the soul of this company, but you'll find the heart somewhere over in the legal department."

It was a feeling that people came increasingly to share as time went by. It was a schizophrenic feeling, as if there were two Disneys. When Disneyland began to give away cars, K. Bourne, who lived nearby, wrote to the *Los Angeles Times*: "Eisner and Wells, it seems, are doing everything they can to destroy Disney's dream. It is absolutely scandalous. They are in the business of making money. What ever happened to making people happy? . . . As if there isn't enough commercialism and competitiveness in the outside world, instead of escaping from the 'real' world for a few hours, as one used to be able to in this 'magic' land of fantasy, one is kept smack dab in the middle of it all. . . . Overall attendance was on a downhill trip from 1982 through 1984, and maybe I didn't visit as often as I used to. But I liked Disneyland a lot more when it wasn't a car lot and was still 'The Happiest Place on Earth.' Walt Disney may be dead, but it doesn't mean his dream must die, too.''

There was the conflict, in two phrases: "Whatever happened to making people happy?" and "Maybe I didn't visit as often as I used to." Walt Disney the man, and Walt Disney the company, spun a web of grandeur and dreams, a web that people came to believe in at a level so unquestioning that they never thought of it as belief. That powerful belief is summed up in that one spontaneous phrase describing what Disney was about: "making people happy." Yet that belief, in itself, was insufficient to support the company: "Maybe I didn't visit as often as I used to"—that was the dilemma at the center of Disney. To make people happy, the company had to make money. But making money could not be the company's only goal. That dilemma goes to the heart of the schism in Disney—and the reason why, touring the parks, one can repeatedly hear people complain that Disney has "gone commercial"—as if this American corporation, at least, is expected to be something other than "commercial."

Oddly enough, this is not true only of Disney. Disney's experience only dramatizes a dilemma that every company faces. Profit is not enough. Profit, as a goal, is insufficient even to sustain profit. Charles Hampden-Turner, a senior research fellow at the London Business School and visiting scholar at MIT, remarked recently that "Business is not 'about' profit. Profit is only one of the measures of a healthy ongoing system; it can be traded off against others. The Japanese, for instance, don't even report profits the same way we do. For them, profit is not as important as market share. Market share is what you've done for other people. Profit is what you get back from doing more for other people, so that you can go on doing more and more for other people. It is not an end in itself."

Money alone is not enough to drive a company. A company has to be about something. Maytag is about reliability. American Express is about service. K-Mart is about low prices. When today's adults were growing up, Disney was not about something as simple as reliability or conservative accounting procedures. It was not, as some Disney people say today's Disney is, about "quality." It was not even about "family entertainment." It was about all that makes life precious: a sense of wonder, of adventure, of striving for greatness, of the genius of creativity. Its tone was moral and its product was myth and magic. Disney was about how to live.

Whether this was substance or show made little difference. (Walt Disney once told illustrator Peter Ellenshaw, "What we produce is pure corn. But it's high-quality corn.") The sense of wonder may have come from the heart, or it may have been just advertising. It didn't matter—Disney came to stand for all those things. If Disney, man and company, was not the real thing, much of America reacted to it as if it were.

Some of today's Disney executives consider this an unfortunate burden. Katzenberg's reaction to the hail of criticism was that Disney is held unfairly to "a stricter standard" than other businesses. But it is exactly this sense of what Disney was about that makes Disney so valuable a company today, and that renders its value so fragile.

Disney is a peculiar company. It is not American Standard, or Exxon, or Paramount. Every corporation has its own personality. There is little mistaking Lockheed for RCA from the inside. But the difference that is Disney goes much deeper into the American consciousness, for this is a company that sells myth and fantasy.

In *Snow White, Sleeping Beauty, Peter Pan, Pinocchio, Fantasia*, and other films, Walt did something no one else had managed: he made the screen tell ancient tales about what it means to be human, to struggle and bear scars and fight the inner wars—tales that bore the weight of myth. He did it not only in animated classics, but in such live-action films as *20,000 Leagues under the Sea, Treasure Island*, and *Davy Crockett*, and even in television serials such as "The Legend of Zorro" and "Johnny Tremain."

Many of the most successful films since Walt Disney's death—the Godfather films, the Indiana Jones films, the Star Wars films, and *E.T.*, for instance—were also able to generate a sense of myth on the screen. And Spielberg and Lucas, who made most of them, openly acknowledge Walt Disney as their inspiration.

As the world has steadily come to seem a more difficult, violent, and valueless place, the value of the classic Disney images has grown, as if they represent for us a well of innocent optimism into which we can dip, in which we can baptize our children in the faith that things will work out, that life can be good and whole.

Some parts of the new Disney are about those core values. Some—Touchstone and Hollywood Pictures and the new Hollywood Records—

are not about anything in particular. They have little in common with the old Disney except a share in the cash flow.

Some of the new Disney films, such as *The Color of Money*, *Tin Men*, and *Good Morning, Vietnam*, are arguably great films. But none beat with the heart of mystery and myth, however simply told, that animated the great Disney classics. *Who Framed Roger Rabbit?* is funny, imaginative, fast-paced, a truly wonderful film, but at heart it has nothing to do with the Disney tradition. It is, in fact, a feature-length homage to the Warner Brothers style of animation. *The Great Mouse Detective* and *Oliver* are charming stories played by animated animals, no more.

Then, in 1989, two films of radically different natures hinted that perhaps the tradition was not completely dead. *The Little Mermaid*, for the first time in decades, dealt directly with mythic motifs. And a completely realistic film, *The Dead Poets Society*, directly challenged the "realistic" values of modern materialist society.

So Disney grew a schism in its heart. Increasingly it was a company held together not by a common vision and mission, but by the personality of the man at the top, a personality that entertwined sweetness and aggressiveness, creativity and ferocity. That's the way it had been when Walt was alive, but now the enterprise was a global conglomerate earning revenues (in 1990) of over $6 billion per year.

As Disney the company grew, it often seemed a juggernaut with the motto: "Hit 'em harder. Be there first with the most. Win." Yet at the top was a man who, at least in his public face, seemed almost whimsical, an earnest school-boy, as if, like Tom Hanks in *Big*, he had simply awakened one morning, a boy in a man's body, to find himself suddenly chairman of his own company.

There was Eisner, every Sunday night on the tube, a family man, not a grandfather but a father with kids—kids in school, with skinned knees, and report cards, and soccer balls behind the car seat, and questions. There was Eisner, reflecting not some kind of austere, formidable corporate EPCOT face of Disney, but the old-fashioned stuff, Main Street and the family dog. Eisner himself was the ideal audience for the Disney attractions and movie projects. As Gordon Weaver put it, "With Michael, you get a person who actually watches TV, who actually is entertained at Disneyland." Yet there was Eisner, in command of this global corporate engine.

The amounts of money that Eisner made grew quickly. By the 1986 fiscal year, his bonus had grown to $2.6 million, plus options on 816,000 shares. The next year it hit $6 million, then $6.7 million the year after that. Together with three years of stock options he exercised in late 1987, his compensation for fiscal 1988 amounted to nearly $41 million—a record at the time for any American executive.

He became a big *macher* on the charity scene in southern California, hosting dinners, giving awards, speaking at fund-raisers. For instance, one night in 1987 at a CalArts dinner, like Michael Anthony in the old "The Millionaire" series, he pulled a surprise check for $1 million from his pocket—donations from the company, himself, and Frank Wells to the school founded by Walt. He became a major checkbook Democrat as well, throwing fund-raising parties and contributing heavily, especially to the coffers of such sound liberals as presidential possibility Senator Bill Bradley.

The mechanics of his personal life changed dramatically. He traveled in the company plane and took limousines. He traveled, moreover, with a retinue that included bodyguards not only for himself but also for his family.

He became a darling of the press. He appeared on the covers of *Business Week*, *Time*, *Newsweek*, *California Business*, and *Premier*. Everywhere, for better or worse, people compared him to Walt.

On Main Street in the Magic Kingdom in Orlando, the panes of the upper windows carry signs for various businesses, as would the upper windows of any small town. The lettering is realistically old-timey, florid, curlicued, gilt, but the businesses are inside jokes. One advertises "Auditors and Bookkeepers," including the name "Michael Bagnall," the chief financial officer forced out to make way for Gary Wilson. Another proclaims: "The Original Dick Nunis Gym, night manager Ron Miller, 24-hr service, turkish baths, supervisor Dick Nunis."

Others read: "Lazy M Cattle Company, Wyoming, Ron and Diane Miller, Proprietors"; and "Dr. Card Walker, Licensed Practitioner of Psychiatry and Justice of the Peace." Another upper-story sign, for an alleged shoemaker, is more poignant: "No shoes too large to fit." The reference, of course, is to the challenge of filling Walt's shoes.

Michael Eisner stepped into Walt's shoes in more ways than one. In introductions to the Disney Sunday Movie, and in trailers shown at Disney World for the studio's coming attractions, he clowned and cavorted, a warm-and-fuzzy dad, with Mickey and Goofy and Roger Rabbit and the rest. When he spends a day at Disney World, he is mobbed for autographs. Once he commented, "I'm not exactly a movie star, but I'm very popular with the under-10 set." He once excitedly called Roy Disney with the discovery that "you only have to change two letters in my name and it's 'Disney!' "

Roy said, "Okay, Michael, calm down."

Like Walt, Eisner is a tinkerer and a poker. Walt used to keep a small apartment in the imagineers building; Eisner continually drops in on the imagineers to talk over new projects and suggest ideas. All over Disney World, ideas are attributed to "Michael": new seat backs for park benches, the *Making of Me* film in the "Wonders of Life" pavilion, the folding seats on the new monorail cars.

He actually manages to outdo Walt in quirkiness, in his ability to imagine the outrageous. This has become a major piece of his public image, and he plays to it.

For example, touring the unopened Disney/MGM Studio Tour back lot with a *Newsweek* reporter and an aide with a clipboard in tow, Eisner pointed to one empty spot and told the aide, "You know what would look great over there? An aircraft carrier!"

"You mean," said the aide, "next to the subway car?"

"Sure, why not? Call some naval bases and see if you can get an aircraft carrier and put it right there."

"Sixty miles from the nearest ocean?"

"Yeah, it'll be fun to look at, don't you think?"

Was he serious? Probably not. After all, there was the reporter, recording the whole thing. And he was far too savvy about the media to pass up a chance to reinforce his image as a fun guy.

Yet he could also humble himself. Remaking *Davy Crockett*, the studio had dismissed the proposals of Fess Parker, the original Disney Crockett, and he had not been in the movie. Meeting Parker later at a party, Eisner had said publicly, "Next time we'll do it right."

Yet for a showman, he is remarkably private. For all that he has put himself forward as the face of the company, and incessantly remarked on his children in the company's annual reports, he shields his family from any public scrutiny, and never allows reporters to meet his children. When his father died in 1987, the obituary in the *New York Times* merely listed among his survivors "a son, Michael, of Los Angeles."

Eisner can be consistently and ferociously upbeat. While he is educated enough to use words like "worldview," he describes his own worldview as "Panglossian," after Dr. Pangloss in Voltaire's *Candide*, who insists in the face of all evidence that "All is for the best in the best of all possible worlds."

Newsweek has called him a "huggable CEO." "Fun" is the operative word in Eisnerland. He says, "I'm like a six-month-old puppy just house-broken." In most of his publicity pictures he's smiling. And it's not a small, neat, polite smile, or a wolfish salesman's grin. It's a wide, open-mouthed, head-cocked smile, full of warmth and sweetness and something indefinably loony, as if the cartoonist had taken care to draw one eyelid slightly higher than the other. He looks like a man having more than a legal amount of fun.

If, as it is said, angels can fly because they take themselves lightly, we might expect Eisner to leave the ground at any moment. At an anniversary dinner marking the fifth birthday of the new management, Disney's division heads "roasted" their bosses in songs and skits about their fat paychecks and their styles of management. Far from returning tit for tat, Eisner can-canned onto the stage, with Wells, Roy Disney, and their wives, singing a spoof of "We Are The World."

Similarly, on an L.A. talk show, deejay Rick Dees asked him, if he could be any Disney character, whom would he select? Eisner didn't hesitate a second. He said, "Oh, clearly, Goofy."

In the aftermath of the takeover attempts of 1984, Eisner had the animation department whip up a short depicting Saul Steinberg and Irwin Jacobs as nasty wolves, the company as Sleeping Beauty, awakened by a kiss from "Michael." In 1989 Shelley Duvall's "Fairy Tale Associates" made a video in which Eisner led Mickey Mouse and Disney back to success by kissing Cinderella. Yet he is perhaps more modest in his public pronouncements than anybody else in the public eye. The phrase "he out-Walts Walt" garners from Eisner the disclaimer: "I'm slightly above average. Walt was way off the scale. I'm less Walt than Walt, by tenfold. People give me credit I don't deserve."

As powerful as Michael Eisner is, he makes fun of his own power. For instance, the trailers for the latest Disney movies shown at the end of the Studio Tour are introduced by a short called "Michael and Mickey." Eisner, in his office, is halfway through a little speech welcoming the viewer when Mickey pops up from behind, playfully covering Eisner's eyes. It's time to go to the screening room, as Michael can see on his Mickey Mouse watch—and as Mickey can see on his Michael Eisner watch, which features a little cartoon Michael pointing to the numbers with his hands. They walk down the halls of the animation building, opening doors, saying, "Come see the film." The halls fill with executives and animators, as well as their creations—dwarfs, walking brooms, wooden soldiers, birds, skunks, Bambi, Dumbo—all marching to the screening room. Settling into his seat, Mickey bumps someone in front of him, who turns, and suddenly towers menacingly over the little mouse, eyes flaring with the flames of hell. It's the devil from the "Night on Bald Mountain" sequence of *Fantasia*. Eisner, taking his seat next to Mickey, says simply, "Sit down, please, it's time for the film." The devil recognizes Eisner and suddenly drops to a grovel: "Oh, sorry, Mr. Eisner, Mr. Chairman, sir, it won't happen again. Sorry."

What kind of man can publicly make fun of his power at the same time that he so aggressively keeps it, exercises it, and extends it? Is all this self-effacement, this shuffle-footed humility, like many another public face in Hollywood, no more than a particularly clever pose?

There are a number of signs that it is not completely pose, but at least in part an accurate display of the man. For instance, Eisner studies. When something interests him, he will hit the books. In the midst of the expansion of the 1980s, Eisner read book after book about how to do something he had never done: manage a corporation in a shrinking economy. When he was preparing to go to Paris for the groundbreaking of Euro Disneyland, he studied French from tapes and hired a French-speaking chauffeur. While trying to decide which architect to hire to design the Swan and the Dolphin, he boned up on modern architecture by study, and by carefully observing, on a family visit to Maui, how his sons made use of the resort hotel they were staying in. A man who takes time to study is not a man who thinks he knows everything worth knowing.

He can be stubborn. Writer-producer Bill Blinn says, "Michael is real hard to move off a concept. If he seems to have a fix on an idea, you can save yourself a lot of time and effort by trying to go with his idea. He is very difficult to shift."

Eisner keeps his hands on the wheel. For all Katzenberg's success and vaunted genius at running the studio, Eisner still reads every script that Katzenberg wants to produce, and reviews every major casting decision. In the few cases in which Katzenberg and Eisner disagree, the younger man easily defers to the elder, not only because he's the chairman, but also because, in Katzenberg's experience, Eisner is usually right.

It takes a certain arrogance to even think you can run a company as big as Disney. And Eisner has an ego that is up to the job. When he went to Disney, it was specifically to take on a challenge. But at the same time, he felt confident he could do better than the previous management. He said, "In addition to more important quality reasons, I wanted to go to a company where you couldn't fall off the floor." After all, he had been a key member of the team that brought ABC from last place to first among the networks, and half of the duo that brought Paramount from last place to first among the major studios.

The confidence was not misplaced. Whether or not Eisner's appointment was right for Disney as a cultural icon, there is little question that it worked for Disney as a business.

It may be that this is what every business needs: a balance of bold, imaginative risk-taking with firm financial discipline, tough deal-making and realistic planning. It may be that this balance must be embodied within the CEO, and within all the company's major players, so that it does not have a creative department whose best ideas are regularly throttled in the cradle by a business affairs department, or a chief financial officer whose intelligence and training are rendered useless by others' indiscipline. It was certainly what Disney needed: a CEO who combined financial savvy and powerful intelligence with a free-roaming, playful, permissive imagination and a strong sense of what would fly.

13

Time and the Kingdom

By 1991, the pace at Disney had noticeably slowed. Eisner was no longer in charge of a Level I Trauma Unit battling desperately to keep the patient alive. The Disney parking lots were not always full "from dawn 'til dark-thirty." Sundays were perceptibly different from the rest of the week. People were known to take vacations and to see their children in the daylight. Even Katzenberg, at the advanced age of 39, his hair thinning a little up front, seemed to have settled in for the long haul. His trainer didn't get to his house until 5:30. His first phone calls did not go out until 6:30, some days even later. He began giving serious interviews to *American Film* and *Premier*, fishing for recognition.

In the six years since Eisner had taken the helm at Disney, the company had grown almost beyond recognition. The parks had spawned dozens of new attractions, one whole new theme park, and the beginnings of a vast multifaceted project outside Paris. The studio had become the foundation for a whole new line of films, and then for a whole new studio. It had come from being an "also-ran" 12th to being consistently one of the top three Hollywood "majors." The company's consumer products division had exploded into a dizzying array of stores across the country, and had plunged at the same time into mainstream publishing and recording. In those six years Eisner had tripled the company's assets, tripled its return on equity, more than tripled its revenues, increased its profit by eight and a half times and the stock price by twelve times. Just as important, he had taken a company once seen as moribund and turned it into a top performer, dominant in its fields.

Eisner's team was still mostly intact, with the major exception of Gary Wilson. In 1988, Wilson had joined the board of Northwest Airlines. Eisner did not allow his executives to join the boards of other companies—the possibility of a conflict of interest was too great. By 1989, the friction between Eisner and Wilson had grown, and Wilson had other plans. In June 1989, he and Checchi bought Northwest Airlines, and by the end of the year he had left Disney, except as an adviser and board member. Before he left, he cashed in the generous stock options he had been given, putting his compensation for 1989 in excess of $50 million— one of the largest amounts of cash ever given as compensation to an American executive, slightly beating the $49 million that Wells received the same year, counting his converted options, and $10 million more than Eisner himself had received the year before.

The Disney team signed new long-term contracts at the end of 1989— Richard Frank, Ricardo Mestres, David Hoberman, Helene Hahn, and Frank Wells for five years, Joe Shapiro for six, Jeffrey Katzenberg for eight, and Eisner for nine.

Yet for all the appearance of continuity, Eisner had not quite settled into a "business as usual" turning of the crank. His dreams of Disney's future were both grand and specific. As one analyst put it, "A lot of big American companies don't even have a five-year plan. Disney has a 20-year plan, with cash flow projections." But many of the strategies that had taken Eisner to this great level of success were coming into question. Some seemed to work still, but were apparently being abandoned; the viability of others seemed questionable in light of changing economics.

In the studio, there were increasing signs that Disney was straying from the formulas that underpinned its success.

The studio had not slowed down its growth. At the end of 1990, over 100 projects were in development at Disney. The studio expected to release 28 films under its three labels in 1991, on its way from 14 in 1988 to a projected 30 per year by 1992. Projects on the way included *Blondie*, based on the venerable comic strip; Andrew Lloyd Webber's musical *Evita*; Tom Hanks and Debra Winger in *Significant Other*; Sylvester Stallone in *Oscar*; and Bill Murray in *What about Bob?* In the second quarter of 1991, the studio for the first time made more money than the parks. Yet as that wild growth continued, it increasingly began to show its costs.

Disney's animation unit, in its tilt-slab warehouse in Glendale, continued to plow forward with ambitious projects, including *Beauty and the Beast*, set for late 1991, *Alladin*, aimed at 1992, and *The King of the Jungle*, for 1993. Spielberg had already signed on to do *Toon Platoon*, another live/animated film, this time focusing on the early life of Roger Rabbit on a farm in Kansas. After the successes of *Roger Rabbit*, *The Little Mermaid*, and *Oliver and Company*, there was no longer any doubt that Disney animation had a future.

But to fill the gaps between the classic films, the company seemed willing to dilute its reputation for high quality in theatrical animation by bringing its made-for-television characters, with their simpler style, into the theaters. The summer release of the French-made *Raiders of the Lost Ark* sendup *DuckTales: The Movie: The Secret of the Lost Lamp* enraged the critics with its low quality. It seemed as if Saturday morning cartoon animation had, indeed, leaked onto the big screen. Charles Solomon, critic for the hometown *Los Angeles Times*, wrote, "In just 73 minutes, the film-makers manage to trash both the Disney tradition of excellence in animation and the Carl Barks comic books on which it is supposedly based. . . . Scrooge and his nephews gesture a lot, but their movements don't express their personalities." The company registered its embarrassment by releasing the film under the rubric of "Funny Flickers," but promised at least one "Funny Flicker" a year in the future.

The studio's calendar of "live" films was no longer filled with low-budget comedies and stars picked up for a pittance on the downside of their careers. Katzenberg paid Murray, to take just one example, $9 million for his role in *Bob*. Katzenberg's costs crept inexorably closer to the industry average, and the industry average continued to shoot up.

Even the costs of the simplest projects began to career out of control. In late 1990 and early 1991, for instance, Katzenberg set first-timer Jerry Rees, who had previously directed the videos that greet visitors at the Studio Tour, to direct Kim Basinger and Alec Baldwin in Neil Simon's *The Marrying Man*. Then Alan King sued Disney, Simon, and producer David Permut for stealing his idea: Simon, he said, had spun the whole script out of one of King's tennis-courtside conversations. That was no sooner settled out of court than the set erupted. Baldwin and Basinger both turned prima donna. What's worse, they fell in love. They would be hours late some mornings, while the rest of the cast and the crew sat around. When they got to the set they would argue with everyone in sight—with Simon over rewrites, with the director of photography over camera angles, with the Disney executives, with Permut, with Rees. Baldwin threw a chair, put his fist into a wall, smashed a camera lens, and jerked a cellular phone out of the hands of a Disney executive. Basinger refused to do retakes, repeatedly stopped takes to "fluff" her hair, and demanded that a Directors' Guild trainee hold a parasol over her constantly to keep the sun off her delicate skin. Eventually the pair got the Disney executives and the line producer banned from the set, and got the cinematographer fired. They finished the film, but not before sending the costs of the production spiraling from $15 million beyond $26 million.

By the turn of the '90s, the Disney studios clearly stood at a crossroads. Katzenberg had built enormous success on a strict, by-the-book formula: pay for stories, not stars; pay for talent, not celebrities; bargain like mad; keep control; never pay retail. Pressures were building to pry Disney away from that formula—ego pressures for higher-profile films and stars, as well as market pressures for higher salaries not just for stars but for directors and writers.

Eisner and Katzenberg were stung by the charge that their formula had made them "the McDonald's of the film industry," as well as by accusations that, as one analyst put it, "Disney hasn't shot very high." Frank Rose, writing in *Premier*, displayed a typical Hollywood opinion—and quoted a heavy-hitting critic to back him:

> Most of Disney's big hits have been variations on a theme, and sooner or later—*Pretty Woman* notwithstanding—that theme is bound to wear thin. For some, it already has. In *The New York Times*, critic Janet Maslin characterized Touchstone films—the comedies in particular—as having a "cookie-cutter feeling" and accused the studio of putting "a definite ceiling on the heights to which film-makers can soar."

Eisner and Katzenberg show signs of loosening up in efforts to join the Hollywood rush to "event" films. *Dick Tracy* was a clear deviation from the "go-for-singles" philosophy, and its failure to become one of the highest-grossing films of all time combined with the threat of war in the Gulf and a general slowing of the economy to pull Disney stock down 50 points to a low of 86 in the summer of 1990. Yet Katzenberg continued searching out more "prestige" product, vehicles that carried the chimera of an Oscar with them, such as Gerald Poner's *Warlords of Crime*, E. L. Doctorow's *Billy Bathgate*, and the autobiography of Natan Sharansky. He more often was willing to pay the going rate for top directors, and removed a cap—which had been set at $1.5 million—on the salaries he would pay them. Katzenberg even began to sidle up to the agency "package deals" that most of Hollywood ran on, that gave so much power to the agencies, and that he and Eisner had always disdained. In the fall of 1990, Katzenberg announced a long-term deal with Andre Vajna's Cinergi, a new company that had just signed a Creative Artists Agency package deal, paying $20 million for one script, and the services of one director, one producer, and one actor on one film. Katzenberg even signed the high-profile team of Don Simpson and Jerry Bruckheimer, makers of big-budget films like *Top Gun* and *Days of Thunder*, after they left a highly publicized deal with Paramount that was less than a year old. Frank Mancuso, at Paramount, had kicked them out because he could not control their costs—*Days of Thunder* racked up a $63-million total—yet Katzenberg felt he could do better.

Far from emulating Eisner and Katzenberg's tightfisted ways, the industry had gone on a spending spree in 1990, spurred in part by Japanese investment and the worldwide appetite for violent action films. Carolco had paid Arnold Schwarznegger $15 million to star in *Terminator II*, which cost $88 million to make, and $10 million for *Total Recall*, a special-effects-laden film that cost more than $60 million. Paramount spent $50 million on *The Godfather, Part III*. Other films in the $50 million category included Universal's *Jurassic Park* and Tri-Star's *Hook* and *Hudson Hawk*. Disney's own *Billy Bathgate* and *Rocketeer* were both pushing past the $30 million mark. Even screenwriters began to participate in the bonanza: Carolco paid writer Joe Ezterhas $3 million for a single screenplay.

The spending spree tended to pull the prices of the whole industry upward. Even those who did not specialize in high explosives and blood had to compete for much of the same writing, acting, and directing talent, and Disney did not remain aloof. Disney's watchword had been Rich Frank's saying, "We won't pay retail." Now, as one executive noted, "They're still tight with a dollar, but they'll pay for the talent they want." Disney began to take chances, and those chances had the capacity to put Disney in the same schmo's game as everyone else in Hollywood.

The big-budget gamble did not always pay off at the box office. What had been true in 1985 was still true in 1990: large budgets, special effects, and big-name stars do not necessarily guarantee profits. The two highest-grossing films of 1990, *Ghost* and Disney's *Pretty Woman*, were both modestly budgeted films about relationships. *Ghost*, the romance of a couple whose love goes beyond the grave, took in over $200 million domestically. *Pretty Woman* capped its $180-million domestic take with $232 million made overseas. Another "small" film, *Home Alone*, released late in the year, eventually beat them both with $213 million in domestic sales.

By early 1991, under the cloud of recession and war, the relationship film and the family film—Disney's and Touchstone's métier—were making a modest comeback in Hollywood. In a much-leaked, much-published, and much-parodied 28-page confidential memo, Katzenberg declared that it was "back to basics" for Disney. *Daily Variety* published the memo in full, all 11,000 words, and Hollywood was in an uproar. He argued that movies cost too much, that too much emphasis is put on big-name stars and not enough on good stories, that not enough effort is put into searching out talent beyond Hollywood's borders, and that Japanese investment was ruining Hollywood. It was a clear and elegant argument, but it was also a catalogue of Katzenberg's own sins. Beating his breast over the *Dick Tracy* fiasco, Katzenberg seemed to admit as much himself, writing that the company had "drifted away from our original vision of how to run our movie business." He added:

> At some point, we seemed to have replaced it with a strategy that might best be called the "Yes, but" philosophy, as in, "Yes, he's expensive but it's a great opportunity for us," or "Yes, that's a lot to spend on marketing, but we have too much at stake not to," or "Yes, the sequel will require a big budget, but it's a potential franchise."

But despite Katzenberg's memo, and the agreement of other industry leaders, and despite the example of such films as *Ghost*, *Pretty Woman*, and *Home Alone*, the march of the big-budget action film seemed to go on unabated. By the spring of 1991, the average film produced in Hollywood cost $26.8 million, a 14 percent jump from the previous year.

Katzenberg had not built his success by taking big risks. Don Simpson responded to the two-decades-old story of Katzenberg getting thrown out of the Bahama casinos by claiming that "Jeffrey's not a gambler. Gamblers have the sort of personality that likes chaos, open-endedness, blind fate. Jeffrey is the antithesis of that. He looks at areas of confusion and says, 'There's a way to get a rope around that one.' He loved being able to beat the odds at blackjack. He didn't play all the games—he only played one, he played it brilliantly, and he won at it. He'd figured out the system."

Another executive called Disney "a rule company, because that's the way Jeffrey lives his life. He eats at the same time, he works out at the same time, he reads at the same time, he plays with his kids at the same time, he comes to the office at the same time. As long as they are dealing with concept comedies, that seems to work. As they get into other kinds of movies, we'll have to see." In trying to explain the success of Disney formula comedies, writer/director Paul Schrader referred to "a secret pact between the audience and Michael Eisner. They're the cinematic equivalent of big-print books."

Of course, Touchstone had produced quite a few successful films that were more complex and daring than the formula. To ignore them would be to leave out, for instance, the singular mix of wrenching drama and wild comedy in *Good Morning, Vietnam*, the meaning and charm of *Dead Poets Society*, the satisfying complexity of *New York Stories*, *The Color of Money*, and *Tin Men*, the technical daring and wild surprise of *Who Framed Roger Rabbit?*, and the classic excellence of *The Little Mermaid*. But the basic argument makes business sense: despite the wonderful exceptions, the core of the expansion of the studios was the inexpensive formula comedy, and the more Eisner and Katzenberg strayed from the formula, by desire or by necessity, the greater the risk in Disney's future.

Television presented Eisner with particularly intractable problems. Disney had yet to find its path in network television. Television shows are usually unprofitable in their original run, even if they are popular. But a popular show can pay off handsomely once it becomes a syndicated rerun package. And indeed, such packages are the "cash cows" of such other studios as Paramount, MCA, and Columbia.

In pursuit of that magic status, Disney had pursued a herky-jerky path, plunging forward, then cutting back, then plunging forward again. Most recently, the studio threw significant amounts of money into long-term contracts with television writer-producers. In 1989 it signed Matt Williams, one of the top writers on "Roseanne," to a $10 million contract, and put him to work producing "Carol and Co." with Carol Burnett. In 1990 it laid out a reported $15 million for the team of Neal Marlens and Carol Black, the writers behind "The Wonder Years." This latest drive toward success produced six shows in prime time in the 1990 season, including the somewhat raunchy and daring "Hull High" (a musical set in a high school), "Lenny," and "Carol and Co." But at the same time, Disney announced that it was giving up on hour dramas, and its association with Garth Ancier, the *Wunderkind* it had brought in to help fix its television problems, ended in noisy recriminations. Within weeks of their opening, CBS put "Lenny" on hiatus, and NBC cancelled "Hull High," after it came in at 86th out of 98 prime-time series. With "Carol and Co.," at least, the money paid off: the show became a hit as soon as it was introduced in the spring of 1990, and combined with

Disney's Witt–Thomas–Harris shows "Empty Nest" and "Golden Girls" to help NBC stay neck and neck with the other networks in the fall.

The company also branched out beyond sitcoms into unusual new types of shows. In the spring of 1991, the company announced it would syndicate a national lottery show, combining 33 state lotteries to create cash pools of millions of dollars, with tie-in promotions available to viewers in the other 17 states. Other syndications were doing equally well. The two-hour "Disney Afternoon" block of cartoon programming was proving profitable, and in the spring of 1991, Disney brought in $125 million by selling a package of 50 movies to television stations. What was most remarkable about the sale was that 33 films were yet to be produced.

If only because Eisner, Katzenberg, Frank, and many of the other broadcast executives came from the networks, or had experience in producing shows for network television, Disney would continue to try mightily for a presence in network television.

The future was much clearer in the parks, where Disney's plans already stretch well into the next century. By 1990 Eisner had poured an estimated $1.5 billion into the parks, and the company was prepared to spend a great deal more in the coming years.

Financial analysts tend to think of theme parks as cash cows. Despite the large investments, theme parks are considered huge money-makers once they are up and running. Operating costs are relatively stable, and any increase in attendance, ticket prices, or the number of days that visitors stay tends to go directly to the bottom line. Analyst Paul C. Marsh of Bateman Eichler, Hill Richards, a Los Angeles brokerage firm, echoes this point of view: "Once it's in place, it just a turnstile game."

But that phrase, "once it's in place," is more complex than it seems. Disney's experience with theme parks in the previous three decades shows clearly that if a company simply opens a park, then sits back and runs it, it is wasting its assets, because the park's profits will never live up to its potential. The majority of the people coming through the gate have been to the park before. If you want to keep people coming back to the park, as well as entice new people, and justify charging them more at the same time, you have to continually re-create the park, rebuilding old sections and adding new attractions, constantly making it new, keeping the charm of the old and familiar in balance with the excitement of the new. You have to spend big money to feed that cash cow.

Michael Eisner understood this more clearly than any other CEO in the industry. For six years he had constantly nurtured and prodded the parks. And that nurturing and prodding were expected to speed up in the '90s, not slow down. Disney, which controlled over 40 percent of the domestic theme park market, more than double the 18 percent of Anheuser-Busch, its nearest competitor, was determined to maintain that lead, and to keep the cash cow in hay. Every part of the Disney universe is expected to see big changes over the next ten years.

There are already plans on the boards for Disney World that include a possible fourth theme park, as well as a Soviet pavilion at EPCOT and seven new hotels. In addition, the imagineers are planning 29 new attractions at the three existing parks.

The 2,000 new hotel rooms that Disney opened in 1990 were only part of a program that will make Disney the owner and operator of 30 hotels and 26,000 rooms worldwide by 1992. By the winter of 1990, bulldozers had already begun to churn the swamp and bush for two more resorts, Port Orleans and Dixie Landing. By the end of the decade seven hotels with more than 5,500 rooms will join them: in 1992 a Mediterranean resort, built in the style of the Greek islands, on the monorail at the edge of the Seven Seas Lagoon near the Magic Kingdom; the following year the Wilderness Lodge and Buffalo Junction, both in the Fort Wilderness Resort and Campground area; and later in the decade, Kingdom Suites near the Magic Kingdom and the Boardwalk resort near EPCOT, along with two hotels with Hollywood themes. By the turn of the decade Walt Disney World will harbor 25 separate resort hotel complexes with more than 20,000 rooms and nearly 400,000 square feet of convention space, from meeting rooms to ballrooms to audiovisual complexes.

In the Magic Kingdom, the Splash Mountain flume ride will open in 1993. Later in the decade the Little Mermaid will carry guests into the world of her father, King Triton. By 1996, the imagineers will turn Tomorrowland into an intergalactic spaceport for arriving aliens.

In the years ahead, Eisner has decided, the Studio Tour will nearly double in size. A "Honey, I Shrunk the Kids Adventure Zone" will terrorize guests with giant insects and lawn sprinklers. The complex will even sprout a new "Main Street." Sunset Boulevard will angle off from the current Hollywood Boulevard to Roger Rabbit's Hollywood, where guests will ride the Toontown Trolley, Bennie the Cab, and even Baby Herman's runaway baby buggy. Along the same street of dreams, guests will fire machine guns from careening antique cars on a Dick Tracy ride, or play with fanciful movie equipment in Mickey's Movieland, a replica of Walt's original studio on Hyperion Avenue in Hollywood.

When Disney's feared rival MCA opened their Universal Studios Tour nearby in Orlando in the summer of 1990, everything went wrong. Many of the most-advertised rides, including "Jaws" and "King Kong," didn't work. People lined up for blocks to demand their money back, and network television news cameras—the very networks that MCA had courted for coverage of its opening day—were there to record it all. For the moment, at least, Disney had little to fear from MCA.

It is at EPCOT's Future World that the most profound changes may emerge. Michael Eisner is a man who thinks about the future. He has shared the podium with Alvin Toffler and other futurists at conferences on the future of technology and society. He has spoken at colleges and universities and association meetings across the country on his vision of that future. He believes in a future in which technology is secondary to the message it carries—it is ideas, not technology, that shape tomorrow. "With apologies to Marshall Macluhan, the medium is not the message," he has said. "The message is far more important, and has a life of its own. The stone tablets that Moses carried down the mountain are lost in the dust of the Sinai. The message written on them survives thousands of years later."

Michael Eisner runs the only corporation in the world that boasts a major institution of popular education focused on the future: EPCOT's Future World. And the message of EPCOT is exactly opposite to what Eisner believes. Furthermore, a number of critics have called the message of EPCOT's Future World empty and outdated. EPCOT may well undergo a transformation in theme. There are already signs that both Eisner and Wells are looking for ways to shift this vast institution.

EPCOT is not at all empty of ideas. It has a coherent guiding philosophy, a central idea, straight from Walt: an unbounded belief in progress, powered by technology. Such a philosophy neatly fits the commercial needs of American corporations marketing their technology—a fact that certainly helped build EPCOT. EPCOT's image of the future is unfailingly sweet, a dictatorship of the nice, with no sense of the chaos, waste, and confusion that make up the real world. It is a technologically inspired utopia of order and harmony. EPCOT (like Disney World as a whole) has no answer for social problems—it just outlaws them, banishing them to the world outside. As a result, whether its designers intended it to or not, EPCOT teaches specific social messages.

Some of the messages are valuable: that you can enhance your health by changing your diet and exercising more (in Metropolitan Life's "The Wonders of Life"); that we should think about what goes into our food (Kraft's "The Land"); that the oceans are a great resource that must be researched more deeply and managed more wisely (United Technologies' "The Living Seas").

But the most prominent messages, all clearly and entertainingly presented with the usual Disney thoroughness and pizzazz, do not seem so benign. The theme song and the ride through General Motors' "World of Motion" clearly equate the personal car with personal freedom, and impresses visitors with the idea that the personal car is the "right" answer to future transportation needs. It also declares that the internal combustion engine is the only reasonable power source for transportation (a large multiscreen animated cartoon in the "World of Motion" ridicules alternative engines).

Another message that is vividly displayed is that more oil exploration is the only viable answer to our energy needs, and other solutions should not be taken seriously. There is a curious irony to the "Universe of Energy," presented by Exxon. Although it is roofed with solar cells, the pavilion shows no sign of being an energy-conscious building. It is just another air-conditioned sealed environment in the Florida heat. The "Energy Exchange," also sponsored by Exxon, displays the various forms of energy. But solar and wind power waste away in a corner like lost lab experiments from a high school science fair. Synthetic fuels are displayed with prominent copy that explains how expensive, difficult, and environmentally dangerous they are. The drama of oil exploration takes up 75 percent of the space, and is portrayed as a heroic exercise in which brave men and women face danger and deprivation in the far corners of the globe to bring the world the energy it needs.

EPCOT also teaches that imagination (in Kodak's "World of the Imagination") is a baffling magical process, rather than an ability that can be nurtured. The idea that invention might in some way spring from individuality, from personal expression or the ability to think differently from other people, is never considered. Ironically, it is that very individuality and creativity that have made Disney so successful.

The most unsettling of the messages of EPCOT, however, is the notion that technology can save us. In the EPCOT worldview, new inventions and processes—floating buildings, undersea villages, computer networks—seem to carry the world to a superior future all by themselves. In this, EPCOT doesn't feel futuristic at all. In fact, there is a whiff of nostalgia about such unchecked enthusiasm for a tech-utopia.

The machines and technology at EPCOT seem to have little to do with the people who operate them or the worlds in which they operate. For instance, a "futuristic" all-terrain bus featured in a General Motors display can carry 50 or more people deep into the desert, the swamp, or the Arctic tundra—but the display gives no hint of the effect that swarms of tourist buses might have on such delicate environments.

The final message of the EPCOT experience is a subtle, but strong emphasis on conformity: be nice, keep your hands and legs inside the car, remain seated, refrain from unscripted behavior.

EPCOT may change its message, if slowly. Eisner and Wells, along with most members of the post-1984 Disney hierarchy, are public, contributing liberal Democrats, with an avid opinion about environmental matters. Liberal Democrats regularly enjoy fund-raisers sponsored by Michael Eisner, often at his house, and on some occasions even on the Disney lot. For instance, Senator Bill Bradley, a Democrat and a friend of Eisner's, received $52,165 from 1986 to 1990 from 59 Disney executives (including the legal maximum of $2,000 each from 12 of them), and another $25,750 from their spouses and children, while Florida governor Bob Graham, also a Democrat, received $25,500 from Disney executives in his successful 1986 race for the Senate. Most of the top executives, including Eisner and Wells, have their own favorite environmental causes.

The dichotomy between Eisner's and Wells' personal beliefs and the messages of EPCOT is vivid. By 1989 and 1990, serious articles criticizing EPCOT had circulated throughout the Disney hierarchy. In early 1990, Frank Wells gave imagineer Randy Bright an assignment: write a white paper detailing how EPCOT could become an environmental showcase in the 1990s. Soon after submitting his study, Bright was killed in a traffic accident while cycling. But his ideas have become a part of Disney, and they may yet become a part of EPCOT.

Eisner has continually asked in private the questions that cannot be asked in public, "Are we overdoing it? Are we saturating the market? Will people get sick of Disney Stores, Disney parks, Disney clothes, Disney cartoons?" He publicly mocks market research, telling stories from his years at ABC. The market research said "Roots" would bomb, so they tried to bury it by showing it all in one week and people called them marketing geniuses; a palm-reading guru hired by the network told them to ditch "All In The Family," and they did. He calls market research "trying to apply numbers to a business ruled by emotion." Yet, privately, he and Wells have agreed that the company desperately needs just such numbers, and have commissioned regular focus groups and customer surveys, as well as surveys among people who don't come to the parks to find out why they don't come. One Disney executive involved in the process said, "We are expanding so rapidly that we keep looking for that resistance. We keep waiting for people to say, 'Enough!' We haven't found it yet."

So the expansion continues, as fast as the company can do it and still give it the "Disney touch." For instance, south of EPCOT, across the freeway, across the line in Osceola County, Disney owns almost 9,000 acres of land, pine barrens laced with nearly 3,500 acres of swamp, drainage watershed, and canals. Here another child of EPCOT will rise over the next 25 years, straddling Interstate 4 with a massive 1.5-million-square-foot, upscale shopping mall, Central Florida's largest, along with as many as 6,000 middle-income and "executive" houses with a starting price of $90,000, 6 to 7 million square feet of office space, over a million square feet of light industrial space, golf courses, and recreation areas. The company estimates the cost of the development at $2.5 billion.

In the 1970s and early 1980s, in the Disney Village and other parts of Walt Disney World, the company had allowed construction of major chain hotels, golf courses, and time-share condos that had nothing "Disney" about them—no unusual ideas, no themes, no stories, no consistent design that would let the visitor know that this was Disney World, rather than Hilton Head or Boca Raton.

According to Peter Rummell, president of the Disney Development Company, Eisner is determined that this not happen again. Every development will extend the Disney idea, defined by Eisner as "creativity, quality, and synergy." In real estate, this means first that every development will carry some kind of story (such as Typhoon Lagoon's conceit that refugees from a typhoon were forced to build a resort from the typhoon's wreckage) and that story will be carried out in every detail, every "design element." It means, second, that every project will have the same legendary Disney attention to detail, cleanliness, proper staffing, sight lines, and traffic planning. It means, finally, that each project will act as a feeder for every other part of the Disney empire. Eisner feels that the name "Disney," and the imagination and quality that the name represents, are the corporation's major assets, and it is foolish to invest in any project that does not take full advantage of them. As Eisner puts it, "Nobody would trek to Florida to go to a 'Michael Eisner World.' Nobody would get on a plane to Anaheim to go to an 'Eisnerland.'"

The Osceola project is a prime example of that attempt to differentiate

Disney projects from anything else. Besides "design elements" and "themes," the project will include a "Disney Institute," a resort that will feature education as recreation, with guests mixing brain-expanding seminars with visits to the Magic Kingdom and Typhoon Lagoon. It was an idea predicted by Dychtwald and Flower in the 1989 futurist book *Age Wave*: that popular education mixed with travel, typified by Elderhostel, the popular low-budget educational travel program for seniors, would soon be taken upscale by an adventurous entrepreneur. *Age Wave* called it one example of "thrill rides of the mind," a phenomenon encouraged by an aging, and increasingly educated, population. Disney is the first to put such plans on the drawing board. Visitors will stay in resortlike surroundings. Corporations can use the grounds for corporate seminars. Other times, Disney will schedule its own seminars on such popular subjects as current affairs, the environment, and self-help. In between seminars, visitors will relax and enjoy the rest of Disney World.

Research and education were part of the original idea for EPCOT, and so was the idea of residents. Walt Disney's original ideas and sketches of EPCOT clearly contemplated residents living in the "community." But residents tend to engage in unscripted behavior. So Disney has never allowed true, independently employed, permanent residents in any of its projects. But the company plans to drop the Osceola development from its Reedy Creek Improvement District and turn it over to Osceola County, which will be a partner in the development. For the first time in Florida, Disney will pay county impact fees for water, sewers, roads, and other services. And for the first time, real voters will live in a Disney development.

With its Orlando experiences in mind, Disney is working hard to keep things smooth in Paris. It has continually negotiated with the French government over how much of the signage and narration will be in French, and how much of the whole project will reflect French culture. When local farmers began resisting selling their land for the project, Disney put a crew on it, doing a miniature PR blitz that included taking scores of French farmers and their wives to Orlando for a free luxury tour of Disney World.

Preparing Europe for the 1992 opening of Euro Disneyland is a vast project. Disney has greatly increased its presence on European television, through annual Christmas extravaganzas and a Sunday morning children's show called "The Disney Club." In February 1991, the company opened an information center at the construction site, and began escorting scores of journalists through the emerging attractions. Arthur D. Little International expects the park to attract 11.7 to 17.8 million visitors in the first year, and Disney expects that first year to be in the black.

Euro Disneyland could face competitors. In 1990, MCA began looking for a site for a theme park of its own, to be opened by 1993. MCA's park chief Jay Stein told the press that MCA would "kick Disney's butt all over Europe." Eisner replied, through the press, that Disney's accomplishments could speak for themselves, but "it won't be our butt that will be getting kicked." And in 1991, Sony announced its intention to build a worldwide chain of theme parks—"Sonylands"—in direct competition with Disney. In the face of all this threatened competition, Eisner's comment might seem like so much bravado. Yet there was some truth in it: so far, no one has shown an ability to beat Disney at the game that Disney invented.

Disneyland, the grandfather of theme parks, will undergo major changes in the 1990s—its first major facelift since Bear Country, now called Critter Country, was added in 1972. The park has always seemed packed, especially compared with its East Coast cousin—crowded with shops, restaurants, rides, and "in-betweens." But in fact, of the 86 acres inside Disneyland's high earthen berm, some 30 acres are still available for new attractions, especially in the northwest section, behind Critter Country, Big Thunder Mountain, and Small World, and in the southeast corner, between Main Street and Tomorrowland. Most of these acres are now used for "backstage operations," including warehouse and maintenance facilities, many of which could be moved outside the park itself. Ripping out aging attractions, such as the outdated Mission to Mars ride in Tomorrowland, will create even more space for new ideas.

The plans—some preliminary, some advanced—include a "Young Indiana Jones" stunt show; a reproduction of the Hollywood Boulevard portion of the Studio Tour; and an attraction based on *The Little Mermaid*. The imagineers are also planning two attractions based on Roger Rabbit and Toon Town, possibly including Dick Tracy (a Dick Tracy stage show opened in the summer of 1990, to go along with the release of the movie); a "character land," where patrons can take photos with all of the Disney characters; the conversion of the now-closed "America Sings" attraction into a hovering spacecraft peopled with "Audio-Animatronic" robot characters; and a complete remodeling of Tomorrowland.

Outside that earthen berm, Disney owns about 66 acres around Disneyland, including a 40-acre strawberry field north of the Disneyland Hotel and 26 acres southwest of the hotel. There are also 120 acres of parking lots that could be replaced with a parking structure. The company has announced plans to build a second gate, and possibly a third gate next to Disneyland, including a copy of the Disney/MGM Studio Tour, and an EPCOT-like park that will combine the technological future with international pavilions, to be called "WESTCOT."

In late 1990 and early 1991, while trying to keep quiet about it, Eisner and Wells set about trying to buy land around Disneyland for expansion. Much of the land was already developed, covered with dozens of hotels and motels, including the 15-story Pan Pacific Hotel, built in 1984. Other parcels were mobile home parks, and some were still farmland, including a 58-acre strawberry farm just south of the Disneyland parking lot.

One parcel after another fell to Wells' agents, but not all. The Pan Pacific's Japanese owners were insulted by Disney's $45-million offer, which was less than they had spent to build it. Disney was baffled, as well, by the resistance of Hiroshi Fujishige, the owner of the strawberry farm. Disney offered him $32 million for a long-term lease, but he didn't want to leave. The 68-year-old farmer figured he was still three or four years away from retirement, and money didn't mean as much to him at the moment as farming. Besides, he was still shadowed by the memory of his brother, Masao. Only five years before, Masao, who owned and worked the land with Hiroshi, had felt his health going, and had felt as well the pressure of developers to buy his property, and pressure from the city to put access roads across it. Masao committed suicide. Hiroshi didn't feel ready to sell and leave the ghost of Masao behind, even when Frank Wells came down to meet with him, and chat about his family. Fujishige was polite, but not overwhelmed. When the *Los Angeles Times* called later to hear about the talks, Fujishige had to ask his bookkeeper for Wells' name. It was not important. Someone else had recently offered him $2 million per acre for the 58 acres, and Fujishige had said no without even finding out the man's name.

With or without the strawberry farm, Disney's plans will go forward. Eisner has announced his intentions to sink $2 billion in a new Disney park somewhere in southern California. The market research that he claims to disdain has shown him that the southern California theme park market is far from saturated. If Disney wants to continue to dominate that market as it has for 35 years, it must move fast, building attractions so big and so different as to deter other competitors from even starting.

The new park might be in Anaheim, or it might be in Long Beach. The two cities are engaged in a battle for the park, each with its own assets and drawbacks. At stake are sales tax revenues: Disneyland and the tourist attractions that have grown up around it brought Anaheim some $15.5 million in sales tax revenue in 1989 alone. Anaheim has nearly four times as many hotels and motels citywide (16,000) as Long Beach (4,400) and its convention center is nine times larger. Long Beach, on the other hand, has one of the most lightly traveled freeways in the Los Angeles area ending at the Disney property, and a light rail line on the way. In Long Beach, the company leases 55 acres from the city and holds the option to develop 256 acres of water surrounding its *Queen Mary–Spruce Goose*–Londontown attraction.

Long Beach would benefit enormously from the revenues and tourists a Disney park would attract. Like many American cities, Long Beach has long been debating what to to do about its downtown: where it can find jobs, how it can attract a larger tax base, how it can be redeveloped, how it can cut down on crime and the misery of the underclass.

The $2-billion Port Disney that Eisner is considering would cover 350 acres—250 of it now under water—with a theme park, luxury hotels, the world's biggest aquarium, waterfront restaurants, artificial tropical reefs, circular structures rising like bubbles out of the water, a marina, and even underwater steel cages where tourists can swim with sharks. Although Port Disney would not open for at least 10 years, in time it could create 10,000 jobs.

As writer Robert Jones pointed out in the *Los Angeles Times*, there is something going on here that goes far beyond a theme park. The "city-side" part of the Disney plan would in fact occupy most of the land along Long Beach's waterfront. For the first time, Disney is proposing not to build a new fantasy city, but to retro-fit an existing real one with themes:

> So now come the Disney people, making an implicit promise. They are saying, "We can theme this city and bring it to life. We can succeed where the city has failed. Our unreal world is more powerful than any reality the city could produce."

> The interesting and sad part is, Disney probably speaks the truth. The company estimates that 13 million people a year would visit their version of Long Beach. I believe them. Perhaps it's because a downtown-by-Disney provides the sense of safety that a real downtown could never offer. Disney's Long Beach will have strolling, shopping, volcanoes—and no risk.

Nor will it require, as do real cities, a willingness to search and explore for the good stuff. Port Disney's secrets will all be revealed in a brochure. You will have the "mysteries" of the sea offered to you inside a glass bubble while outside, just yards away, the real sea will glimmer quietly in the moonlight. And, somehow, the real thing will seem slightly diminished.

Nonetheless, we will love it. We will be fed, entertained, and finally monorailed to our hotel for the evening. A safe hotel. A place where we can fall asleep and dream that, truly, this is urban life without a downside. The way it should be.

Perhaps the strangest and most interesting result of the Disney expansions, this leaking of Disney theme park development into "real life," into streets and neighborhoods, hotels, and business parks, is not the result of some imagineers' cabal determined to "theme the world." It is merely that, as Peter Rummell, president of Disney development, put it, "We want to control the periphery. If we build a theme park in Long Beach, someone is going to develop hotels on the land across the inlet. We want to do it, so that we can incorporate it into our design concepts, so that we can control what kind of development it is, and so that we can profit from it." Yet it is happening on a growing scale in Anaheim, in Orlando, in Paris, in Tokyo, where a series of new hotels linked with the Magic Kingdom have been built, and in Burbank where giant statues of the seven dwarfs holding up the dome of the new corporate headquarters stare out high above the frame bungalows and apartments of Burbank. It is an approach to architecture never seen in quite this form before: the linking of individual elements of large-scale projects through themes that go far beyond visual accents or "design elements" to actual stories, "let's pretend" scenarios that seduce the employee and the visitor into a bit of play.

It is relatively predictable that the existing theme parks will expand, and new ones will be built. How quickly the changes take place will depend upon how many visitors Disney is able to pull through the gates of the existing parks, and of each new project as it opens. If Disney's cash flow continues at its current high level, and if it is not seriously affected by a major recession, the company not only will be able to continue expanding, it will need to, in order to turn the cash into profitable internal investments, and not leave it sitting around as takeover bait.

The "go" decision on such projects is a matter of intense consideration. Each project requires intensive investments, both of capital and of highly skilled in-house labor, especially by the imagineers, much of which simply cannot be bought elsewhere. Each project takes from six months (for the stage shows) to five years to complete. Counting political maneuvering, environmental impact reports, and building such pieces of the infrastructure as freeways, drainage canals, and sewage capacity, such large-scale projects as the Osceola "dream-city" could take a decade to put in place. Yet, especially for projects within established facilities— within Reedy Creek, for instance, or at the Disneyland site—Eisner and Wells have considerable flexibility in deciding when to expand and what to build.

The people driving into the parking lots in Florida and Anaheim, and getting off the trains in Paris and Tokyo, are the engine that has powered Disney's great expansion. The central questions for Disney in the 1990s become: Will that engine falter? And will Eisner and Wells know what to do if it does? By the summer of 1990, the great economic expansion of the 1980s was clearly over, and the rapid fundamental changes in the Middle East, Eastern Europe, and the Soviet Union made the future seem less and less predictable.

The questions have a certain fascination to them. There are few models on which we can base our forecasts. If there is a serious worldwide recession, what will happen to the theme parks? No firm has a longer or broader experience in the theme park business than Disney. But Disney's own experience in recessions is ambiguous. The few recessions the country has had during Disney's brief history have not seemed to affect the parks deeply. To be sure, unemployment rises in a recession. But some of those laid off treated the layoff period as an enforced vacation, during which they might finally take the kids to Disneyland or Disney World. The experience of the past shows that if a recession is relatively short, people tend to keep up or even increase their level of leisure spending, especially for less expensive items such as toys and movies. But that experience comes from a time before Disney's huge price increases— from a time when going to Disneyland, for instance, was relatively inexpensive entertainment, with a ticket costing only two or three times the cost of a ticket to a movie. Will the price increases make the theme parks more vulnerable to a recession today? No one knows yet. Already, as the economy slowed in the fall of 1990 and the beginning of 1991, Disneyland and Disney World declared temporary price reductions to shore up a park attendance that Eisner admitted was "crummy."

What if a recession were brought on, in part, by gasoline that cost $5 per gallon or more? During the 1973/74 oil crisis, attendance at Disney World and Disneyland dropped nearly 6.5 percent. Nonetheless, the new Disney, with its large cash flow, has the capacity and the incentive to subsidize air fares in the eastern corridor, if necessary, and possibly even to buy its own shuttle airline, to encourage travel to Disney. If a recession were stronger in the United States than elsewhere in the world, and if it were accompanied by a weak dollar, as the mild recession of the early 1980s was, any drop in American attendance would likely be replaced, at least in part, by a surge of foreign visitors.

Similarly, the entire video industry has grown up since the last recession. A recession might actually be good for the video rental business: videos are the cheap entertainment that movies were during the Depression. Films might also benefit in the short run, as people with more time on their hands look for something to fill it. But with movie tickets costing two to six times as much as video rentals, films might suffer as a long recession began to bite. Television would suffer, especially from a lengthy recession: viewers would have plenty of time on their hands, but advertisers would have less money to spend. Most of the other leisure businesses in which Disney is expanding—books, records, toys, retail stores—would probably feel little effects from a short recession, but be vulnerable to a long one.

The most vulnerable part of the Disney business would appear to be the attempt to attract the business traveler to Disney World through expanding convention facilities. The convention/association/seminar business is very vulnerable to recessions, since a ticket to another conference, especially at a fun place like Disney World, is one of the first things a business cuts out of a tightened budget. Fortunately for Disney, this is but a small part of Disney's business.

For a global entertainment conglomerate like Disney, with significant investments in many industries on several continents, the question of how it will do in a recession, and what is the right course for its managers to take, is highly complex. It is made more complex by lack of experience: neither Eisner nor Wells has had CEO responsibilities for a company during a recession. During the 1970s, with its oil crisis and "stagflation," Wells rose to co-chief executive of Warner Brothers, a division of Warner Communications. Similarly, Eisner rose to president of Paramount Pictures Corporation, a division of Gulf & Western (now renamed Paramount). To some extent, the concerns of the directors who preferred Stanfill in 1984 remain valid today: before his tenure at Disney, Eisner had never dealt with a board, never fought off a takeover attempt, never managed a company in a stagnant or shrinking economy. After the 1987 stock market crash, Eisner had researchers find him the best books available on how to manage in bad economic times. It's comforting that he put in the effort, but the effort only underscores his lack of experience. Managing in bad times is not something you can learn in a book.

And the books may well be wrong. There is no relevant pool of experience from which to draw. It has been decades since the entire world economy suffered a simultaneous recession, and in that time the economies of the world have grown increasingly interdependent and complex. Nobody in any company has yet experienced a serious global recession in an international economy so intimately involved as this one.

New theories of economic systems may give us some perspective on Disney. These emerging theories, based on recent studies of disturbed dynamic systems, stand in clear contrast to classic theories.

Classic economic theories suggest that systems tend toward equilibrium through negative feedback. For instance, lower demand for shoes drops the prices of shoes, which allows more people to think about buying shoes, increasing the demand, and eventually driving the prices up again. Any sudden jolt to the system, or any early advantage of one company quickly calls forth countervailing events, and are nullified. An oil crisis raises the price of oil, so wells are sunk in more marginal areas, more oil is produced, and the price stops rising and starts to fall. If one company comes out with a better argyle sock and captures more of the market, competitors are driven to come up with even better products, and gain back market share.

Knowledge-based industries, on the other hand, seem to respond to positive feedback. The more a company succeeds in the early going, the more knowledge it will have about how the product works, how it can be manufactured, and what research areas appear promising. At the same time, its potential customers gain more knowledge about its products and more comfort in making use of them. Early leads tend to widen if they are pursued vigorously.

Disney is just such a knowledge-based industry. Since it is large and aggressively run and has a substantial cash flow, this suggests that it will continue to grow and outflank its rivals in areas where it has already established a substantial lead (such as theme parks and character-based merchandising), or in areas in which it can quickly establish one through aggressive action in a changing situation (as it did in theatrical movies and video). In some of the areas that it is now exploring (such as television, retail merchandising, restaurants, mainstream book publishing, and recording), it has no such lead. This has two effects: it makes it exponentially more difficult for the company to advance in these areas, and it can cause the company to act inappropriately, throwing its weight around in industries where it has no weight.

The kind of management that is needed in knowledge-based industries has to have great sensitivity to trends and timing, a marvelous feel for the moment. It must be aggressive, able to capitalize rapidly on opportunities presented by the changing environment. It must be nearly ego-less, willing and able to shift nimbly, starting and abandoning projects as shifting circumstances dictate. And finally, it has to be lucky.

Michael Eisner and the team around him seem to have some of these qualities. He is as sensitive as a man in such a corporate Olympus can be, and he has transmitted that quality to his company. *The Little Mermaid* came out so rapidly on video because Disney executives literally stood outside theaters and listened to the comments of people who had just seen it. Eisner continues to go to the theaters to see the films of other companies, continues to tour the parks. Occasionally he even works in them. In December, 1990, he spent an evening soda-jerking on Main Street in Disneyland during a "free for the Armed Forces" night.

As we have seen in an earlier chapter, the company's aggressiveness under the new management, its constant willingness to go to the mat for what it wants, has become legendary. And Eisner, for all his happy-go-lucky public face, is the driving wheel of that aggressiveness.

Yet, most of the time, Eisner's ego mostly expresses itself in a desire to make himself a public figure, a "Daddy" figure for America, rather than an insistence that he is always right. He has willingly abandoned one idea after another when the numbers don't work out. In most major corporate decisions, Eisner has shown little desire to prove himself infallible, to hang onto losing projects.

The new Disney faces no more uncertainty than any other company, and has great resources of money, talent, and momentum to help it over the bumps. All these factors are important, but even they are overshadowed by the incomparable power of the name "Disney." In 1990, Landor Associates of San Francisco, the country's leading corporate identity firm, surveyed 5,000 Americans, 3,000 Europeans and 1,000 Japanese to discover the world's most powerful "brands." Using survey results that combined the familiarity of the brand with a measure of its esteem, they found that the five most powerful brands in the world were Coca-Cola, Sony, Mercedes-Benz, Kodak, and Disney. No other entertainment company made the top ten. This powerful name remains the company's largest resource, an asset that would be difficult if not impossible for any other company to build or buy. While Disney may suffer setbacks in particular areas, and may even abandon some businesses, it is likely that, all things considered, the company will continue to grow faster and more safely through the next decade than the average American company.

All through the late '80s and into the '90s rumors continued to swirl through Hollywood and Wall Street that Disney was about to make an offer for CBS, NBC, MCA, or Paramount. The rumors were based not on inside information but astute observation and the usual Wall Street love of bodies in motion. Eisner had the momentum, debt capacity, and cash flow to buy something really big. The industry was moving toward consolidation. One entertainment company after another had been swallowed up by larger entities. Capital Cities had bought ABC, and General Electric had bought NBC. CBS was the only independent network left, and rumors of its sale constantly festered on the perennially glum outlook of its chairman and chief stockholder, Lawrence Tisch. On one day in August 1990, CBS stock rose almost seven points on another gust of rumor that Disney was ready to take it over. In November of the same year, Disney rose four points on the rumor that it would buy NBC from GE.

But Eisner kept denying the rumors and, by spring of 1991, none of them had proven true. In mid-1990, though, Eisner reportedly had held discussions with Tisch. Eisner had long been friendly with Larry Tisch and his brother Preston Robert, who together control the Loew's Corporation. Eisner balked mainly because Tisch wanted $300 per share, more than 50 percent higher than their open market value.

Eisner has shown no tendency to gobble up enterprises just because he has the money, especially when he would have to pay premium prices. Eisner is tightfisted, and complains regularly that businesses he is interested in—television stations, for instance—cost too much. The structure of the entertainment industry would make such a purchase attractive for Disney, but not imperative. And, in the midst of its continuing expansion, Disney would have to worry about the capacity of the python to swallow the pig—big companies with far different corporate cultures and no loyalty to the increasingly thin idea that is "Disney."

Yet the possibility of buying CBS remained alive, especially after the network announced in December 1990 that it was using $2 billion in cash to buy back some of its own stock. This, along with CBS' continually eroding market position, would tend to lower its value, and encourage a merger with an aggressive, visionary management that could rebuild its formerly dominant position. For Disney, the possibility became more real in April 1990, when the FCC changed its rules to allow networks to own the syndication rights to television shows. For Eisner, a takeover of CBS may well represent his final unfulfilled ambition: running his own television network.

Could someone take over Disney? Or is it finally safe from raiders? With shareholders' equity of $3.5 billion and total assets of over $8 billion, this pig would be very large for any python to swallow. The shareholders of any enterprise that wanted to buy it might well rebel at either having their stock watered down by a new offering large enough to trade shares for Disney stock, or taking on enough debt to simply buy and retire the shares. Furthermore, the easy-money junk-bond era of the '80s is past: leveraged buyouts, accomplished effectively with the cash flow of the target company, are far more difficult in the regulatory and investment banking climate of the 1990s.

Potential raiders would have great difficulty convincing potential investors that they could wring more value from the Disney assets than the current management. And, given the rewards that they have gotten from Disney, the current management has few personal financial concerns. In a hostile takeover, they would be likely to leave—and most investors would consider that a bad outcome.

In fact, Eisner and company have bought the deep loyalty of most current Disney shareholders through the company's steady growth. Unless the stock price goes into a long-term stagnation, it would take sizable crowbars to budge most of them into throwing in with a hostile raider.

But these factors weigh differently measured against the cash of a large foreign investor looking for software that would make a synergetic match with its hardware. In the late 1980s foreign investors, particularly the Japanese and other Asians, showed up in Hollywood, eager to buy up what they could of this most American industry. By 1991 Disney was the only one of the seven major studios that remained independent and in the hands of the company that had founded it. Paramount had long been the property of Gulf & Western (which in 1989 changed its name to Paramount Communications). Warner had become part of the Time-

Warner empire. Sony had bought Columbia Pictures, the Italian-controlled Pathé had bought MGM/UA, Rupert Murdoch's News Corporation had bought 20th Century Fox. MCA, Disney's would-be rival in the theme park business as well as on the silver screen, was having difficulties in both arenas and it eventually fell to Matsushita for $6.6 billion, which outsiders considered a bargain price.

Other Asian companies were waiting in the wings. The Samsung Group, a $35-billion-a-year Korean conglomerate *chaebol* (family-owned company), rated by *Fortune* as the world's 20th largest industrial concern, began angling for the debt-plagued Orion Pictures Corporation. Japanese investors poured money into independent production firms such as Carolco Pictures and Largo Entertainment, which landed $100 million from JVC in 1989. In May 1990 Nomura Babcock and Brown (80 percent of which was owned by Nomura Securities, Japan's largest securities firm, and the rest by American investment bankers Babcock & Brown) invested $100 million in Morgan Creek Productions. In 1989 and 1990 alone, Japanese investors sank over $13 billion into Hollywood.

Eisner would not be left out of this rush for Asian money. By mid-September 1990, his foray into Japan the previous year bore fruit. Yamaichi Securities of Japan put together a $600-million investment in Disney films, raising the money through banks and a limited partnership called Touchwood Pacific Partners. Nomura Securities struck a deal with Disney and Interscope Communications that would eventually push as much as $250 million in Japanese money into Disney films. Interscope had already produced such hits as *Three Men and a Baby*, *Cocktail*, and *Outrageous Fortune* for Disney. At the time Interscope signed the deal, they had 16 projects in development on the Disney lot. In the new pact, Nomura agreed to match Disney's investment in Interscope films dollar for dollar for four years.

Eisner, it seemed, had availed himself of Japanese capital without giving up any control over the company. Yet these pacts could be just the toe in the door. It is quite possible that Disney, now the lone holdout, could be swallowed whole. Such Japanese electronic giants as Toshiba and Hitachi, already roving the American landscape in search of entertainment "software" to match their hardware, are among a select group of international companies large enough to foot a price tag estimated at upwards of $10 billion. By early 1990, American consultants specializing in takeovers were already receiving visits from groups of Japanese investors and companies testing out the possibility of buying Disney. One such consultant, visited by Japanese investors in the spring of 1990, told them that it would be politically and culturally impossible. After the purchase of MCA in the fall of 1990, though, he said that he felt the situation had changed. Hollywood shared his opinion. It came alive with rumors of a Disney sale. It was Eisner's friend Michael Ovitz who had helped with the Sony deal and brokered the Matsushita deal, and much of his office staff's time was taken up by dealing with floods of inquiries from other potential Japanese investors. Eisner and Wells became increasingly involved in internal strategy discussions about the possibility, recognizing that Disney was widely known and admired in Japan, and that a Japanese attempt to take over the Magic Kingdom was quite possible. Some Japanese investments had already come to grief, financing films that bombed and pouring money into companies that have yet to find a profit. This has caused the Japanese to focus even harder on companies that have consistent records and a reputation for sound management. And the biggest such company is Michael Eisner's Disney.

Any turn of the tarot on Disney's future has to end where it began: with the man at the top. Could Disney continue to grow without Michael Eisner? What would happen to the company if Eisner decided tomorrow to go off and climb mountains, as Wells did at his age? Some analysts argue that he is no longer really needed. They say that, now that he has reshaped the company, stocked it with powerful personalities, and moved it into new businesses, his absence likely would not damage the company irretrievably. They point out that, although he makes many creative decisions, he is not, as Walt was, the font of all independent creative thought for the company.

The danger of Eisner leaving Disney is more subtle: as the company expands into ever more far-flung enterprises, businesses that have less and less to do with the core of the Disney mythos, it craves a center. It needs a face, a personality, that embodies all of it — the intelligence, the charm and innocence, the business acumen of the Disney image. Eisner does that. And just as important, he is the man who built the new Disney. To its employees, its investors, its suppliers, and its competitors, he is the stem of this hardy bush. It would be difficult, if not impossible, to find his replacement. Without him, the tensions inherent in its rapidly expanding diversity might begin to tear the company apart and degrade its businesses. The company would become more vulnerable to centrifugal forces, such as takeover and dismemberment, and the forces of decay that infested it before 1984. Such a diverse company needs a strong and highly visible driving wheel.

But what would cause Eisner to leave Disney? Money? He already makes $8 to 10 million per year, not counting stock options. Power? Influence? He is already widely considered one of the most powerful men in Hollywood. Within his universe of Disney and the entertainment industry, he has a good deal more freedom of action than most political leaders.

It is hard to imagine him leaving for a job that more closely fits his personality, because it is hard to imagine a better match of man and job than he has as chairman of Disney. He could leave simply because he is bored, because he wants a career shift, because he is going through a life stage change. It is hard enough to know what will go on in our own hearts tomorrow, without pretending to know the hearts of others. But in his career Michael Eisner has seemed singularly steady. He has had only three real jobs in his life, has lived in only three houses as an adult, has stuck with the same wife he married decades ago. Eisner is not a man given to wild emotional gyrations.

He could leave because, like former Disney CFO Gary Wilson, he wants the opportunity to own his own company. Yet his situation now, at Disney, would not be much different if the company were his to play with. He could hardly have more freedom of action than he has now.

He could, like his predecessors, be forced out in a power struggle within the company. But, now that Wilson has left, it is hard to find a center of discontent among those who would have the leverage—the stockholders, the board, and the other high officers of the company. As long as the company remains successful, such discontent, if it existed, would have no rallying cry. Of course, if the company stumbles badly, he would be vulnerable, whether or not he could be blamed for the stumble.

Michael Eisner has been prince of the Magic Kingdom for seven years already, a long time by Hollywood standards. Watching any trajectory so powerful as Disney's during those years, viewers are tempted to ascribe to it a permanence and power it may not possess. In the study of chaotic systems, a straight-line extrapolation of the current trend is, in the long run, the least likely outcome of all. Michael Eisner could be gone from Disney soon, or he could be at the company's helm well into the next century. Because of his staying power, because of the success and growth of Disney, and because of his agile mind, his influence in the world of entertainment will likely continue to grow. If—and the odds on this are steep—Disney is as successful in television, retailing, restaurants, publishing, recording, and real estate development as it has been in movies, video, characters, and theme parks, it could become one of the giants of the world, an entertainment General Motors with the touch of Walt. But whatever its future, Disney's rescue and turnaround, with Michael Eisner as its prince, is one of the great business bedtime stories, one that would end—if only the world of business allowed such definite endings— "and they lived happily ever after."

Index